The Architecture of America

The Architecture of America

of America

A Social and Cultural History

by JOHN BURCHARD
and ALBERT BUSH-BROWN

LONDON
VICTOR GOLLANCZ LTD
1967

The authors wish to thank the following for permission to reprint
material from published books and magazines:

Cornell University Press for Edward Chase Kirkland's DREAM AND
THOUGHT IN THE BUSINESS COMMUNITY, 1860-1900.

Dodd, Mead & Company for Fabian Franklin's THE LIFE OF
DANIEL COIT GILMAN.

Duell, Sloan & Pearce, Inc., for FRANK LLOYD WRIGHT ON ARCHI-
TECTURE, edited by Frederick Gutheim, copyright 1941 by Duell,
Sloan & Pearce, Inc.

Houghton Mifflin Company for AUTOBIOGRAPHY OF ANDREW CAR-
NEGIE and THE EDUCATION OF HENRY ADAMS.

Hoyle, Doran & Berry for Ralph Adams Cram's MY LIFE IN ARCHI-
TECTURE.

Massachusetts Historical Society for "The Atkinson Papers" as
quoted in Edward Chase Kirkland's DREAM AND THOUGHT IN THE
BUSINESS COMMUNITY, 1860-1900.

Oxford University Press, Inc., for Talbot Hamlin's GREEK REVIVAL
ARCHITECTURE IN AMERICA.

Studio Books, London, for Bruno Taut's MODERN ARCHITECTURE.

PRINTED IN GREAT BRITAIN BY
LOWE AND BRYDONE (PRINTERS) LTD, LONDON

Publisher's Note

The Architecture of America was first published in the
United States in 1961, under the sponsorship of the
American Institute of Architects, who had originally
commissioned it for their Centennial Celebration. That
edition was never published in this country. What we
now offer to the British public is an edition abridged and
revised by the authors, who have undertaken it for the
reasons set out by them on pages xi and xii.

For Marjorie *and* Frances

I suppose, if Lacedaemon were to become desolate, and the temples and the foundations of the public buildings were left, that as time went on there would be a strong disposition with posterity to refuse to accept her fame as true evidence of her power. . . . But if Athens were to suffer the same misfortune, I suppose that any inference from the appearance presented to the eye would make her power to have been twice as great as it is.

— THUCYDIDES, *The History of the Peloponnesian War*, I, 10
(translated by Sir R. W. Livingstone)

Foreword

A GOOD five years before the centennial celebration of The American Institute of Architects in 1957, it was suggested that a fitting, if not essential, by-product of the celebration would be publication of a history of the Institute's first hundred years. The proposal seemed not without merit. After some search of the records, it was found, however, that the history of an organization, even that of The American Institute of Architects, was not exactly apt to titillate the public and, at best, would interest the membership but slightly: It seemed scarcely a subject for a major endeavor. It then occurred to the Executive Director that instead of a history of the Institute, it would be well for the A.I.A. to publish a book on American architecture during the Institute's lifetime. The book, he felt, should relate more to the impact of our changing society on the profession and the resulting architecture, than construe a tenuous, if flattering, premise that things happened the other way around. In other words, he asked for a scholarly treatise — one which would call for skill.

The Committee on the Centennial Celebration enthusiastically adopted the proposal. The Chairman, Alexander Robinson, III, appointed a subcommittee under the chairmanship of Dean Wurster, who, with his customary foresight and enthusiasm, persuaded Dean John E. Burchard of the School of Humanities and Social Studies, Massachusetts Institute of Technology, to undertake the task. Subsequently, Professor Albert Bush-Brown of M.I.T. was enlisted as co-author.

As it turned out, it was impossible to even ask that a work of such magnitude, demanding such staggering amounts and depth of research, be completed, let alone printed, in time for the A.I.A. Centennial in 1957. It was therefore agreed that it would be better to have the job done well than hurriedly.

A*

This decision was wise, for the authors have succeeded far beyond the anticipations of anyone to produce a book which should and will, I think, prove to be *the* major work on American architecture of the past century.

The American Institute of Architects is proud to lend its name and sponsorship to this work.

Edmund R. Purves, FAIA
Executive Director
The American Institute of Architects

The Octagon
Washington, D. C.
September 1960

Foreword to the Abridged Edition

THIS abridgment has been made mostly to put our book in easier financial reach of students. It corrects errors of fact which we have noted. It responds to minor points of criticism which we have felt were well taken. Naturally it does not respond to those sometimes polar critics who wanted us to write a number of different books we did not set out to write. It remains an effort to write a social history of American architecture, to subordinate personal biographies, analyses of individual buildings, and discussions of theory to the attempt to assess building types and social process and the position of architects in all this. That architecture thus sometimes seems a matter of fashion, that architects sometimes seem less than God-like is not our fault. Nor is it our fault that we are human beings and thus, like all other critics, subjective. Unlike some we admit it.

Except for a complete excision of the preliminary essay on architectural design and the two great historic examples of Athens and Chartres, the abridgment is quite uniform throughout. It tends to delete details of the general historical ambiance rather more than to lessen the examples of buildings, but we hope and believe that the historical currents have not been muddied thereby.

When one does a book over, even after as short a span as five years, it is tempting to try to bring it down to date. Insofar as the text itself is concerned we have resisted this temptation. We have, however, added a signature of photographs of buildings of importance which have been completed since 1960. We may not insist that all these buildings are fine ones and we might not even agree fully as to which ones were the finer. But we have supplied buildings which we believe to have been important and we have not included any we would regard as caricatures.

The later work seems to us to do nothing to change our larger conclusions. Pop and op art have come and are going with no serious effect on architecture. Concrete buildings with heavy shadow-casting projections are gaining ground on mirror-glass, shadowless screens but the atomization of architecture is if anything more complete. No important new victory has been recorded by the city in its struggle against the freeway and the motor car. Whether the brief Age of Kennedy has introduced an important new note into American cultural aspirations it is still too early to tell though tepid billboard laws, and tree-planting programs may seem a weak denouement, as does the small appropriation for a National Foundation for the Humanities and the Arts, equaling $\frac{1}{400}$th of that for NASA and $\frac{1}{2000}$th of that for the Federal Highway Program. What does emerge in the new pictures, which were not selected with a view to demonstrating it, is that the leadership in encouraging imaginative architecture may have passed from the industrial corporation to the universities, whose sluggishness in this regard we tended to deplore in the original text. This has made it an exciting time on many campuses; whether campuses as a whole have been improved we decline to testify. Conceivably campuses like cities would have gained more by a lesser range of innovation in any one neighborhood.

In the belief that scholars can find their way to sources and other references through the original edition, we have deleted elaborate indices, bibliography and notes from this version and confined ourselves to a single index.

In addition to the acknowledgments which were made in the original edition we should thank the American Institute of Architects for permitting this edition on generous terms; and John Burchard must thank the Carnegie Corporation for a grant which has helped him to put time on many recent works of which the labor of revision here is one.

John Burchard
Albert Bush-Brown

Cambridge and
Providence
June 1965

Contents

I

1600-1860

FIRST there was the land.

Each of its details was nearly duplicated somewhere in the world. But when you put all the American land together it seemed different. Abraham Lincoln said it was a land suited for one people, but it took a large mind to see that. Individuals loved the details.

The details began at the shores. There was the sheer bare geometry of the rock cliffs at Castle Head, Mount Desert, where the waves dashed against the rock and the brittle spray fell back into a dark cold sea. There were the gentle estuaries dotted with piles of salt-water hay near Newburyport. There were the tall waving pampas grasses of the Jersey meadows, the ragged scarred palms on the tiny hill of a sandy beach in Florida, the ominous boom of the Pacific as it rode under the kelp to the steep sides of the Big Sur, or the rough and foggy coast of California north of Fort Ross where lumber schooners tied precariously near while redwood logs were lowered down to their decks. But the coasts were not places where many people might live. They were often too bold or too marshy or too sandy. We can remember our coastal architecture, its lighthouses, its salt-gray shingles beaten by the weather, but for America most of the buildings were inland. Some American writers wrote of the seacoast but it was the inland continent that entranced most of them.

Thomas Wolfe told of the New England autumn with its frost "sharp and quick as driven nails," its blazing, bitter red maples, and other leaves "yellow like a living light . . . falling about you like small pieces of the sun."

The winter of old England was clammier. In Minnesota or Montana the winds blew more bitterly. Blizzards from the west piled the snow higher around Buffalo, but New England would come first to mind when you read in Henry Adams of "straight, gloomy streets, piled with six feet of snow in the middle; frosts that made the snow sing under wheels or runners."

Very little of the land was east of the Appalachians. As you crossed them, you might, if you had never been farther west, agree with Jefferson that the "passage of the Potomac through the Blue Ridge is, perhaps, one of the most stupendous scenes in nature," admire the small catch of blue horizon through the cleft, speak of the "terrible precipices hanging in fragments over you." There were other water gaps like the calm one of the Delaware below Stroudsburg, and beyond the Blue Ridge were many rivers: the French Broad as it poured out of the Smokies or the serpentine Tennessee as it meandered around Chattanooga and the wind-and-water-scooped rocks of Lookout Mountain. In the end all the rivers of the western Appalachian slopes would take you to the Mississippi but before that there was the Ohio valley and before you came to the Great River there were the remote lands of its fertile eastern basin as Hamlin Garland came to know them in the late 1860s.

Here Green's Coulee, Wisconsin, offered timbered knolls and little steep ravines, obdurate oak stumps and ditch-demanding marshes dotted with lakes which made the West seem "a fairer field of conquest."

Before the West there was the Mississippi. It dominated a great deal of American thought. Like multifold American nature, the Mississippi was many rivers. It was the steep-banked sky-blue stream of Hennepin and Hiawatha and the flat black bayou of Evangeline. But for most Americans it was the broad and muddy river of Huckleberry Finn with its coves, knee-deep above sandy bottoms, its bullfrogs, its gray sunrises, its rafts and its snags, its log cabins, and its fresh morning breezes, "and everything smiling in the sun, and the song-birds just going it!"

After New England and Virginia and the Appalachians and Wisconsin and The River there was the prairie coursed by the wide Missouri and its muddy tributaries. The Garlands came there, to the meadows so wide that they stretched unfettered to the western rim, to the "grass tall as ripe wheat," to the remote, dim clumps of trees, to "the hawks lazily wheeling in the air," and to the land billowing "like a russet ocean."

West of the plains and before the mountains there were the
Bad Lands. Frank Lloyd Wright saw the Bad Lands of the Da-
kotas as architecture—"a distant architecture, ethereal, touched,
only touched with a sense of Egyptian, Mayan drift and silhouette. . . . Endless trabeations surmounted by or rising into pyramid (obelisk) and temple, ethereal in color and exquisitely chis-
eled in endless detail . . ."

Entry to the plains, crossing them, was to be a dominating and
persistent part of American experience. The Spaniards had
known it, too, oppressed as De Voto reminds us by the ball-
shaped sky-surrounded land, the dusty willows and cottonwoods
along the shallow watercourses, and the incessant grass which
"bent as the wind trod it; the line of horsemen bent it too as they
crossed; it rose again from wind and hoof and closed behind them
and no sign of their passing had been left."

In the long run, whether through the Bad Lands or through
the grasses, you came to the Rockies, laminated and sheer as they
were in Montana, pointed and serrated as they were in Wyoming,
massive and dry as they were in Colorado, sculptured into monuments as they dwindled south into Arizona and New Mexico.
They were hard enough to pass but the low and tractable places
could be found. Then you met the sand, the insistent barrier of
all American transcontinental experience. The desert could not
be avoided. It subsumed the world's experience of deserts. Walter
Prescott Webb has called it the overriding influence that shaped
the West, its one unifying force, permeating the plains, climbing
the mountains to strip them of their vegetation, drying up the
inland lakes, plunging "down the Pacific slope to argue with the
sea."

To the north the desert was sometimes kind. The good dirt
might be carried from Washington and Oregon on to the rolling
dunes that covered the great lava beds of Idaho and a handsome
fertile wheat belt like the Palouse could be born. Beyond the rolling hills that would some day bear the great grain crops were the
wet and wooded Cascades, the gorge of the Columbia, where Indians precariously speared the salmon, and the expansive coni-
fered region of Puget Sound. But to the south the desert was
more insistent and after you had crossed it there was still the

Sierra, that fantastic mountain range that Clarence King knew and loved so well, its eastern foreground of whitened plain, its sapphire mirages, its frowning eastern wall, marked with the shoreline of an ancient sea. But when you saw it from the west the brown foothills were gentle, now purple, now full of orange-colored flowers, the sky was beryl, the summits sharp but unforbidding, the green-roofed pines separating the foothills with their rusty mining-town ravines from the not quite perpetual snows which at sundown "burned for a moment in the violet sky, and at last went out."

Beyond there was only the complex Pacific, here craggy-beached, there sandy, here bearing fog-laden forests of giant trees, there sun and scattered live oaks, madrones and clumps of manzanita, but the end of the line for America unless subtropical Hawaii and arctic Alaska were to be counted.

This was the majestic framework. The land offered every splendor except those of the tropics and the Arctic, the whole range of nature's palette, varieties of sight and sound, of animal and bird, or wet and dry, of heat and cold, of light and dark, of eminence and depression, of fertility and sterility, all often in close and dramatic contrast.

It provided almost every kind of material for building: hard and soft woods, woods that were white or red or blue, woods that came curling clean off a plane and woods that splintered at a touch, close-grained oak, tractable pine, wild-grained fir, cherry, maple, cypress, redwood; and tropical woods were not far away. It offered many clays that would provide hard bricks and soft bricks, warm red ones, delicate pink ones, simple grays and dirty yellows. It supported icy granite and burning lime, sandstones and limestones that carved easily, a variety of marbles. It had dirt for adobe, and grass for thatch, and all the building metals, copper, zinc, lead, aluminum and the bounteous supplies of iron and coal and flux which made steel easy to come by. Whatever the climate demanded of the architecture, the land responded to with useful and handsome building materials. But like the climate and the terrain the range was fantastic.

In almost any condition, except the American condition, this land would have dominated a variety of peoples, have preserved and intensified their differences, have supported an interesting range of diverse architecture, dress, food, speech, ways of life. It began that way in America too. But the wave of technology undammed by national frontiers was as inexorable for men's buildings as it was for their clothes and their food and even their thoughts. By 1960 it had filled even the coves of the black mountains of Tennessee and Kentucky and justified Jesse Stuart's plea, "If there are ballads left among us, they should be gathered now."

In the beginning the land seemed vast. The vastness had impressed St. John de Crèvecoeur, back in the eighteenth century, when he reported that no European foot had traveled half the continent and that it would take many ages to "see the shores of our great lakes replenished with inland nations." But before the airplane and not much more than a hundred years after de Crèvecoeur, a Middle-western historian, Frederick Jackson Turner, announced, perhaps prematurely, that the vastness had been consumed.

In the century between de Crèvecoeur and Turner many Americans had a wide variety of love affairs with American nature. But the characteristic American romance with nature involved more conquest and pillage than love and care. De Tocqueville understood this well enough in 1831:

> . . . the Americans themselves . . . are insensible to the wonders of inanimate nature and they may be said not to perceive the mighty forests that surround them till they fall beneath the hatchet. Their eyes are fixed upon another sight: the American people views its own march across these wilds, draining swamps, turning the course of rivers, peopling solitudes, and subduing nature.

Later on, the American romance of nature was composed of a strange mixture of admiration for ancestral self-reliance and a belief in change, of nostalgia for a past that was gone and a craving for the exotic that may never have been. But when the chips were down and the choice needed to be made between the virgin forest and the bulldozer, there would be no doubt which the American people would choose. Against this choice the land was not impregnable though it did have endurance and resiliency.

The ultimate American uniformity did not come about solely through the leveling ministrations of the machine or the pollen of American nomadism. It was also prepared for by the shared mysticism that a man was a different man the moment he set foot on the new continent and that the continent had a mystic unity. You can find this belief in many famous passages from John Winthrop and de Crèvecoeur down to the present. But the early Europeans, like de Crèvecoeur, holding an eighteenth-century European view of nature, thought that the Americans, "incorporated into one of the finest systems of population which had ever appeared," would in the long run "become distinct by the power of the different climates they inhabit." They did not, could not, foresee that Americans would reverse previous human procedures. Instead of being affected very long by the power of the land and the climate, they would affect the land and the climate by their power. It would even seem more important to Americans to apply the power than to be careful not to apply it carelessly or adversely.

This spirit would boil up in little ways and big ways. It could produce an impression such as the St. Louis Exposition did on Henry Adams in 1904, when he saw

> . . . a third-rate town of half-a-million people without history, education, unity or art . . . doing what London, Paris, or New York would have shrunk from attempting. This new social conglomerate, with no tie but its steam-power and not much of that, threw away thirty or forty million dollars on a pageant as ephemeral as a stage flat.

It was something that Adams found possible to enjoy with "iniquitous rapture"; it gave hope to a "pilgrim of power," it foreshadowed that Americans would soon have all the power they wanted to throw away. But Adams also noted another American characteristic in St. Louis. It "industriously ignored" its only element of natural interest, the River.

The spirit of the frontier laid waste the hills of West Virginia, the cut-over areas of northern Michigan, the rivers of the California gold dredges; brought grime and flood to the confluence of the Allegheny and Monongahela and called it a Golden Triangle; shrouded the Sierra Madres in smog; ignored minor desolation in every city every day so that Mencken could justifiably talk of the American libido for the ugly; it was never patient enough to work out the destiny of one place before it pulled up stakes and moved on to another. But it also made Rockefeller Center and the Tennessee Valley Authority; it carried the waters of inner Colorado through the massive Front Range to bring bloom to the eastern slopes. You might love a more intimate nature and pray that grand nature would not be demeaned by man, you might deplore desecrations, weep over the ruthless, thoughtless, even aimless despoliation of natural resources, but you would generally be loving, praying, deploring and weeping in a small company. You might dream yourself back into the imagined richness and integrity of an eighteenth-century New England village or Virginia manor. You might seek desperately to pour water on the dead roots of a never flourishing regionalism, you might hate the machine and the city, you might insist on a diversity for America which Americans did not want, but all your dreaming, seeking, hating and insisting would be quite in vain. Jeremiads would not cancel either the record or the promise. There was the land and its continental embrace, its enormous scale, its indirect and elusive unity, and there was the pioneer, always changing the scene he stopped briefly to change, always moving on until there was nowhere else to move; but then going back to remake what had in the meanwhile become desolate. So the frontier returned from the West to Pittsburgh, Chicago, Detroit, New York and Boston to begin a new cycle. This circular frontier had no end.

There was the great basic fact that man had come to alter nature and not to be altered by it. You might love this or hate it, admire it or fear it, or you might just try to be indifferent to it, but you would not have much chance of understanding what was good and what was bad about American architecture if you tried to pretend that this relation of the American man to the American land was different than it was.

On this land decisions had to be made, some deliberately, some only as things developed. Instead of a garland of small countries, speaking different languages and remembering different history, jealously preserving several cultural differences, America became a continental nation with an essentially English underpinning.

In the Civil War we abolished the feudalism, if not all the other realities, of slavery and in general concluded not to be a pair of nations, one agrarian, one industrial; one feudal, one almost democratic; one educated and scientific, the other gentlemanly and vague.

We decided to exterminate the indigenous peoples, as de Tocqueville put it, "tranquilly, legally, philanthropically, without shedding blood, and without violating a single great principle of morality in the eyes of the world"; in the same moment we essentially rejected the influence of their symbolic, irrational, ritualistic cultures.

In a spirit of generosity about our gift of freedom we encouraged for a long time immigrations, first of British or German Protestants, then Gaelic and Italian Catholics, finally Russians, Poles, Romanians, Greeks, Croats, Levantines, many of whom were Jews. These were indispensable for the arts which for a long time might not have survived at all without immigrants, permanent or temporary. For most "old" Americans were not expected to join the ranks of painters, sculptors, architects, musicians, cooks, decorators, opera singers and actors, though they might venture at being poets. For a long time American parents thought it tragedy when their children sought careers in art, and perhaps still do. But the later immigrants produced progeny who, American-born and half American-bred, had talents resting in both worlds. The puritan ethic might have held it unsound for a scion to be either painter or scientist. The European view was different. In the end it might even be fashionable for an American whose ancestors had arrived in 1620.

There were decisions about how American wealth should be distributed. We say America has become one great middle class; and we are partly right. This has a great deal to do with what our architecture has been and what it is likely to be. It has meant, for example, an upgrading of the standard of the average dwelling. But an average standard, which might have produced some elegant uniformities as it has in other times and places, has been degraded by an absurd demand for an insecure individuality. The leveling of incomes offers the risk that a comfortable middle class may supply no patrons interested enough in architecture to aspire to the best.

Then there was the decision about farm and city which continued to provoke debate long after it had been taken. It was not a conscious decision but it was none the less real; the surge to the city was relentless, beyond the power of any critical Canutes to halt. In the rush to the cities Americans, never strong at long-range planning, overlooked, even lost, the real advantages of urban life. But the consequences of the decision to be urban if not urbane ran through all of American history after 1880.

Finally, there was the difficult, halfhearted decision that we should play a leading role in world affairs. For American architecture this meant many things. There was the infusion of new architectural ideas brought by foreign visitors or by Americans who had sojourned in many lands. The things Americans wanted, the things they would accept were influenced. The opportunity to build abroad had a similar result. The result might be superficial and appear in thoughtless imitations of the Katsura Palace or the Masjid-i-Shah at Isfahan as happened in the nineteenth century. But later on, the experience seemed to settle into the spirit and be distilled later in forms that were not imitative.

All these decisions were debated before the backdrop of "the American dream." The dream existed long before James Truslow Adams named it about a quarter-century ago, "that dream of a better, richer, and happier life for all our citizens of every rank which is the greatest contribution we have as yet made to the thought and welfare of the world." Almost all Americans subscribe to the dream, no matter how they differ about what is better, what richer, what happier.

Despite its illusory nature, despite many disillusionments, the dream has been durable. It has three main ideas. First, there is the idea of progress, perfectibility, the new and better life. Second, there is the idea of a democracy forming a new kind of commonwealth. These alone could not define the American dream, for they have been imagined by other dreamers of dreams, for Edens, Utopias, Atlantises. The dream became American when the powerful conviction was added that it could come true and in a specific place and that the specific place was America. The idea that "this is the place" is the conviction of most Americans and of many foreigners, too. It runs through most American documents from Edward Johnson's seventeenth-century *Wonder-Working Providence* through Emerson and Whitman to the Four Freedoms. It is in the Declaration of Independence, Brook Farm, the TVA, and Frank Lloyd Wright's proposal for Broadacre City.

The dream sought reality in countless specific examples, some in architecture. There was for example an early American prison in Virginia, the first one conceived architecturally in America, whose cornerstone was laid in 1797. When French experts criticized the plan, it was the American dream which answered that the prison was different because "it was planned to emphasize reform and hope."

Observers like Frederic I. Carpenter have suggested that the dream at its best thought of universal freedom, not of nationalism; of the advance of science, not of materialism; of the intelligent cooperation of educated individuals, not compulsory social reform; of self-realization through struggle, not simple individualistic successes in pragmatic terms. The recurrent ejaculations have been "freedom," "progress," "democracy." They were powerful words, sometimes mouthed uncritically, sometimes not quite believed, but always powerful; and whenever they seemed negated we felt apprehensive.

2

AMERICA, like every other country, had its own primitive, naïve and indigenous original architecture. But this was the architecture of Indians — the bark houses of the Penobscots, the long houses of the Iroquois, the tipis of the Crows, the mounds of the Mandans, the pueblos of the Zuñi, the hogans of the Navajos, the log dwellings of Puget Sound. Indian words and Indian foods passed into the American culture but nothing important from the Indian architecture, save a belated effort to imitate the form but not the function of the pueblos, the ornament and decoration but not the meaning of the Maya. This was not surprising, for the evolution of buildings from comparable European primitive types had gone a long way before English, French, and Dutch settlers came to America. Their own experience and their memories provided them with more advanced solutions than those of the Indians.

The arts of the pre-Columbian Indians of Mexico and Peru were rejected by the Spaniards who saw in them nothing worth adopting or even something idolatrous to be shatteringly repudiated. So Spanish-American buildings recapitulated the achievements of Spain on land which had much in common with the Spanish land, just as the English efforts were to be on land which, in New England, if not in Virginia, had much in common with English land.

Of the European invaders only the English left a large, durable and extensive residue. The purposes of the French were not to establish permanent settlements; the *coureurs de bois* and the *voyageurs* were brilliant explorers and trappers and they opened up the great rivers; they brought an interesting vertical version of the log cabin up the Mississippi, perhaps a better version than the horizontal, but in the long run their influence was trivial; and the great contemporary and monumental styles of France were inappropriate for poor Frenchmen in America even while French colonization was vigorous.

It was a little different with the Spaniards. The church and the army marched hand in hand, and though the main search was for gold there was also the matter of converting souls. The churches of Mexico did leave a mark. It was the mark of the Spanish Gothic and later of the Renaissance and baroque. Such churches appeared briefly in the United States, too, as in the eighteenth-century St. Xavier del Bac in Tucson. Florida's St. Augustine contained the Spanish Governor's house and cathedral. But they are not so important as the more primitive missions of California built by Father Juniper Serra later, long after the conquistadores, not long before the conquest of California and Texas by the United States. The missions are handsome in their honest and human simplicity; and touching when they contain examples, as at Ventura, of the Indian primitive rendering of ancient Biblical subjects. They were fine of their kind but came only at the end of a Spanish influence, and did not move into the main stream of the indigenous California building which would endure. So they have not had the durable and insistent influence on America that the transplanted English house did via Massachusetts, Virginia and South Carolina.

The California "adobe" did have such an influence, for it was a good design for California living so long as California was to be a land of far-riding rancheros. It offered enough combination of outdoors and indoors, enough free ventilation with its through rooms and its double verandas so that it was useful for much other Californian life, too, and it can be called genuinely indigenous. It has been resilient, even in modern hands. But there is at least a good chance that the "adobe" was not Spanish at all. Its primary form may well have been brought to Monterey by Thomas Oliver Larkin, who had lived in South Carolina before he came. Whatever its source, the California indigenous was real; but its influence was not widespread nor really durable. Easterners like Richard Henry Dana, coming by Monterey in 1834, thought it pretty and exotic; but fifteen years later it was dying away and Bayard Taylor came to examine what seemed to be the last of the old Spanish way of life; while the semblance of Mexico was all on the surface by 1890.

It is not necessary to dwell on details brought early from other parts of Europe, as in the Vieux Carré of New Orleans; or even late in the nineteenth century and duplicated from memory by Germans, Swedes, Danes, Norwegians in various parts of the agrarian West; or on the earlier contributions of the Danes or the Dutch to localized regional architecture in the East. This implies no disrespect for the Swedish introduction into Delaware of the log cabin, which would spread across the Appalachians and have a powerful, if ephemeral, life on the frontier, or the French use of timber-and-nogging walls in New Orleans as early as 1716, or the stilted first floors and long porch designs of the French for a tropical climate of the lower Mississippi, or the yellow-brick kilns of the Dutch that provided stepped gables for early Albany (1657), or the cloisters of the Baptists at Ephrata. Some of the buildings are handsome and characteristic. All partake of the same fine qualities as the English development in New England and Vir-

ginia and Carolina; all endured the same later history; in the long
run they remain less as influences than as memories.

As soon as the colonists emerged from their temporary burrows,
such as they dug at Concord, they began to build their version of
the English medieval development from the Saxon cruck house.
Wood was plentiful as bricks were not.

The houses did not long resemble their medieval prototypes,
perhaps no longer than the first winter. The exposed Elizabethan
struts, stuffed with bricks or lath and plaster, simply let in too
much air and the American addition of heavy siding was urgent.
Otherwise the houses still had a distinctly medieval cast. But
within fifty years after their arrival the colonists had developed a
style of house which had distinctive American characteristics. The
chimney was the dominant factor in this, and out of it in the long
run came four basic plans, one with a great central hearth, one
with a chimney at each end, one with two chimneys set in the
center of each of two wings, and one with four chimneys, two at
each end.

Such primitive constructions were refined rapidly. In other parts
of the colonies a few other American innovations were being
made, such as the gambrel roof which the Dutch seem to have
invented here. But though we can still see a few of these ancient
American houses, they are not really what we associate with New
England. The buildings that come most readily to mind are of
later date and the result at first of considerable native development, then modified by self-conscious efforts at refinement of details, first from memory, then with the aid of books, and finally by
the efforts of professional architects. Between 1607 and 1800 dor-
mer windows had appeared, thatched roofs had disappeared, and
stick chimneys had been abandoned for brick. The roofs were
flatter, the second-story overhang was disappearing. Iron railings
had become readily available, houses could be built even as high
as five stories.

This architecture, though it would be carried far and wide over
the land, was not necessarily well fitted to serve every terrain and
every climate that was now to be encountered. As the Romans
had marched across Europe and deposited the atrium wherever

they marched, so the English and their descendants now marched across America and most of the time deposited the New England house. As it became less and less suited to its surroundings, it also suffered depreciation.

Before it spread to the prairie, this architecture had gone beyond the primitive, was self-conscious, was relying in part upon the book to jog a failing memory or to supply what memory never had. As the carpenters, armed with their simple books of proportions and their own manual skills, began their embellishments of windows, edges, chimney tops, pediments, cornices, quoins, and corbeling, they followed well-established patterns almost as traditional as the original peasant style itself, patterns for details that were originally in stone, as the granite façades of Georgian London were reproduced in wooden house façades of 1716 Portsmouth, New Hampshire. The results were of high quality in New England. Was this because it originated there and was sensible there, or because craftsmen were better, or because New England was richer, or because New Englanders cared more, or because their memories were greener, less plagued by the daily grinds and desolation of the west-bound frontier? Something of all of these, no doubt, but was there something more, as Lewis Mumford insists, the result of the "common spirit, nourished by men who had divided the land fairly and who shared adversity and good fortune together"?

3

IN the period between 1800 and 1860 the central part of the North American continent was joined to the United States whose boundaries would soon touch the Pacific. But at the turn of the century (save for New Orleans) everything that was really civilized in this land stood east of the Alleghenies. It was a testimonial to people who built well.

Even today, a town like Shirley Center, Massachusetts, settled in 1750, makes a happy impression. Its triangular green stands at the intersection of three roads leading through rock-fenced fields bordered by deciduous woods. Its meetinghouse and town hall are white and large enough to dominate the town while proclaiming

their communal functions. Nearby, along the roads, trim houses
stand four-square beneath arching elms, facing the green or the
roads, backed by sprays of cedars, maples and oaks. The common
character of the village is asserted by double-pitched roofs, red-
brick chimneys, white clapboards, modulated windows, dark trim.
Other towns of that day, like Salem or Newburyport or New
Bedford, perhaps more prosperous, perhaps more worldly, sometimes have a more elegant architecture: but the plans and scale of
all speak of orderly societies whose enormously independent
builders contrived to produce individual houses that did not con-
tradict the whole.

What they built looked well in many landscapes, served efficiently in many climates, could be built of many materials, permitted a good amount of adaptation. It was less elegant than romance depicts it; it cannot solve all the problems of today but it
is one of our finest architectural heirlooms. What one sees today
at Williamsburg or Cooperstown is glamorized historical fiction
and may lead to the belief that a historical style, rather than scale
and town planning of spaces and a way of life, was the source of
what is admirable. But Shirley Center, where time stopped in
1860, is a genuine witness to the sure eye of builders who, while
working sincerely in the style of their period, insisted on the good
design of spaces. Thus they created comfortable, dignified houses
and handsome public and religious edifices even in quite remote
and small places.

It was not long before New Englanders demanded greater
amenity and elegance than their early architecture afforded.
Many Americans, especially in the South, had risen well past
primitivism by 1800. Only a few surviving houses, like the Fairbanks House in Dedham, Massachusetts, or the John Ward House
in Salem, recalled the privations and hardships of colonial life.
Unsubstantial wooden structures like the many-gabled Old College at Harvard had long since rotted, burned or been demolished. Even Williamsburg's Capitol had nearly disappeared, and
the so-called Wren Building at the College of William and Mary
no longer satisfied eighteenth-century men like Thomas Jefferson
who called it a "den of noise, of filth and of fetid air."

Urbane, cosmopolitan people readily felt at home in some of

the American cities. Many had a special and personal character:
there were the rows and stoops of Baltimore and Philadelphia;
the squares of Savannah; the gracious verandas of Charleston; the
gold-domed State House on Beacon Hill rising above the Boston
Common. Local flavor was Spanish and French in New Orleans,
Quaker and German in Philadelphia, English in Boston, Dutch
in New York whose step-gables had not yet been replaced by
ubiquitous brownstones.

Dugouts, sod houses, tents and shacks were emblems of the
frontier or of the destitute. On the frontier there were log forts
like those at Marietta, Ohio; Harrodsburg, Kentucky; and Fox
River, Wisconsin, but as the Indians were pushed westward by
wars like the Black Hawk of 1831, more substantial dwellings appeared on the rivers and even in clearings at the very edge of the
forest. The Swedish log cabin was never regarded in America as
anything more than a makeshift on the way to better things and
by 1840 it was well down in the social scale and with less political
leverage than the myths suggest.

The westward expansion tended to reduce diversity and erase
primitive enclaves. New England houses were provided in California and Oregon during the Gold Rush as New England pianos
and window curtains were ferried around the Horn. Mormons,
moving westward from New York, left a trail of buildings in Kirt-
land, Ohio; Nauvoo, Illinois; St. Joseph, Missouri; and finally in
Salt Lake City. As more up-to-date ways of building came to the
frontier, they were quickly adopted, usually more coarsely than in
their Eastern prototypes.

A major factor in the diminishing regional differences was the
national acceptance of a professional architecture, American
Georgian. Derived from Palladio, the sixteenth-century Italian
architect, this style had been modified in England by architects
like Sir Christopher Wren and James Gibbs, whose work was
known in America through books like William Salmon's *Palladio
Londinensis, or the London Art of Building*, first published in
1734.

The cast of American Georgian architecture is well exemplified
by a famous eighteenth-century Virginia house, Westover, located twenty-five miles above Williamsburg on the James River,

built for William Byrd II about 1730-1734. Educated in London, Byrd was a wealthy plantation owner who directed public affairs in the colony. One of our finest national monuments, his mansion is approached from the north side through wrought-iron gates that open beneath a scrolled overthrow. On either side, brick piers, bearing large birds, mark the beginning of handsomely wrought fences that stretch across the forecourt to the house. The entrance façade is symmetrical while the first floor is raised three feet above grade on an English basement. The central doorway is the fulcrum of the composition, reached by a pyramidal flight of stairs. The windows in the two main stories, spanned by low brick arches, form a regular rhythm clearly centered on the axis of the doorway. The roof rises steeply to a sharp ridge which is stopped by two pairs of end chimneys. A belt course and the main cornice, with rows of dentils and modillions, wrap the whole design. The south or garden façade is identical except for the doors, which were modeled after plates in Salmon's book and may have been imported from London with the wrought-iron entrance gates. The fore-hall is off center to gain light from one of the windows; beneath the stair landing it opens into a more commodious after-hall whence one may enter a music room, a drawing room, a dining hall or a library. Each has its own deep fireplace and is fully paneled to the height of cornice moldings.

Houses such as this, or Carter's Grove, or the ballroom wing of the Williamsburg Palace, the product of skillful imported master carpenters like Richard Bayliss and master designers like Richard Taliaferro, perfectly exhibit the character of Georgian architecture. They shame the better-known architecture of Monticello or Mount Vernon. Their fine compositions overrode all minor differences. An English house, designed by James Gibbs and published in his *Book of Architecture*, served perfectly well, for example, for the south front of Mount Airy in Richmond County, Virginia, built by John Tayloe in 1758-1762; differences in national origin, site and terrain might affect the level of craftsmanship or cause minor adjustments to windows and chimneys, but they did not seem important enough to require modification in the basic harmonies of Gibbs's design. They were not always good; Mount Vernon was so flawed that it was criticized later by

B

professional architects like Benjamin Henry Latrobe, who thought it a result of "indifferent taste."

Still the best Georgian managed to reconcile beautiful form with useful performance, and that excellence so endured that what was essentially an English style continued to fascinate Americans from 1700 until 1850 even while they were toying with other ways. The strength of the Georgian lay in its unerring aim at beautiful form and respose and the modesty of its scale. It permitted considerable variety, particularly as houses were adapted to tropical or temperate climates to produce differences such as those between the Gibbes House in Charleston, South Carolina, and the Jeremiah Lee House in Marblehead, Massachusetts. But this variety did not disturb the basic homogeneity of the form. Even public buildings resembled houses so that Independence Hall in Philadelphia or the Old Colony House at Newport have a domestic character.

It was possible for a gifted man to study Georgian precedents and produce fine buildings. Thus Peter Harrison, of Newport, often called the first American architect, achieved notable successes in his Touro Synagogue and Redwood Library in Newport, his King's Chapel at Boston and Christ Church at Cambridge; all are beautiful and dignified buildings, especially admirable inside, and all are within the common tradition he had studied in his books. Where, as in Salem, such scholarship was combined with the skill of a great woodcarver like Samuel McIntire, the general beauty imparted by formal composition was enriched by mantelpieces and paneling, as in the Gardner-White-Pingree House. It was a tradition that set American architecture upon a good beginning; we should not be making the mistake of trying to continue it in modern Lexington or Shaker Heights; but what remains of it should be zealously preserved and will always enhance our landscape and our life while it lasts.

But the serenity of the Georgian experience was threatened by the Revolution and by the subsequent demand for a new expression of the new land in every sphere of American life. One could sense this in the first national architectural competition, held for the Capitol in Washington in 1792. Naturally, it drew a group of designs in the accepted Georgian idioms. Some were amateurish, like Philip Hart's badly scaled and ineptly phrased elevations; others like James Diamond's clutter of roof trusses, arches, pediments, domes and other discrete elements failed to provide the desired dignity. Several were surprisingly competent, notably McIntire's, a well-proportioned and monumental English palace. But Washington and Jefferson looked for something more classical than any of these. Such a spirit appeared in the domed and porticoed designs submitted by Samuel Dobie, Stephen Hallet and Dr. William Thornton. Thornton's design won the competition, and to it are due the general scale and features of the old Capitol, still visible in the rebuilt east façade. Hallet was asked to modify details and to supply a technical competence which Dr. Thornton lacked. Later, Latrobe executed much of the interior work and the dome over the Halls; in 1818 Charles Bulfinch was called from Boston by President Madison to redesign the portico and to achieve a better unity between the wings. Still later, in 1851-1867, Thomas Ustick Walter raised the great dome over the center and constructed two outlying wings whose heavier scale balanced the dome and the central block. This succession of designs was often the result of bitter political and aesthetic bickering. The atmosphere was normally one of great personal rivalry, machination, anger. Men were freely accused of incompetence, extravagance, even venality. Congress and the President were forever interfering. But the fact that so many designers, working in such an unhappy climate, could nonetheless achieve improvement, and maintain an essential architectural unity as they worked across the sixty years, indicates the basic unanimity of agreement about classic design. To compare the situation with the present, we have only to ponder the disruptive proposals made for the completion of the crossing of St. John the Divine, or the additions our contemporaries make to the Grand Central Station in New York. The history of the Capitol reveals also that local traditions were disappearing as the "national" art emerged. The Capitol set the mark for later government buildings like the Department of State and the old General Post Office in Washington, and most of our state capitols have since reflected it.

The decay of the Georgian and regional architecture was brought about by several forces; there were the designers themselves who began, self-consciously, to import English architecture through books, often incompetently, unimaginatively, merely degrading the native traditions; there was the decay incident to careless handling of details on a frontier indifferent to details since it was always preparing to move on; there was the decay implicit in attempting to put a form where it did not belong, in modification to make it more useful, destroying the old but not creating a good new one since the limitations of the residue were too cramping; there was the decay incident to the unification of a land, tending to level out ways of life. Decay by design could be best seen in the old places where the original memories were greenest, decay by neglect could be seen across the prairie, decay by modification could be seen in the more prosperous parts of the Middle West, and decay by unification was a national experience.

The designers took the low rectangular houses and made them square and high, attached classical pilasters and cupolas and captains' walks, cut wood to look like stone. Soon the men who had used the books fancied themselves competent enough to get along without them. So the style decayed; a glance might not show that the proportions had changed, but closer inspection revealed that ornaments had become an "illiterate reminiscence," that windows were bare openings; as Lewis Mumford observed, "Alas for a bookish architecture when the taste for reading disappears!"

What in Kentucky and Ohio, on the very edge of the frontier, had been made with skill and beauty and even refinement, farther west became crude and transient; the versions of the now much changed and aged vernacular became unrecognizable without emerging into a clear local type. The early Oregon houses of New England type built under the guidance of the early settler Dr. John McLoughlin look interesting in Oregon but would seem inconsequential in any old New England town. The efforts of the men of the mining towns, whether in Colorado or along the Mother Lode of California, often move us and remind us of something we like from Mark Twain or Bret Harte but their architecture will not stand any real analysis. The charm of the Victorian relics of Aspen, Colorado, should not lead us to overestimate their absolute excellence. They are all betrayals of architectural illiteracy rather than of any desire to build something particularly suited to the place, the times and the conditions. The old courthouses at Guthrie, Oklahoma, or Tombstone, Arizona, for example, are but two among many mute witnesses to an effort at architecture by someone without any understanding of it.

But the greatest leveler was the development of a national instead of a regional pattern of life. This was substantially a product of technology.

The balloon frame was such a leveler. For the critic-historians John Kouwenhoven and Sigfried Giedion it is a symbol of the properties of the American "vernacular." Certainly this light wooden frame covered by boards was an American invention. The quick, economical and often insubstantial way to assemble a house was soon adopted after Augustine Taylor of Hartford, Connecticut, arrived in Chicago in 1833 and proceeded to build St. Mary's Church on such a frame. First described in Gervase Wheeler's *Homes for the People*, of 1855, this structural system soon replaced the old heavy methods of timber framing. Its speed of erection permitted whole towns to spring up overnight looking much the same wherever they rose.

The professional architects were less enthusiastic about the invention and were not necessarily blind in this attitude. Not imaginative enough to see what could be done with it, they were all too reasonably depressed by what was being done. Thus Calvert Vaux called the new buildings of 1857 "bare, bald white cubes." Distressed by these, his strange remedy was to use the frame to build Moorish arcades and Chinese balconies.

That the indigenous and the regional would decay was seen as early as 1819 by Latrobe when he entered in his diary of January 25 the note that the French flavor of New Orleans would be reduced to the standards of Baltimore and Philadelphia. "We shall introduce many grand & profitable improvements, but they will take the place of much elegance, ease, and some convenience."

4

THIS did not happen overnight. As Americans stood poised in 1800 for the great western expansion, they were still rural-minded, racially homogeneous, economically differentiated, regionally oriented, unprepared for the onslaught of technology. They lived in a clear architectural tradition of neat domestic buildings in which a city was only a larger village. The natural expectation was that these cultural traditions would simply spread westwards with the men who carried them. But the West itself, together with the rapid change in industrial technology, declined such a conclusion; first the results and in the end the aspirations as well.

In retrospect, the early Federalist days may seem more attractive than they actually were, but attractive or not they must now pass. Industrialism was beginning to stamp the new pattern. Its rise prompted Emerson to remark, "a cleavage is occurring in the hitherto firm granite of the past and a new era is nearly arrived."

In the sixty years after 1800 Americans occupied the most productive parts of their continent from ocean to ocean and the western expansion on the land flowed from the industrial expansion of the East. Furs, farms, speculative land profits, and precious metals had drawn Americans westward in that order. By 1849 all these magnets still had power. At the time of Lincoln's inauguration, however, the total population mustered but a little over thirty millions; the center of it was only at Chillicothe, Ohio, though it had moved steadily westward along the thirty-ninth parallel from Baltimore, where it lay at the end of the Revolution. Now the industrial Middle West had joined the older New England and Middle Atlantic states in accounting for three fifths of the population and almost all of the industrial wealth; another three tenths were in the Southern states east of the great river; only a tenth of the Americans lived west of the Mississippi; only a handful had reached California. The coming years belonged to the Middle West, and nowhere was this more clear than in the Civil War itself, which was won by U. S. Grant in the valley of the Mississippi despite the brilliance of Jackson and Lee in the valley of Virginia.

The people of the United States, with the exception of the Negro slaves and a declining number of Indians, continued to be essentially a single race, and it was not until the reactionary troubles in Europe of the 1840s that Germans came to change the long-enduring pattern of an immigration ninety per cent of which had been from the United Kingdom. But the Germans, quantitatively significant, did not offer any problems of assimilation or any serious change in the cultural outlook.

America was moving toward urbanism, but slowly. If five thousand people were a city, then perhaps one fifth of Americans lived in cities in 1860. The area around New York held a million people but no other American city came near to it. There was but one other with more than half a million, only nine altogether to boast more than 100,000 while only one twelfth of the people lived in such great congregations. Three fifths of all of the workers were in agriculture, even before you counted the Southern slaves. We were still basically a rural people following the pattern that Thomas Jefferson had laid down a half century before.

Major technological changes were preparing in the wings but the actors on the stage were horses, whale oil, and illuminating gas, canals, and paddle wheels; even the locomotive now snorting its way across the Mississippi was a romantic adolescent.

Only a prophetic man might have noted that the independent yeoman of Jefferson would soon be replaced by the businessman farmer of the prairie. The transportation system had just begun to open the markets to Western agriculture; the new wide fields encouraged the use of horse-drawn machines that might not have been maneuvered over a rocky hillside or in a forest glade. Machines cost money and the farmer began to yield some self-sufficiency for more cash, to become an employer of semispecialized transient labor. By 1860 this was not an uncommon practice in Ohio, Indiana, Illinois, and Michigan; crop specialization had begun; more machines demanded larger acreage and required fewer hands; so the agrarian exodus was prepared if not in full swing.

In the city, urbanity was uncommon. City streets when they were lighted at all relied on gas which had increased in popularity from Murdock's inventions of 1798 and particularly after the demonstration of street lighting on Pall Mall in 1807. Domestic lighting came from gas or candles or the whale oil of Nantucket and New Bedford. Electricity was still a matter of scientific curiosity. In the century after Franklin caught the lightning with his kite, noteworthy and fundamental discoveries about currents, voltages, resistances, electromagnetism, and induction had been made, so that by 1830 the essentials for electric lighting and power had been prepared. But for the time they lay unapplied and there was a still greater delay in applying the discoveries of the late '50s of the use of lead in a storage battery or of the glow on the glass wall near the cathode of a gas-filled tube.

Electricity whether as a source of light or power had no significant effect on architectural developments between 1800 and 1860. Neither did petroleum. In 1859 a well was dug near Titusville, Pennsylvania, but the few who saw riches at the bottom of the pipe thought in terms of kerosene and a way to light homes. To be sure, an Englishman named Samuel Brown had succeeded in exploding gas in an atmospheric engine as early as 1823 and had moved to some exploitation of the internal combustion principle for stationary engine purposes at Croydon. Thus the knowledge of internal combustion, the storage battery, and the fuel to be used were all ready but it would be a long time before architecture would become servant of the automobile.

On the other hand the people of these sixty years moved rapidly to develop water and rail transportation. In the sixty years after Fitch, Fulton and Stevens carried out their faltering demonstrations, the trans-oceanic steamship became a clear success, reasonably safe, reasonably comfortable. Over much of the period, canal and river-boat systems were important modifiers of American development. The Erie Canal began to operate in 1825; it brought prosperity to the state and city of New York and produced backwaters in Massachusetts and Pennsylvania. The Ohio and Mississippi were alive with paddle wheels. Ideas and people moved with the steamer; and despite the picture of wide-hatted, long-cigarred, drooping-mustached gamblers in fancy vests, the arts traveled more smoothly on the river boats than they did on the prairie schooners. Architecture and building materials alike moved down the Ohio from the English East and up the Mississippi from the French New Orleans; they met at St. Louis. Even the architectural fashions were reflected in the river boats and from the river boats to the adjacent land.

But of all the advances in transportation, the growth of the railroads was most prophetic. It had taken more than forty years to get from Newcomen's pumps (1726) to Watt's condenser (1769) and almost as long again to Stephenson's locomotives. In 1830 the engine Tom Thumb raced against a horse for the Baltimore and Ohio Railroad — and lost, but it was almost the last defeat for a century. In the next thirty years the rails entered Chicago and crossed the Mississippi. By 1830 there were 31,000 miles of railroad track, heavily concentrated however in the Northeast. As the rails pushed through the land they too carried ideas and materials to hammer at the palisades of regionalism; but for the moment transportation charges discouraged the architectural use of exogenous materials, and the main effect of the rails was to cut the cities in pieces, to create perpetual blight along their smoke-blackened rights of way, and to begin the demand for some less matter-of-fact approaches to the station whence a traveler would launch his exciting journey and at which he would alight at journey's end.

In 1860 the larger cities had some horse-drawn cars which had been used in old towns like Boston for more than a quarter of a century. They were fast enough for existing urban needs. There were portents of how they could be faster in London's new underground railroad.

The power which made the locomotive possible had also been harnessed to manufacturing. Indeed, the two things went together for without a strong manufacturing industry there would have been no need for the railroads. There had been a productive textile industry for a long time and by 1798 Eli Whitney had taught the virtue of interchangeable parts. Americans were ingenious in developing the machine tools which lie at the base of any serious industrial expansion. They had found ways to make other articles in considerable supply by standardizing their designs and though these ways were tentative it was sensed that standardization is essential for large-scale manufacture, and that it is not *ipso facto* harmful.

The most exciting promise for architecture was no doubt the new metallic material, steel. The recent inventions of Bessemer in England and the less well-known American, Kelly, were being

B*

adopted by 1860 in America for rolled rails, but the beams and the columns were yet to come, so the promise of steel for architecture could only be felt in a future time.

Thus the period was rather one of preparation for a technological-industrial nation than of its realization. It was an age of horses, gas, coal, steam, iron; not an age of automobiles, electricity, petroleum and steel. It was an age in which education was either remarkably theoretical and classical or overly practical. Technological education was in its infancy. West Point and Rensselaer Polytechnic Institute were the only senior institutions in which rudiments of a technological training might be sought.

Nor had the development of industry yet led to significant changes in the lot of the workingman. Organized labor was inconsequential and unorganized labor could not play a forceful role in architecture.

What was more evident was the physical devastation of the countryside brought on by careless applications of the new technology. Where once painters had delighted in the apparition of gleaming and gay locomotives chugging across an English moor, now a poet like Wordsworth could see only the desecration of the land and the degradation of the cottager. Even the optimistic Dickens turned from the cheery prophecies of *Pickwick Papers* to the dismay of *Hard Times*, after the Chartist riots. No doubt the dinginess and despair of industrial England were greater than the dinginess and despair of industrial America, for England was at the moment moving at a faster pace. But the results were the same in America. The new industrial works *were* dirtier than a New England village; they *did* produce smoke and grime; the rails *did* chew up the hillsides to get through; and the conditions of labor *were* uncomfortable and unsafe. In this stage of its development, industrial America destroyed more beauty than it produced, uprooted better habits of life than the substitutes it proffered.

Despite the enthusiasms of the innovators and the pioneers, the people were clearly ambivalent about what they were doing. Industrialism was exciting and promising but it was also dirty and vulgar; it needed counterpoint in a different world. For the moment anyway the gate between the two worlds could be shut and safely guarded and there was little doubt which was the more pleasant side of the gate. It is not surprising that the artists were the greatest victims of this ambivalence.

The depiction of American historical events which had fascinated painters like Benjamin West and John Trumbull no longer seemed to fascinate. The painters were preoccupied with classical subjects which had little relation to the lives or education of the Americans who were living in the industrial towns spread out near the factories. Some did understand and love the American rural landscape cast in the romantic haze of English landscape painting as it might be by Thomas Cole and others of the Hudson River School. Indeed, the bolder excursions of Inness on the Delaware were troubling. A closer documentation of the real America did wake interest when men as talented as Audubon, Catlin, and Bingham or Mount portrayed the details of the birds, Indians, or life on the rivers. But even the frontier ought not to look too raw and it was the romantic Bierstadt who knew what kind of West was wanted in the salon.

The gargantuan industrial infant did not often seem a suitable subject for any painter, just as novelists did not know how to come to grips with business and, saving Hawthorne, did not even seem to want to try. A painter like John Neagle might idealize a blacksmith as a representative of American technology, but the blacksmith was remarkably clean and really a symbol of the village rather than the industrial economy. Despite a few exceptions it was left to Currier and Ives to see the excitement of a steamboat, a railroad, or a steel mill.

The *cognoscenti* were few in number, aloof, and self-satisfied. They looked to Europe for their references in the arts, were happy that the "best" painters like William Morris Hunt should study with and be influenced by Millet or the classicist Gérôme and not by the more contemporary Delacroix and Courbet. They looked to Europe but overlooked industrial England as firmly as they overlooked industrial America. When murals were needed for the national Capitol they turned naturally to Italy and the subjects were not to be those of the frontier or the factory but rather abstractions in the form of classical allegories.

Beyond the *cognoscenti* nobody cared about painting. Benja-

min West had learned this earlier; Samuel F. B. Morse epitomized it when he deserted painting for electricity. Whistler
wasted no time in leaving America for good. It was not surprising
that Americans painted less well than Europeans; seldom studied
with *avant-garde* painters; invariably lagged behind the European
movements by a quarter century or more. It was even less surprising that their subject matter avoided the forces which, outside the
arts, were most moving America.

If this were true for our painters it was even more true of our
sculptors, who went in for the literal interpretation of native
subjects or of heroes from the American scene or for the rendering of a few imagined classical topics. Powers's *Greek Slave* which
was so much admired from 1840 on had literally nothing to do
with anything that ever had existed in America. Rogers's groups
were more indigenous and homely, and found their way, as Max-
field Parrish would later, to many an American parlor.

The trail of the American writers was more complex. Whatever
the talents of the tragic Melville and the dark Poe, they did not
grapple directly with the American industrial scene, whether or
not they blamed it for the defeat of the American dream. Together with the more popular Hawthorne and Emerson they were
later to be identified as the American giants. But while Paris met
Les Fleurs du Mal and *Madame Bovary*, Boston and New York
savored the *Song of Hiawatha* or *The Autocrat of the Breakfast
Table*. The contest between Americans and Europeans was
hardly more equal in letters than it was in the visual arts. Despite
all of Emerson's fanfares the shackles of colonialism had by no
means all been severed by 1860.

For architecture, American engineers and particularly their European stimulators had paved a road more brilliant and daring
than was yet to be trod. The Howe and Pratt trusses were well
known. Roebling's cables at the Niagara Bridge had demonstrated the potentialities of suspension. Labrouste, Horeau, and
Baltard in France and Paxton in England had built or proposed
highly imaginative iron structures at the Library of Ste.
Geneviève, the Bibliothèque Nationale, Les Halles Centrales,
and at the later Crystal Palace of 1851 in London. James Bogardus had demonstrated a five-story iron factory in New York; in

1853 Elisha Graves Otis showed that an elevator could be safe; steel was just around the corner while Aspidin's Portland cement was known from 1824. In a humbler sphere the balloon frame, as we have seen, had opened wide flexibility for wooden structures.

Thus from 1830 on, technological opportunities beckoned feverishly to the architects. By 1860 most of the potentially revolutionary materials and methods had at least made their debut. Bunning's iron-domed Coal Exchange in London could have been visited any time after 1849. If American architecture chose, on the whole, to look rather to the neo-Renaissance gentilities of Barry's Reform Club or the Red House built in 1859 on Bexley Heath by Philip Webb and William Morris, it was not exactly the fault of the engineers, although most of them had a taste in architecture which was even more conservative than that of the architects. And if the various American architectural efforts seem to have centered around matters of eclectic choice, the architects were not behaving differently than other Americans. The whole long debate about whether American buildings should be Georgian or Greek or Gothic or Egyptian was quite unrelated to the fact that Americans were moving westward, that railroads were building, that the big shift from an agricultural life to an industrial one had clearly begun to accelerate.

There were few specialists in those early days and they were good at more than one thing. A doctor, Thornton, won the architectural competition for the national Capitol; a painter, Peale, was a skillful inventor of mechanical devices; an architect, Latrobe, was a good engineer, wise enough to be commissioned by the American Philosophical Society to make the official response to an inquiry from Holland on the state of engines in America. A President, Madison, personally sought a new architect for the Capitol and had the sure taste to choose Bulfinch; another President, Jefferson, had ideas of his own about architecture and they were not naïve or untutored. He was the last, even the only American President, of whom this could be said.

The American society still thought essentially in village patterns, even in the city; expected to solve all the problems of Federalism in the terms of Madison rather than those of Calhoun; found it reasonable that the finest buildings should be devoted to the offices of democracy and to the service of the church. And at the beginning Americans knew how to build such buildings.

During the sixty years before the Civil War they forgot how to build so well and so beautifully. They left the security of the Georgian rules but found no compensating security elsewhere. They experimented with rationalistic architecture as proposed by Latrobe. They left this promising theory before it was mature, to dabble with a variety of associational ideas about nature and about earlier buildings. From the experiments with association they gleaned a moment of dignified aesthetic success in the Classic Revival; and a more dubious sense of moral fulfillment in the first Gothic Revival. But associationalism also led to importations from Egypt, India, China, via Victorian England, in two orgies of eclectic fashion which left their cities without dignity or repose. At the end rationalism was recalled in a utilitarian cast-iron architecture which had some good qualities. Once the Georgian convention had been abandoned, though, the experiments swirled through time with no clean-cut beginning and end. Always the choices seemed to involve little concern with the vital questions of the needs of the new cities, of industry, of technology.

We shall never forget the charm of Charleston, South Carolina, even though we may never again achieve it. That it has lasted so long depends upon its failure to keep pace with the times after the Civil War. But admire its ancient glories as we may, we must not forget that the streets of Charleston below Broad Street represent the Indian summer of a way of life and owe their continued elegance to an escape from reality, though there has been a time when Charleston was not an escape.

5

AT the end architects were divided into camps, each championing a style. If you listened to them all you might come out like young George B. Post, who began to study architecture about 1860; to him it seemed as though there were only confusion. Medievalists saw no merit in classic art; devotees of the Renaissance thought modern Gothic beneath contempt. Over all, Post noted that American painters and sculptors frankly stated that they believed there was no art in architecture.

Post's bewilderment was understandable. By 1860 there was little agreement about any of the big architectural questions. Some new men supported regionalism as others had once favored a national architecture. Other new architects sought something more personal than the anonymous classical results. Some argued, as more talented men have done since, that nature should be the chief determinant of architecture; but others insisted that geometry and formal composition should not be abandoned. No one could escape the great argument between those who wanted to derive a national architecture from Europe and those who exhorted young artists to aim at all costs for something indigenous. One might want to cling to the faith that churches would remain the dominant symbols of American society; but he could not ignore Bogardus's successful prefabricated-iron emblems of business enterprise. Was America to remain a collection of picturesque, peaceful, rural villages, or to become a nation of large and elegant cities, or a nation of small planned industrial communities? Where was each American to stand on questions of taste — with the naïve Jacksonian hope for egalitarian art, with Jefferson's distrust in it, with the effort of Calvert Vaux to find a democratic way of controlling it? There was an easy way (and there always has been) to avoid such questions. Men like George Post took it. Like most architects, before and since, they drifted with the crowd, willingly adopting what was fashionable at the moment even though the changes were frequent and violent. Those who did debate the questions were naturally less content than Post to satisfy current fashion, more willing, even anxious, to affront it.

By 1840 a young aspirant to architecture might gain only a confused picture of America by walking, for example, the streets of New York. At Hudson Park there was a serene moment in the contemplation of John McComb's dignified St. John's Church of 1803-1807, but nearby the Infant School Society met in a ramshackle basement. Wall Street clearly revealed a society in transition; plain brick houses alternated with Greek temples, occupied by banks or the Merchants' Exchange, and here too were drab houses for insurance companies and newspapers. At the Fulton Street Market in 1821 one might walk along cobblestoned streets, past arcaded stalls, only to pick a way among barrels, casks, wheelbarrows, hucksters' wagons and horses toward the tower of an undistinguished church. From the ferry at Brooklyn Heights one could see Underhill's handsome Colonnade Buildings, while at the North River he would meet a jumbled assemblage of utilitarian brick buildings forming an iron foundry where locomotive parts were made. Or one might visit Henry Brevoort's Ionic-porticoed three-story brownstone at Fifth and Ninth, designed by Alexander Jackson Davis. All its interior spaces, from the library and parlor to the entrance with its curved stair, announced a New Yorker of taste and distinction; yet not far away at the headquarters of the Fourteenth Ward on Broadway in 1840 the presidential campaign of William Henry Harrison was conducted from a synthetic log cabin fitted chiefly with hard cider. It would be easy to wonder which was the true America, and perplexity might mount when one compared Rogers's Mercantile Exchange of 1836-1842 and its giant Ionic portico and large Pantheonic dome with Barnum's Museum on Broadway, its upper face covered with a giant billboard showing the picture of a menacing serpent. A note of the future was suggested in James Bogardus's cast-iron house; or by 1857 in the Haughwout Store at Broadway and Broome, where Elisha Graves Otis installed the first passenger elevator with automatic safety devices; but these were still incidents within a city that was undecided about its future form, as indeed it still is. The chaos of 1840 may not seem remarkable to an American who knows the contrasts of Manhattan in 1960 but it was more perceptible then, standing as it did against the background of a time when cities had managed more unity, dignity and repose.

Indeed, not all American cities had yet followed the example of New York. Philadelphia, more than most of the others, demonstrated that a commercial architecture might be dignified. From her eighteenth-century heritage she had retained an orderly plan, a small scale and attractive residential squares. Latrobe's Bank of Pennsylvania, 1799-1801, with its Ionic portico and rotunda banking room, had shown that art and commerce were not intrinsically enemies. William Strickland's Second Bank of the United States (later the Customs House) had a fine banking room framed by Ionic colonnades under a barrel-vaulted ceiling; its Doric porticoes were modeled after those of the Parthenon. With Thomas U. Walter's Philadelphia Saving Fund Society Building of 1839-1840, these established a classic precedent for banks. Anyone who knew the Burlington Arcade in London would have noticed similar corridors of interior shops in John Haviland's Arcade of 1827. More elaborate Greek Revival architecture could be found at the Merchants' Exchange designed by Strickland in 1832-1834; its Doric west front, its curved Corinthian façade at the east, and its finial from the Choragic Monument taught lessons in archeology, a gentlemanly study. There were innovative structures too like the cast-iron plated office building Cummings erected for the Penn Mutual Life Insurance Company of 1850-1851. A prescient visitor might have seen in William Johnston's ten-story Jayne Building, of 1849, a premonition of the skyscrapers that would rise soon enough. Altogether few Americans would deny that commerce was well served by art in Philadelphia and that it might happen elsewhere.

English visitors from Mrs. Trollope in 1827 to Charles Dickens in 1842 had more reservations. The lady concluded very soon, as British tourists had and have a way of doing, that we were not doing well and were harbingers of a decaying European civilization. Dickens felt that America was seldom so refined as at The Tremont House in Boston. But many Americans preferred the advice of Robert Mills, "Go not to the Old World for your examples . . . it is our destiny to lead, not to be led," despite the clumsy proportions and details of Mills's own buildings.

Everybody held the national capital in scorn despite its pretensions. Though it later became America's best tribute to monumental urban design, Washington was nearly ruined by abuse in the period before the Civil War. The term "magnificent distances" was used in scorn. Abigail Adams who was used to only modest luxury in Quincy complained about the mud of Washington; she was forced to use the incompleted East Room of the White House as a drying room for her laundry, there was no running water, and only temporary stairs afforded access to the upper story. Conditions were not much better at the time of Lincoln's first inaugural. Even after the Executive Mansion was burned by the British in 1814 (and its blackened sandstone walls were painted white), successive Congresses begrudged any funds spent upon improving its furnishings and setting; they permitted public and private architecture to destroy the brilliance of the city plan that the French engineer, Major Pierre Charles L'Enfant, had laid down for Washington beginning in 1791. This plan proposed a grand development of the area on the land lying at the confluence of the Potomac and Anacostia Rivers. The best sites were to be reserved for principal buildings, of which the most important, the Capitol, would stand on Jenkins Hill, a plateau some eighty feet above the rivers: it was "a pedestal waiting for a monument," said L'Enfant. On a line westward from the Capitol he laid out a grand avenue, four hundred feet wide, where foreign ministers might have spacious houses and gardens. A mile and a half northwest along the Mall, a second axis would strike north and south, leading from the White House to the Washington Monument's knoll and southward to the marshy estuary of Tiber Creek, which L'Enfant proposed to canalize. Such principal sites were to be coordinated upon a gridiron of streets running east-west and north-south. Broad diagonal avenues or "lines of direct communication" would connect principal points. Where two or more diagonals intersected there would be squares or circles, carefully adjusted to afford "reciprocity of sight" from one civic space to another. The squares and principal sites would provide opportunities for fountains, statues, a national church, residences and small churches, colleges, academies and buildings for various societies. Leading from one large square, near the White House, L'Enfant proposed to have an avenue lined with shops and an arched covering over the pavement. But his intention — to "unite the useful with the commodious and agreeable" — almost went unrealized at all and was never realized in full. The scale of his avenues acted as a challenge to later architects to erect overblown classic buildings. His formal scheme was not protected from those who tried to turn the Mall into a romantic garden and built the Smithsonian Institution, an ugly red-sandstone building, a medieval castle with towers and turrets, designed by James Renwick. Washington developed westward rather than eastward as the planner had proposed; the site of the Washington Monument was shifted southeast so that the axes were thrown off; Tiber Creek was allowed to become a menace to health. Beginning in 1835, the tracks of the Baltimore and Ohio Railroad were laid to the capital, and the Pennsylvania Railroad built a terminal on the Mall itself. Areas but a block away from the great avenues, even near the Capitol, became squalid slums. L'Enfant languished in poverty and obscurity until his death in 1825, and his plan was progressively misinterpreted, disfigured and neglected until a commission appointed by Senator James McMillan of Michigan revived it in 1901. Unfortunately, no similar enlightened interest has resurrected the comparably urbane plans made for Detroit and Indianapolis, which fell victim to the disregard that destroyed the eighteenth-century American city plans and left the cities that had them in not much better shape than the cities with none.

The arts had still to struggle against three old things: utilitarian standards, commercial expediency and puritanical suspicion. James Jackson Jarves thought that the spirit that sustains trade could do nothing except debase art. Evidence for such a belief was bountiful. Even the railroad stations, which should have intimated America's future architecture, were uniformly bad, though dull, utilitarian buildings like Baltimore's Clare Street Station were occasionally offset by a whimsical pavilion like Austin's New Haven station of 1848. The adventure of traveling was often announced by bizarre entrances, like the Egyptian portico of New Bedford's Old Pearl Street Depot. Such absurdities in the name of the arts were enough to damage them even in the eyes of those who were not unsympathetic.

6

THE first major attempt to bring some higher degree of order to American architecture was made by rationalist architects. Beginning in France and England, they questioned classic unity. They argued that form should be a rational expression of spaces that were arranged strictly for use. Critics and architects alike heaped scorn on Palladian excesses that permitted false windows and façades which masked interior functions as at Mount Vernon. Architecture, the rationalists asserted, must be adapted to use, to climate, to structure, not to abstract principles of unified form. Adaptation became the basis for a new international architecture. The Italian Lodoli expressed an extreme view: "In architecture only that shall show that has a definite function, and which derives from the strictest necessity."

Such ideas gained support in America through the circulation of writings by English or Scottish philosophers like Francis Hutcheson or Archibald Alison, whose essays on taste written in 1790 were republished in Hartford, Connecticut, in 1821: " . . . all machines or instruments," he wrote, "are called beautiful by the artists, which are well adapted to the end of their arts."

Such avowed espousals of mechanism are too easily misread by modernists, as premonitions of the machine aesthetic to be announced fully almost a century later, in 1925. But Lodoli, Hutcheson and Alison had no such intentions even when they said that forms should be adapted to use. The forms they had in mind were classic elements; the point was that they should be composed on non-classical rules and without regard to the classical principles of unity.

Rationalism led to a new architecture, distinctly different from the preceding Georgian and its Renaissance precursor. The movement began in Europe, in such works as Sir John Soane's Bank of England or the Barrière de la Villette by Nicholas Ledoux in 1785-1789. Valadier and Piranesi announced it in Italy; Persius, Gilly and even Schinkel in Germany. By the early nineteenth century when it came to America, the style had even invaded Russia.

St. Chad's at Shrewsbury, England, designed by George Steuart (1791), exhibits the major characteristics of rational architecture. It has four parts: an entrance hall preceded by a portico, a two-storied tower, a staircase leading to galleries, and a large church hall. Each part is distinct; the cylinders are opposed to each other; from the exterior they exhibit an array of self-centered, independent rooms of different shapes. Unlike baroque effusive architecture, St. Chad's is reserved, and baroque unity disappears as parts are placed in strong isolation so that they rebel against any blending and harmony; they are juxtaposed without easy rhythms, regular cadence or suave intersecting curves. This composition of pure geometric shapes — with classic features — is a presage of an aesthetic that gains dynamism by ignoring unity, and gains useful disposition of interior spaces by refusing to be ruled by classical balance, hierarchy or axial arrangement.

The Frenchmen Joseph Jacques Ramée, L'Enfant, Joseph F. Mangin and Maximilian Godefroy were principally responsible for bringing rationalism to America. Ramée's design for Union College at Schenectady was characteristic. So was Godefroy's First Unitarian Church in Baltimore of 1817-1818, a single cube capped by a hemispherical dome, with a deep entrance designated by a triangular pediment that is carried upon arches supported by columns. The massive, simple geometry, the monumental scale, and the bold juxtaposition of strong shapes are all quite different from such Georgian buildings as the neighboring Otterbein Church of 1784. Subsequently, architects who were born in America took up the style; Robert Mills in the Sansom Street Baptist Church in Philadelphia, Isaiah Rogers in his hotels, and Alexander Parris in the Quincy Markets at Boston. Towards the end of his career, even Charles Bulfinch began to move towards rationalism with his University Hall at Harvard and the Church of Christ at Lancaster, Massachusetts.

But the most important American designer in the new style was the English-born Benjamin Henry Latrobe, whose architectural and other knowledge merited the respect of Jefferson. Latrobe recognized that architects must seek more than harmony of form. He was almost unique in early nineteenth-century America for achieving an integration of "firmness, commodity and delight" within forms that were expressive as well. His deprecations of Mount Vernon must be understood in terms of that synthesis. It led him to deplore the misdeeds of carpenter-builders like those who submitted plans for the national Capitol; it also led him to disagree with gentleman-architects like Jefferson who, the "apostle of individualism" himself, paradoxically chose "as his first master in architecture, Palladio, who passes as the chief representative of dogmatic authority."

In Center Square, Philadelphia, in 1799, Latrobe built an engine house for the pumps that raised water from the Schuylkill

River. The building had a parallelepiped base that supported a tall cylinder terminated by a low dome. Its basic conformation was similar to Ledoux's Barrière at Paris. Like the French building, its proportions, emphatically unclassical, were tall at the top and low at the base. No blending ameliorated the abrupt junctions of the strong geometrical parts. The building announced the architect's intention to utilize classical elements, like columns, within pure geometric forms, to keep the buildings simple in silhouette and allow use to be the major determinant in the composition. "I would never put a cupola on any spherical dome. It is not the *ornament*, it is the *use* I want," he once wrote.

The Merchants' Exchange and Custom House at Baltimore, begun in 1816 and opened in 1820, a collaborative work of Latrobe and Godefroy, again had a boldly geometrical composition and was eminently well fitted for the stock exchange and bank it housed. These were nineteenth-century institutions; no ancient formalism, whether Greek, Roman or Renaissance, would produce buildings suitable for their use. "Our religion," Latrobe wrote, "requires churches wholly different from the [Greek and Roman] temples, our Government, our legislative assemblies, and our courts of justice, buildings of entirely different principles from their basilicas; and our amusements could not possibly be performed in their theaters or amphitheaters." He insisted that architectural form proceed from the character of the institution it was intended to house, rather than from books about design. This led him in 1807 to try to invent new minor architectural elements as well, such as the American maize capital for the new vestibule of the Old Senate or the tobacco-plant capital for the Senate Rotunda.

Similarly his Roman Catholic Cathedral in Baltimore begun in 1808 and dedicated in 1821, was a succession of surely designed spaces, which were rational volumetric interpretations of a liturgical plan, clearly expressed in elevation. Latrobe began with a freedom of planning and expression unknown to Georgian formalism and produced this remarkable concatenation of unblended elementary spaces and masses. There are classical details to be sure and they were made more classical by the porch added in the

1870s but they are combined non-classically in a composition that is sustained only by the balancing of pure, elementary geometry.

No matter how much he respected Latrobe's rational exposition of useful forms, and though he frequently consulted him about his plans for the University of Virginia, Thomas Jefferson was never able to bring himself fully to relinquish formalism.

His initial proposal for the University was a direct attack on the problem, seeking a practical correction of the defects he had criticized in the dormitory at William and Mary, but the solution lacked architectural character. Following some suggestions made by Latrobe, Jefferson revised the plan so that it provided for an academic community centered on a dominant rotunda, the library, which stood upon an eminence, whence lawns descended in a series of terraces. Two rows of parallel buildings stood on each side of the lawn. The innermost row contained pavilions for classrooms or faculty residences. These were connected by covered passageways that gave access also to low buildings where some of the students lived. Beyond the first row, or lawn, there were gardens enclosed by serpentine walls; these were closed by the second row of buildings, called "ranges," providing more dormitories. The excellent site plan achieved a community of buildings each of which served a definite purpose; it permitted variety within an over-all integration; it protected the community against the spread of fire or disease; it isolated noise. Thus far it obeyed good rational principles. But Jefferson could not follow rationalism to the end. Instead, he ransacked Palladio's books to find temple façades for his pavilions; he studied drawings of the Pantheon, made them more classical by altering the proportions of the porch, and transformed the library into a half-sized Pantheon which he called the perfect model of "spherical architecture."

Thus Jefferson represented the two sides of the architectural coin in America at the turn of the century; the eminently practical builder who insisted upon precise cost estimates and good performance; the amateur gentleman-architect who demanded correctness of form, who was willing to copy earlier buildings no matter how incompatible or disjunctive the resulting combinations might be. It did not disturb him at all to hang a practical balcony from the center of the columns in an otherwise classical façade, or to propose that the White House imitate the Villa Rotonda.

The dichotomy amazed some of Jefferson's friends. Latrobe, for example, disliked the reliance upon precedent which appeared again in the house at Monticello. Here the principal façade was a restudy of a design made by the English architect Robert Adam. But this overt formalism was incompatible with Jefferson's other interests so the classical sophistication was at once denied by the lobby of Monticello. George Ticknor, an urbane student of cosmopolitan life, did not like the contrast when he met, in the entrance hall, many kinds of ingenious mechanical clocks, weathervanes, buffalo heads, Indian maps on leather, in short the paraphernalia of Jefferson's private *Wunderkammer*.

We do not find such extravaganzas surprising in the nineteenth-century home of Theodore Roosevelt at Oyster Bay but they are less easily associated with Jefferson, whose boundless curiosity is still unappreciated. Yet Jefferson prized both the enclosure and the museum. The ambivalence was very Jeffersonian — and very American.

Latrobe's attempt at developing an American architecture with classical elements composed in a useful, rational exposition of spaces was rapidly submerged after 1825 by romanticism and formalism of the kind Jefferson displayed at Monticello.

7

Now the whole encyclopedic history of architecture became a possible mine for American buildings. In 1829 the *American Quarterly Review* devoted forty pages of its March issue to Egyptian architecture. The *American Monthly Magazine* for April, 1835, contained an editorial, "Architectural Designs," which was a savage attack upon Town and Davis's design for the New York Customs House, an "utterly monstrous and barbarous" sin, combining a dome with the temple form of a Greek Parthenon or Thesion (Hephaistaion). The editorial praised Haviland's Egyptian prison at New York, the morbid "Tombs." In 1844, Arthur Gilman advised architects to seize upon Renaissance styles and develop them further. His own approach was fully eclectic: his Arlington Street Unitarian Church in Boston, he said, was based on the English Renaissance of Gibbs on the exterior, while its interior was inspired by the Santa Annunziata at Genoa. Americans now built villas modeled after Tuscan country houses and Chinese temples; from Asia, Indian sources were invoked, too, as at Armsmere and at P. T. Barnum's Iranistan near Bridgeport, Connecticut. Barnum said he hoped to repeat in America the success scored by King George's Brighton Pavilion, but in the end Iranistan was not a copy. Instead, it was an American country house with a square central block and balanced wings but it was all bedecked with bulbous domes and exotic minarets. Easily seen from the New Haven railroad trains, it was an early example of American architectural advertising from 1848 when it was built to 1857 when it burned down. All this was, it must be said, not merely an American extravaganza. Again the Europeans were leading the way and with more *brio*. Now the lead was notably English again and the pipers to this architectural masque played even more boldly and of course much earlier in the motherland, where Jesuit missionaries to China and Japan brought back an irregular and asymmetrical way of gardening called Sharawadgi. Horace Walpole converted his country house at Twickenham into a "Gothick" castle he called "Strawberry Hill," and Richard Payne Knight, influenced by the landscapes of Claude Lorraine and the Poussins, set Downton Castle in a wild, irregular terrain where trees had torn and shredded shapes, where dead branches were scarred, even burnt, looked menacing by moonlight, as in some of the romantic scenes of Fuseli, Blake, or Schinkel; waterfalls and precipitous crags, rude bridges and ruins announced nature as wild and uncontrollable, the destroyer of man's artifacts, unencompassable by formal geometry or reason.

In 1761 William Chambers adorned Kew Gardens with a fullsized Chinese pagoda, and Hindu, Turkish and other exotic motives were imported from the "mysterious East" or the "barbarian Goths." William Wrighte's book of 1790 dealing with "Grotesque Architecture, or Rural Amusement" and offering plans for "Huts, Retreats, Summer and Winter Hermitages, Terminaries, Chinese, Gothic, and Natural Grottos, Cascades, Baths,

Mosques, Moresque Pavilions, Grotesque and Rustic Seats" came to America in 1835 after the conventional time lag. Americans could not be immune to such temptation in the days of their high romanticism; they are scarcely immune yet. But again their native sobriety and restraint made their picturesque work less extreme and therefore less effective than the work in Europe. Whatever might happen in American literature, American architectural romanticism was nearer to the spirit of Cooper or Irving than to that of Poe.

Much of eclectic architecture depended for its impact upon what has been called associationalism. Here the chief merit of a building was thought to lie not in its power to present a clear and distinct sensory impression, nor in its power to display the useful and structural organization of volumes of space, but rather in its power to evoke secondary reactions generally associated with the form. Those reactions might be subjective, personal, local or national; they might be purely literary. Such a view was derived from the philosopher and precursor of logical positivism, Hume: "Beauty is no quality in things themselves: It exists merely in the mind which contemplates them. . . ." What was admired was not necessarily beautiful; it was expressive, or, as Burke called it, "sublime."

8

ASSOCIATIONALISM spawned many progeny, sphinxes and ziggurats; an Egyptian hospital in Richmond, Virginia; Chinese temples in rural New York; artificially ruined castles in a St. Louis park. It led to a careless or a careful Gothic revival, but it also led back to a tender reconsideration of Greece and Rome. One of our finest architectural residues, the products of the Classic Revival, must thus be numbered among the offspring of associationalism.

It was perfectly possible, then, indeed easy, to be romantic about this most regular of architectures, especially if one looked upon it as the product of democratic societies, entertaining incomplete notions about the Periclean orations or the character of the early Roman Republic whose stalwart farmer citizens might seem to resemble the citizens of the new American Republic. It

was many years later that other Americans, not much more sure-
footed about their history, insisted on construing the classic symbols as those of imperialism. For the day they were taken as the
symbols of democracy and heartily welcomed on that ground.
Again European archeological knowledge supplied the preliminary fodder in a spate of books from England, France and Germany, detailing the ruins of Athens, Spalato, Palmyra, Baalbek,
Herculaneum and Pompeii. Winckelmann praised the political,
social and intellectual conditions that underlay the "noble simplicity and tranquil greatness," of Greek art. Chambers began scientific reconstruction when he built a Temple of the Sun in Kew
Gardens, in 1760. It was derived from Baalbek. In 1774 Clérisseau published a volume on Les Monuments de Nîmes which
included the famous Maison Carrée. As soon as the war was over
Jefferson posted to Nîmes and soon after, in collaboration with
Clérisseau, imitated the Maison Carrée in his design for the
Richmond Capitol. As Fiske Kimball points out, this portico
"was a frontispiece to all Virginia." He adds that in the classical
movement America was a leader not a follower in pressing it to its
extreme consequences.

Architects constantly railed against such subservience to precedent and warned of the shortcomings of formalism. "Wherever
the Grecian style can be copied without impropriety, I love to be
a . . . slavish . . . copyist," Latrobe wrote in his most patroniz-
ing way, but hastened to add that classical styles are inapplicable
to modern uses and climates. At the Franklin Institute in 1840
Thomas U. Walter, the architect of the dome on the Capitol at
Washington, lectured: "The popular idea that to design a building in Grecian taste is nothing more than to copy a Grecian building, is altogether erroneous. . . . If architects would oftener aim
to think as the Greeks thought, than to do as the Greeks did, our
columnar architecture would possess a higher degree of originality, and its character and expression would gradually become con-
formed to the local circumstances of the country, and the repub-
lican spirit of its institutions."

But clients and amateurs demanded correctness rather than
adaptation. In February, 1838, Philip Hone recorded in his diary:
"How strange it is that in all the inventions of modern times

architecture alone seems to admit of no improvement — every departure from the classical models of antiquity in this science is a departure from grace and beauty." Such a feeling among patrons of art stifled art; as Talbot Hamlin, the historian of the Greek Revival, noted, "at last, under the heavy blanket of correctness, it was smothered to death."

Thinking of that sort brought on the fiasco at Girard College in Philadelphia. Stephen Girard, the merchant-financier, had specified in his will the exact dimensions of the building he intended to have for instructing the orphans at the college he founded. He offered a premium for the best plan submitted in a closed architectural competition. The contest was won by Walter, whose plan did not please Nicholas Biddle, president of the National Bank, traveler in Greece, admirer of Byron, and amateur, who immediately wedged his way into membership on the building committee. He weaned Walter from the original plan and persuaded him to "take advantage of this rare opportunity of immortalizing himself by a perfect, chaste specimen of Grecian architecture." The trustees and councils hesitated, thinking a Greek temple out of character with Girard's request for a simple building; but Biddle rallied them to lay the foundation stone on July 4, 1833, and the Corinthian temple with elliptical groin-vaulted classrooms was warped to fit the dimensions specified in Girard's will. When, in 1847, the main building at Girard was completed, the taste of the day was again affirmed by a client, a literary man, not an architect. Joseph Chandler spoke of it as "the whited sepulchre of ancient art [that] shall . . . become the temple of moral life."

No style since the Georgian captured American hearts more fully than the classical, especially the Greek Revival. Scale and workmanship were often exquisite; the best results may vie with the best Georgian as America's finest effort to date. A Greek Revival town is a fine and handsome assembly of stately colonnades and well-turned building masses. One can catch glimpses of this civic beauty at Nantucket, where the whaling captains built Greek Revival houses, churches, banks and libraries in 1840-1860. The style moved westward to grace Saratoga Springs and Ovid in New York, Dayton, Ravenna and Newark in Ohio, Detroit and

Chicago; it moved south to Frankfort, Kentucky, to Tuscaloosa, Alabama, and Athens, Georgia. The buildings in those towns were not reproductions of whole Greek or Roman buildings; at most their porticoes or cornices were copies; but largely they should be regarded first in terms of their plans and sections, where the results were practical and graceful, and then in terms of their details whose refinement was frequently original as in Mills's Customs House at New Bedford or the church at Wickford, Rhode Island.

The vitality of Greek Revival design stemmed from a sure sense of architecture as a combination of use, construction and beauty, first of all in spaces. This can be clearly seen in the old Capitol at Frankfort, Kentucky, by Gideon Shryock. It has an excellent plan, in which an axial arrangement admits visitors past a portico to a one-story hall and then to a central, double circular stair of marble, built as a curved arch, which rises gracefully beneath the overarching dome. The spaces for the court of appeals, library, offices and committees are clustered on the first floor around the stair hall. Ingenious planning enabled the architect to gather the House of Representatives and Senate Chamber at the front and rear of the second floor. A section through the building shows a sure grasp of the space under the rotunda; the circular stair spirals gracefully upward through the space, which is pinched inward at the summit and funneled into a side-lighted cupola. According to Shryock, the inspiration for this old Kentucky Capitol was the temple of Athena Polias at Priene in Ionia; but he referred only to the portico; the arrangement of the whole building is as original, practical, and modern as it is beautiful; no Greek temple ever had a rotunda or staircase like those of the Capitol; none had a dome and lantern. Shryock thought as the Greeks thought, but he did not do as the Greeks did.

The Greek Revival moved across the land until it dried up in the plains. Besides Shryock, there were other fine practitioners like another of Latrobe's apprentices, William Strickland, the Philadelphia architect who designed the State Capitol at Nashville as well as St. Mary's Church there. Belmont, near Nashville, reveals once again the sureness of geometry which Strickland shared with other Greek Revival architects. Others like Francis Costigan showed more caprice but still dealt skillfully and with charm in buildings such as the Lanier House (1844) at Madison, Indiana, or the many-domed Institute for the Blind at Louisville (1851).

Houses like the Roper House in Charleston and Belo in Winston-Salem revealed to what a degree Southern taste in architectural matters would be missed after the Civil War. This impression is borne out as one moves into Prince Street in Athens, Georgia, or into Tuscaloosa, Alabama, where the house for the President at the University reveals an architectural taste that Northern cities neglected to their detriment during the '80s and '90s. No hotel in the North could boast greater elegance, magnificence or lavish formality than the rotunda of the St. Louis Hotel at New Orleans, designed by Jacques Bussière de Pouilly and built in 1836-1840. Urbane and monumental, its polychromed interiors were superb, reaching their climax in the columned rotunda and dome at the center. In the lower Mississippi Valley, the Greek Revival reached an apogee of refinement, with attenuated columns like those in Stanton Hall at Natchez and the Governor's Mansion at Jackson, Mississippi, and with original detail like the faceted blocks in the frieze of Shryock's State Capitol at Little Rock, Arkansas. The Greek Revival was especially popular for schools, like the one built at Norwalk, Ohio, in 1848, where Ionic columns, as graceful as any in the East, punctuate the façade. At Columbus, Ohio, the State Capitol exhibited the strong geometric forms of the style, and even farmhouses in remote Michigan, Gordon Hall at Dexter, for example, had a practical plan graced with a Doric portico. As it moved westward, the style declined; but federal buildings carried it nationally and even the gross scale of the United States Mint in San Francisco shows that the Greek Revival was a national style that was seldom used so poorly as to prevent its buildings from remaining superior to most in any city.

9

DURING the 1840s and '50s the Greek Revival, especially in the copied forms amateurs and clients often insisted on, was attacked by many critics. The most effective were associationalists who de-

nied the democratic association to argue instead that Greek forms
spoke of a pagan civilization incompatible with a modern Christian nation whose true architecture should be the Gothic. When
Alexander Jackson Davis completed his Gothic hall for New York
University, the critic Henry Cleveland, writing in the *North
American Review* of 1836, declared his pleasure upon learning
that Gore Hall Library at Harvard would also be Gothic, restud-
ied from King's College Chapel at Cambridge, England. Cleveland admired Gothic. He criticized Egyptian and Greek architecture because their religions were pagan, not Christian, disgusting,
absurd, superstitious. Gothic, he said, besides being Christian, allowed close adaptation of form to use. But expression was more
important than use: "There is a style of architecture which be-
longs peculiarly to Christianity . . . whose very ornaments remind one of the joys of life beyond the grave; whose lofty vaults
and arches are crowded with the forms of prophets and martyrs
and beatified spirits, and seem to resound with the choral hymns
of angels and archangels . . . the architecture of Christianity,
the sublime, the glorious Gothic."

Cleveland's sentimental yearning reflected a growing amateur
taste for Gothic architecture, which had gripped England in the
Oxford Movement and the Camden Society, which had initiated
greater liturgical ceremony within the Church of England and
influenced architects to follow medieval precedent. The eighteenth-century "Gothick" of Walpole's Strawberry Hill had already been undermined by archeological investigations into true
Gothic buildings which Rickman, Britton and Pugin published in
1805-1821. One notable architectural success in the perpendicular
style, Barry's and Pugin's Houses of Parliament, encouraged a
taste for better modern Gothic buildings. The older "Gothick"
succumbed. The zealous high priest of the new Revival in England was Augustus Welby Pugin, whose *True Principles of
Christian Architecture* confounded aesthetics and ethics in the
assertion that Gothic was a Christian architecture, and Gothic
buildings would influence people in Christian ways and beliefs.
Gothic churches inspire moral behavior, he thought, and medieval
towns were better than those of the nineteenth century. The idea
came to America in essays like Cleveland's and in one small

American book of naïve drawings, Bishop John Henry Hopkins's *Essay on Gothic Architecture*, published in 1836.

The early Gothic Revival, which entranced Americans in 1830-1860, simulated effects by any available means, rather than building in accordance with Gothic as a whole structural system. The climax of many designs was a lath-and-plaster vault carved to imitate stone, as in Richard Bond's Gore Hall at Harvard. Such faults were not corrected until Ruskin's freer interpretation of the Gothic Revival insisted upon honest construction. When this was coupled with the serious scholarship of Viollet-le-Duc, original compositions employing Gothic structural principles began to appear after 1860. Meanwhile, the typical church was Gothic only in having buttresses, vaults and pointed windows; notably deficient in the sculpture and stained glass that were essential features of true Gothic architecture. Only rarely an Anglo-Catholic church such as Notman's St. Mark's in Philadelphia of 1848 displayed the colorful, picturesque masses that would characterize the later Ruskinian churches.

The most interesting and famous architect of the early American Gothic Revival was Richard Upjohn, the architect of Trinity Church in New York, who once concluded "that he could not conscientiously furnish a plan for a Unitarian Church, he being an Episcopalian."

The best feature of Upjohn's architecture was the freedom of planning he achieved by using many separate Gothic units, dispersed siting and picturesque silhouettes, but his Gothic was still mainly pictorial. Oaklands, the R. H. Gardiner House at Gardiner, Maine, of 1835-1836, has an L-shaped plan and an extended symmetrical wing from which a semi-hexagon is extruded; each room is shaped well so that the spaces are firmly modeled and flow through the plan. Churches allowed Upjohn no comparable freedom nor did he have the imagination to demand it. Trinity at New York, 1839-1846, is an English country parish church. Except for a soaring spire, it is boxlike, decorated with planar sculptural ornament, and lacks the depth and plasticity of true Gothic. Its plaster vaults and ribs mark a heavy geometry that depresses a space which refuses to be shaped by the wide nave and boxed-in side aisles; the nave arcade bifurcates the interior, a fault that

Shirley Center, Massachusetts

Charles City Co., Virginia, "Westover," ca. 1730

Salem, Massachusetts, Gardiner-White-Pingree house, 1810,
Samuel McIntire, arch.

Charlottesville, Virginia, University of Virginia, 1817-1826,
Thomas Jefferson, arch.

Shrewsbury, England, St. Chad's Church, 1791, George Steuart, arch.

Philadelphia, Girard College, 1833-1847, Thomas U. Walter, arch.

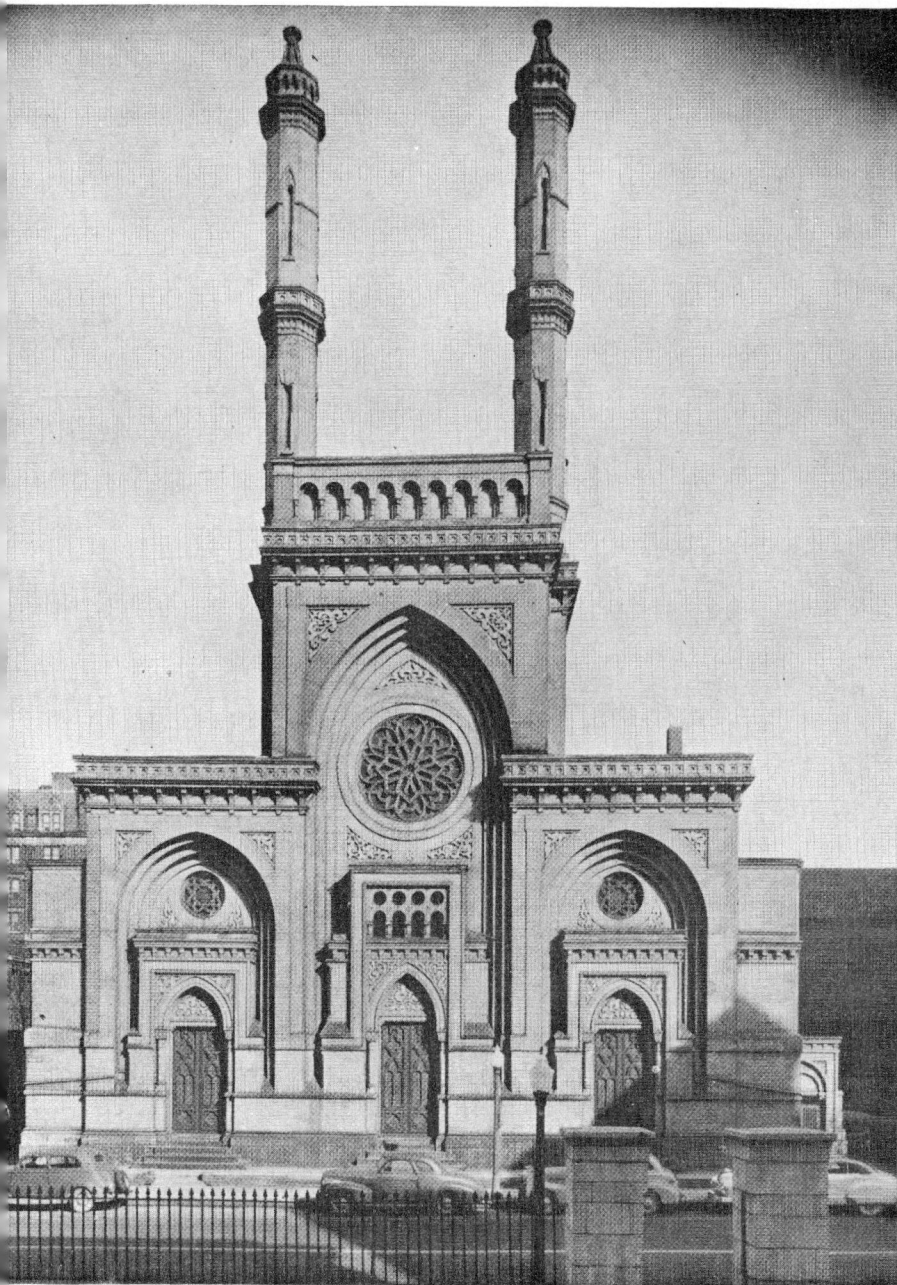

Cincinnati, Ohio, Plum Street Jewish Temple, 1866, J. Wilson, arch.

Cambridge, Massachusetts, First Parish Church (Unitarian), 1833,
Isaiah Rogers, arch., seen from Harvard Yard

New York, St. Patrick's Cathedral, interior, 1858-1879,
James Renwick, Jr., arch.

New York, Haughwout Store, 1857, J. P. Gaynor, arch.

New York, Old Grand Central Depot, 1869-1871, Isaac C. Buckhout and
J. B. Snook, archs.

Gothic architects had corrected by using the triforium gallery.
Upjohn was more successful in simpler, rural churches like St.
Mary's at Burlington, New Jersey, of 1846-1854. There, stone
walls and buttresses retain a brittle character which gives "punch"
to the sharp spire on the tower, and wooden rafters and hammer-
beam vaults are sufficiently heavy to indicate that they truly support the roof over a space that is well proportioned and well sustained by the Gothic arch at the crossing. In fact, the more rustic
and modest they were, the more successful were Upjohn's designs. His board-and-batten churches, like St. Thomas's at Hamilton, New York, of 1847, have vigorous forms that are well scaled
by the shadows of the battens, while the truss that supports the
roof is a complex foil to the austere simplicity of the white walls
on the interior. Upjohn's best work carried Gothic Revival into
an original phase. It was not nearly so fine as the classic moments
of the Greek Revival, but it deserved at least part of the eulogy of
Thomas U. Walter, who praised the "purer and more artistic
forms of medieval art" that Upjohn developed.

10

BEGINNING with buildings like Hugh Reinagle's Masonic Hall on
Broadway, started in 1826, the American landscape had long supported a weird collection of foreign visitors. But now the flood-
gates of eclecticism opened wide. There were picturesque Gothic
rural villas like Upjohn's Edward King House at Newport of
1845. Stranger still was Wilson's Moorish temple on Plum Street
in Cincinnati, complete with minarets, serving ironically as a Jewish temple, and a prime illustration of the fact that there was no
Jewish-American architectural tradition (and there still is none).
A church at Sag Harbor, Long Island, erected in 1844, was Egyptian, designed by Minard Lafever whose crude archeological notions led him to suppose it recalled the Temple of Solomon.
Alexander Jackson Davis's Pauper Lunatic Asylum on Blackwell's
Island, New York, presaged more Italianate developments, like
Notman's "Prospect" at Princeton and later villas by Davis, in-
cluding the Litchfield House in Prospect Park of 1853-1854. At
Washington, the National Soldiers' Home of 1851 was a foretaste

c

of Ruskinian Gothic. It was a time of the Roman and Tuscan villa, the Lombard church, the Roman of Pliny and Palmyra, Vitruvian, Norman, American farm or country house, suburban Greek, Regency Moorish and the Byzantine cottage. If we rely solely upon the names they assigned their work, we shall miss seeing that architects accomplished more than novelty of effect. They also apportioned spaces rationally and freed planning and silhouettes from the limitations of strict Greek and Gothic forms. One could notice this in the creative though eclectic work of architects like Detlef Lienau, whose commercial buildings like the Noel and Saurel Warehouses in New York, of 1864-1865, stem from the eclectic architectural tradition that developed strongly in the '40s; underlying his use of picturesque forms like the mansard roof on the Schermerhorn House of 1859 was the strong insistence upon adaptation to use which eclecticism sometimes fostered when it was not mere façadism.

It did not seem to occur to many designers that the new plans and performances might yield their own new appearance. We need raise no eyebrows at this. It was natural for the men of a society which liked to adorn its steam engines and machines with fluted Ionic columns in iron, carefully placed where they would not interfere with the practical workings. It was a sincere, if inept, search for something good-looking, no less sincere than the flight to streamlining three quarters of a century later. There were some voices speaking the other way. In *Hints on Public Architecture*, an account of the eclectic Smithsonian Institution at Washington, Robert D. Owen advanced the view that "in planning any edifice, public or private, we ought to begin *from within*; that we should just suffer the specific wants and conveniences demanded . . . and then adjust . . . its architecture . . . to the individual form." But at the same time he praised the elevations of Renwick's Smithsonian building, which were Lombard Romanesque, for reflecting the plan and he did not doubt that they were well adapted to America or to Washington in 1849.

Use and expression — the watchwords of eclecticism — were the mainstays of the diet Andrew Jackson Downing fed his readers. *Cottage Residences*, which he published in 1842, offered a strange paean to rusticity in a nation which was headed for industrialization and which had already produced such urbane cities as Philadelphia and Charleston. His most ambitious publication, *The Architecture of Country Houses*, published in 1850, showed a genuine, almost overwrought, attention to natural landscape. He insisted that houses be adapted to the rocks and ground, the trees and plants, where they stood. A house should look "domestic" and fit its environment. Expression was for him merely a matter of style. He showed Italian villas, Swiss houses, Gothic rustic cottages and English rural houses, championing the fallacious notion that each style was suited to a particular landscape, and he wanted "harmoniously [to] combine rural architecture and rural scenery."

Even the meanest mechanic knew better. In 1838 some of the mechanics in Michigan were setting themselves up as architects and engineers. They were incensed at Alexander Jackson Davis's proposal for a Gothic hall for the University of Michigan. One of them wrote to ask why the Lieutenant Governor had not given the citizens of his state a chance before calling in a New Yorker. "I suppose," wrote one man, "it was because the Mechanics of Michigan do not assume that dignified name called *Architect!* or any of those *lofty* titles as Esq'rs &c." He found nothing "attractive about this Gothic elevation, without it is those towers of Babel between 200 and 300 feet high, and the two negroes in the attitude of skating in front of the plan." "Pray, why does Michigan want to imitate the fooleries and splendid extravagances of Europe? The whole of the funds appropriated will be expended before there will be conveniences for a single professor. Why are those four mammoth windows necessary, and the large chapel which will require a fortune to provide fuel to keep it comfortably warm in winter?"

In *Rural Architecture*, of 1852, Lewis F. Allen urged farmers to be as simple as they were alleged to be and "leave all this vanity to town-folk, who have nothing better — or who, at least, think they have — to amuse themselves." In *Village and Farm Cottages*, published in 1856, the authors, Cleaveland and Backus, gained the confidence of suspicious farmers by remarking about the Greek Revival that they hoped "this folly has had its day." They proposed a way to develop varied, useful plans into picturesque, rural compositions. Again there was the American dream, announced in Messianic terms, that a proletarian art would bring good housing for everyone. At its wildest, this could lead to the proposals of Orson S. Fowler, a phrenologist, who wrote *A Home for All, or the Gravel Wall and Octagon Mode of Building*. In this he prescribed the spiritually medicinal properties to be found in concrete octagonal houses such as those by Goodrich which he had seen near Janesville, Wisconsin.

The musings of medicine men and mechanics were anathema to professional arbiters of taste; yet they, too, paid lip tribute to use and morality. Downing shot darts at the "coarse and brutal" frontier: "So long as men are forced to dwell in log huts and follow the hunter's life, we must not be surprised at lynch law and the use of the bowie knife. But, when smiling lawns and tasteful cottages begin to embellish a country, we know that order and culture are established." Here, again, was the curious belief about good architecture: that it improved moral conduct! Americans guiltily demanded and demand some justification for beauty to be found beyond beauty itself; they naïvely confounded and confound aesthetics and ethics — to the disservice of architecture and ethics as well. Not quite convinced of the alliance, Downing stepped into a second and still seductive trap; joining aesthetics with economics, he intended to prove that the superior, beautiful and harmonious forms "may be had at the same cost and with the same labor as a clumsy dwelling, and its uncouth and ill designed accessories."

He argued too for expression of purpose, that is, that banks should look like banks, churches like churches, and not all be confused together behind common, impassive, impersonal, Greek porticoes or Georgian façades. But the appropriateness was not to be unlimited. The building must still be rustic and "natural" in a strictly romantic sense. Here was an exultant affirmation of the countryside over the city; of the alleged farm purity over urban decadence. Downing's village mind recoiled at the urban houses that expressed "sensuality instead of hospitality"; setting the stage for the later censures of John Bascom, he thought that "gaudy and garish apartments . . . will express pride and vanity" since "a house which is beautiful . . . deadens or destroys its beauty by overlaying its fair features with a corrupt or vicious expression." Small wonder that the *Broadway Journal* poked fun at Downing's books.

But journalists could not stem the tide of picturesque eclecticism. Thomas Cole depicted "sublime" landscapes such as *The Architect's Dream* where piles rise high in a kind of classic Xanadu. But he was more at home when commissioned to paint some landscapes in 1826 by Robert Gilmor, Jr., of Baltimore. Gilmor insisted that they be the kind of setting Downing and Davis envisaged for their houses: "Water should be introduced in one, and would be well in both, one being *falling water*, and the other *still lake*, reflecting the play of light on a slight motion of part of it, which may also be effected by introducing deer or cattle drinking or a canoe with Indians paddling on it. The boat race in Mr. Cooper's last novel would be a happy introduction. . . . It would give animation and interest to the whole; — I should also like to have in the other some *known* subject from Cooper's novels to enliven the landscape." Thus the literary quality of the visual arts was affirmed.

Indeed, Cooper had greatly fortified the canons of the picturesque tradition. His views on architecture were set forth in *The Pioneers, Home as Found* and *Afloat and Ashore*; he sided with the Goths. In *The Pioneers* he ridiculed the Jones-Doolittle attempt at turning the Templeton manor into a Greek Revival temple; in *Home as Found* the Effingham family went up the Hudson expressing scorn for the "vulgar pretension" of the Greek Revival country seats and public buildings they saw; John Effingham thought it a sickness: "One such temple well placed in a wood, might be a pleasant object enough; but to see a river lined with them, with children trundling hoops before their doors, beef carried into their kitchens, and smoke issuing, moreover, from those unclassical objects, chimneys, it is too much even for a high taste." It was no surprise to Cooper's contemporaries at Cooperstown when the novelist got Samuel F. B. Morse to remodel his father's house from the Greek Revival to a Gothic dwelling; though the hoop-rolling children were no more compatible. His voice was markedly different from that of Mark Twain whose *Life on the Mississippi* spat tobacco juice at the Gothic pretensions of the State House of Louisiana.

All of this was a long way from the rationalism of Latrobe and the best Greek Revival architects. None of the leading intellectuals of the '40s and '50s was duped by picturesque eclecticism. They shared the farmer's suspicion of the Europeanized architect and distrusted the aristocratic arbiters of taste. The opinion of leading writers like Greenough and Emerson was far removed from that of Downing, while scientists seem to have received favorably the aesthetic ideas of the physicist Joseph Henry, of the Smithsonian Institution, whose speech at the meeting of the American Association for the Advancement of Science in 1854 was a strong avowal of utilitarian building — a point of view we shall meet later in other scientists like John Shaw Billings, Thomas Huxley and Charles William Eliot.

Henry, like Latrobe before him, insisted that buildings should be planned from the inside. They should have a character expressive of their age. The Greek temple was intended for external worship and "an old Greek would laugh to see us construct a Grecian temple for a treasury building or a meeting house . . . architecture should be looked upon more as a *useful* than a *fine* art."

It seemed to many that machines and clipper ships showed how strict adherence to utility might produce a beautiful architecture. James Russell Lowell, Samuel A. Eliot and Clarence Cook praised the new American ships about 1850. Emerson, writing in *The Dial*, in 1840-1841, described how a tyrannical nature forces men's designs to be subordinated to her wishes: "It is the law of the fluids that prescribes the shape of the boat — keel, rudder, and bows, — and, in the finer fluid above, the form and tackle of the sails." As early as 1836, John Willis Griffiths, who designed the first extreme clipper ship, began lecturing about new mechanistic bases for ship design. His *Rainbow* and *Sea Witch*, launched in 1846, were revolutionary: "We have spread our banner to the breeze bearing our motto of *fitness for the purpose, and proportion to effect the same.*" That was Griffiths's definition of beauty as well as his guarantee of performance.

Behind the image of the ship lay the notion that nature herself demanded functional form. Nature was regarded as the selector of the form best adapted to perform well in a given environment. The idea was proposed as a law to describe evolution when Darwin published his *Origin of Species* in 1859. The idea was particularly attractive to men of the Darwinian days when descriptive biology was at its height. Nature, always a favorite of poets, could now be scrutinized at least in a pseudo-scientific way. It is not an accident that *The Chambered Nautilus* should appear at the same time that architects, engineers and critics were once more proclaiming that nature offered models of excellent adaptation. Marc Isambard Brunel constructed the Great Shield that enabled him to tunnel beneath the River Thames by taking as his model the structural shell that enclosed the wood-gnawing mollusc, *Teredo natalis*. The structure Joseph Paxton invented for the Crystal Palace of 1851 developed from observation he made of a water lily, the *Victoria regia*, and a year earlier he had described the beautiful engineering in the underside of that Amazonian plant: "Nature was the engineer. Nature has provided the leaf with longitudinal and transverse girders and supports that I, borrowing from it, have adopted in this building." From similar examples of engineering based upon organic forms, Emerson developed a principle about nature's resources for engineers: "Smeaton built Eddystone lighthouse on the model of an oak tree, as being the form in nature best designed to resist a constant assailing force. Dollond formed his achromatic telescope on the model of the human eye. Duhamel built a bridge, by letting in a piece of stronger timber for the middle of the under surface, getting his hint from the structure of the shinbone."

Of all the men who rode these currents at their full, Horatio Greenough was the most convincing as a writer if not as a sculptor. He sensed the urge of America to become a new and great civilization; he was saddened by our youthful misadventures, by our failure to learn deep lessons from Europe, by our insistence on founding institutions on hope rather than experience. It is tempting to interpret Greenough as a seer, well ahead of his time, a precursor of the architecture that Le Corbusier, Wright and Mies van der Rohe developed in the twentieth century. His criticism has been read that way. But Greenough was no more seeking a mechanistic architecture in his treatise than he had abandoned classical tradition in his sculpture of Washington or Lafayette. He sought adaptation *within* the classical tradition. He thought no architecture complete unless it were ornamented; he opposed reconstructions of Greek temples but not the kind of rationally planned classical work that Latrobe and Isaiah Rogers had designed. In fact, he championed a future development of the rational architecture that had been the most vital work in Europe during the 1830s when he was living in Italy. "Instead of forcing the functions of every sort of building into one general form, adopting an outward shape for the sake of the eye or of association, without reference to the inner distribution, let us begin from the heart as a nucleus and work outwards."

Girard College, Greenough wrote scornfully to his architect brother Henry, was like "seeing the Pitt diamond upon an Indian squaw." Some indication of an architecture Greenough might have approved is the work of his brother Henry; buildings like the Orthodox Church in Cambridge and the Museum of Comparative Zoology at Harvard were pragmatic and utilitarian; severely plain masses revealed the shape and apportionment of useful spaces.

Use and expression, the two standards of eighteenth-century criticism, are also the chief themes of Greenough's writings. There were, he said, two distinct kinds of building: what he called the monumental and the organic. The *organic* is "formed to meet the wants of their occupants"; the *monumental* is "addressed to the sympathies, the faith, or the taste of a people." They had separate rules. The organic had its own laws: ". . . the laws of structure and apportionment, depending on definite wants, obey a demonstrable rule. They may be called machines, each individual of which must be formed with reference to the abstract type of its species." But different laws guided the monumental: they occupied "the positions and assume the forms best calculated to render their parent feeling." Greenough offered a concise summary of the architectural philosophy of "organic adaptation" in a letter he wrote to Emerson which was later published in *The Dial*: "Here is my theory of structure: A scientific arrangement of spaces and forms to functions and to site: an emphasis on features proportioned to their graduated importance in function; color and ornament to be decided and arranged and varied by strictly organic laws."

The American client and his architect were not often mindful of the nationalism that Greenough thought should divorce us from Europe; nor were they willing to espouse Greenough's belief in a vernacular art, or an architecture similar to "the trotting wagon and the yacht America." They might agree that "If a flat sail goes nearest the wind, a bellying sail, though picturesque, must be given up," but they saw no point in transferring this metaphor to architecture. Least of all did they agree with him that if we could "carry into our civil architecture the responsibilities that weigh upon our ship-building, we should ere long have edifices as superior to the Parthenon, for the purposes we require, as the Constitution or the Pennsylvania is to the galley of the Argonauts."

All of this met favor with Greenough's friend Emerson, who subscribed to Coleridge's idea of how the artist should shape form: "The organic form . . . is innate; it shapes, as it develops itself from within." The process of designing a building should then be natural, not literary; spontaneous; aimed at giving good performance first. Consult nature; once consulted, nature revealed an authority that allowed small scope for choice. Emerson attacked the revivalists, both Greek and Gothic, and insisted in his essay on self-reliance that architecture should be expressive of American aspirations. That idea was promoted by his circle of friends, including the architect Samuel Gray Ward, whose "Notes on Art and Architecture," published in *The Dial* of 1843, advocated organic adaptation and an architecture in which a cornice — "a wreath of thistles and burdocks curiously carved or cast"— might express the American landscape.

Indeed, Americans at mid-century revealed a growing sense of "natural" landscape. Downing thought buildings should form a harmonious part of their settings, and Olmsted and Vaux, who created Central Park in New York City, valued romantic landscapes within urban settings.

This was a nature the urban, classic and conventionalized man

c*

would soon lose. It remained real for Thoreau. There was a purity
and a simplicity in nature which led Thoreau to question, even if
self-consciously, whether civilization had improved man's condition. "I would rather sit on a pumpkin and have it all to myself,
than to be crowded on a velvet cushion."

Neither Thoreau's primitivism nor Greenough's organic adaptation was to be the way of architecture. The city was to invade
Thoreau's wilderness; European taste vanquished Greenough's
pleas. When Thoreau speculated that a man might be well
content with a shelter that was a mere box where railroad men
kept their tools, he effectively drew a curtain between himself and
all but the most romantic Americans, and he did not even often
live that way himself.

11

THE future of America, for better, for worse, lay along the canals
and waterfalls of the New England rivers, not in the quiet shal-
lows of Walden Pond. It lay in Fall River and Woonsocket and
Pawtucket where Samuel Slater had established the first cotton
mill back in 1793. It lay in the factories of Manchester, Nashua,
Lawrence and Lowell. At first they were easily accommodated in
buildings that preserved much of Renaissance design, such as the
Mill at Lowell, founded about 1827. They were neat, attractive
buildings, standing in open countrysides; races brought water and
dropped it over giant wheels. Nearby, as at Harris, Rhode Island,
stood trim, white cottages for workers; their communities were
villages in the traditional sense with well-appointed churches,
schools and stores. By 1850 the older means of wooden architecture no longer provided the strength or size or safety demanded
by the new heavy machinery. Wood beams carried on cast-iron
columns were tried in many large brick factories like those at
Lawrence, Massachusetts. They lost the scale and grace of the
early mills. Crowding and massiveness became characteristic of
the later development of Lowell. Workers' houses deteriorated in
quality. Architects and engineers had not yet developed adequate
architecture or city planning for the burgeoning industrial society.
Nor had they found an adequate substitute for the Renaissance

tradition, once the magnitude of the industrial city overstepped the Renaissance scale.

The possibilities of a new pattern for the environment of industrial society made initial appearances in the '50s. Some architects seized upon relatively new materials like cast iron to develop new structural forms. Sometimes it supported traditional forms, as when Walter produced his brilliant design of wrought and cast iron for the dome of the Capitol at Washington. Often used in sheets as exterior sheathing, it was only a means of simulating stone. The greater potentialities of iron as structure began to be realized about 1850. James Bogardus's Harper Building in New York, done in collaboration with the architect John B. Corlies, employed iron to form a cage of columns, discontinuous at each story, which supported beams made of wrought-iron tension members and cast-iron compression supports. Foundries, like Badger's Iron Works, began to turn out prefabricated parts that were assembled to form columns and capitals made of iron. Most of these still simulated classic and Gothic forms. But increasingly a form more suited to iron appeared in buildings like the *Baltimore Sun*'s iron building, R. G. Hatfield's design of 1851, or in the interior of Baltimore's Peabody Institute Library. Many of the cast-iron buildings achieved a dignity that had not been seen in city streets since the 1820s, owed to the modular design of cast-iron prefabrication and to classical principles of composition, as they appeared in New York's Broadway Manufacturing Supply Company of 1857 by J. P. Gaynor, and the Haughwout store of 1857 on Broadway at Broome. Neither of these had the spatial excitement that Paxton achieved in London's Crystal Palace, nor the soaring adventure of Bunning's rotunda and his iron skeleton dome on London's Coal Exchange. Even when Walter followed the precedent of the remarkable cast-iron dome of the Cathedral of St. Isaac's at St. Petersburg, Russia (erected 1840-1842), he was too cautious to press that experiment to a new stage. In 1853-1854 a competition was held for the Crystal Palace to be erected at New York's international exhibition. Bogardus with Hoppin and Leopold Eidlitz proposed to build a roof that would be suspended by wrought-iron chains from a central tower; but their radical design lost out to a pedestrian and pale reflection of Paxton's building, prepared by G. J. B. Carstensen. Americans valued iron for the ease with which it could be erected and because it was an economical way of gaining the effect of stone in structure and ornament. But they were a little ashamed of it, too! By 1859, some of its possibilities were visible, notably to the architect Henry Van Brunt who read an important paper to the American Institute of Architects. He approved the repetition he saw in cast-iron buildings: far from being a deficiency, that repetition was a correct expression of standardized industrial production. "As regards truth of material," Van Brunt said, "monotony in iron is as noble as variety in stone." Such ideas opened a new field for design — one that the picturesque tradition had not contemplated.

In the years just before the Civil War and right after it, the cast-iron façade waxed in America. Foundries in San Francisco made parts for buildings in Portland, Oregon, and so it was throughout the land. Thus a national façade developed rather rapidly. The details of the castings were often atrocious, and sometimes the proportions of the columniation too. But on the whole the fabrication imposed a kind of order and regularity which was not lacking in vigor and architectural interest. It could be found from east to west, from north to south. It embellished the river fronts of Cincinnati, Louisville, and St. Louis, and the streets of many cities. It even invaded old cities like Charleston, where it came to the landward side of Broad Street. Charlestonians still try to forget that it is there, and wrongly. It does not have the great quality of the residences south of Broad but it is not without dignity and it was an effort to say that new things could happen in Charleston as well as old. If we wish to select a representative of the style of America just before the shelling of Fort Sumter we must choose the iron façade.

Unfortunately, no comparable progress was made in city planning for industrial communities. Villages and towns rapidly became choked by new growth. Utopians tried to establish new agrarian-industrial communities like New Harmony, Indiana, with indifferent success; but when Robert Owen attempted to interest Congress in planning for industrial communities, it turned a deaf ear to the Scotsman in spite of his years of experience with industrialism in Scotland. Nothing comparable to Saltaire, England, established near Bradford in 1850, was erected in the United States.

Some could see now that the commercial agricultural community was a thing of the past, and the Civil War would seal its doom. It was obvious that Georgian and classical and medieval architectures were not the right forms for industry. But whether they could still be warped to serve was the question that perplexed many architects. There was little to suggest that the vernacular or the democratic might guide industry into a cultural form that was meaningful. Yet, if one were a democrat, that assumption was part of the American dream. Thus Greenough had an unlimited naïve, Jacksonian faith in the common man: "It is the great multitude that has decided the rank of the statesmen, the poets, and the artists of the world. It is the great multitude for whom all really great things are done, and said, and suffered. The great multitude desires the best of everything, and in the long run is the best judge of it."

Such an egalitarian basis for the American dream seemed false to many cultivated and serious-minded men who had seen the collapse of Georgian taste and saw now only the ugly side of the industrial *sequitur*. The common man seemed neither to want nor to get the best.

It was not surprising that, at this juncture, architects climaxed nearly thirty years of ineffective efforts to be recognized as professionals by founding the American Institute of Architects under the leadership of Richard Upjohn, who remained its president until 1876. The aim of the founders was to establish a concerted effort at improving architecture by exchanging ideas, establishing ethical codes and fees, and publicizing the way their functions differed from those of the ordinary builder. But the way of the professional architect remained almost as difficult as it had been in 1820 when Latrobe had complained bitterly about it.

Calvert Vaux sensed the difficulty of the professional architect in a democracy where cultural integrity had been destroyed by a violent social change; in 1857 he wrote in *Villas and Cottages*:

Continuous ease and leisure readily welcome art, while constant action and industry require time to become acquainted with its merits. . . . The industrious classes . . . decide the national standard of architectural taste. . . . How is this universal taste to be improved? . . . To secure any thing permanently satisfactory . . . , professors . . . , workmen . . . , and an appreciative, able public are necessary. . . . The press is the improving power that is to be mainly looked to. Cheap popular works on architecture . . . , popular lectures, popular engravings . . . are the . . . means . . . to influence the public.

It seemed a strangely weak conclusion to a period that had started so well. It had started so well because it knew what it wanted and procured it simply yet elegantly. It ended in confusion because America was becoming industrial. Not very many wanted to stop it, while no one knew how. America might continue to pretend that this was not happening by the witness of her architecture or she might admit that she was what she was and try to display it proudly. It would take her nearly three quarters of a century before she could bring herself to the latter alternative.

II

1860-1885

AMERICANS were always teetering between a desire to imitate the culture of Europe and a chauvinism which insisted that the American democracy would inevitably evoke a new culture, a break with the aesthetic past as the American republic seemed a break with the political past.

But the devastation wrought by the expanding and uncontrolled industrialization in the wake of the Union victory was more apparent than the improvement. This led some sensitive Americans to yearn both for the handsome past which was being stamped out and for a European approach to the fine arts. Men like Richard Morris Hunt who led such movements gained their understanding of what was happening in Europe mainly from capital cities like Paris and London which felt the impact of industrialization for the most part on the exchanges, or in the villages of Provence which felt it not at all; they ignored Manchester and Sheffield and Lille, which were the centers of the industrial movement and which were, if anything, more dismal than their American counterparts.

Those who coveted the European way were by no means characteristic of the groundswell of America. They might seem important in the salons of New York, but were only the butt for merriment on the frontier; they were repudiated by Twain and Whitman; and in the long run of history they were swimming upstream. The adverse current that would sweep them under was the current of advancing technology and industry.

If less turbulent times can be epitomized by one or two buildings, the contentious themes of the post-Civil War period require nearly a dozen. Shirley Center was now a memory, its place in the sun pre-empted by such industrial metropolises as Cleveland, where crass expediency downtown was coupled with an ideology about cultural institutions which romantically decked them in Gothic and classic costumes. Concurrently there were vigorous, uncouth striplings, the bald working machines of commerce, or useful expedient buildings for the new sciences. There were emblems of the new technology and wealth, skyscrapers and Gothic mansions affirming the wealth, denying the technology. At the opposite end from the pragmatic, there were the Victorian Gothic buildings of cultural institutions. There were also signs of a titanic energy, nascent and undecided, perhaps best felt in the rustic, Romanesque buildings of Henry Hobson Richardson. Collectively they betrayed a schizoid culture. In 1864 James Jackson Jarves proclaimed that "the one intense, barren fact which stares us fixedly in the face is, that, were we annihilated tomorrow, nothing could be learned of us, as a distinctive race, from our architecture."

The brighter side of our coin might show only if, as Jarves predicted, future scholars fell upon "the mechanical features of our civilization . . . our ocean-clippers, river-steamers, and industrial machines . . . They bespeak an enterprise, invention and development of the practical arts that proclaim the Americans to be a remarkable people." But at the end of the period, the evidences of American personality, especially the city, continued to disturb artists.

1

IN America, up to the Civil War, the city had not been much more than an overgrown village. Its congestion was not much greater, its pace not much faster. The country was not remotely different. But now the industrial peripheries and even the industrial centers made the city into a different thing. The countryman could no longer feel at ease in the city street or the city man in a rural hedgerow.

The country suggests freedom to most men, and the virtues of the country were imputed also to the countryman by philosophers as well as farmers. The countryman was supposed for practical reasons to be naturally frugal, disinterested in profit, more intelligent and resourceful, more versatile than the factory worker, because he had not been required to, nor was he able to, specialize his task as much. He made a better soldier because he was healthier and more resourceful. And the country tended also to preserve his morality, if only by keeping an eye on it.

In America, Irving painted a picture of the aesthetic peasant in *The Sketch Book*, a life full of wonderful observances and rituals and ceremonies; in England Wordsworth mourned the industrial desecration of the countryside and the degradation of the peasant thereby; but neither was picturing a peasantry he had ever known; instead, they were harking back to the conjectural peasantry of Elizabethan England.

Protests like those of Wordsworth were not heard so soon in the New World. The appeal of the country or the woods, with or without peasants, was couched in different terms, notably those of Thoreau who went to the woods "to live deliberately, to front only the essential facts of life." But the deterioration of farm life bothered countrymen like Whittier.

> Our yeoman should be equal to his home
> Set in the fair, green valleys, purple-walled,
> A man to match his mountains, not to creep
> Dwarfed and debased below them.

The pictures the poets remembered were becoming harder to see; the single haycart creaking down the hill, with the driver asleep on top, the drowsy smell of heliotrope, white clover, and mignonette, the locust stabbing the sharp silence of noon, could be matched by curtainless windows, shiftless rags, rubbish piled up the chimney's back, rampant honeysuckle and burdock.

But the agrarian myth was more durable in America where there were no peasants and where agriculture was less central than in older countries such as France where there were peasants and where agriculture provided the heart of the economy. What America wanted, of course, was to have it both ways. So the agrarian myth was a happy one which has only recently been deflated by scholars like Richard Hofstadter, who coined the phrase for what he was to deflate.

The speculative nature of the western expansion was matched by the life of the speculator in land. Thus the image of the sturdy and virtuous yeoman wandered farther and farther from the truth. Many of the pioneers were, in effect, not farmers at all but land speculators, men of Mark Twain's *Gilded Age*, constantly seeking the end of the rainbow, like Squire Hawkins of Obedstown in East Tennessee. Such men did not always move on because they thought the land might be more fertile farther west, although many clung to that illusion even when the green grass of Iowa gave way to the brown grass of Kansas and both in turn to the sandy desert. But the need to move on, the dream of the oasis over the hill, the craving for speculative profit, became all mixed up. De Tocqueville had noted this even in 1831.

America had no Zola to tell the truth about life on the farm and among the peasants. As the city gained on the country, as the city represented machines, immigrants, bewilderment and expense, it looked even to unemotional people as though there were some menace in the metropolis. People of the country came to view the city as a godless and parasitical growth upon the country. The banks to whom the farmer owed money were there; the immigrant and the foreigner were there; the urban slum was more apparent than the rural slum; urban immorality was gayer and more constructive but also more visible than what went on behind the barn and in the hayloft.

The myth of the village was at least as durable as the agrarian myth. Again it conjured up a group of self-reliant, tolerant, charitable and understanding citizens, communicating with each other, loving each other, working at a "human" scale, acting, in other words, as village-lovers think all human beings should act. The Georgian village had perhaps some of these characteristics. But that villages can also be narrow, circumscribing, censorious, bitter, was well known to many who had been brought up in them and who could dispel the fogs of sentimental memory. They knew all this well enough before Sinclair Lewis peeled a layer of skin off Gopher Prairie. If the city created anonymity, the village insisted upon surveillance. Yet this myth too died hard and at the Corning, New York, conference in 1951 there were still many city men weeping for the villages to which they had no intention of returning.

Village myth or not, the evolution of American architecture had to take place in the growing city. But for most American cities industrialization succeeded in retaining the less desirable village characteristics while destroying the village virtues. Thus few American cities were really metropolises. They grew too fast without enjoying the centuries of evolution which had characterized the great centers of Europe and Asia. New York was no real exception. It never became truly urbane. Los Angeles was obviously a city of farmers and milkmaids. In Atlanta the Governor of Georgia was supposed to keep a supply of red mud to smear on his boots when he walked the streets at campaign time; Boston and Philadelphia owed most of their charm to the dignity of their early village remains; and there was no greater rural scene than Broadway at night, enjoying much the same kind of events that used to line the carnival streets of a small town, right down to the frequent chances to see Little Egypt. It was the agrarian or village mind quite as much as the Puritan inheritance which imposed restraint on the splendor and elegance of American buildings.

Peasants have traditionally made handsome objects and provided the beginnings of art but they have not needed very sophisticated art. American countrymen were more, and unhappily less, than peasants. The anonymous peasant art and craft was replaced for them by the produce of the machine; they lost the aesthetic instincts of the peasant but retained his narrow prejudices. So the agrarian and the village mind became, in the end, the enemy of art and architecture in an America where there were few urbane minds to offer opposition. American architecture, produced by village-bred architects for village-bred clients, has had to breast the adverse stream of rural intuition. It is only in the last quarter-century that most of the leading architects of America have been brought up in cities, while the ultimate arbiters of their work particularly in Congress are still victims of the village background.

But the rural mind caused an even greater difficulty. Americans were not really ready to have great cities. Instinctively they followed the gospel of the country and the village and lived by the country and the village myths. Thus they preferred to travel long distances to suburbs to avoid the responsibility and the privilege of making and paying for great cities. The early suburbs had perhaps some autonomy and some sense of differentiated communal life, but the modern collections of anonymous buildings betray city and country alike — too scattered to provide any of the advantages of the city, too anonymous to provide any of the community spirit of the village. Distilling a process which began in the '80s, Americans, following their rural noses, succeeded in averaging down both the city and the village.

2

AFTER the Civil War the national population soared from 31 million to 55 million. Its center moved farther westward along the 39th Parallel from Chillicothe, Ohio, to a point just inside the eastern Indiana border. The industrial eastern quarter of the nation held a slightly smaller per cent of all the people but still had half and remained the heart of the nation. The relative position of the South dropped abruptly. The agrarian West. was a large gainer and by 1885 had doubled the 7 per cent it held in 1860, marking the high point of immigration into the rich farmlands. The Southwest, whose petroleum reserves were still not much coveted or even imagined, was beginning a slow gain; the Pacific states showed a large proportional gain but were negligible on any absolute basis. The center of the stage, which had been on the Massachusetts-Virginia axis in colonial days and located around New York and Philadelphia for the first half of the century, was now between New York and Chicago or at the farthest St. Louis. The Mississippi River valley was about to become the aorta of the nation. San Francisco and Los Angeles may have been romantic, Portland and Seattle tempting, but their contribution to the national economy or the national culture was not yet serious.

There was still the frontier, small in size, dramatic in the eyes of all, a place where a single second-rate villain or a minor cavalry officer could be blown up to extravagant proportions by the tall tale, romantic for its associations, meaningless for its architecture. You can wander down the deserted streets of Nevada City or Grass Valley or Volcano in California, or the later Cripple Creek or Leadville in Colorado, and find buildings or sites (hanging-trees) to cause a sigh of remembrance. The buildings are sometimes quaint, even bizarre, and there is always a Chinaman's shack and a simple Assay Office. It is not hard to feel nostalgia among these backdrops for Bret Harte. But they have little to do with serious American architectural history. The people of the boom towns built cheaply and clumsily. When they aimed higher they usually became fantastic. An occasional building like the old hotel in Georgetown, Colorado, peers through its modern revisions to suggest a shadow of dignity; the simple brick of the much restored Columbia, California, suggests that a rare town may have had repose. At their best the magnates of the mining frontier imported what they could afford and recaptured the best recollection they could of what their surroundings might have been like had they lived in the East. Their memories were faulty.

While population was growing on the frontier, in the East the movement to the city accelerated. Two fifths of the people now lived in "cities." New York remained the only city of a million but by 1880 there were four cities of more than half a million; the expansion of smaller cities was even more amazing. It was these larger cities that would determine the urban patterns. In 1860 one twelfth of all the Americans lived in cities of 100,000 or more, in 1880 one eighth, and in 1900 nearly one fifth. There was a corresponding decrease in the proportion of farmers but America had not yet become an industrial or a city-dominated society. Almost half of the working population was still on the farm.

Though it was a period of heavy immigration, the immigrants did not have an important effect on the architecture of the cities. There was little of Norway in Minneapolis, of Germany in Milwaukee or Chicago, of Italy in New York. Picturesque ghettoes or enclaves like Chinatown added some local color on the coasts but did not influence the art of American architecture. A strong effect of the Far East on American taste could be experienced only much later, after Americans had gone to China and Japan and encountered the real thing. In the long run the culture immigrants brought was more modified than the culture to which they came. They all became Americans.

Despite the earlier notable contributions of imported architects like Latrobe, L'Enfant, and Upjohn, despite the work of imported contemporaries like Vaux, Americans were learning more by visiting Europe than from European visitors. It is not so clear that the American architects visiting abroad were looking at the

right things or working on the right problems. Before Richard
Morris Hunt came to Europe, Cubitt had provided a forceful expression of the train shed of King's Cross Station in London and
Duquesney, the provocative Gare de l'Est at Paris, but they interested Hunt less than Lefuel's classic addition to the Louvre.

3

STILL less was he or any other influential American architect prepared to understand or care about what was happening on the
frontiers of science. These frontiers were alive with the magnetic
field theory of Maxwell, the electromagnetism of Hertz, the
vacuum tubes of Crookes, the hybrids of Mendel, the phase rule
of Gibbs, the light-velocity measurements of Michelson, the psychological experiments of Wundt, the tubercle bacillus of Koch
and the work of Burbank on the crossbreeding of plants, but they
had no interest for nineteenth-century architects or their architecture.

What did make an impression was the theory of Darwin announced just before 1860. Orthodox theologians and scientists
locked horns. On the face of it architects were not lively debaters
of these issues, at least until the later generation of Louis Henri
Sullivan. But like other successful entrepreneurs they were no
doubt happy to credit their successes to a strained interpretation
of the meaning of the comforting phrase "survival of the fittest"
and to expect that architecture too might evolve, even be subject
to the processes of "natural selection," so that nothing that was
not fitting could survive, and what did survive was, ipso facto,
fitting.

It was a time for many new learned societies and professional
organizations, and of great expansion in university and college
systems.

Commerce, mining, industry, agriculture — all demanded men
trained in science, engineering, and the practical arts. The traditional liberal arts colleges, none too interested in utilitarian education anyway, dealing by habit with theology and teaching,
grudgingly with medicine and the law, were doing almost nothing
about preparing men for demanding industrial careers. West

Point and Rensselaer Polytechnic Institute were inadequate to the national demand. With the founding of the Massachusetts Institute of Technology in 1861, William Barton Rogers, its first president, saw the realization of a prophecy made by his brother Henry a decade earlier, "an important revolution. . . . The old institutions with their vast funds, educating youth at enormous expense, yet fitting them for nothing truly useful or calculated to advance the age, must soon meet the rivalry of institutions which will embody modern ideas."

M.I.T. was only the vanguard. Many followed, and soon. In 1862 Congress passed the Morrill Act for Agricultural Colleges which applied to engineering colleges as well. Not only did this foster the engineering taught at older state universities, but it stimulated the founding of twenty new ones. The first American Ph.D. was granted at Yale in 1861. From the outset Hopkins and Stanford were interested in science. In 1869 Harvard made the revolutionary choice of a layman and a chemist, Charles William Eliot, as its president. That there was a technological wind blowing through American education there could be no doubt. Whether architects would feel it was more questionable.

The question was real despite the fact that the first American architectural schools were located in schools of engineering. Prior to 1860 the only way to qualify for practice in America had been by the English pupilage method, although some design had been taught as part of the science of building. The first independent course in architecture was established at the Massachusetts Institute of Technology in 1866 and schools soon followed in departments of engineering at Cornell (1871) and Illinois (1870). The first one to be seated in a deliberately liberal arts environment was at Harvard in 1890.

Most of the architects in America at this time were under the influence of English romanticism, but the engineering faculties, in so far as they taught design at all, leaned on the classics as interpreted by Vignola. Conflict was bound to ensue. Architectural students fled abroad when they could and began their misguided worship of the École des Beaux-Arts in Paris which few of them really ever understood. Had they but known it, American engineers had a fleeting chance to develop in nascent architects an understanding of the relation of technology to architecture. Instead, they themselves ignored the relationship, took refuge from it in aping the classics. Thus the architects were alienated both from engineering and from the growing activity of their times. The alienation left a stubborn residue in the mutual distrust between architects and engineers. It meant that the architects would never really understand their quarter-century, would try to deny what they did understand, and would usually join the anti-scientific and anti-rational forces of the day. The things they built would betray this all too clearly as would the experiments they failed to make. Most of all perhaps the attitude would be betrayed by the contempt in which architects and clients held the most important building types of their generation. Indeed, manufacturing seemed so vulgar as to be beneath the attention of most of them.

A seminal influence in communications was in preparation when Alexander Graham Bell sent his historic message to Mr. Watson on March 10, 1876. The new device caught on rapidly enough after it was demonstrated at the Philadelphia Centennial of the same year. One year after the demonstration there were 1300 commercial telephones. By 1880 there were nearly 50,000 but this was still a little less than one phone per 1000 population. Its potential influence on building was enormous. It was one of the devices which collaborated to make life in a big building or a high building possible. It opened many opportunites for planning a city, including imaginative decentralization. But in the beginning, like most innovations, it was treated as a novelty. Jordan Marsh of Boston was quick to install it. It would speed internal communication and it was regarded as good business for a store to be able to say, as witness of its modernity, that it had telephones. For the moment the main effect on the urban landscape was a proliferation of unsightly poles, joined later by those for electricity and still standing gauntly on most rural roads and village and city streets, though we have learned not to notice them.

Just as the intimations of the telephone would be felt only in later buildings, so it was for the automobile whose faint shadows were cast by Otto's four-stroke internal combustion engine of 1876 and Daimler's motorcycle of 1885.

Now Americans left the rivers for the rails. For the railroads it was the time of enormous consolidations; of transcontinental expansions assisted by federal land grants; the time of Leland Stanford and Collis Huntington; of Cornelius Vanderbilt and Jay Cooke and Henry Villard. In 1869 at Promontory Point in Utah the first transcontinental link was forged. A first through car came from the Pacific Coast to New York City the following year. By 1879 Cornelius Vanderbilt had moved the railroads into the region of finance capitalism and what was bad for the railroads was bad for the country. Still through financial reverses and panics the rails stretched on and by 1883 there were three transcontinental lines, one north and one south of the pioneer venture. In the same year four standard time zones for the nation were suggested and gained by the railroads.

The major effect of the railroads on architecture was as a transporter of goods, people, and ideas which broke down regional differences. But there was a railroad architecture as well, and it was not good. The rights of way destroyed the unity of most towns, introduced an area of blight, often established a right and wrong side of the tracks. Union Pacific yellow adorned the Western landscape. Stockyard towns were born. Pullman cars fostered some ideas of interior elegance that might better have gone unfostered. But the railroads made rich men who like Huntington and Stanford gave away large fortunes in the founding of great libraries and universities. The railroad men, pirates or not, were among the giant builders of America and some of them were substantial patrons of architecture.

But they were not the only giants. There was Andrew Carnegie, entering the steel industry during the time when the American production would multiply ninefold by 1885 from the 190,000 long tons of 1867 — an exaggerated example of what was going on all over America, what was happening to a number of people. By 1901 his United States Steel Corporation had a capitalization of almost one and a half billion dollars. The whilom bobbin boy Carnegie was clearly one of the leaders of his society.

Other consolidations of the day were going on in oil, in flour, in meat-packing. Montgomery Ward was rising as the first large mail-order house, starting with a single-sheet catalogue in 1872.

Appropriately, Horatio Alger published his first book, *Ragged Dick*, in 1867 and advanced the obvious thesis, "There's always room at the top."

So the country was alive with innovation and growth, with building and rebuilding, with consolidation and speculation. Enormous fortunes were made and sometimes lost. It was a country of soot and grime, of ugly cuts in the landscape made by the thrusting rails, but it was a busy country, and an exciting country, in which the opportunities for some at least were unlimited.

Observing these new institutions, exulting in the patent successes of the new technology, progressives could not help but look forward to an era of material prosperity and progress. President Daniel Coit Gilman of Johns Hopkins prophesied, "The improvements that result from the employment of steam and iron . . . are so varied that those communities will henceforth be most prosperous and happy where intelligence is allied to Industry and where appropriate education is most widely diffused."

As the period advanced, though, there seemed less reason to be so optimistic about the diffusion of education or the alliance with industry. The laboring force did not seem more prosperous or happier and the towns were certainly getting uglier. Even among those who cared almost nothing about the lot of the working class there were those who did not like what they saw. But men like Charles Eliot Norton of Harvard or President Noah Porter of Yale, however much they detested and inveighed against the aesthetic and moral temper of the times, could not reverse the ugly utilitarianism of a society made prosperous by mining and industry and made profligate by rapacious victories won by mutually beneficial monopolies. At best they could offer, at Harvard or Yale, a genteel education, oriented towards European, especially upper-class English, values, capable of producing a Henry Adams who was able to master the ideals and the ways of the agrarian and commercial society that was disappearing but unprepared to understand, much less master, the symbol of his age, the dynamo. Destined to glorify the Federalist period as America's Golden Age, such a product was bound to see his hopes betrayed by the degradation of the democratic dogma. Unfortunately for American architecture, too many architects had the same instinctive revulsion from coal and iron.

The changes of scale were enormous. In the 1880s men could still remember when a farm worth $1500 was a sign of prosperity and when a fortune of $50,000 would earn the title of "magnate." But when Carnegie sold his holdings to United States Steel in 1901 his daily income was estimated at $40,000. At the end of the Civil War there were but a handful of millionaires; by 1892 there were more than four thousand.

4

MEANWHILE changes in urban transportation were beginning to make larger cities possible and to change the requirements for an urban building. By 1890 American cities employed 105,000 horses and mules to pull 28,000 cars along 6600 miles of track. Despite the importance of cable cars on the hills of San Francisco in 1873 and trials of their remarkable techniques in Washington, New York, Seattle, and a few other cities, notably Chicago, they never accounted for more than one tenth of the urban systems. Electricity for urban transport was introduced by Siemens in Germany in 1881 and caught on rapidly, first in Richmond, Virginia, but the period was clearly one dominated by the horsecar.

Although the London Underground had been in existence for some time and experiments were conducted in New York in 1867 with a cable-driven elevated railroad on Ninth Avenue, off-street transport had a setback when the cables failed and steam locomotives had to be used as an unsatisfactory substitute. Subways did not come to America for another generation.

The development of fixed lines of urban mass transportation froze the city plans, congested the city centers, determined the kinds of building that would go in the centers. The horse-drawn streetcar made it possible to conceive of a great department store located at the convergence of the various lines. There was a big development of horse-drawn buses in Paris in the early 1850s and in 1852 Boucicaut founded the first department store, the Bon Marché. Lord and Taylor and Jordan Marsh had begun business in America well before this innovation but had confined their business to traditional retail lines, mostly dry goods. But now wider horizons could be viewed, wider markets served; Stewart in New York, Wanamaker in Philadelphia and Marshall Field in Chicago were the first to expand into department stores. Others followed. They created a demand for an entirely new type of building.

But the rails had other effects. The Loop beckoned to any activity that much of the population might patronize. Theaters, museums, central libraries sought to be near the focus of urban travel. Companies that needed many office employees could draw and hold them better if the office building were in the center. The cross-country railroad brought the visitor to the center and his hotel ought also to be nearby.

The urban rails represented a big investment and they were not easily moved. Cars on a street meant a noisy street. So the character of streets was defined, almost irrevocably. People tried to get their houses near a car line but not on it. Small neighborhood shops profited by being on the line. Streets like North Halsted in Chicago or Sixth Avenue in New York were colored by the passing trolley or El and their complexion was not easily changed later even after the rails and the pillars were taken away.

Had there been a pneumatic tire, had there been a smooth pavement that horses would not slip on, had there been a better omnibus so that rails were not needed for comfort, the system might not have been so rigid. The coils of the city might not have been so inexorably laid. For the want of a tire, perhaps a city was lost. It was not inevitable, despite the rail, that the city pattern should have become as desolate as it did; the absence of a rail does not guarantee serenity to a city, or even flexibility, as modern Los Angeles attests. But certainly the urban rails did not make the city problem easier. In this decision about shape through *laissez faire* the other technical services below the surface of the street were also staking out rigid boundaries. The result was seldom attractive and a century later cities were spending colossal sums to free themselves from their self-imposed chains while new and free cities were spending as much on divisive superhighways to impose new ones.

Americans brought up in villages had a hard time deciding how to live in a city. The *American Architect and Building News* of 1876 reported that living in flats was spreading. It had long prevailed in Edinburgh but had been resisted in England. It was of course much more common on the Continent. Paris led the way. "It seems . . . to be the best contrivance of modern times, for the secure and comfortable housing of a large number of people of different conditions, in the narrow spaces of the city." But a year later the same journal noted that New Yorkers were spending an hour each way in transit between home and work. It remarked that the Americans (and the English) in contrast to the French had tended to separate commercial and residential quarters and suggested that we too build dwellings above stores. All this offered American architects an opportunity to provide more urbane cities, had the clients desired them. But Americans generally did not want them. They approved rather the morality of Van Osdel, Potter Palmer's architect, who refused to build "French" apartments, fearing they would destroy family life. Most Americans clung, as they still do, to the notion of "owning" a single-family and detached "home" — even when the "owning" consisted of so small an equity that it could be wiped out by a small business reverse and the detachment consisted of nothing more than a six-foot strip of grass between neighbors' bedroom windows. Insistence upon the detached dwelling made the cities larger in area, stretched out the lines of public transport to the point where they were too thin. Some of the ills of the American city of the twentieth century stem from the determination of nineteenth-century Americans not to live like Europeans.

The urban transportation had a great deal to do with the kinds of building that might be required downtown but not much with what they would be like. Other innovations, seemingly far from architecture, played roles in this. Sholes invented his typewriter in 1868. After Remington exhibited it at the Philadelphia Centennial in 1876, it caught on quickly. Edison invented the mimeograph in 1876. This with the typewriter, the telephone, the electric light bulb had much to say about what urban buildings would become. But since the same innovations were available in European cities which did not make skyscrapers, evidently there was another competitive and symbolic ingredient belonging exclusively to the American scene at the moment.

The commercial prestige attached to height could not be realized until passenger elevators were available. The idea of elevators was an old one. They had long been employed for hoisting goods to the tops of warehouses, often by horse power. By the middle of the '50s steam-powered grain elevators were common in America. When the future Edward VII visited Chicago in 1860 he was most fascinated by Sturgis and Buckingham's Elevator B, a block from his hotel. A year later Anthony Trollope saw it too and thought it interesting enough to describe in his book *North America*.

Such elevators were for freight and were sold almost exclusively to warehouses and factories. The change came after Elisha Graves Otis demonstrated his safe passenger elevator at the New York Crystal Palace Exhibition of 1853. It was not long before hydraulic elevators became as important a part of modern hotel advertising as bathrooms later were to be. When the Tremont House was refitted to be the largest hotel in Chicago, in 1867, its proprietor, John B. Drake, advertised that it had all the modern improvements and illustrated this specifically by only one example, "including a passenger elevator." A year later the Sherman Hotel made the same point.

The ability to generate electricity by steam was demonstrated at the Philadelphia Centennial and soon the necessary inventions of alternating current, central power stations, the arc light for streets and the incandescent bulb for buildings had been made. Brush arc lighting systems were installed on the streets of Cleveland and San Francisco in 1879, a year before Edison brought New Yorkers to Menlo Park on a special train to see his demonstration of three hundred lamps. But Welsbach's new gas mantle in 1885 postponed the decline of gas lighting for many years. The numbers of electric light bulbs were small, even sketchy until 1890. Indeed, Sullivan's use of them to light the Chicago Auditorium at that time was thought a daring experiment. And one often saw a gas lamplighter working the streets of Chicago in the dusk of 1910.

Innovations in building techniques were more quickly adopted.

By 1867 cast-iron columns had reached their peak in the Paris show. In 1871 Jules Saulnier built the first building of true iron skeleton in the modern sense, at Noisiel-sur-Marne near Paris. It was widely published. But the problem of building intelligently with iron and later with steel was not solved overnight or by a single inventor, whether the claim be made for Leroy S. Buffington of Minneapolis or William Le Baron Jenney of Chicago.

The city of Chicago did offer a specially fertile field for the innovations of the moment. Having burned down in 1871, it needed a great deal of building in a hurry. During that fire hundreds of tons of pig iron in the McCormick reaper yards had melted and flowed in rivulets and this made the builders realize that iron buildings were not necessarily fireproof. The same fire had shown that a "fireproof building" like the Grannis Block, made of heavy mill construction, could burn down and this had caused a shock. Whether Major William Le Baron Jenney was forced to the steel framing of the upper part of the Home Insurance Building in 1883 by a bricklayers' strike, or whether, as Henry Ericsson suggests, Jenney got the idea from the accident of laying a heavy book on Mrs. Jenney's wire birdcage, we may leave to the romancers. In any event the steel frame and the notion of using stone or brick, not to support loads, but to form curtain walls and to fireproof the metal, were born at this time.

In a short time the engineering, if not the architectural, possibilities of the frame were realized throughout America. The chance to use them often was augmented by the development in 1878 of the Thomas alkali process for making open-hearth steel.

As the frames came along, the cast-iron fronts had to go. From Bogardus on, they had permitted great speed of construction but they were not so fire-resistant as people had hoped. Cast iron had brought a certain dignity and even elegance to an age in which elegance and dignity were rare. The skyscraper as it evolved from Jenney's preliminary use would not always acquire an equal dignity.

Reinforced concrete, one of the great building materials of modern times, was not yet available. Natural cements were still the most useful and continued to be common until the end of the century. They were less dependable than artificial Portland ce-

D

ments were to become and they were not available in large quantities. The manufacture of artificial Portland cement began in the
United States at Lehigh, Pennsylvania, in 1875 but a decade later
the material was still not an important ingredient in building construction. Indeed, it could not be until a great deal of experiment
had been conducted. Concrete is strong in compression and weak
in tension. The Romans had used their pozzolanic cements only
in compression systems of arches and domes and these forms were
not always suitable for building needs of the nineteenth century.
Using concrete in blocks simply offered an alternative masonry
material no more plastic than a brick. Perhaps it was the French
gardener Monier who in 1868 first thought of using wire mesh to
strengthen the concrete of some water basins he was casting. In
any event, the idea was born at about that time and it could not
be worked out for serious building construction in a hurry.

Thus the society of 1860-1885 was one in which railroads were
the dominant transportation, gas the dominant lighting, the telegraph the dominant means of fast communication, wall-bearing
buildings and cast-iron fronts the dominant ways of building important buildings, the horsecar the dominant means of urban
travel. Iron was more common than steel, natural cement more
common than artificial. But in this time electric lights, telephones, electric streetcars, elevators, steel frames, fireproofing,
and reinforced concrete were all suggested. In terms of the
changes of daily life they implied, the innovations of 1860-1885
were explosive.

5

As agrarian influence diminished and more wealth was associated with business, you heard less scorn of merchants, bankers,
and manufacturers. Once men had seemed blessed of God when
they succeeded, for God would not bless the unrighteous with
success. But as Calvinism became less convincing, a successful
man found it harder to believe that his successes had been or-
dained by God. A misconstruction of Darwin might be substituted. If "survival of the fittest" could be construed broadly, then
the man who went to the top was but a justification of the laws

of nature while the poor man in general was obviously unfit, a man for whom "a litany might be sung" but who was not much to be regretted.

It is not surprising that Herbert Spencer was given an ovational banquet at Delmonico's when he came to America in 1882. Even the barons with the larger consciences admired him. In 1868 Andrew Carnegie thought that the amassing of wealth was the worst sort of idolatry. But after he had misinterpreted Herbert Spencer's misinterpretation of Darwin he proclaimed that he had "got rid of theology and the supernatural" and "found the truth of evolution. 'All is well since all grows better' became my motto, my true source of comfort." The new millionaires continued variations on the theme well into the oncoming century.

The fortune-makers were of many types from sharp bargainers like Andrew Carnegie, who valued his Lord Rectorship of St. Andrews above a favorable listing at the hands of Ward McAllister's social twenty-five, to the rough, tough, public-scorning Vanderbilts, to socially registered speculators like Jay Gould, to Jim Fisk, the onetime circus hand, hotel waiter, peddler, dry-goods salesman, stockbroker, and consistent briber of legislatures and judges. The most serious enterprises could play fast and loose with economic morals. But hardly anyone except Boss Tweed was ever convicted and it was the temper of the times to feel rather sympathetic with the charming and wealthy scoundrels who were, alas, often the best patrons of art and architecture. The quality of their patronage was not proportioned by their morality or lack of it.

But in the '60s there were already those like John Bascom who worried about the possible corruption of the millionaires, reiterated Downing's moral concern, asked whether a house with forty rooms could provide a family with a "pure" life. In his *Aesthetics, or Science of Beauty*, published in 1862, he railed against extravagance and luxury with a puritanism unexcelled even in the seventeenth century: "Extravagant dimensions and elaborate ornament bespeak an expenditure utterly uncalled for by the end to be reached . . . it speaks of an eager, selfish gluttony of enjoyments . . . A baronial mansion implies superior rights, deep-seated hereditary inequalities . . . The dwelling which shows the lavish prodigality of fortune toward a favorite teaches the immorality of chance government and of irresponsible expenditure." Here was a note indicating that further excesses would arouse voices of reform, a preview of positions to be taken in later days by social critics like Thorstein Veblen. A report of the Senate Committee on Education and Labor as early as 1885 spoke of legislation to put a ceiling on the amount a millionaire might spend for a house.

Despite the long hours of work, the terrible working conditions, and the poor wages in most of the new industries, labor organizations were only beginning to be effective. Until Samuel Gompers organized the Federation of Organized Trades and Labor Unions of the United States and Canada at Pittsburgh in 1881, most of the efforts of the various labor groups were politically oriented and consistently abortive. Strikes did begin, grew more violent and occasionally successful. Conflict reached a momentary peak in 1886 when 610,000 workers were out with a monetary loss of 35 million dollars, which was enormous for the times. But in all this labor gained little. Gompers had done away with the Utopian political proposals of earlier groups, had introduced pragmatic policies of a gradualist sort, declining to define any ultimate ends but working on the problems of the here and now. Yet even he was not very successful. The Gompers Federation began to lose strength soon after it was founded and in 1884, when the eight-hour day became its issue, the membership was cool.

A lack of interest in communism or socialism went hand in hand with an apathy, even among labor leaders, toward efforts at public or any other form of communal housing. Lewis Mumford was not exaggerating a great deal when he wrote, "at no period in American history has the working class in America been more desperately enslaved."

In contrast, a few wealthy men in New York engaged in increasingly extravagant and snobbish actions. The Saratoga race track was opened by John C. Morrissey. The foppish Ward McAllister organized the Patriarchs, a group of twenty-five socially impeccable gentlemen who were prepared to censor the guest lists for social gatherings in Manhattan and who played this trivial role for years.

The architects' social choice was clear enough. They were more interested in building mansions for Vanderbilt than railroad stations for him. They preferred a McAllister to a Gompers every time. With a few striking exceptions architects have not been great friends of the poor or even very interested in the common man or in the waves of reform that have swept the land. They have not often manned the barricades of causes.

Indeed, all through the period the *American Architect and Building News* was clucking nervously about the labor situation. In 1877 and 1878 it was particularly apprehensive. It gave accounts of trade unionism in London and expressed fear for its spread. It thought that labor revolts indicated a "gradual consolidation of the men into a united class with class-feelings, class-prejudices, class-aims and class-politics." Such a class, it believed, might become completely stratified and might be used as a tool of the politically ambitious or the unscrupulous. It did not ask whether McAllister's twenty-five were stratified; did not consider that there was danger in the cohesive unity and power of Vanderbilt's associates. "It is not much, perhaps, that architects can do, but it becomes them since they continually have to do with workmen, to keep some watch on them, to understand as well as they can their aims and feelings, and to be awake to what good influences it may be in their own power to favor."

Although the time is generally regarded as high, wide and handsome, the fact is that many important reform movements got their quiet start in this boisterous era. It was a time when many legislative controls had their inception, the first tenement law in New York City, the Civil Service Commission, state boards of health in some of the leading Eastern states, railroad and warehouse commissions with power to fix minimum rates and to prohibit discrimination. Women could practice before the United States Supreme Court. Societies for the prevention of cruelty to animals and later to children, for barring obscene literature from the mails, for national prohibition, for divorce reform had their start. The first pure-food laws were enacted in New

York, New Jersey, Michigan, and Illinois. An intimation of another future set of controlling actions was given in the publication in the *Atlantic Monthly* of Henry Demarest Lloyd's attacks
on the Standard Oil Company in 1881, called "The Story of a
Great Monopoly." With political and social reform there were
new bursts of charity such as gifts to hospitals and universities.
Characteristically the Salvation Army and the Red Cross were
founded in this time. In 1890 Andrew Carnegie endowed his first
American public library at Allegheny and this was an event of
great importance to the ultimate culture of America if not to
American architecture.

6

The culture of the moment, effervescent as it was, needed to be
understood by the American artists if understanding was possible.
The painters did not help much. Vedder, Homer, Eakins, William Morris Hunt, Inness, Whistler were not necessarily inferior
in absolute skill to their European contemporaries, Manet, Monet,
Renoir, the young Cézanne, Van Gogh and Seurat. The differences went deeper. The Europeans were more imaginative and
daring experimenters. Even in the work of Whistler and Inness
there was nothing so bold as the switch from pleinairism to impressionism or as Monet's interest in railway sheds.

It must not, of course, be imagined that European society as a
whole or European critics generally took kindly to the new experiments. Both Manet and Monet were attacked. There had to be a
Salon des Refusés. The European painters were at the cutting
edge of experiment in painting, the Americans were living in the
past and when they came nearer to the present there is no suggestion that they were anything but derivative.

Neither group could be said to be avid as documentarians of
their own day. It could be argued that Winslow Homer's pictures
of prisoners during the Civil War or of the parasoled ladies standing on the cliffs at Long Branch, New Jersey, were just as observant of a society as Degas's pictures of ballet dancers or of the orchestra at the opera, or the cotton office in New Orleans, or other
French painters' pictures of each other in boats or on picnics.

Eakins's careful painting of *The Gross Clinic* might be called an effort to understand and portray one element of the advancing technology of the day. But it can hardly be placed on the same footing with the general discovery by the Europeans of the city as a proper landscape and more particularly with the announcement by Monet that the train shed and the locomotives and the smoke and steam of the Gare St. Lazare were suitable subjects for an important painter in the age of coal. Little protest would be found in either group outside of Daumier unless one wanted to call Van Gogh's *Potato Eaters* of 1885 a form of protest. On the contrary, when American painters did come near to industry they made it look more than presentable. Anshutz's painting of *Steel-workers' Noontime*, for example, offers a bland description of a contented group of men amiably flexing their bare biceps in the sunshine. Finally, there were few counterparts in Europe to Vedder's fantastic *Lair of the Sea Serpent* or to the romantic classical allegory *The Flight into Night* prepared by William Morris Hunt for the State Capitol in Albany in 1875. Hunt's Albany mural with its rearing horses and gods and goddesses perched atop cumulus clouds was an absurd statement for the halls of the capitol of New York State at the end of the nineteenth century.

The American painters, indeed, had little affection for the whole American scene and seemed to love only those parts of it which were reminders of a past that was quite clearly slipping away, or romantic fragments of a West which occupied the place of science fiction in our day, or enclaves in the halls of Vanderbilt where the throbbing pulse of America outside could not be heard. Thus though this was precisely the time when most of the famous art museums of America were established, they were evidently designed for the art of history and not the art of the day. If prophecy were to be sought in the American arts, it was better to examine the photographs of Muybridge or Matthew Brady. To the artists the world was evidently a troublesome one, full of manufactured goods in which the machine had replaced the hand. Did this foretell the destruction of the "beautiful" ? Were machine-produced and machine-ornamented articles implicitly ugly?

In 1876 the Centennial at Philadelphia made the question

more explicit. The Corliss engine was a prominent exhibit and its calibrated, sheer lines were much admired; but nearby there were exhibits of manufactured bric-à-brac suggesting only that machine tools might be a bountiful source of meretricious ornament.

But even if the industrial designers of 1885 had been more skillful than they were, even if they had not tried to clothe sewing machines in classic capitals, still there would have been a gap between them and the architects and painters just as there is today. If the serious artists failed to understand or to want to be a part of their new society, others would.

The physical and economic conditions in a French mine were not much worse than those in America; yet it was the Frenchman Zola who wrote *Germinal* and there was no serious American counterpart in this generation. American novelists and poets had hardly known how to come to grips with the businessman after Hawthorne had tried and failed. Surely they knew that in business lay part of the American strength, even part of the dream. But they could not bring themselves to try to understand it and left it to muckrakers while they cultivated American regionalism. *Huckleberry Finn*, the regional classic, may be eternal. *The Gilded Age*, which dealt with larger social forces, is ephemeral. On any terms, as Edward Chase Kirkland has said, "Business affairs and activities were dirty, dusty and personal and occupied a low priority in any absolute scheme of values. Ideas on religion and politics might be literary material; conceptions about making a living were not such stuff as books and articles were made of."

In one sense some American writers tried to come to terms at least with a new audience. Mark Twain asserted that he never attempted "in even one single instance . . . to help cultivate the cultivated classes." Even William Dean Howells, who did not scorn the cultured, thought that the more important audiences were among the masses. At the head of the list of those who preached the notion of art for all, especially for the common man, was Walt Whitman, whose affection for the crowd never abated. He at least could see in a glass works a paean to the colors of the glowing molten mass of silica, could hear a melody in the "see-saw music of the steam machinery," could sense architecture in the "vast, rude, halls, with immense play of shifting shade, and slow-moving currents of smoke and steam, and shafts of light," as he wrote in *November Boughs*. He was not offended by the stench of steel and did not try to look the other way. Indeed he spoke of "effects that would have fill'd Michel Angelo with rapture." No American musician at this time had found a comparable stimulus to his music; no significant painter had yet seen the beauty in technology and industry and their potentials for humanity. The question for architecture was whether it too might have a Whitman. No influential architect was prepared for the role; nor did society clamor that any one should essay the part.

In retrospect not available to the architect of the time, it seems clear enough what the architectural problems of the age were. First, there had to be an understanding of the new technology and a skill in taking advantage of it, a way of making the most of elevators, glass, steel, fire-proofing, new foundation schemes, typewriters, telephones, and electric lights. Second, there was the problem of accepting the new building types as significant and therefore of developing them ardently and excellently, types such as office buildings, railroad stations, large banks, department stores. Beyond this was the clearly impending need of being more foresighted than this and thinking about new forms for cities, housing and schools. Last, and possibly most difficult of all, there was the question of developing an aesthetic expression commensurate with the importance of the new technology and the new culture, which required in the first place an understanding of the times and in the second an enthusiasm for them. One would not do without the other.

In a general way architects did understand that all these problems existed, except perhaps the problem of the city. With greater or less success they made some effort to solve each of them. But surveying the scene of industrial might and millionaires' fortunes, they most often envisioned themselves in the role of cultural impresarios, experts in matters of taste, cultivated in all matters of European fashion, ready to provide the stage where the merchant prince might strut. They allied themselves not with the new institutions, not with the scientist and engineer, but with his critic; not with Daniel Coit Gilman and Thomas Huxley but with Noah Porter and James McCosh and Charles Eliot Norton, who attempted to polish the raw edges of industrial society with European grace and sentiment. The architects, no less than the clients, sought to ignore the ultimate sources of wealth, in industry, with the consequent conflict between a technology underlying prosperity and an art that ignored or denied the technology. They were themselves divided as was the society. They did not know whether they coveted an advance or a retreat; they were not sure they could preserve all the serenities of the old while enjoying all the practical advantages of the new.

Their indecision made them inattentive to the Frenchman Viollet-le-Duc, who prophesied an architecture of metal and glass, or the suggestion of Sir Joseph Paxton, whose Crystal Palace alerted the English historian James Fergusson to note that "at a time when men were puzzling themselves over domes to rival the Pantheon, or halls to surpass those of the Baths of Caracalla," it was wonderful to see the magnificent conservatory made in iron and glass, "the most fairy-like production of Architectural Art that had yet been produced."

Yet the fact now seems obvious: the first exhibition of the industrial world, held in 1851, had inaugurated a new architecture.

But these calls to the future no more alerted Americans than they inspired most Englishmen. Each remained content to fritter away his opportunity by improvising on Gothic and Renaissance themes. Thus a curious paradox underlay the architecture: the age that proclaimed their art of building to be concerned with beauty *and* social improvement refused to treat the centers of mining and manufacture as architectural problems, even though they were the ultimate sources of prosperity and ultimately might even become, through neglect, sources of powerful social protest. The paradox, it is true, alarmed several people. It alarmed Ruskin; it provoked William Morris to start reforms in design and education; and it encouraged Charles Eliot Norton to inaugurate housing reforms, to write about the need for better architecture and to take active part on building committees. But the suggestion they made for solving the paradox was to roll back history, bring about a moral reform, and build once again a handicraft architecture. That answer was all too acceptable to trustees of institutions and even to business managers.

7

In earlier days factory towns built at Lowell or Pawtucket had
been communities; they were small, complete villages. Now this
planning sense was lost. In the coal towns, the oil towns, the mining villages, there were only shacks, wooden stores, saloons, warehouses and the necessary or abandoned rigs and pitheads.

The advances made in industrial architecture at this time were
more technological than aesthetic. Following the series of factory
reform laws enacted during the '60s and '70s, mills were forced to
meet minimum state requirements for health and safety. Still,
good design of a producing unit was not yet identified with advertising and prestige; nor were the social, economic, and political
pressures to provide amenities for workers exerting any great force.

Industrial architecture consisted, then, simply of those buildings needed for the storage of raw materials and the manufacture,
storage and distribution of finished products all on a very simple
basis. The mill engineer's chief objective was to put together an
inexpensive, stable, fire-resistant building which would withstand
the motions of heavy, vibrating machinery, to protect this from
the dangers of fire or boiler explosion, and to keep the whole
arrangement compact so that materials could be moved without
long hauls and so that power could be transmitted by pulleys and
belts with minimal loss. He met these objectives by using "slow-
burning" or "mill" construction whose brick walls enclosed a
frame of thick wooden columns, carrying heavy wood beams and
plank floors. Later the wooden columns were replaced by cast
iron.

Occasional attempts to give architectural character to such
mills ought not to mislead us into thinking that they were common. Just as Paul Nelson in the twentieth century drew theoretical hospitals, so young architects like Hapgood and Whiting drew
factories in the nineteenth; these were speculative if not completely theoretical designs for ideal mill buildings. More rarely a
successful architect, such as Thomas Tefft, whose early brick factory at Cannelton, Indiana, evoked praise during the '80s, attempted to create industrial architecture. But these exceptional

forecasts should not confuse us about the general situation. Neither the client nor the architect regarded factory architecture as a subject fit for a first-class and fashionable artist. The view was held by Charles Follen McKim and Richard Morris Hunt and even by Henry Hobson Richardson despite the fact that he did design railroad stations and warehouses and proclaim that he craved to design a Mississippi River steamboat. Factory owners did not ask great architects to work on their problems; great architects might not have deigned to try. Instead the owners who tried any dressing up at all were content to borrow architectural or decorative trappings, to trick out a factory in the fashionable French baroque of the Louvre pavilion as they did at the New Harmony Mills in Cohoes, New York.

The plain fact is that almost no industrialist then regarded the seats of production as aesthetically significant or even thought much about their other cultural significances; nor did his architect when he had one.

We may recall that the early factories such as the ones at Lowell were set in large spaces, laid out on axes, and that such schemes persisted as late as 1850. But thirteen years later Lowell was crowded. Transportation had not been developed to bring workers to an out-of-town factory. So the old buildings were kept for economic reasons while the needed new ones were simply crowded onto the same sites. Bleak canyons, spaces choked of air and light, deprived of vista, were inevitable.

The steady degradation of housing for the employees was equally characteristic. The older paternalism had prompted industrialists to attract workers, especially farm women, with offers of comfortable houses in a community containing churches, schools, libraries, recreation halls, even lyceums. Now the utopianism of the early mill village was replaced by real-estate exploitation; the industrialist went by on the other side; the laborer found only row housing of inferior quality, the tenement, the slum. In the big cities the exterior alleviations for the slum were harder to come by and pressure for reform of the physical conditions of the dwellings was steadier. But even then improvements such as those made in the railroad and dumbbell apartments of New York were minimal. They left a fine vision of misery for the cameras of Jacob Riis and other reformers of the next generation.

The significant generalization about American architecture of 1860-1885 is that the most needed building types of the period, that is, the factory and its supporting housing, were excluded from architecture altogether.

If industrial architecture and housing lay outside the responsibilities of the architect this was no longer so for centers of commerce, distribution, management and professional services. The architect soon was identified in the public mind as a creator of symbols of commercial prestige, of lures for catching patrons. He was supposed to make banks seem substantial and reliable, stores enticing, offices imposing. Following English practice, the banks emulated Barry's Travellers Club and Reform Club in London. They were modestly monumental buildings designed to resemble small Italian Renaissance palaces such as the one Leopold Eidlitz created in his American Exchange Building of 1857-1859 in New York. Alternatively and following a turn in England towards the medieval, they appeared in Gothic dress, popularized by Russell Sturgis at Albany and Frank Furness at Philadelphia (Provident Trust Company, 1879).

This commercial demand for architectural advertising rapidly destroyed the older type of coherent shopping district. There, as in the Washington Stores in New York (1845), identical small units had provided a homogeneous pattern with uniform bays, floor lines, windows, all under one roof. Stores were distinguishable by modest displays and emblems or by discreetly lettered names. Now even the small retail store departed from this pattern. Thus Bruce Price tried to attract attention to a small store in Wilkes-Barre by protruding a large show window from a deep recess and surmounting it with richly ornamental brick details. Stores demanded show windows surrounded by ornamental frames. Even architects whose instinct was literally archeological were tempted to become adventuresome, to capitalize upon the long spans and thin mullions obtainable with iron to invent vigorous modern ornament.

Although commerce encouraged architects to cherish such new

ideas, few did. One could satisfy most commercial clients and
their buying publics by forcing the new institutions into older
architectural plans and fashioning new materials to resemble
older ones. The shopping area developing in New York between
City Hall and Twenty-third Street was made up of fashionable
retail shops and large department stores. The goods were set out
on counters with the prices clearly marked. The whole atmosphere of such establishments called for a different relation between buyer and salesman than the whispered confidences prevailing in the small shops of a nineteenth-century Savile Row.
Buildings to serve this sort of enterprise needed large display windows on the ground floor combined with inviting, almost grasping, entrances. They demanded large well-lighted floors for displaying goods in separated areas. They needed storage space. Over
all they needed to create the atmosphere of a fashionable bazaar,
incessantly exciting the window shopper to buy. In 1876, comparable requirements for the new Bon Marché in Paris had led Eiffel
and Boileau to design a superb store. Its large glass surfaces forming the show windows were protected by a glass canopy carried
across the whole front. A prominent pavilion was set at the corner. The interior was divided and perforated by iron columns and
bridges to offer a series of courts. It was lighted through skylight
canopies billowing above the floor spaces and mezzanines. American architects were not so imaginative or straightforward in designing their commercial buildings. They took from English precedent the idea that a store should resemble a palace outside and
a group of private chambers inside, ignoring the better English
and even Russian practice of arcades which had also been used in
America earlier. Thus, New York's Haughwout Store of 1857,
previously mentioned, foretold the future development of the
American department store. While J. P. Gaynor, the designer of
this building, availed himself of two technological advances, the
elevator and ready-made cast-iron columns, lintels and capitals,
the plan and the envelope were each conceived in terms inherited
from masonry buildings. The result was naturally not much
different from the masonry building Griffith Thomas had erected
for Lord and Taylor's on the corner of Grand Street and Broad-

way in 1859. This, the *New York Times* noted, was "more like an Italian palace than a place for the sale of broadcloth."

Thus, for the moment, the elevator, the building materials and the functional requirements of the department store were not permitted to condition architectural design. The iron front was not adopted for its own properties, but for its commercial value; as William John Fryer wrote in 1869, ". . . place two merchants respectively in a stone front and an iron front store, side by side, and he in the clean, bright, attractive front will do the most business, and can afford to pay the highest rent."

Advertisements for iron fronts produced by Daniel Badger's Iron Works about 1865 emphasized that they could reproduce any historical architectural form, obtain a sharper outline, achieve more elaborate ornamentation, and do all this at less cost than stone. A product of the requirement that each store have a distinctive façade, an iconography that would advertise itself and attract customers, such versatility further stimulated the demand. The palace-type store, such as the enormous A. T. Stewart store (later Wanamaker's) in New York, designed by John Kellum in 1859-1863, with its dignified rhythmic repetition of standard elements, was bound in these circumstances to go out of fashion. The Grover and Baker Sewing Machine Company was no more ready to use cast iron in a structurally direct way in buildings than in its sewing machine legs. The company erected a store at 495 Broadway with a front suggesting an entrance to a large Gothic cathedral. In 1875 Richard Morris Hunt designed a Moorish cast-iron façade for another store. To be sure, the more pretentious and vulgar of these façades brought contempt from some, and considerably simpler, less cumbersome designs occasionally seemed to indicate a chastening taste. But later buildings, such as the Mercantile Exchange of 1882 by Herman J. Schwarzmann, suggest that idiosyncratic and lavish ornament continued to serve the inferred demands of advertising better than good design.

The office building, too, was clothed in an architectural dress intended to make its form an advertisement and its offices attractive to renters. Architecture was now a financial investment, not a tribute to the Virgin. The growing complexity of modern commerce, not yet much aided by the telephone, required quick physical connections between stock markets, banks, railroad offices, factories and warehouses, and even with a sales force. Physical propinquity was the only immediately satisfactory solution. This demanded concentrated administrative centers to house large office staffs. Since the areas adjacent to leading banks, stores, restaurants and hotels were already densely crowded, the land use was now intensified. This swelled land prices, made it seem important to maximize the use of each square foot, to support on it as much rentable office space as possible. The buildings also advertised the company that owned them. Both forces suggested that buildings be higher.

Early insurance offices, for example, were small, usually simple, even when they looked a little like the houses of Italian merchant princes of the Renaissance. But in New York the Mutual Life Insurance Company outgrew such modest accommodations in the thirty-six years between its founding in 1843 and the day in 1879 when it was acclaimed as the largest corporation in the world with more than ninety thousand policies and gross assets of ninety million dollars. Specifically designed to house the Mutual and two tenants, John Kellum prepared a new building in 1865. It was still a palazzo but much larger. Tenancy turned out to be so attractive that Henry Baldwin Hyde, Vice President of the Equitable Life Insurance Company, persuaded his colleagues to erect a new building in New York which would include six floors of rentable office space. Hyde saw that the limitation upon financial income from leases on properly located properties was not imposed so much by building construction as by the difficulty of making the top floors conveniently accessible. By using an elevator, which had proved successful in stores and hotels, he hoped to attract renters even on the top story in the roof which was 130 feet above the street. It now seems strange that this idea was timidly accepted as a speculation. Designed by Gilman, Kendall and Post and erected at 120 Broadway in 1870, the new building proved so popular that the architect, George Post, who had agreed to rent a suite of offices there as token of his faith in the idea, sold his lease six months later at a profit of $6000.

Having broken through the traditional restrictions upon

height, office buildings started the flight skyward. In 1865 New York was a city of four- and five-story buildings. By 1875 several office buildings had attained nine or ten stories. The change was accomplished without any alteration in building structure. The elevator alone had enabled investors to stretch wall-bearing construction to give as much rentable space as possible. Nor was there any change in street dimensions or in aesthetic conception, even when the new masses strained traditional architectural vocabularies. Ornate Renaissance detail, domes, tympana and giant orders gave a confused and ridiculous appearance to a 110-foot building like that of the Domestic Sewing Machine Company. They dwarfed its scale, much as the *New York Evening Post's* domestically dimensioned windows exaggerated its true size.

The quest for rentable space drove buildings still higher, long before there were any new technological or aesthetic solutions for the skyscraper. In 1873-1875 George Post built the Western Union Telegraph Building and Richard Morris Hunt the *New York Tribune* building. They rose to vie in height with the dome of St. Peter's at Rome by reaching 260 and 230 feet, respectively. Yet both were of wall-bearing construction. Each was a large block which sprouted into a tall tower. Each appeared as a sequence of floors, separated by band courses and cornices, grouped by giant pilasters, capped by a tall roof. Neither design had any sense of unity. Neither had a scale which represented the building. Neither intimated the relationships that existed between the interior spaces or the nature of the vertical or horizontal circulation. These matters were unimportant to the client so long as renters did not mind. The space was expected to have commercial and not aesthetic value and the tenant would have subscribed to the same view had he ever thought about it at all.

The commercial, advertising and prestige values of the skyscraper, were accepted throughout the country. Chicago in particular soon developed the financial and urban conditions which gave rise to concentrated office buildings. Largely razed by the fire of 1871, she now began the erection of large commercial structures. But before taller buildings could be erected on its mud flats, Chicago needed a lighter form of construction. Each floor must weigh less if there were to be more floors. The foundation would have to ride on the mud. The great fire was a vivid memory and fireproofing would have to be achieved. The city sky was already dark with the promise of abundant industrial smoke and so there must be as many large windows as possible. Finally, the speed of construction must be increased.

Such technological problems had to be solved before the aesthetic problem could even be considered. They were solved, brilliantly, and mostly in the Middle West by George Johnson and his hollow-tile fireproofing in the Kendall Building of 1872, by Burnham and Root with their raft foundations under the Montauk Building of 1882. But the buildings were still earthbound as long as the outside walls must be of masonry.

Each floor added its weight to be supported. Each increment of weight required a thicker wall. So the higher the building, the thicker its outside wall must be at the ground. As it got thicker, it had also to have smaller or fewer windows. Thus the commercially desirable window and floor space was smallest precisely where it was most valuable, that is, on the accessible ground floor. So the metal-cage theories revealed in Leroy S. Buffington's patents and the practices of Major William Le Baron Jenney were the great liberators. The break-through seems to have been realized when Jenney erected the Home Insurance Company Building in Chicago in 1883-1885. Once skeletal or hung-masonry construction had been invented and proved, the main technological barrier to higher buildings had been removed. The technical questions, if not those of aesthetics, remaining for later generations were distinctly minor, at least until the buildings rose so tall that the question of wind-bracing became difficult; or demanded so much climatic control that the problem of where to put the air-conditioning units became a dominant one. In the meantime the problems centered on what materials to use on the armature, how to relate the spandrels and the windows in the curtain walls.

It was characteristic of this generation that it would find ingenious, if unrefined, solutions to its technological problems but pay little attention to the aesthetic ones. Essentially, the aesthetic problem was twofold; whatever its structure, the tall building should have a unified composition in which a single theme dominated and ordered windows, piers, and spandrels; and second, the elevations should express the organization of space, structure, circulation and use within the building. Neither of these was solved by Post or Hunt in New York; they were designing their tall buildings on the formula of a multi-layered tower. Stripped of all its Gothic and Renaissance ornament, the Montauk Building in Chicago by Burnham and Root was, on the contrary, something radically bold. The vertical piers somewhat dominated segmentally arched window openings which were slightly recessed. But the small windows were not phrased so as to form a composition equal to the scale of the whole.

The aesthetic problem intrigued the young architect, Louis Henri Sullivan, who had come to Chicago from his Boston birth and early upbringing, from brief stays for the study of architecture at the Massachusetts Institute of Technology and L'École des Beaux-Arts in Paris. Each he had quickly rejected although he had more good things to say for the Paris than for the Boston school. He had worked for a time for Frank Furness in Philadelphia and owed his skill as a delineator and perhaps some of his affection for detail to this experience. A rebellious, inconsistent, poetic, iconoclastic and utterly romantic Irishman, he found his spiritual home in Chicago even in the very days when he was calling it a pigsty. Imaginative as he already was, and great as he later became, Sullivan did not find a solution to the problem of the skyscraper in the short time he practiced before 1885; and it is even stretching things to pretend that in his experiments of this time he was working in a straight line to the great solutions which he ultimately provided a few years later in St. Louis and Buffalo. In the Borden Block of 1879-1880 he made the horizontals dominate. His Rothschild Store of 1881 reversed the premises with assertive verticals. But each was covered with a profusion of heavy and crude ornament which concealed the simple organization he was trying to achieve.

Nor was the engineer any more effective. Major Jenney covered the technological progressiveness of the Home Insurance Building with a jumble of rustication, ineffective arcades, giant pilasters, all breaking up the mass. The aesthetic problem of the tall building was simply not solved in the days of its youth.

8

MEANWHILE the tall building emphasized and intensified the shortcomings·in the total urban form. In the absence of zoning controls, factories and warehouses were built at points where discontinuities in transportation by water, rail, or street conveyance suggested a way of capitalizing upon the transfer of goods and people from one means of conveyance to another. Warehouses were piled on wharves; foundries and factories filled the ocean or river flats, alternating with dump heaps. Tenements were stuck anywhere. Retail stores crept out along the streetcar lines and invaded squares which formerly had been residential or reserved for civic buildings. Dense concentration of tall buildings choked space and movement in the commercial centers. Factories extended out along the railroad, slicing through the city. The city became increasingly a daytime place of work, a residence mainly for poor families, and a place for entertainment.

The growth of Cleveland during this time offers an example. With the completion of the Erie Canal in 1825, western trade funneled through the Lakes to New York. Cleveland had an advantageous location. She drew iron ore from the North, over the Lakes, coal from the South, over the rails. So she grew in eighteen years from the small commercial city of 25,000 in 1852 to an industrial center of almost 93,000 in 1870. Railroads, industry, and large-scale immigration stretched the city boundaries eastwards and westwards along the lake. The commercial warehouses and stores on the Cuyahoga River front disappeared as the river flats were cut by canals to carry heavy ore-laden freighters, crisscrossed by railroads, sidings, freight yards, roundhouses, repair barns, foundries, fabrication plants and their retinue of materials dumps and slag heaps. Dozens of competing railroads, encouraged by grants of land and subsidies from state and town, carved rights of way, disrupting the natural terrain, tearing·through residential and commercial areas, crossing traffic arteries. The Cleveland and Erie preempted the shore line of Lake Erie and spawned a wall of industrial plants that prevented subsequent use of the area for residential and recreational purposes; Clinton Park, a protected

residential area on a fine site near the lake was destroyed by another railroad. Wedges of blackening desolation and confused
congestion were driven upstream by railroads and factories; rivers
were fouled by sewage and industrial waste, land made barren and
corrupt by slag heaps and dumps, air polluted by smoke and
stench. Even the public square which had been Cleveland's civic
center was not inviolate; mercantile firms and retail businesses
transformed it from a village green to a commercial center, further decreasing the capacity of the central core to serve as the
cultural and civic mecca of the city.

While obviously ruining Cleveland for generations to come, it
was also clear that prosperity had created material advances and
economic development. But the society never solved the basic issue, namely, how to make private wealth serve common wealth,
how to ensure that private enterprise would not undermine public interest. Here the private interests enlisted the support of their
newspapers to threaten voters with personal loss of income and
property should controls be placed upon their "free" enterprises.
A proposal for an ordinance aimed at controlling the smoke problem met determined opposition in 1860 from a prominent newspaper, the *Cleveland Leader:* "This action should be spiked at
once. If coal oil can't be refined in the city, no other factory
should be allowed to produce in the city." By indicting a railroad
iron mill company as a nuisance, a grand jury raised the ire of the
Leader: "The idea of striking a blow at industry and prosperity
. . . is an act that should and will be reprobated by the whole
community." Reform had no appeal. An ordinance of 1857
against polluting the Cuyahoga River with refuse was followed in
1861 by a motion to repeal. "This petition," the *Leader* said,
"should be granted. To refuse to do it, is to pursue the same
policy toward manufactures that has diverted trade and business
to other more favorable points, and has greatly retarded the legitimate growth of our city. Our prosperity hereafter will be measured by our manufactures '. . . Pittsburgh is not a pleasant city,
but under its dense smoke, and its begrimed atmosphere, it has a
sub-stratum of manufactures that will enable it to bid fair defiance to all ordinary panics and dull seasons. . . . Cleveland, on
the other hand, indicts her rolling mills because they smoke, and

prohibits coal refineries because they smell badly, and gets laughed at by all her sister cities." If there were a progressive architect, what was he to do when this was the set of his society?

Bradford, Pennsylvania, offers a possibly extreme suggestion of temporary expediency and shortsighted exploitation, accompanying the drill, pump, and move-on mining industry. Oil was discovered at Bradford in 1860, only a year after the first discovery at Titusville. Thus Bradford began its existence as a town only a generation or so after eastern rural towns like Shirley Center or Woodstock had revealed the orderly settled plan of late New England. Bradford lay on an ingratiating terrain. But the purposes of the men who came to Bradford were different from the purposes of those who had come to Shirley. They had no intention of staying. So Bradford grew up as a boom town. A photograph of 1880 shows its horror. The scene is full of eroded hills, denuded of trees, a creek glutted with refuse, covered by oil slick; temporary wooden shacks, pitched at random, hang crazily on the slopes. A few steeples offer a feeble counterpoint to the desolate stores and saloons; they clearly are subordinate to the bristling oil derricks, perhaps appropriately since these were the reason for the town. Indeed, the derricks may be the least repulsive feature of the entire aggregation when viewed from a distance and in a favorable light. The town shows no evident symbols of education or of government. It displays none of the order that would indicate a population intent upon cultivating land, and caring for it by returning part of the usufruct to insure productivity for future generations. We know now that one can extract oil under precisely the conditions of Bradford without desolating the oil area, and without requiring the extractors to lead a desolate life; but even with our knowledge we do not do much about it save occasionally in Latin America. In 1860-1865 Americans did not know how, did not care, did nothing.

Indeed, whether or not Bradford was horrible may have depended upon your point of view. The neat Andrew Carnegie visited the comparable Oil Creek in 1862 and was not repelled. He was impressed with the ingenuity and adaptability shown by the men in managing places to sleep and eat, and, above all, with the good humor of those working there. "It was a vast picnic."

Carnegie did not, of course, have to linger on and see the refuse from the picnic. He could repair instead to Skibo.

But Carnegie saw more than most men of his station. He came home to Pittsburgh in 1860 and found it disagreeable. "Any accurate description of Pittsburgh at that time would be set down as a piece of the grossest exaggeration. The smoke permeated and penetrated everything. If you placed your hand on the balustrade of the stair it came away black; if you washed face and hands they were as dirty as ever in an hour. The soot gathered in the hair and irritated the skin, and for a time after our return from the mountain atmosphere of Altoona, life was more or less miserable." The Carnegies escaped to suburban Homewood as soon as possible.

Yet above the congestion and pollution of their cores American cities began to present soaring skylines. None of these was studied as a whole, from an aesthetic, social or any other point of view. They were the result of chance and of competition for rentals or prestige waged under the most lenient conditions of *laissez faire* and with almost no concern for anything other than economic gain. Yet they were not always ugly. From the Brooklyn Bridge, from Hoboken, and especially from the Lower Harbor, the tip of Manhattan Island began to take on its handsome, aspiring shape, so reminiscent of Mont St. Michel in form, so different in meaning. But whatever the promise from afar, as soon as one went ashore into the deepening canyons, the appearances were less amiable. People no doubt soon learned not to see .the impedimenta of poles, wires and arrogant street signs which still clutter the American urban landscape from New York to San Francisco and which we also have learned not to see. Worse than this disorder, which might have made some plea of necessity, were the long rows of high tenements, wooden lodgings, the alleys of stores and lofts for sweatshops. The elevated railroads added trestles, ramps, stairs and stations plus an endless rumble to many streets; any street they contaminated was unlikely ever really to recover. Vast areas of the cities with the shining front towers were slums where immigrants managed to cling to a little of their traditional culture but which, all too often, were, like New York's Tenth Ward, foci of infection threatening the whole city with disease and crime.

As is so often the case in the throes of economic growth, the slums far outweighed any feeble efforts at reform as represented, for example, by new tenement laws or by model tenements such as those of Calvert Vaux. Occasionally there were new, fore-sighted park systems such as R. U. Copeland's pioneering "city plan" in Boston or Frederick Law Olmsted's magnificently conceived Central Park in New York. But even these, ample as they seemed for the moment, did not have a scale which could do much to alleviate the despair of the writhing ghettos.

Occasional industrialists such as the men of the Ames family established local philanthropies in towns like North Easton, Massachusetts, attempting to improve their factory town by hiring a man like Richardson to design town hall, post office, library and railroad station. But even North Easton, a monument to one of our greatest architects, did not achieve the over-all plan or the communal character of an earlier village like Shirley Center, the harmonious product of several generations. It was less complete, put together too suddenly, and did not have the advantage of the cooperative effort of the townsfolk as well as the benefice of the patron. Perhaps it did not have enough history.

Of all the new towns of this quarter-century, Pullman, Illinois, can best be compared with Shirley Center. But it, too, although designed as a whole and by an architect, S. S. Beman of Chicago, fell far short of the earlier village and very likely for the same reason as North Easton. But even with their shortcomings, villages like North Easton or Pullman were more typical of the thinking of the men of several generations later than of their own times. Ordinarily the villages of this time were low in quality. Many company towns had but a brief existence as such. It was difficult for the management to evict striker-tenants for non-payment of rent; in days of violence it might even have been impossible. Yet, if not evicted, the tenants were, in effect, being subsidized by the employer in their strike against him. Considerations of this sort, rather than that of avoiding paternalism, caused most manufacturers in the long run to turn against the idea of providing housing for their workers and generally to maintain this position to the present day. All too often this reasonable business decision led them also to ignore other responsibilities to the manufacturing community.

In addition to the experiments with company villages there were a few civic movements for reform. Early tenement laws had failed to correct the slum conditions. Occasionally a society in Boston or New York would produce an isolated example of something better such as the White model tenements in Brooklyn. The legislation passed in New York in 1879 was stronger than the earlier laws, called for better construction, assumed higher standards of living in the tenements. But the writing of laws guarantees little; the enforcement of the regulations was often, perhaps usually, slack. Moreover even those tenements which faithfully adhered to all the requirements of the new laws did not reach the standards at which the reformers were aiming. Thus it was that a new model tenement built at First Avenue north of Seventy-first Street by Calvert Vaux in 1880 was publicized by pamphlets with engravings and descriptions and exhortations to others to go and do likewise.

But many people thought it impossible, under a *laissez-faire* system which few wished to change, to achieve enough reform housing to begin to cope with the need. Most people were quite indifferent to the whole question. Others thought that major alleviations might be provided as they seemed to have been in some European cities, if only there were enough grass and open space and playgrounds so that the brutal confinement of the week could be atoned for by a Sunday in the Park. But the quarter-century seldom succeeded in providing even such alleviations. The trend was the other way. Philadelphia continued to fill in her grid plan as it had been laid down in the seventeenth century by William Penn, not even reserving the squares he had then proposed. Detroit and Indianapolis followed the example of Washington and neglected the radiating avenues and circles proposed by their early planners. Even when cities and states created land artificially, the use of these lands seldom was well controlled.

Boston did better than most. Here a large portion of the Back Bay marshes was filled in by the Commonwealth of Massachusetts and the city, working with several private corporations. A semi-cultural center was put on the filled land, developed as Copley Square, which is still something of an ornament to the city; Commonwealth Avenue stretching out towards the higher ground became a broad, green, arbored boulevard with generous pedestrian walks down the middle, ending in what would become the distinguished Public Garden which led in turn to the Boston Common in the heart of the retail district, a group of features which together with the Charles River Basin combined to provide the main ingredient in Boston's pleasant flavor and one which has been remarkably resistant to later desecration of the Back Bay, though not serving the urban poor in any constructive way. But otherwise the plan was an unimaginative grid which forced commercial developments to be made along traffic arteries, prevented all but one row of houses from having a view of the river, laid major streets east and west so that their sidewalks could catch the full blast of the prevailing winds while the houses fronting them would receive a minimum of sunshine, if they received any at all.

Meanwhile the foresight of Olmsted and the designing skill of Vaux had succeeded in persuading New York City to protect the large area of Central Park from being divided into the gridiron proposed by the Commissioners of 1801. Instead, the area was laid out into rustic woods, gardens and ponds, crisscrossed by a network of paths for pedestrians and roads for vehicles, with pedestrian bridges where the paths crossed the roads. Most of the Park begun in 1859 was completed by 1876. Some cities followed the New York example as best they could or to the extent they willed; but few willed enough to overcome the difficulties in acquiring substantial land holdings at their cores and so Central Park remains the largest single public area of open space in the center of any American city. As transportation has changed, peripheral elements of the park system may have become more interesting to some urban dwellers, but the flight from the city might have been less vigorous if all the cities had preserved spaces like that of Central Park. But Central Park was not enough. Manhattan needed many Washington Squares and Gramercy Parks; it made little effort to find new ones; it did not preserve all the ones it first had.

It is possible to live a healthy, perhaps even a happy life in the woods or in a village in Iowa, under physical conditions which would be intolerable in a metropolis. Consequently the rural slum has never been so frightening as its big brother in the city. Nevertheless the frontier was one big rural slum, saved only by the fact that the open spaces were not far away, by the general optimism, even gaiety of the life, by the openhanded attitudes of men and women who had little to lose today but expected to gain a great deal tomorrow.

It did not matter whether such towns were in the cattle kingdom or in Golconda. A place like Miles City, Montana, not so romantic as a gold-rush town, takes on a certain glamour when it is reported by contemporaries of the '80s like Brown and Felton. But the biggest glamour is picaresque, associated with gun fights, or gala balls, or strange conduct at the opening of a hotel or opera house. The architecture was as romantically synthetic as the pleasure. All the commercial buildings had false fronts. Brick was the front of prestige and naturally the first brick was plastered onto the First National Bank. The heart may easily go out to those who toiled to bring the bricks all the way from St. Louis at a cost of about seventy-five cents a brick laid in the wall. But no yearning will make this anonymous architecture good architecture. The hope and the aspiration were not matched by the performance. A town like Miles City burned frequently, and gradually most of the wooden buildings were replaced by two-story brick affairs. But every sequential photograph shows that Miles City was an architectural mess, as it still is. So is almost every other town which was once on the frontier and which boasts a residual Main Street, every town from Keokuk, Iowa, to Placerville, California. The development of a university in a town as at Iowa City can work minor ameliorations; an unusual number of trees and minor buildings by Louis Sullivan and Walter Burley Griffin may add a little interest to Grinnell; Frank Lloyd Wright sometimes made small islands like the one he created in a miniature gorge at Mason City; there were occasional, but only occasional, better things in Denver or Salt Lake City or Kansas City; Lincoln, Nebraska, has gained spires by Bertram Goodhue and H. Van Buren Magonigle. But the average Western town from the

Mississippi to the Sierra cannot be spoken of in the same breath with Concord, Massachusetts, or Pendleton, South Carolina, or Marietta, Ohio. This was not a question of money, geography, climate, water or flora. It was a question of indifference.

9

IN the cities where rich people were building what were then taken to be sophisticated mansions, these mansarded palaces were lavish, comfortable, a flagrant display of wealth and of a half-perceived European taste. It was about the same for Stewart's house on Fifth Avenue and Thirty-fourth Street, Cyrus McCormick's on Rush Street in Chicago, or the Vaile Mansion in Independence, Missouri. They reached their apogee or their nadir depending on how you look at it in the ludicrous Carson House at Eureka, California, of 1880-1886 which stands in the landscape of that northern coast, piling dome on tower, thrusting dormers through mansard roofs, mounting story on story in castellated hyperbole, adding insult to insult until its swagger betrays a man of wealth who wistfully hoped to acquire prestige through foreign forms, no matter how grossly mishandled, while ignoring the wealth of resource that California could have yielded.

The grandest of all these mansions was the one executed with great skill by Richard Morris Hunt for William K. Vanderbilt. Built at 660 Fifth Avenue, on the corner of Fifty-second Street, it alerted a whole city of modest brownstones to recognize how French sixteenth-century architecture might advertise wealth and social position and be the stage for the social maneuvers of the choice Four Hundred selected by Ward McAllister's committee of twenty-five. The family of patriarch William H. Vanderbilt lived lavishly enough, in brownstones on the block between Fifty-first and Fifty-second Streets on the west side of Fifth Avenue designed by the Herter Brothers. But these houses were architecturally careless. None was a brilliant success until Richard Morris Hunt turned a millionaire's house from a bourgeois mansion into a palace.

Having begun his training in Switzerland and spent the nine years between 1845 and 1854 studying at the École des Beaux-Arts

in Paris, Hunt was without any rival; he was the best-trained architect on the American scene in the immediate post-Civil War period. Under his *patron*, Hector Lefuel, he had served as inspector
in charge of work upon a new pavilion at the Louvre, and he was
conversant with that charming architecture, combining Gothic
and Renaissance forms, which flourished during the fifteenth and
sixteenth centuries in France. An increasing affection for it
prompted him to abandon the heaviness and spottiness of his earlier buildings, such as the Yale Divinity School and the Rossiter
House. The late French Gothic of the Palais de Justice at Rouen,
of the Hôtel de Cluny at Paris, and Francis I's château at Blois
showed him how to compose masses upon a varied asymmetrical
plan, capping each with tall, steep roofs, keeping the base of the
building massive but lightening the effect with carved ornament
to produce a rich skyline. Hunt carried off a successful design in
this style for the Vanderbilt House so brilliantly that later architects, notably McKim, derived special satisfaction in looking at it
over and over again. Whether one studied the gray limestone
walls or the hood moldings around the windows or the carved
figures, one saw the result of refined attention to design escaping
the traps of ostentation and vulgarity that pervaded the millionaires' row on Fifth Avenue. Nonetheless Louis Sullivan would
later poke fun at the contrast between the silk-hatted Vanderbilt
and the feather-hatted architecture of his house. The fun was justified, not by the bad quality of Hunt's design but by its false
premises. For Hunt's job was a first-class development of a theme
which had no relation to the real meaning either of the society or
of the owner. The evasion was at least as much the fault of the
client as of the architect. It was inevitable that this first-class
achievement could have no important place in serious architectural history.

There were other houses besides those for the millionaires. A
retinue of lesser dwellings elbowed each other for room near the
elite. There were new row houses, usually more elegant than those
designed in earlier periods. In the hands of an architect like Lienau, they could be designed so as to constitute a fine street façade, as in the houses of 1869 for Mrs. Colford Jones at Fifty-fifth
and Fifty-sixth Streets and Fifth Avenue. The apartment house,

too, was introduced at this period, though it could not have great popularity in an age when servants were liberally supplied by open immigration practices. But Hunt designed the Stuyvesant apartment house complete with a *concierge* living on the ground floor, and J. C. Cady designed the Aurelia, which provided ample apartments for those who wanted to experiment with a way of living well known in Europe. Alongside the houses and apartment houses were gymnasiums and libraries and clubs. Perhaps the best of these was the Union League built at Philadelphia in 1864-1865, a bit of the French Louvre transported to Broad Street. Many such buildings deserve to be given large places in local histories of architecture but they were not representative; they were merely intimations of building types that would become important in the future.

10

OTHER building types also enriched the urban scene. The hotel, for example, introduced during the earlier period, loomed much larger on the cityscape. The Grand Central in New York offered visiting businessmen and tourists a great lobby, small shops, dining rooms, elevators, and suites of rooms fitted with modern conveniences. It could not accommodate conventions of Shriners and businessmen and professional societies, for conventions did not yet seek hotels, but it was the stage for parties and debuts, and the decoration of its grand rooms therefore rivaled in show if not in quality the lavish mansions of the rich.

Besides the office buildings and the mansions and the hotels, the American city occasionally suggested the future. By 1865 Europeans had built a number of magnificent railroad termini. There were the earlier Parisian stations like the Gare de l'Est (1847-1852) and the Gare Montparnasse (1850-1852) in which the brilliant engineering of the train shed was boldly emphasized on the façade. But Chicago's Great Central Station of 1855-1856 and the New York, Harlem and New Haven Terminal of 1857 were little more than ugly tunnels in or through nondescript edifices. The Columbus, Ohio, Union Depot of 1862 was almost exactly a barn, the Boston and Maine Depot in Salem a kind of castellated tunnel. They were in striking contrast to more opulent examples in Europe, such as the St. Pancras Station of 1863-1876 and the second Paddington Station of 1852-1854, both in London, and the earlier magnificence of Hardwick's Grand Hall for London's Euston Station (1846-1849).

Arriving at such European stations or departing from them was exciting; they were truly the gateways to the city. One entered an office building or perhaps a hotel, arrived at a large lobby filled with activity; then boarded the train in a separate building, the train shed, a single vast structure spanning the tracks. Great vaults above the tracks were filled with glass supported on iron arches, creating a space filled with steam and smoke and muffled sounds. These train sheds caught the spirit of adventure and comfort then associated with railroad travel, as Monet was to show in his studies of the Gare St. Lazare. America lagged in building such train sheds and it would not be until the '70s and later that American railroads followed the insurance companies and banks by building an architecture expressive of themselves.

A certain quaintness had been achieved occasionally at way stations such as Henry Austin's amazingly exuberant Union Station for New Haven (1848-1849) or Thomas Tefft's more restrained Lombard tower and Romanesque cloister for Providence (1848). But for the most part the early railroad tycoons, the Vanderbilts, Huntingtons, Stanfords, Villards and Cassatts, displayed the wealth and power of their railroads by the visible evidence of the president's house and not by the railroad station, whose machicolated towers could not conceal the fact that the train shed, the waiting rooms and other important elements of train use were casually studied or ignored.

The single glowing exception was the Grand Central Depot at New York, built in 1869-1871. The important elements of a railroad station, the train shed and waiting room, were not handled equally well. Nor did the designers, Buckhout and Snook, follow the excellent European practice of making the exciting canopy of the train shed a principal element of the façade. Nevertheless, if one could push oneself blindfolded past the entrance façade, escaping the menacing riot of quoins and arches, pilasters, pediments and mansard roofs, the train shed spoke in earnest of the

three railroads, the New York and Harlem, the New York, New
Haven and Hartford, and the New York Central and Hudson,
pusillanimously announced by small signs affixed to the three
pavilions on Forty-second Street. Perhaps few people ever seriously considered the architectural character of the train shed; we
can be certain that even fewer saw the rear entrance to it, which
had the stately rhythms of a ferry slip or pier head, directly expressing its purpose, the work obviously of an engineer who, left
alone, accomplished something greater than the Forty-second
Street entrance. But if one ignores the shell surrounding the great
vaulted space, the train shed at the old Grand Central was magnificent. It was spanned by trussed arches that formed spider-web
patterns against the clear glass of the ribbon lighting at the top
and sides of the vault.

The railroads seldom demanded great architecture; they frequently ruined many potentially fine sections of cities, but they
also supplied a means for escaping the city. Commuting was sufficiently common by 1885 so that English visitors were amazed to
find how many people followed the railroad lines to places which
had been countryside only five years previously. Suburban villas
were starting up like mushrooms, according to an English observer, and the value of property everywhere, but especially along
the various lines of railroads, was increasing at an incredible rate.
Clusters of villages and estates grew within twenty-five minutes of
downtown offices. Boarding the train was ceremonial then, as we
may learn from Edward Lampson Henry's painting, *The 9:45
A.M. Accommodation, Stratford, Connecticut*, of 1867. Migration
to suburbia was actively encouraged by railroads, which purchased
rights of way, laid out towns, developed residential communities
and advertised their advantages. The Marietta Railroad published
a brochure at Cincinnati in 1874 inviting businessmen to buy
large, comfortable houses set in parklike communities with all the
allurements of schools, churches and restricted admission.

Outlying communities, tied to the city by railroads, excluded industry and most commerce. An existing street or turnpike, such as
the Lancaster Pike in Philadelphia, might support intermittent
sequences of clustered stores, taverns and inns. But the residential
area serviced by these and by the railroad was a romantic park,

mbridge, Massachusetts, Memorial Hall,
1866-1878, William Ware and
Henry Van Brunt, archs.

Cambridge, Massachusetts,
Memorial Hall, interior

New York, National Academy of Design, 1865, Peter Bonnett Wight, arch.

Hartford, Connecticut, Trinity College, 1876, William Burges, arch.

Cincinnati, Ohio, John Shillito Company, 1877, J. McLaughlin, arch.

Baltimore, Maryland, Johns Hopkins Hospital, Isolation Ward Pavilion, ca. 1888, John Shaw Billings, engineer

Eureka, California, Carson House, 1886, Samuel and Joseph Newson, archs.

New York, W. K. Vanderbilt House, 1881, R. M. Hunt, arch.

Washington, D. C., State, War and Navy Building (Executive Offices), 1871-1875, Alfred B. Mullett, arch.

Boston, Trinity Church (John Hancock Building in background), 1872-1877, Henry Hobson Richardson, arch.

Boston, Trinity Church, interior (chancel remodeled b
Maginnis and Walsh, 1938)

Cambridge, Massachusetts, Harvard University,
Austin Hall, 1883, Henry Hobson Richardson, arch.

Cambridge, Massachusetts, Harvard University,
Austin Hall, detail

North Easton, Massachusetts, Library, 1881, Henry Hobson Richardson, arch.

Chicago, Illinois, Marshall Field Wholesale Warehouse, 1885-1887,
Henry Hobson Richardson, arch.

with winding drives leading to large houses set in wooded land. Many of the villas built there resembled large Elizabethan manor houses. Such a house was built on the Main Line in 1869 by Alexander J. Cassatt, of the Pennsylvania Railroad. But more noteworthy were later houses created by a number of highly able American designers. The new country residences were remarkably free from historical ornament; their plans took advantage of irregular sites and orientation, and met the prevailing demand for many large specialized rooms with different moods. Frequently, entrance vestibules, drawing rooms, dining rooms and libraries were interlocked spaces; areas were defined but not enclosed, and sequences of walls, windows and columns produced some of the vistas characteristic of modern open planning. The Stoughton House in Cambridge, Massachusetts, of 1882-1883, is an especially vivid example of this new sort of house. Here on a corner lot Richardson developed the house on an L-shaped plan, filling the angle in the garden with a curved bay containing the staircase. Rooms opening off the main hall are variously shaped, and their strong volumes are enclosed by exterior walls covered with shingles.

Hastings, Price, McKim, Stevens and Emerson left fine suburban and country houses whose plans and shapes came to be highly regarded by architects during the twentieth century. There was no real counterpart to these houses in Europe. They were peculiarly well suited to American materials, climate, workmanship, terrain, and to American domestic life during the '70s and '80s. They seemed in that period to epitomize what so many had felt about the American landscape. No civilization would want to rest its architectural case only on its domestic buildings, especially if they were built of a material as ephemeral as wood, but the Stoughton House and its progeny captured the heart of a society whose major interests lay within the family and the private house, not in the cathedral or market place or in the cafés along an urban boulevard. The American tourist might participate as much as any foreigner in the night life of Paris or Berlin, but in his own land the *"boulevardier"* came home after work to a dwelling eminently private and lordly (and comfortable).

Through the open lands beyond the suburbs, railroads carried a

E

small clique of rich Americans to country places, not yet so re-mote as Florida but to Long Island and to Saratoga Springs and even to Bar Harbor. At Saratoga the grandiose United States Hotel of 1875 was an enormous Mississippi River steamboat planted on turf, with a veranda in place of promenade decks and serving much the same function. There one could take the wa-ters follow the races, and gaze at the Vanderbilts. Saratoga Springs lost out in the end to Newport, Rhode Island, which had long welcomed a small colony of visitors but now became the summer capital of American society.

Gradually the face of Newport was transformed by the new elite. The eighteenth-century houses and libraries and churches had been set around the cove and on the hill nearby. About 1835 and farther to the south, Edward King had built a fine Gothic villa designed by Upjohn. Even the summer houses of the '50s were small and rustic, while the small mansards of the '60s hardly intimidated old-time all-year-round residents. But now these were dwarfed by new extravagant mansions, euphemistically labeled "cottages" by the Newporters. Richardson, whose recognized tal-ents now rivaled and would soon surpass Hunt's, created a large manor house for Watts Sherman in 1874-1876, of stone, red brick, and half-timber; it sturdily carried great sweeping roofs punctu-ated by tall chimneys and dormers. It had the most domestic character of any of the large country estates at Newport, but these merits were not appreciated by people like the Fearings, who built their lavish cottage in the form of a French château in 1871-1872. Succeeding "cottages" like the Château au Mer by Hunt of 1877, Robert Goelet's house of 1883, and others by the rising young firm of McKim, Mead and White went full tilt towards the Renaissance palace, providing their owners with colossal halls less fitting to their lives than to those of the Italian princes who had invented them.

Shadows of this taste stole westward, where the meridian of fashion was at least a decade behind the East. Western taste was epitomized by the steamboats *Thompson Dean* (1871), *Grand Republic* (1876), and *J. M. White III* (1878), which churned the Mississippi sporting 260-foot dining saloons with gleaming

white filigreed wood, plush red carpets, and extravagant chande-
liers.

Peter Bonnett Wight, who had pro-Eastern and Ruskinian
ideas, reported on the Western states in 1880 that only their
commercial buildings had quality. What the architects of the
West called Renaissance had little in common with the historical
Renaissance of Italy and France; the style commonly called
Gothic had only a vague resemblance to the original. Chicago was
still behind New York, but many years ahead of San Francisco.

In that romantic coastal city the transformation of Nob Hill
had begun. Its abrupt raw heights were the setting where Mark
Hopkins, Charles Crocker, and Leland Stanford chose to erect
their grandiose palaces of brick and wood, often relying upon
sheer mass for magnificence, with towers, battlements, and fortified walls. Crocker's house cost $1,250,000 and had a 76-foot ob-
servation tower overlooking the harbor. One contemporary observer of Nob Hill thought the builders had carried " 'a bit of
ancient Carcassonne to the shores of the Pacific'; another labeled
Crocker's home 'a delirium of the wood carver' and asserted the
common feature of the whole architectural array was an expense
which could not be taken away from it." This the Nob Hill Franciscans — not then absorbed with the necessity for an "indigenous Bay architecture" — might have gleefully admitted.

But if San Francisco was not yet self-conscious, the Middle
West was beginning to be. In a few places one could, indeed, find
intimations of an approach to architecture that would be independent of historical eclecticism, suggesting a basis for today's
design. The flavor of the West was evident if one compared the
cast-iron Gantt Building in St. Louis of the '70s with the ornate
classical arcades of iron buildings in New York. The St. Louis
waterfront buildings displayed their iron for what it was, a cast
metal, crisp and sharp, made in sections, handsomest when laid
out as lintels and posts with no emulation of classical or Gothic
forms. Even the Easterner Peter Bonnett Wight, who did not
like it, saw that this commercial architecture was Western, identified by straight lintels, flush with the walls, continuous band
courses and sills, cornices intended only to protect the walls, not

to cast a great shadow, minimizing an ornament that was confined to the surface of the walls. A little-known store for the John Shillito Company at Cincinnati, erected in 1876, showed these features brought to a scale and organization that anticipated the solution of skyscraper design worked out in the late '80s. Pier and spandrels were separated, as in some English warehouses and stores of the period; the theme was one of dominant verticals standing in front of recessed horizontal planes.

But such buildings appealed no more to other Eastern architects than they did to Wight. To them it was a "vernacular" or mechanic's style, perhaps acceptable for industrial buildings, even for some kinds of commercial buildings, but hardly architecture at all. Certainly it could not be satisfactory as the "national" style campaigned for so fervently by architects in the new American Institute of Architects and by architectural magazines such as the *American Architect and Building News*, based on the conviction that theirs was clearly a new age demanding a new style in architecture, that it must express this new national unit, America. The current theme was that the new age ought not be frighteningly new. America might be a new phase of European history, but not a complete departure from Western heritage. Their interpretation of the relation resulted in the magnificent historical inconsequence that the new architectural style should be a continuation of the last phase of Gothic, having at most an admixture of Renaissance elements, all mixed up with the idea that great architecture can effect moral and social improvement, and that it was the architect's duty to improve his society.

11

No one in the English-speaking world split these various currents of architectural sentiment more fully than John Ruskin. *Seven Lamps of Architecture*, 1849, and *Stones of Venice*, 1851, were widely read and more editions of them were published in America than in England. American architects followed Ruskinian doctrine even more literally than Deane and Woodward had in designing the Oxford Museum.

During the '40s Ruskin had seen in England the horrifying

spectacle of industrialization that would appear later in American cities. He despised its disintegrating effect on urban life, its mechanized products, its degraded workmen. Believing that lasting reform could come only through education, he organized museums of art and science, taught at Oxford, established lecture programs for factory workers and artisans, emphasizing always the influence of good art on morality. His interests were wide-ranging, sometimes progressive as in his support of housing reforms and his critical appreciation of the painter Turner; sometimes scientific, though his affection for geology tempered his dislike of any science that enjoyed anatomical dissection; but his disposition was mainly historical and religious, even mystic, and this led him to an unqualified admiration for the medieval guilds. He drew well and wrote with passion. When he looked at a sunrise, one of Ruskin's friends remarked, he doubted there could ever be a sunset. He was the leading spokesman for the dubious idea that art and architecture must contain moral expression, insisting that good architecture makes men good. His lectures about art, as well as his books, were Messianic sermons, pontifically pronounced, melodiously phrased, and they spellbound his audiences and his readers into believing that Gothic architecture, alone, was appropriate for use in a Christian society and that its revival was necessary to correct modern paganism and to temper the onslaught of industry.

Such sermons were well received in America, particularly by those who despaired of factories, cities like Cleveland, or the Vanderbilt mansions. They ignored the rational architecture proposed by Latrobe and Greenough, preferred the conversion to medieval piety offered by this English high priest. By 1875 a few people discredited Ruskin but most of the disenchantment had to wait for later generations. Few in the '60s had the discrimination necessary to discern Ruskin's art, to separate his knowledge from it, or to measure his genius.

Groups in New York, Boston and Philadelphia set out to emulate his example. Their love affairs with Victorian Gothic are commemorated on many college campuses today. Some of the buildings like Memorial Hall at Harvard and the Chancellor Green Library at Princeton have long since ceased to serve their original purposes and modern students perhaps too readily wish them ill. But their colorful ornament and rich silhouettes endear them to others, especially if the later architecture seems excessively bald and inexorably ruled by straight lines. The American acceptance of Ruskin diverted her leaders from industrial horrors to the ultimate loss or at least postponement of great opportunities.

Ruskin's inaccurate observations and *non sequiturs* were well suited to beguile Victorian sentiments and open Victorian pocketbooks. It was not surprising that a group of young architects and critics living in New York in 1863 should have founded an astonishingly naïve society, The Association for the Advancement of Truth in Art. Dedicated to promoting Ruskinian principles, the Society's magazine, *The New Path*, attacked the Renaissance style, whose morality they judged corrupt as Ruskin had also: "It is base, unnatural, unfruitful, unenjoyable and impious." The Society could find no American architecture worthy of praise before the National Academy of Design was constructed at New York between 1862 and 1865. Polychromed and carved enough to make spectators giddy, the building was designed by Peter Bonnett Wight. It was the Society's greatest triumph, a colorful palace more or less in Venetian Gothic, a bit of whimsy livening the commercial scene with tracery and brick patterns polychromed in reds, ochers and yellows. Ruskin had set an example at the Oxford Museum when he brought plants to the brothers O'Shea which they copied into the capitals. Now Wight followed this and brought indigenous foliage to the stone carvers to be studied as models. For he subscribed to Ruskin's belief in the moral efficacy of having workmen who were craftsmen and creative artists; he wanted "to give workmen opportunity to think."

Having moralized the stones of New York, the Ruskinian muse perched on the shoulder of Charles Eliot Norton at Cambridge, where this distinguished Harvard professor of fine arts successfully inspired many an undergraduate to believe that "we have, as a nation, painfully displayed our disregard of the ennobling influences of fine architecture upon national character." Like his close friend Ruskin, Norton believed that morality and aesthetics were inseparable. This belief led Norton to attempt to enhance the beauty and presumably the morality of the Harvard environment by taking an active part in overseeing the character of Memorial Hall, built in 1866-1878.

Norton wanted Memorial Hall to be Gothic. His hopes were high when Ware and Van Brunt's Gothic design won the competition, and he even solicited Ruskin to express interest in the building. The architects designed a cathedral form, the nave becoming the dining hall, the apse a theater, and the transepts a Memorial surmounted by a tall ornate tower. When completed, it was a picturesque and solemn monument to the Civil War dead, an imposing mass of red brick with colorful designs in the shingled roofs and topped by a cast-iron coxcomb — dreadfully effective when washed by moonlight. But it was a tragedy of errors in design all the way from a scale that violated the collegiate theme established in the Yard to the moralizing inscriptions that seem to modern students so maudlin and contrived. Norton himself was disappointed in the result. It was his misfortune, as it was for many Americans versed in the best European traditions, not to find any modern architecture that met his standards for beauty and morality; he was to have his hopes for something better revived during the age of reform but as late as 1904, still dissatisfied, he continued to seek in aesthetics an ethical ideal, "fine architecture as an influence in the education of youth."

Norton's disenchantment with Ruskinian medievalism did not prevent a whole American generation from erecting Victorian Gothic buildings for their cultural institutions. In the Gothic, American trustees found a "civilized" style; they would not often use it for factories or machines nor would they attempt by and large to surround their workers with the kind of environment the Society for the Advancement of Truth in Art tried to promote. When acting not as practical businessmen but as preservers of culture they took on the *alter ego* of trustee personality and insisted upon having "important" institutions housed in buildings redolent of history, perfumed with the spices of France and Italy. It was a style with some merits: it permitted highly utilitarian, informal planning. It offered large open areas between buttresses where good lighting could be obtained. Frequently such a building provided a drab town with its only Xanadu, its one spot of fantasy, exoticism, color or romance. This Victorian Gothic floridity was balm to a soul divided and a feverish attempt to compensate for the ugliness produced by machinery run solely for economic advantage.

Indeed, the Memorial Hall of Harvard and the Chancellor Green of Princeton as well as many less exuberant Old Mains on American campuses, fail as they may in absolute architectural terms, deserve preservation as part of American university history and even applause as graceful reminders of our enchanting interlude with Ruskin.

Victorian Gothic was not the only competitor to become the American "national" style. Dr. E. A. Freeman, an Englishman who visited Albany in 1883, was convinced after seeing Richardson's Capitol that the true style for America, the one that "really flourished best on American soil," was the style of Pisa and Lucca, that is, Italian Romanesque. The *American Architect and Building News* in 1885 was convinced that the Théâtre Lyrique and the Chatelet in Paris proclaimed the style of the century which would be that of Louis Philippe and Napoleon III. Out in Chicago John Wellborn Root was expressing a liking for Flemish Gothic but he understood history too well to mock it as the Victorian Gothicists unwittingly did. What Root said about the classic could as well have been heeded by the nineteenth-century Gothicists, "this very perfection, which was only attainable when life was simple and the world was young, . . . makes it forever impossible that Greek detail should be successfully 'adapted' to modern buildings." The Middle Ages too had been young.

At first glance it might have been expected that ecclesiastical buildings would express differences in ritual or creed. But denominational differences soon could not be distinguished in an architecture which, for the moment, was drowned by Gothic.

It was during this period in Boston that Unitarians built their Gothic First Church, by Ware and Van Brunt, the Congregationalists their Gothic New Old South Church, by Cummings and Sears, the Episcopalians their Gothic Church of the Advent by Sturgis and Brigham. The distinctions among these remained more in plan than in elevation or detail, but even planning differ-

ences tended to disappear as social aspects of church activity became increasingly prominent and the shrine was correspondingly
reduced.

Identification of Victorian Gothic architecture with the liberal
arts was common. The American collegiate tradition was so firmly
rooted in English institutions that the President of Trinity College journeyed to England in 1875 to find an architect capable of
designing a massive medieval pile in the tradition of ancient Oxford and Cambridge, to be built in Hartford, Connecticut, a place
the architect did not know and would never see. He found William Burges who conjured up a whole Gothic monastic collegiate
community for this unfamiliar place and land. Princeton, Harvard, Yale, the Union Theological Seminary, Columbia and
Knox College all emulated the quadrangles of Oxford, and it was
a durable idea as the University of Chicago proved from 1892 to
the 1940s. The whole dream was totally unrelated to the potential
for a new aesthetic residing in science and industry. One could
sense the dichotomy at Cornell, where one side of the campus
displayed rude, calloused academic and dormitory buildings and
utilitarian machine shops, all erected by the businessman Ezra
Cornell, while on the other side were Victorian Gothic "sermons
in stone," as President Andrew Dickson White called them.

With all of this some scientists and those awake to the potentials of the new civilization were quite out of sympathy, hoping
that money would be spent on good laboratory space rather than
on art. That simple building could also be art occurred to no one.

Official architecture for government buildings was less uniform,
but equally impervious to utility or vernacularism. The official
style varied with the man who was acting as Supervising Architect
of the Treasury. Under Assistant Supervising Architect Alfred B.
Mullett, aggrandized versions of the Louvre pavilions appeared in
the post offices of New York and Philadelphia and Portland, Oregon, and in the State, War and Navy Building in Washington,
and were emulated in the City Halls of Boston and Philadelphia.
When the State, War and Navy Building was completed it was
described by deB. Randolph Keim as "the finest edifice of the
kind in the world." Its "Roman, Doric, originally treated" was

E*

much admired. Now known as the Executive Office Building, it is no longer listed even in the *World Almanac* as one of the buildings to see in Washington.

The official buildings veered to Victorian Gothic when Supervising Architect William Appleton Potter covered the Middle South with courthouses and post offices in the Ruskinian vein. The impending controversy over what our official national architecture ought to be became of more public concern after the State Capitol at Albany was taken from Thomas Fuller's office and given to Richardson and Leopold Eidlitz. Then Richardson built a grandiloquent Senate chamber and entrance in the Romanesque style, whose appropriateness evoked the praise of the Englishman, Freeman, already cited.

All of this dabbling in archeological styles in an attempt to find something appropriate for an emergent Americian culture was enforced by a literary, musical and philosophical heritage quite unrelated to, indeed regarded as an amelioration to, rather than an expression of, the industrial civilization. The schism in the culture was revealed by the Centennial Exhibition at Philadelphia in 1876. There were many wonderful things there. Japan sent a sectionalized house and workmen to erect it; Germany sent a fascinating exhibit of Froebelian educational methods. Both of these would profoundly affect later American culture and American architecture, and not only through Frank Lloyd Wright, whose mother learned from the Froebel exhibit a system of three-dimensional block training which Wright claimed gave him his start. But architectural progressivism hardly was the dominant theme of the Fair. American steam locomotives amazed a Russian engineer by their functionalism. Many a visitor caught the sense of power appearing in the Corliss engine. But these were housed in buildings that suggested no architectural recognition of mechanism. Turning his back upon the Crystal Palace, the architect Schwarzmann tricked out Horticultural Hall in Moorish fantasies.

Surveying the architectural scene in 1876, then, one saw the same confusion of tongues that one saw in the society. Victorian Gothic threatened to become a national style, but other languages abounded. Architects shared and abetted this confusion.

Asked to enter a competition for completing the Washington Monument, most of them submitted fantastic proposals for completing it in Gothic, Romanesque, or mansard styles.

Worse yet were proposals submitted for a "national" style. Such a proposal appeared from the hands of John Moser in 1884 when he suggested a building for the American Institute of Architects, to be built at New York. In his description of the building, Moser advised an explicit eclecticism: from bottom to top it was to go from Egyptian to Victorian Gothic, "an embodiment of the history of our art . . . where every epoch in architectural history shall be represented by details from the best examples now obtainable, following each other in regular and orderly sequence."

This was no indication of the prophetic design nascent in the earlier John Shillito Building; it was rather a synopsis of the architects' library of plates, not so well composed nor so consistent as *The Architect's Dream* of 1840, painted by Thomas Cole for the neo-classic architect Ithiel Town, where the essentially Roman cityscape was overshadowed by the Great Pyramid of Cheops. Erastus Salisbury Field's *Historic Monument of the American Republic*, of 1876, was a similar compendium of ten skyscraper towers covered with archeological remains. "Progress" had been backward.

12

THIS sort of archeological architecture was attacked by several kinds of critics, all of whom sensed in the American scene a destiny different from that of the "tastemakers." Clarence Cook, a convert from a youthful confirmation in Ruskin's parish, excoriated the tastemaker architect and his merchant-prince client: "Where architects abound, the art of building always deteriorates." He thought the trouble lay in the ascendancy the professional architect enjoyed over the vernacular builder: "and in architecture . . . the field has fallen into the possession of a set of clever, accomplished, but over-cultivated young men who have come back from French and English studios, offices, and pedestrian trips, with a plenty of 'material' in their sketch books." It seemed to Cook as to many other thoughtful people that American architecture had run steadily downhill from Independence Hall to Memorial Hall.

Cook's attack upon the architectural profession, though bitterly rebutted in the architectural press, simply drove home the wedge of functionalism which was being fashioned by nineteenth-century industrial engineers and scientists. For them, adaptation to use was a simple principle that guaranteed performance, of course, but that might frequently result in beauty as well. To prove it there was always the Corliss engine. Daniel Coit Gilman, President of Johns Hopkins, made the conventional, unimaginative, almost irresponsive, pragmatic answer, testifying that machinery "brings to every cottage of our day comforts and adornments which in the days of Queen Bess . . . were not known outside of the palace." But Gilman also saw machinery as a source of beauty as well as comfort. It was apparent to him in the Brooklyn Bridge, in ships like the *Aurania*, in complex machine tools such as Rowland's dividing engine which "has beauty of its own; not that of the human form nor that of a running brook, but the beauty of perfect adaptation to purpose," much as some contemporary scientists assert that a beautiful formula is a poem. Quite obviously a man like Gilman would not want medieval buildings for his university at Baltimore, but rather serviceable, economical structures. Gilman coupled a dislike for the modern medievalism he saw at the University of Glasgow or in the plan for Trinity College with a disdain for professional architects whom he considered both ignorant and incompetent in technical matters. He wrote gleefully about architects' failures to provide drains from roofs and courts, of bad orientations, of long staircases, of doors too narrow to pass machines and laboratory equipment, of the absence of lifts or ventilating hoods. He wanted buildings at Hopkins which would have good machinery for heating and ventilation, be well supplied with gas, water and light, with ways of removing noxious dust or gas from the laboratories, all arranged, without architectural assistance, by a "professor who looks after these things in advance — instead of an architect who forgets them altogether."

Bad as the architects doubtless were, the professors were worse.

What Gilman got was an array of remodeled houses, carriage sheds, bald laboratories erected to suit the taste of professors of physics, chemistry, biology and philology. Developed in the middle of Baltimore, the University grew without guidance from a master plan. The utilitarian aspect of Hopkins attracted only local attention, however, until the notoriously contentious Thomas Huxley journeyed to Baltimore in 1876 to participate in opening the new University. His speech made headlines and raised the hackles of the architectural profession. He was not disappointed by the utilitarian appearance of Hopkins. On the contrary, he said, "It has been my fate to see great educational funds fossilise into mere bricks and mortar, in the petrifying springs of architecture, with nothing left to work the institution they were intended to support . . . whenever you do build, get an honest bricklayer, and make him build . . . just such rooms as you really want, leaving ample space for expansion." Huxley envisioned the future Hopkins as having serviceable laboratories and museums of science, "then, if you have a few hundred thousand dollars you don't know what to do with, send for an architect and tell him to put up a façade. If American is similar to British experience, any other course will probably lead you into having some stately structures, good for your architect's fame, but not in the least what you want."

Huxley's attack upon the architectural profession, which many a reader may still relish, upset architects almost as much as his theories about evolution had angered religious fundamentalists. They were pressing by concerted action against American apathy towards the arts and American reliance upon the "honest bricklayers" in matters of building. Their task was not made easier when a well-known scientist espoused amateurism. Huxley's opinion moreover denied the claims of European-oriented architects such as Hunt and Eidlitz that America would have no worthy culture until she was refaced in the image of Bourges or the Baths of Caracalla.

But it was on exactly this score that Europeans and Americans sensitive to what was best for America disagreed with the professional architects. Huxley did not want us to repeat the errors made at Oxford. Physicians who saw monumental hospitals de-

signed more like palaces than as places for the sick and wounded
cautioned us not to build architecturally. Architects seldom accepted the advice. Hunt's Episcopal Hospital at Philadelphia as
well as his Presbyterian Hospital in New York, built in 1872, were
multi-story structures with dark interiors, monumental stairways,
all in medieval dress, more attractive to donors and trustees than
to nurses, physicians and patients. What the physician wanted
was a hospital built as a series of independent ward-pavilions supplied with good lighting and ventilation, easy to supervise, easily
cleaned, easily separable for the isolation of disease. A ward-
pavilion at the Johns Hopkins Hospital was the ideal. It was designed by a physician, John Shaw Billings, who was asked by the
benefactor, Johns Hopkins, to make a modern institution built
upon a plan fit to obtain "ventilation and heating and light and
sunshine, as curative agents." He adopted the idea of one-story
detached pavilion wards which had been advocated by experts
like Florence Nightingale, based upon observations made during
the Crimean War. Set upon north-south axes so that the sun
gained access to both sides during the day, each pavilion, standing
apart from the others, would have ventilation and sunlight.
Walls were double, enclosing a hollow space that insulated the
ward. Further attention to utility appeared in abundant provisions for heating and ventilation, consolidation of plumbing,
elimination of all moldings and ornament to facilitate cleaning,
and a plan which enabled a single nurse easily to supervise a large
number of patients. These arrangements made the ward as efficient a machine as a hospital management could then conjecture.

Physicians had long hoped to be able to operate such a machine. One doctor blamed architects and trustees for the backward state of hospital design, and nearly all physicians echoed
Huxley's lament about the useless expenditures made by architects; thus Dr. Francis Henry Brown wrote in 1879: "Architects
are tempted with permanent materials in their hands to devote
too large an expenditure to display and effect, making the buildings expensive in indirect proportion to the use for which they are
intended."

But perhaps the most serious of the charges physicians made
against the architect was that he strove for permanence and

monumentality. Experience during the Civil War with temporary wooden barracks convinced Surgeon-General Woodworth that "The old, magnificent hospitals, built as monuments for all time, will be abandoned for the simple pavilion of indefinite existence." Dr. Billings agreed: "no hospital should be constructed with a view to its being used more than fifteen years."

Nonetheless Billings was forced by the donor's will to make a city monument out of the façade of his Johns Hopkins Hospital. This task was entrusted to Cabot and Chandler who produced an unbelievably bad composition, and the investment conditions required that the pavilions be permanent instead of the ephemeral ones Billings thought wiser. But despite these fundamental difficulties he persisted in the primacy of utility and achieved a building that performed well while lacking any architectural merit. It was a bald brick working machine sprouting ventilators, windows, and chimneys in ugly disarray.

The medical success of such a building caused scientists to suspect the assumptions underlying professional architecture. Charles William Eliot, President of Harvard, once a chemist, struck at the heart of associationalism when he observed that art and morality were two separate things. He was suspicious of anything involving mysticism or ritual, identified medieval architecture with Catholicism which he thought idolatrous — regarded cathedrals as bad things because they were unsuited for rational worship. The seat of all virtue for Eliot lay in the intellect. The emotional and the intuitive he discounted as vague and deceptive. His democratic taste countenanced no high priests of the arts. He was repelled by Ruskin's remark, "It is not to the public that the judgment is intrusted. It is by the chosen few, by our nobility, and men of taste and talent, that the decision is made." He too suspected professional architects, and preferred the "honest bricklayer" to any tastemaker. Architects might insist, with Leopold Eidlitz, that "An architect who consents . . . to permit a layman to decide upon the merit of his work, to gauge it, correct it, accept it or refuse it — has already given up his position as a professional man." This was a professional posture, a sentiment that would be respected by many an architect right down to such different men as Frank Lloyd Wright and Ralph Walker, but it was not a sentiment many other Americans would accept. On the whole, they would agree rather with Greenough's apostrophe to the common man, previously cited, "The great multitude desires the best of everything, and in the long run is the best judge of it."

Such desires and judgments as "an honest bricklayer" might entertain would, it was thought, inevitably align architecture with progress. Buildings should be useful, extendable, temporary, flexible, expendable. Having seen the difficulties of remodeling various monumental buildings at Harvard, Eliot expressed a common American thought which had been voiced long before in *The House of the Seven Gables*: "our way of building for the present generation only is the best way. . . . It is not well that a house should last a century — it becomes unsuited to the improved habits of succeeding generations. The same is true of public buildings."

Utility, then, conditioned the plan and bleak appearance of the University Museum at Harvard begun in 1858. The museum is largely a monument to one scientist, Louis Agassiz, the biologist, who intended it to be a center for object-directed education about flora and fauna and the laws governing their growth, though not their evolution which he was not to accept. The museum's factory-type structure, consisting of cast-iron columns embedded in brick, carrying brick vaults, enclosed many isolated and fireproof rooms, two stories high, with balconies around their perimeters. Such rooms enabled Agassiz to display a series of biological ideas, assembling within one exhibition all the animals and plants, mammoth to microscopic, stuffed specimens or fossils, that might be needed to show a new typology. Here was a museum building, lacking any effort at artistic merit, which enabled scientists to provide public education in the "best connection between animals, both fossils and modern."

The uniqueness of the Museum, generally unobserved by professional and European-minded American architectural writers and architects, was not lost upon the Europeans themselves.

The sacrifice of architecture to science pleased one of the great naturalists of the day, Alfred Russel Wallace, especially, for he had come to dislike Victorian Gothic monuments such as the Museum of Natural History at South Kensington because they taught nothing about biology. A dozen visits to the Museum at London would not distill the lesson so clearly told at Harvard — "the lesson that each continent has its peculiar forms of life, and that the greatest similarity in geographical position and climate may be accompanied by a complete diversity in the animal inhabitants."

It was ironic that such compliments to a product of American culture should come at the very moment when the American merchant and his tastemaker architect were attempting to reproduce in America an overlay of European art culture, when we were seeking to borrow exactly what the most creative and forward-looking Europeans were trying to discard.

But the functional view had its myopia too. "Honest bricklayers" did not abound nor did they build beautifully. For this there was plenty of evidence from Cambridge, Massachusetts, to Guthrie, Oklahoma.

13

A MAJOR reconciliation, and intelligent and sensitive intellectual and intuitive synthesis between the demands of science and the needs of art, between pragmatism and idealism, between the real and the imaginative, the material and the human, was manifestly needed in architecture.

Among the architects who were the leaders of the period there were surely few who could even essay such a synthesis — a synthesis which compromised neither commodity nor delight. The power was not in Jenney, despite his functional ingenuity, for he had no skill in composition and no understanding of symbolism. It was not in the symbolists like Van Brunt, whose worship of architectural "morality" left them indifferent to the building needs. It was not in eccentrics like Furness; nor in followers of stereotypes like Mullett and Potter. It was not in the arrogant would-be tastemakers led by Hunt who denied their day altogether.

In the next period men like Sullivan and Root would come nearer to the goal though they too would fail to reach it. But that utility could be accommodated to design might not have seemed to them a thing to be believed had it not been for the incomplete examples offered by the greatest American architect of his day, one of the few great American architects of all time, Henry Hobson Richardson.

He entered an America ready for an architectural catalyst. There was, on the one hand, the boisterous roar of a colossally energetic and utilitarian nation. There were on the other hand the picayune and often effeminate pratings of a people who did not yet know that their own aesthetic and intellectual resources were good enough, who sought to emulate the surface flourishes of European manners and customs. Men like Henry James and Whistler might flee to Europe; men like Henry Adams might worry ineffectually about the dynamo and the Virgin of Chartres. What was needed was something lusty and American. For architecture, the first useful image was provided by Richardson. That his image resolved the dilemma of his culture, at least in architecture, was sensed by many of his contemporaries, though, in retrospect, it clearly fell short of this.

A poll conducted by the *American Architect and Building News* in 1885, when Richardson was forty-eight, showed well enough that architects favored large, imposing buildings, regardless of the style of their interiors. Voting for the ten best buildings in the United States, seventy-five architects selected a total of 175 different buildings. None of those selected dated from before 1790; only two were of the period prior to the Civil War. These were the United States Capitol, placed second, and Upjohn's Trinity Church, New York, fourth. Five of the top ten buildings were the work of Richardson. Hunt's Vanderbilt House, it is true, was a favorite, gaining third place. But Hunt had definitely lost to Richardson whose Trinity Church in Boston stood easily in first place with 84 per cent of the votes; and this was followed in various positions by his Albany City Hall, Sever Hall at Harvard, the State Capitol at Albany, and the Town Hall at North Easton, each a unified, strong building. This was amazing acclaim for a man who was still young. It goes far to prove that he was indeed a hero, but a hero respected in his lifetime, not a hero in revolt against a time that did not understand him. The heroes of architecture do not always work in the face of unbelievable opposition.

The Johns Hopkins Hospital with its utilitarian wards masked by a gilded front would not do. Neither would Memorial Hall's infatuation with Ruskinian moral symbolism. It was no longer possible for an engineer like Jenney to be satisfied merely with technical innovation. It was no longer possible for Hunt to pretend that the new, huge, commercial buildings would achieve dignity and visual prestige with awkward silohuettes festooned with pages from history. The buildings and their builders had to acknowledge technology, and be concerned with total form at the new enlarged scale.

Ironically, the building that did this was not technologically progressive at all. This was Richardson's wholesale warehouse for Marshall Field, built in Chicago in 1885-1887, now unhappily destroyed. Here Chicago saw great architecture for the first time, and the impression struck home. The building was one great, single, plastic mass, with all the grandeur of a simple form which springs boldly from the ground, which is precisely defined at all points, which is terminated by a fine and decisive cornice. Throughout, each mass and space meant what it said. Everything was clearly organized, emphatically stated, whether one followed the superb rhythms of the arches or studied the heavily textured walls. Here in the sight of this building, Sullivan found what others would find later, a way of form so that the technical need not be ugly and the aesthetic need be neither borrowed nor flimsy. Richardson gave to young architects a goal of quality, an index of scale, a sense of stateliness possible in architecture for an industrial civilization.

Thus 1885, just before Richardson's death, was a point of climax. The dichotomy between symbolism and utility had produced a clientele which might demand a new sort of architecture. After Richardson such an architecture was possible and it became evident very soon.

Richardson, himself, seems to have sensed the fact that the American architectural scene needed a living hero. He came from a rich and cultivated plantation family in New Orleans, and

might have been a Henry Howard, designing elegant houses for
the landed gentry. He was popular at Harvard, where he won
membership in the Porcellian. Thus he might have rivaled Hunt
as aesthetic docent to Northern Society. He studied at the École
des Beaux-Arts and might have transplanted the architecture of
the Second Empire to America. But he did none of these things.

The Civil War cut him off from his family funds; his friends in
the North dissuaded him from returning South after the war. He
was to become the architect for many wealthy people, including
industrialists like the men of the Ames family, but he thought
money was best used on architecture to which posterity might
point with pride. He refused to transplant a French architecture
to America, saying that "it would not cost me a bit of trouble to
build French buildings that should reach from here to Philadelphia, but that is not what I want to do."

If you will know Richardson, you must look at some of his
sketches. No one else on the American scene could plan with his
authority. Nor had anyone else yet grasped the majesty of the
elementary forms he drew in a composition for a lighthouse or an
icehouse beside a small pond with its sheds and long chute leading down to the water. Contrasted to the work of Downing or
Upjohn, Richardson's sketches seem to have dropped all that
smacks of interior decoration, effeminate scale, two-dimensional
picturesqueness. Contrasted to those of Jefferson, whose scholarly
habit ruled rigorously straight lines on blocked paper and showed
the façades of different temples, annotated with statistics of materials and costs, Richardson's sketches reveal an architect who
seeks the organizational whole of spaces and masses first, plunges
into the composition emotionally, and preserves all the fire of first
impression. He worked with builders and masons and artists, altering his design on the site until it lay "in stone, beyond recovery." Nothing could be more different from Jefferson's rational
way of working than Richardson's creed. "The architect acts on
his building, but his building reacts on him — helps to build itself. His work is plastic work, and, like the sculptor's, cannot be
finished in a drawing. It cannot be fully judged except in concrete
shape and color, amid actual lights and shadows and its own particular surroundings; and if when it is begun it fails to look as it

should, it is not only the architect's privilege but his duty to alter it in any way he can."

Few great architects should be remembered for their first works; Richardson was no exception. The 1870s saw him mature. The tower of the Brattle Square Church (1870-1872) gave some intimation of the masses and the interior, a hint of the large expansive spaces he would later develop.

Trinity Church at Boston, which he won in a competition over Hunt, brought him to the manner which would become identified with his name. Although the exterior was still a combination of many fragmented parts and some reminiscences of Arles and Salamanca, the interior presented a strongly unified space arranged for the preaching of Phillips Brooks. Among other things it was the first American church to have a whole interior decorated by any single painter of ability, John La Farge. What Richardson learned at Trinity about handling a total mass and volume appeared fully in the Cheney Building at Hartford in 1875-1876, with its massive and stately arches framing smaller parts. This office building is progressive in the highest degree.

By 1878-1879 he had achieved something more than a new imported style. He had learned how to plan great and complex series of spaces and to surround them with elementary masses vigorously proportioned, varied in shape, balanced on the land, and energetically counterbalanced by each other. We can see this in the Town Hall at North Easton, which sits on the crest of a hill, rising mountainlike from ledges of granite. The great circuitous approach stair undulates with the land. The Library below sits on the side of the hill. Its arched entry forms a point of balance between the long handsome stack wing with its irregularly rhythmed windows and the tall tower on the lower side. The railroad station at North Easton again displays simple, big forms. The Ames gate house may be the prize. Here huge glacial boulders project two feet or more from the surface, but never escape their imprisonment in the battered walls that shape a rough geometry. All this is executed in autumnal browns and reds and earthy colors. A giant conceived of those stones, not a man inspired by Godey's *Lady's Book*. Van Brunt was right when he said it was "a specimen of boisterous Titanic gamboling."

In the '80s and particularly in his last four culminating years, after his trip to southern France and northern Italy and Spain, all of Richardson's work tended in the direction of simplicity of forms, compactness of mass, monumentality of scale. But this was not a copied inspiration from a new foreign source, merely a recognition of some fundamental principles with which he found himself in accord. Austin Hall, at Harvard, with its assymmetric stair tower, library fenestration, and extended classrooms, was a bold and original presentation of the program devised to house Professor Langdell's case method of teaching law. The designs were always conceived as a whole; the rhythms were always all-inclusive whether the building was a library in Quincy or a bridge over Boston's Fenway. The materials became more natural, the planning more "open." The series of railroad stations and small public libraries of the '80s all led him to segregate functions, to envelop them with basic geometric shapes, and to weld these into an over-all design. Sever Hall, at Harvard, begun in 1878, reveals his ability to handle brick beautifully, to gain a monumental envelope, even if in this case he followed the lead of other great architects by compromising the spaces, circulation and lighting within the building. It shows also how he could strike his own theme while yet making his building compatible with others, even with such ancient buildings as Bulfinch's august University Hall which lies opposite to the west.

Contrasted with these, his buildings in Pittsburgh and Chicago were simpler still. Seldom has any architect handled a difficult problem better than Richardson did when he designed the Allegheny Courthouse and Jail at Pittsburgh of 1885-1887. One can imagine Hunt attacking this problem with a quotation from European town halls. Richardson did no such thing. Even the Bridge of Sighs became in his hands a massive arch springing between the buildings. Giant stones in walls and arched openings fairly scream the custodial finality of the jail. No doubt Richardson here thought himself working with all his power; he believed it would be his greatest achievement, and said, "Let me but have time to finish Pittsburgh . . . and I should be content without another day."

All this work of Richardson's came to fruition in the Marshall

Field warehouse. Here was his *chef d'oeuvre* and his swan song. It suggested to his successors how they might begin to make the details of a fine city of industrial buildings. It did not propose the larger truth that a great city must be more than a collection of fine individual buildings. There is nothing to suggest that this idea ever occurred to Richardson, much less to any other architect of this period. That revelation was saved for the age of reform and for Daniel Burnham of Chicago.

Yet Richardson, dying before he was fifty, had done enough. He was a hero. Henry Adams said Richardson was the only really big man he had ever known. He loved the remark of a German admirer, "*Mein Gott*, how he looks like his own buildings." He would have loved the epitaph by Phillips Brooks in the *Harvard Monthly* for October, 1886: "The man and the work are absolutely one. The man is in the work and the work is in the man."

14

STILL it was not enough for the post-Civil War generation to have one great architect, nor is it ever sufficient even when he is as creative as a Richardson or a Wright. Richardson's greatness, like Wright's, lay in a personal achievement that could not easily be wrenched from the personality that made it. His was a personal triumph over the society in which he lived, but his art could not become a universal expression like the genuine Gothic, nor attain the universality of the Georgian. His personal stature majestically commanded a following among young architects who carried the Romanesque throughout his empire, but as their weaker versions of Richardsonian royalty revealed John L. Faxon, Robert H. Robertson, or Frank M. Howe in disguise, the style languished and its passing carried away the most important lessons of design Richardson had taught. A later generation thought of Richardson as the purveyor of still another foreign style, the Romanesque. In the *Atlantic Monthly* of 1886, Van Brunt hoped for something gentler, more cultivated and urbane, with less of "savage and brutal strength." It seemed to him that Richardson's experiments were "often open to the charge of an affectation of barbarism and heaviness inconsistent with our civilization."

Thus the next generation begun in 1885 had still the pressing problem of developing a beautiful and amenable architecture and a plan for industrial cities. Neither the idealism of European-minded architects like Hunt and critics like Norton nor the pragmatism of Huxley and Gilman had found a way of improving the slums that mocked the American dream. The opening of the West had not carried with it an architecture commensurate with the landscape; the South no longer could offer examples of an aristocratic architecture; and as agriculture declined in importance, the city, with its swollen immigrations, became entangled in a paradox in which cultural institutions were preoccupied with European achievements and architectural dress, while the industry and commerce that supported those institutions addressed themselves to the utilitarian and expedient. The vernacular might sometimes reflect the great movements in science, as it did in the Johns Hopkins Hospital and the Museum of Comparative Zoology at Harvard; but the cultivated architect preferred to ignore science while he erected a National Academy of Design or a Memorial Hall. By their sheer bulk alone, a Mutual Life Insurance Building or Western Union Telegraph Building indicated the power of national business concerns, but their architecture preferred to hide rather than exalt the telegraph, telephone, rails, steamships, typewriters, elevators, electric lighting, iron and steel, and oil that were the great technology of the time. Richardson showed an artistic way past the Home Insurance Building, by his jails and warehouses, but even he did not seize upon the technological resources available to him. Lesser architects, like those who designed the Cathedral of St. John the Divine or the proposed building for the American Institute of Architects, could not be expected to do so. The resources were great, but there was little to suggest in 1885 that architects might ever learn how to use them.

III

1885-1913

Before they could expect to learn to use the resources, American architects had first to face squarely the question: Do you welcome the science and the technology of industrial America or do you prefer to pretend they are not there? The next quarter-century intensified it as Lilienthal's gliders developed to Sikorsky's four-engine aircraft; Daimler's erratic internal combustion engine matured, was abetted by Kettering's self-starter, and one million automobiles thronged American roads.

Serene Parisians carrying their umbrellas over the sward of the *Grand Jatte* of Seurat were succeeded by the violence of Chagall's drinking soldier or the emptiness of Chirico's lonely spaces. Saint-Gaudens's statue of Lincoln became less moving to new generations than Lehmbruck's *Standing Youth.* The buccaneers of American industry gave way to the barons. It was a time of bitter polemic, and of transient reform.

It saw the "passing of the frontier," the emergence of Chicago as a national center. It experienced a culmination of the antagonisms that farmers felt toward city men, the West toward Wall Street and the East. It saw us begin to assert a national belligerence built on a faith in manifest destiny, which, despite disclaimers, often seemed imperialistic.

Federal government was rising. Did this demand or deserve a new or a refurbished architectural symbol? Large business corporations were beginning to do business on a national scale. Ought one to try to produce a corporate architecture? There was interest in social settlements and in alleviating the lot of the poor. Did this call for a social architecture? Reform was in the air. Could there be such a thing as a reform architecture? Should there be, would there be a bimetallic architecture, a Populist architecture, a Granger architecture, a labor architecture, a Western architecture? Clearly enough America was yearning for world influence. Would her architecture turn imperial, too? Many people thought too many buildings were designed for the taste and use only of the rich and powerful and that this was undemocratic. Beyond that there was a mystique. Men like Sullivan and might cried for "democratic" architecture. Was there, could there be any such thing?

The American dream persisted; but it was too vague to be expressed in some democratic symbol as unequivocal as a Thomist cathedral.

1

Now the discussion of the past and the future was carried on in a new key. In the beginning it had been mostly a denial of Europe, a solicitude about preserving the special and vaguely defined American treasure against the corruption of the Old World. It was often manifested by demands for a national art, a national literature, even the unifying and different national language proposed by Noah Webster. It had reached its peak in the ringing words of Emerson's 1837 Phi Beta Kappa oration, *The American Scholar*. This was far more than a mere declaration of literary independence. It applied to all employments of the mind.

Whitman added egalitarianism. He enjoined the muse to "migrate from Greece and Ionia" not only because America was to be self-reliant but because she was the absolute antithesis of Europe, a place where the average man, with the most common qualities, could be divine.

Now the true issue was the more general one of change against tradition, the urgent necessity, felt by many Americans, to lift the heavy bolt of the past which barred the door to the future. In the beginning the barrier was epitomized by Europe, ignoring how many innovations were, in fact, coming from the "tradition-fettered" and "tired" Old World. Later on the same mistake was made about the Eastern seaboard.

But even among the wise extremists of either side there was an American ambivalence, one which Santayana noted when he said that America was really a country with two mentalities: "one a survival of the beliefs and standards of the fathers, the other an expression of the instincts, practises and discoveries of the younger generation."

2

REJECTION of Europe and of the past was but a face of the contest between the transcendental sword of self-reliance and the historical shield of the genteel tradition. Each had its romance. The
men of the tradition loved a Europe that may never have been.
The transcendentalists imagined a frontier that never was.

For the transcendental romance, the frontier was the cutting
edge. Viewed another way the frontier was then and now an escape from failure; but to the transcendental mind, failure was
synonymous with the past, and the past was always in the East,
European or American as it might be. The pioneer obviously had
to be self-reliant; the self-reliance involved in coping alone or
almost alone with elemental forces was more evident than the
self-reliance that might be required to cope with the complex
problems of the settled community. Now towards the end of the
century as the obvious frontier was disappearing, it was around
the frontier that the controversy swirled.

On this vanishing frontier the rage against the East was hot
and deep. Already life on the land was becoming marginal and
after 100,000 "boomers" had poured into the Cherokee Strip in
1893, there were no more great reserves of land worth stealing,
annexing, bartering, or "buying."

On July 12 of the same year, Frederick Jackson Turner, the
Wisconsin historian, delivered his classic address, *The Significance of the Frontier in American History,* and it was appropriate
that it should have been delivered in Chicago. "The existence of
an area of free land, its continuous recession, and the advance of
American settlement westward, explain American development."
The region of sparse settlement to the west, "the frontier," was
"the meeting point between savagery and civilization." In that lay
its strength. As the frontier went west, it moved farther away
from the influence of Europe and this meant a steady growth of
independence along strictly American and, therefore, better lines.
When the frontier closed there would be a real risk of decay.
Such a theory naturally distrusted the industrialized and urban-
ized civilization of the East, where, nevertheless, the government

was beginning to think about the problems of the farmer. Of long-range significance were the federal surveys of the arid regions of the West and the New Lands Reclamation Act of 1902 which authorized the government to build great irrigation projects served by such structures as Wyoming's Shoshone Dam or the Roosevelt Dam on the Salt River of Arizona. The great conservation movement was on, supported by President Cleveland and especially by President Theodore Roosevelt, in whose administration almost 150 million acres were set apart for the public domain, establishing reserves of minerals and forests, conserving watersheds, providing the prospect of bounteous national parks.

But even the most direct benefits of such programs did not appear to farmers a sufficient recompense for the drain on their slender cash which seemed always to be flowing to the city and to the East. The interests of farmers in Oregon and Nebraska, of silver owners in Nevada or Colorado, united in a suspicion of financiers, of cities, of the East. Some motives were economic, some psychological. But they pooled their often contradictory resentments and ambitions; they voiced political discontents which were really economic discontents. In the end they coalesced into the Populist party.

The high-water mark for Populism was reached in 1896 when William Jennings Bryan came nearest to victory. But for a long time after that he was still indefatigable and a durable symbol with his bald head, his fringes of side hair, his rumpled linen suit, his incessant palm-leaf fan, spellbinding the Westerners at fairgrounds and under Chautauqua tents, standing against wealth, against the East, against bankers, against the gold standard, against alcohol, against the theory of evolution, against science, against culture.

What could a movement like this do for or to architecture? The frontier was an abandonment of architecture by the nature of its mobility. It never settled long enough in one place to develop the log cabin or the sod house into architecture. The Populist movement had the same characteristics. Bryan was symbolically anti-architectural.

But there was an ideological residue of importance for American architecture. For Sullivan and other architects the frontier

theory provided the genesis for an insistence on "regional architecture" and the belief that American architecture could be born
only in the West.

Sullivan fancied himself a poet and wrote a great deal of flam-
boyantly bad poetry. A professed nature lover, his words seldom
revealed any close observation say of the blade of flax bent by the
wind or the ruffled underfeathers of a blackbird's wing. His ornament, unlike that of medieval Bourges or Chartres, was not often
drawn from the neighborhood, the immediate prairie sources. His
detailed observations when there were any came mainly not from
Illinois where he worked but from Biloxi where he occasionally
played. But his Byronic terms were broad and general. He wrote
of "surging forests," "vasty plains," "angry waves," "forest mon-
archs," "the lily's aromatic luxury," and spoke most often of
"flotsam and jetsam." In architecture he almost never dealt in
clichés; in poetry he seldom wrote anything else. Thus it was with
his views of democracy. They centered not on the political process but on the one thing he felt essential, the full development of
every individual as an individual. But Sullivan's interpretation of
individualism was as confusing as his interpretation of feudalism.
Feudalism meant, roughly, the men who had power and money
in his day, mostly, though not all, in the East. Individualism
meant the farmer standing alone in his fields facing the rain. Of
world peoples he asserted, "Their ancient polychromatic thought
is turning white."

Sullivan thought that both New York and Chicago were fatally
bad. The belief that few great men are born in the city, that the
individualist will always be associated with the noble countryman,
the perpetuation of the agrarian myth of the stalwart yeoman, the
notion that the Western city always had a better chance of regen-
eration than the Eastern — all these are Populist. But this does
not make Sullivan's architecture Populist. The Prudential Building for Buffalo could have been for St. Louis; the Wainwright
Building of St. Louis could have been in New York. Thus the
words and the architecture were almost unrelated. It is the architecture that matters.

Frank Lloyd Wright's prose often betrayed the influence of
Populist thought, soaked in Carlyle and Thoreau. The doctrine of

individuality colored all his pronouncements though he did not
often stretch this doctrine to include the right of other individuals to do the awful things they did. In his definitions of democracy, Wright like Sullivan often sounded transcendental.
Wright's picture of Sullivan and himself suggests the lonely revolt they led against any classic school of design, even a contemporary one. It was an extreme statement of the transcendental
notions of the self-reliant pioneer, appropriate to the "frontier"
climate of Chicago.

But despite the brilliance of men like Wright and Sullivan and
despite the underlying national affection for transcendentalism,
men of the genteel tradition were in the saddle during the whole
quarter-century. The polemical debates were almost always won
by the transcendentalists but when it came to getting important
commissions or leading their professional societies it was the traditionalists who came out on top.

3

THE nationalist debate went on. At its lowest level a chauvinistic
view simply manifested itself in uncritical statements about
American buildings. In 1887, for example, the *American Architect and Building News* asserted that Henry G. Marquand's new
house in New York was going to be the most beautiful in the
world. Such hyperboles run through American criticism but were
usually balanced by equally strong statements to the effect that
American work was the worst in the world.

Even thoughtful and temperate Americans like John Wellborn
Root, one of the most sensitive leaders of the architectural development of Chicago in the '90s, were not immune to the mysticism of the American dream voiced in architectural terms: "In
the American works we find strength and fitness and a certain
spontaneity and freshness, as of stately music or a song in green
woods."

Against the nationalist view there were those Americans who
thought American productions in general were uncouth. This was
potentially a sound corrective to chauvinism; but when it extended to accepting only things from abroad it was absurd. So

much of the argument for a national style roared out of Chicago instead of New York that the debate appears in part to have been between Fifth Avenue and Newport on the one hand and Halsted Street and the Loop on the other, the "cultured and leisured" versus "the uncouth and untutored," the East against the West, a regional argument conducted in national terms.

John Wellborn Root thought we might have a national style because American students, "reinforced by what is now conceded to be a great national spirit," had the advantage of having no ignoble history; this might more than compensate for the lack of a great national art history. "They are, therefore, free; free in a deep and significant sense." To this the genteel would of course have countered that it was necessary for Americans to turn to European pasts precisely because they had no history of their own.

But quite aside from the question of freedom from history there was the persistent feeling that Utopia was just around the corner and that the corner would be located in America, which believers from William Penn and Bishop Berkeley to John Middleton Murry and D. H. Lawrence thought offered an escape from the corruptions of the Old World, so that Wyndham Lewis could call America "the antechamber of a world state."

Freedom from Europe, from the East, from history, Utopian necessity, separation from other nations, progressive government, all these spoke in the '80s and '90s to Chicago architects like Root, Sullivan, Wright and George W. Maher for a particular American style.

It was, of course, to be a democratic architecture as Sullivan was asserting in *Kindergarten Chats*. "Arrange your architecture for Democracy" because "a certain function, democracy, is seeking a certain form of expression, democratic architecture." What this meant no one really knew. Was it Jeffersonian classicism or Sullivan's bank at Owatonna? Was Hunt's Japanese teahouse for the Belmonts at Newport less "democratic" than the Missouri State Capitol or the Egyptian obelisk, taken from a totalitarian scene, planted on an artificial knoll near the Potomac? Was the White House democratic simply because its fences seemed frail? Despite the confusion, it was easy enough for architects who do

F

not enjoy long stays in the realm of rigorous argument to fall back
on the main theme; there is such a thing as democracy; there can
be such a thing as a democratic architecture; America is a democracy; there are differences in democracies, and America's, though
not the only one, is a different democracy. Therefore it should
have a different democratic architecture. This will be American
architecture.

4

REGIONALISM, deeply loved, stood in antithesis to nationalism,
just as doctrines of states' rights struggled with federalism. Men
of a self-loving region could argue that a nationalism which represented all regions would inevitably destroy the loved special qualities of each.

To those regionalists who thought national architecture undesirable, there were added those who thought it impossible. Frederick G. Corser, a Minnesotan, writing in 1885, took an equally
strong stance against both importers and nationalists. The best
periods of art, he said, had always been those when art was indigenous. Better buildings were made, even if they were crude, when
they were "done in response to the living needs of a people." The
climate of Versailles, he liked to remind his readers, was not the
climate of Minneapolis; and St. Paul boasted no Louis XIV.

Beyond those who thought that a national style would either
be impossible or would shackle regionalism, there were those who
opposed it as a shackling of independence in general. This was
really Wright's position although he was identified by the *Architectural Record* of 1908 as an exponent of the New Nationalism.
In fact Wright denied Americanism or regionalism in favor of a
much broader kind of individuality which should be consistent
with the personalities of clients, artists, terrains and climates. "A
man who has individuality (and what man lacks it?) has a right
to its expression in his own environment." Adherence to such a
doctrine not only means that there could not be a national style,
but that even an international style could not properly develop.
"I do not believe we will ever again have the uniformity of type
which has characterized the so-called great 'styles.' Conditions

have changed; our ideal is democracy, the highest possible expression of the individual as a unit not inconsistent with a harmonious whole." But was this idea in itself so American that the expressions which would arise from it would in themselves define an American architecture of maximized diversity? To call such architecture American was probably to avoid the issue; and surely it was the antithesis of what the ardent nationalists were looking for.

Even among those who wanted a national style there was no agreement as to what it should be. The national eclectics wanted to repeat the works of the Georgian past. The traditionalists wanted Americans to work out their own version of Roman architecture which would somehow have a new national flavor. The innovators insisted that eclecticism of all sorts be abandoned, historical models discarded entirely, even those from the American past.

Thus the architects were, as usual, arguing about too many things at the same time; did we need a national style at all; how could we get it; must it be eclectic; should the eclecticism be national or world-wide? Where should eclecticism stop and innovation begin? These were questions that could be answered categorically only by the opinionated. The more thoughtful were, perhaps, in the camp of Root when he said, "broad influences of climate, of national habits, and institutions will in time create the type, and this is the only style worth considering."

But the sober Root tried nonetheless to state the American traits that might be expected to appear in an American architecture. He did his best in his main address at the Illinois symposium of 1887. It was about as well as anyone has ever done. He thought American architecture would be catholic:

The American people . . . tend to the adoption of any new thing, provided it merely seem better than the old, which often leads to a too sudden abandonment of older modes cutting off slow and yet promising developments and inflicting the newer fashion with certain harshness and crudity. . . .

It will be grave. . . . Though Americans are really grave,

the gravity . . . has a humorous complement, strongly
marked, which will give to the architecture of the future, a
certain "lightness" . . . grace of detail . . . or . . . occasional touches of fancy, or even whimsicalness. . . .

Our architecture will probably remain practical. This
means not only that structures of purely decorative character
will be few in number, but that each important detail of a
building must have some immediate, easily recognized and
practical use.

Perhaps as afterthought, he suggested it might also show some
trend toward splendor.

5

SUCH self-conscious introspection into American personality to
discover what the American dream meant for architecture came
in a period of drastic changes in population, cities, science, technology, business organization and labor patterns.

The population of 1913 was double the fifty million of 1880. Its
westward drift persisted, still along the 39th Parallel, its center
reaching Bloomington, Indiana. The Pacific Coast and Mountain
states grew at two or three times the national rate but still
claimed a mere fifteenth of the population. The farmlands of the
Middle West were about full. The industrial states around the
Great Lakes continued to expand vigorously but the industrial
northeast quarter of the country still held more than half the
population and vastly more than half of the wealth, monetary,
productive, or intellectual.

The long swing from country to city was now more apparent.
Agricultural valuations accounted now for only a fourth of the
national wealth; only a third of the gainfully employed were engaged in farming. About a quarter of the people had lived in
"urban territory" in 1880; by 1910 it was nearly a half. Chicago's
population doubled in a single decade. Others exploded as vio-
lently. The twenty cities of more than 100,000 became fifty. A
great many of the new urbanites were alien.

After 1882 immigration had increased precipitously. By 1910

one seventh of the whole population was foreign-born, amounting to almost half the people in some of the larger cities so that the native stocks of Boston, Philadelphia and New York were outnumbered by the unassimilated foreign-born and their immediate children. Rudyard Kipling, who had no affection or respect for "lesser" races, described the government of New York City as a "despotism of the alien, by the alien, for the alien." And after 1880 the ethnic composition of the immigrants changed drastically from the middle-class burghers and farmers of northern Europe to Italians, Greeks, Hungarians, Poles, Czechs, and Balts, often from the ghettos to the ghettos, doomed for a time to huddle together in urban distress, to suffer in bewilderment and submission. While the advocates of good government sniffed and drew their coats away from the stench and the sordid dwellings, local agents of the bosses helped the new citizens, won their loyalty, forged a chain of power and graft in municipal services. Lord Bryce thought American municipal government the worst failure of democracy in the United States. Andrew D. White asserted in 1890 that American city governments were the worst in the world.

But the cities were not the result only of this torrent of immigration. There had also been a substantial migration of native Americans from the farms. These were small-town people, usually Protestant, usually accustomed to familiar neighbors and to a simple and superficially virtuous life. They were depressed by the anonymity of the city, confused by its crowding and its noise, astonished and repelled by the blatant exhibition of extremes of wealth and poverty, angered by vice and crime and corruption, ill-concealed, often jubilantly paraded. All of this they blamed on the alien and "idolatrous" newcomers. With Josiah Strong they proclaimed that "The first city was built by the first murderer, and crime and vice and wretchedness have festered in it ever since." With Hamlin Garland they entertained lurid dreams of the dangers attendant upon a callow youth who might venture to walk across downtown Chicago even at midday. But it was the new immigrants who were most resented. The Populist hero, Ignatius Donnelly, asserted that America was "united by a ligament to a corpse — Europe!" By 1914 Professor Edward A. Ross had

produced a tract to show that the new immigrants were destroying America. They had forced down the living standards of all
labor "toward their 'pigsty mode of life,' just as they brought
social standards down to 'their brawls and their animal pleasures.'
They were unhygienic and alcoholic, they raised the rates of illiteracy and insanity, they fostered crime and bad morals . . . they
threatened the position of women with their coarse peasant philosophy of sex and debased the educational system with parochial
schools; they spurred the monstrous overgrowth of cities . . .
they threatened to overwhelm 'American blood' and bastardize
American civilization."

The smooth face of American buildings seemed unwrinkled by
these intolerances but what was going on had its effect on American architecture nevertheless. The migration made the American
metropolis what it was to become. It produced large congregations of people calling for large and important buildings for government, education, commerce, religion, recreation. To support
activities that would have languished in the villages, it demanded
concert halls, opera houses, theaters, coliseums, libraries, museums, railroad stations, cathedrals. The ingredients for urbanity
were there and in the moment the desire as well. But at the same
time the growth of the city was too rapid, too thoughtless, too
indigestible. The city lost what traditions it had, dissipated its
early order, became a jungle. The immigrants contributed to the
jungle; though they brought new tastes and ultimate support for
music and painting, and the promise of new artists to come,
urban indigestion was the most obvious immediate consequence
of their arrival.

6

WHILE ordinary immigrants and older Americans were milling
about, seeking to accommodate themselves to each other, scientists, principally in Europe, were preparing a connection of conclusions which would be earth-shaking, yielding unparalleled
weapons of destruction, unparalleled sources of potential peaceful
energy, unimagined opportunities to alter what would once have
been thought to be immutable substance or immutable theology.

The ideas of Planck, Bohr and Einstein were difficult ideas, not well comprehended in the beginning even by many members of the scientific community. They could not so easily be explained to the public as the theory of evolution, for example, had been. No social Einsteinism or social quantum theory came to replace social Darwinism.

Outside the domain of natural science there were other influential theories and observations. This was the time when Freud published his three great studies of hysteria, dreams and sexual theory, soon followed by Jung's investigations of the unconscious. All these came quickly to America, as the ideas of Darwin had before.

The effect of Freud and Jung on later twentieth-century thought, education, literature, painting, medicine was enormous. But in this moment there was no obvious effect on the thinking of American architects. Though men's minds were marching close to the gates of Heaven or the jaws of Hell in this quarter-century, there was nothing on the American architectural scene to indicate such a fearsome crisis of the intellect.

If a time is producing brilliant science, must it be concluded that it will also produce brilliant art? Even if all the efforts of men are not equally well displayed in any given era, would not the *Zeitgeist* at least expect that the participants might interact with each other? By the end of the nineteenth century the different voices were becoming unintelligible, even antagonistic to each other, and interaction was becoming more difficult and less likely; perhaps even less desired.

7

WHETHER the intellectuals or the artists or the public had any basis for an accord with the scientists' science, everyone could see and most would applaud the accompanying technological revolution, based as always on preceding accomplishments of science. The break-throughs were, on their own terms, as astounding as those of science.

From basic European inventions of engines and transmissions by Daimler and Benz, and pneumatic tires by Dunlop, through the struggle in which the steamer and the electric automobile lost the field, the noisy, stuttering, explosive gasoline buggy gradually came to the throne under such king-makers as Charles E. Duryea and Henry Ford. Ford wheeled his contraption out of the barn for its initial road test in 1893. Seven years later there were 8000 automobiles in the United States but only 150 miles of hard-surface roads. In 1903 the first transcontinental automobile trip was made from San Francisco to New York, taking ten weeks. That was the year the Ford Motor Company was formed; five years later it brought its classic four-cylinder Model T to the market; in another five it had adopted assembly-line techniques in a new and modern building by Albert Kahn. From the first sputtering hand-cranked engine to self-starters and assembly lines had taken only twenty-eight years; the 8000 registered cars of 1900 grew to two and a half million by 1915.

Experiments in aircraft were not less spectacular, culminating at Kitty Hawk in 1903 and quickly followed by longer, higher, faster, more hazardous flights by such pioneers as Blériot and Glenn Curtis. In 1911, Galbraith P. Rogers flew a plane from New York to Pasadena in 82 hours of flight but the elapsed time imposed by repairs and weather was seven weeks. Air transport and its great effect on cities seemed far away.

Despite the excitement and portent of these events the important immediate change was in urban transportation. By 1890 there were a hundred electric street railways in the United States. The first elevated railroad was built in Chicago in 1892; the first real American subway in 1904, preceded by a rudimentary one in Boston. In 1905 the London Underground was electrified. With new and relatively comfortable urban transportation the concentration and the dispersion of the city began in earnest, abetted by an enormous expansion in telephones; by now there was an instrument for every dozen people instead of every thousand. The public transportation of New York was one of the things essential to permit a Woolworth Building. But it did not demand one.

Overland long-distance travel still belonged overwhelmingly to the railroads. The transcontinental lines grew to seven. Now the goods of the nation could be carried almost anywhere. Passengers in sleepers and dining cars found physical comforts not all of them could enjoy at home. All this new comfort and success evoked an interest in impressive railroad stations; it seemed fitting that a new Grand Central Terminal should arise in New York City and it did not seem absurd to stretch a red carpet under those who boarded the Twentieth Century Limited. So the quarter-century saw the flowering of the American railway empire and of an imperial railway architecture to fit it.

Despite the recognized successes of Marconi's experiments, including the rescue of passengers at sea, radio and television were still far away. The movies, born in France and New Jersey, moved in a quarter-century from the day when a few people went, for a novelty, to a basement of the Grand Café in Paris to see a short film by the Lumières to an audience of ten million Americans. It is amusing but not particularly important to recall the black-topped movie tents that toured Kansas or the special, if modest, establishment, "Parisiana, the King of the Cinemas," built in Paris in 1911. The important thing is that by 1910 so many people were sharing common theatrical and other visual experiences.

While the population was doubling, the energy consumption was increasing more than fivefold. Almost 90 per cent of it came from coal even in 1910 and most of this was soft coal. Thus the factories were still limited in location to places where coal was easily found or delivered and the urban air grew grimier. By 1912, much as hydroelectric installations may have impressed men like Senator Norris, they provided a negligible amount of the power. After Laval's turbine generators of 1889 and Westinghouse's experimental alternating-current plants, electric energy was finally to permit the city to explode into the country. For the moment it was used for transportation, horizontal and vertical, in small amounts for communication and chiefly for illumination. Progress in the design of the lamps followed the happy demonstration at the White City in Chicago in 1893. Production increased thirty times between 1891 and 1919 and each American citizen had twenty-two times as many lamps on the latter date while these yielded 230 times as many lumens of light. The electric light had arrived.

Architects had a potentially new design force in electricity. For

F*

the city as a whole it meant that it could be a twenty-four-hour place. For buildings it meant that the forms need not be seen only as white in the day and black in the night against a dimly lighted sky. It meant that the night forms could be revealed by floodlights, or reversed from the daylight form by lighting visible interiors. It meant that buildings no longer had to catch every minute of daylight from the ever dingier industrial skies, that the effort to get larger and larger windows could abate; indeed that there could be a complete retreat from the window if this was desired, as soon as better ventilation could be found, and this too was implicit in electricity. The large bay window was no longer essential even in Chicago. Within the building electricity called for the inauguration of a new kind of lighting fixtures and asked the question, still not well answered by architects or decorators, whether the electric light should inspire its own forms. A few men like Adler and Sullivan tried, as in the Chicago auditorium, to come to grips with the new lighting, and McKim made a different try in Boston's Symphony Hall, but for most architects of the day the electric light was simply a convenience and not a stimulus. Not many architectural oversights have been greater.

These were the influential or potentially influential technologi-cal achievements of the generation on the large scale. In building technology itself Hall developed his process for extracting alumi-num from ore but aluminum buildings did not spring up for fifty years. The first successful electric elevator was installed in 1889, the escalator in 1900. But the most important of these develop-ments for the building art was the enormous increase in the pro-duction and use of steel.

In 1885 the country made three million long tons of rolled iron and steel, but probably half of it was iron. By 1894 the Carnegie-Phipps Company of Pittsburgh had circularized a trade catalogue of standardized steel sections for use in the building industry, and in 1910 there were 21 million tons of rolled shapes, practically all of steel.

What this meant for architecture was that there was plenty of steel to let the buildings thrust skywards. At the same time there was a more modest improvement in concrete technology though not so dramatic as the introduction of the open-hearth process. A

Montgomery-Ward warehouse of reinforced concrete was built in 1908 in Chicago; one concrete skyscraper of modest size appeared in the Ingalls Building in Cincinnati, a building of no distinction save for its innovation; but the imaginative uses of this resourceful plastic material were to be deferred to a later day, although Europe had begun to reveal its potential. The steel, the subway, the elevator, the telephone, the typewriter, the adding machine, the electric light, all stood ready to conspire to give to men's vaulting ambitions a vehicle for trying to scratch the skies.

To scratch the skies required the collaboration of engineers and the desire of businessmen. Whether the architect could cope successfully with either seemed for a time in doubt. Of the two marriages, that with the engineer was the more precarious. When the Forth Bridge was revealed in 1890, William Morris called it the "supremest specimen of all ugliness." Sir Benjamin Baker, the designer of the Forth Bridge, replied in a lecture he gave at the Edinburgh Literary Society on November 27, 1890: "beauty relates to function." This was the essence of the debate. The architect looked on the engineer as a servant, a kind of Caliban to do the behests of the architectural Ariel; the engineer thought the architect an effete fool. Montgomery Schuyler, the leading American critic of the day, saw the dichotomy: "The architect resents the engineer as a barbarian; the engineer makes light of the architect as a dilettante. It is difficult to deny that each is largely in the right. The artistic insensibility of the modern engineer is not more fatal to architectural progress than the artistic irrelevancy of the modern architect. In general, engineering is at least progressive, while architecture is at most stationary."

8

WITH the businessman, the architect could find more in common. Thorstein Veblen was not speaking for architects when he castigated the aesthetic standards of the rich of 1899. The funds they spent on endowed buildings showed, according to him, the "pervasive guidance of the canons of conspicuous waste and predatory exploit." According to Marxist theory the businessmen's ideology would be heavily conservative so they would demand, as James Fitch says, "imperial symbols for their new imperialism." As a diagnosis of the dilemma of architecture in the '90s the comment was valid; as an analysis of "capitalist architecture" it was wide of the mark, as the USSR's architecture of 1950 would show.

The trend of business was certainly toward empire. The quarter-century was the scene of titanic struggles between businessmen trying successfully to build influential monopolies and reformers trying to curb them. But despite antitrust legislation like the Sherman Act of 1890, a few families became very, very rich, a few men sat in seats of enormous power, and corporations could not be kept small. Every time a judge cut off a business head with a court decree, a larger hydra appeared.

By 1900 large corporations produced two thirds of all our manufactured goods. In 1904 John Moody in *The Truth about the Trusts* listed 318 corporations of great size. A company like that of Morgan easily controlled the interlocking managements of diverse operating companies. So did the Rockefellers, who influenced not only oil but the National City Bank and the Union and Southern Pacific Railroads. The larger the growth, the louder the protest, by Theodore Roosevelt, Lincoln Steffens, Ida M. Tarbell, Ray Stannard Baker, Charles E. Russell, Thomas W. Lawson. Now the tide began to turn toward the reformers. There were Employer's Liability Acts, Pure Food and Drug Acts, Meat Inspection Acts, the prohibition of corporate contributions to election campaigns, an extension of Interstate Commerce Commission's jurisdiction to telephone, telegraph, cable, and wireless companies. Roosevelt made his declaration for the New Nationalism at Ossawatomie, Kansas: "I stand for the square deal — property shall be the servant and not the master of the Commonwealth." But despite Woodrow Wilson and the Supreme Court the bigness did not die so easily. In 1913 the Pujo Committee brought in its report which said that the people who were attached to the Morgan interests held 341 directorships in 112 corporations, banks, trust companies, transportation systems, insurance companies, manufacturing and trading companies and public utilities with total resources or capitalization of 22 billions. Louis D. Brandeis estimated that this was "more than three times

the assessed value of all the property, real and personal, in all
New England. . . . It is more than twice the assessed value of all
the property in the thirteen Southern states. It is more than the
assessed value of all the property in the twenty-two states, north
and south, lying west of the Mississippi River."

The polemic writing of the time has left an unfair residual picture of the barons. They had much to be blamed for, but they
ought not to go unpraised. To management they brought new
efficiency and not all of it was fiscal; they built better plants; they
introduced the methods of Frederick W. Taylor with corresponding large increases in productivity per hour of a man's work; they
improved materials as Rockefeller did when he employed chem-
ists to salvage the evil-smelling oil of Ohio. They consolidated
railroads and utilities, and the consolidated units usually gave
better services than the unconsolidated. They made notable contributions to education and to culture with massive, usually un-
impeded gifts. It is inconceivable that anything like the same
funds and the same freedoms could have been found from any
other sources in those days, and to imagine the importance of the
barons we need only to recall the memorials, foundations, hospitals, institutes and universities that bear their names and the great
collections of paintings and sculpture and books that distinguish
our museums and libraries. In these men there was a certain
statesmanship, a certain magnanimity, not often to be found in
the writing or the legacies of their detractors.

Yet the detractors were right on the main issue, which was how
much raw power could be left in the hands of private individuals.
Unfortunately their attacks were not often pitched at this level.
We know little, for example, about Ida Tarbell's own taste. But
we do know how she attacked that of John D. Rockefeller. Of
him she said that his houses showed him to have "no pleasure in
noble architecture, to appreciate nothing of the beauty of fine
lines and decorations." But in such a discussion an overly rich
man could not win. If he built a fine house of its kind, as Morgan
and Henry Frick did, then he was subjected to the opposite attack
of being over-luxurious, perhaps even immoral. Certainly Rockefeller's taste was quite irrelevant to Tarbell's main hunt. Neither
good nor bad taste would justify the operations of the Standard

Oil if they were wrong; and if they were right, then Rockefeller's personal taste was a matter of no concern. The reformers caught on wherever they could. Henry Demarest Lloyd spoke of the power kings as one-generation men, "Without restraints of culture, experience, the pride, or even the inherited caution of class or rank." Joseph Medill Patterson's *A Little Brother of the Rich*, published in 1908, described a Watteau-like fete given for the Anti-Vivisectionist Society of Boston. A Brahmin dilettante read Chaucer with a Middle English accent. His soft and white hands, Patterson commented, were kept so by child labor in the mills of South Carolina. Cartoons in *Life* showed the idle rich treading elegant marble floors upheld by starving men and women.

There were stupid rich men like Harry Lehr, who dined his friends' dogs, or those who rode horses into ballrooms and lighted cigars on hundred-dollar bills. The real men of power, the Morgans, the Rockefellers, the Carnegies, danced on few marble floors, recited little Middle English. But they were callous enough and after the writers were through with them, after the reforms had been made, the imperial men never looked so glamorous again.

But they were imperial men. Social Darwinism was slow in dying. It was still persuasive, for example, to E. L. Godkin. In *Forum* for 1894 he wrote an article called "The Duty of Educated Men in a Democracy": "The great law which nature seems to have prescribed for the government of the world . . . is that the more intelligent and thoughtful of the race shall inherit the earth and have the best time, and that all others shall find life on the whole dull and unprofitable." This was the spirit which moved the powerful Charles Elliott Perkins to write Edward Atkinson in 1881, "I think it would answer an extremely useful purpose if as able a pen as yours would show what I suppose to be the fact, that the Standard Oil Company is simply a product of natural laws and laws which it is not safe to touch."

Men like this might have had a certain respect for the bold defiance of young Frank Lloyd Wright but they would prefer the classical architecture of Stanford White. They were conservative about art and they desired, consciously or unconsciously, an imperial architecture. They wanted it for their offices, their railroad stations, their houses, their libraries, their museums, their universities. And they had a way of getting what they wanted.

9

THE imperialism went abroad too. The Keiths built a railroad in Costa Rica and then developed a banana business to justify it. The Guggenheims sought copper and silver estates in Mexico and South America; others exploited sugar in Cuba and oil in Venezuela. With finance went naval diplomacy and the frequent report that the U. S. Marines had landed and were preserving democracy. Our coup d'état in Colombia to promote the secession of Panama was flagrant. Secretary Olney reasserted the Monroe Doctrine and did not hesitate to cite our naval power. Senator Beveridge envisioned a world covered with the American merchant marine. Senator Champ Clark hoped "to see the day when the American flag will float over every square foot of British-North American possessions clear to the North Pole."

There was another and more amiable side. It was Americans who promoted the Pan-American Conferences, the Pan-American Union, the Pan-American Exposition, the American Court of Justice. It was a citizen of the United States, Carnegie, who built the Peace Palace at The Hague, and paid for the Pan-American Union Building at Washington, who established the Carnegie Endowment for International Peace. It was another American, Ginn, who founded and endowed the World Peace Foundation. The divided personality represented two views of America's new position in the world, which no longer could rest on a policy of isolation. Americans *were* affected by the agricultural, industrial, and commercial successes and failures in other lands; Americans *were* genuinely sympathetic to the human plight of Armenians and Chinese.

Whether benign or sinister, the new world view in the United States made it inevitable that the doors of America were opened to an influx of ideas from the East and from Europe. There was, for example, the acceleration of the strange, long-drawn-out, love-hate affair between America and Japan. Japan held some fascination for America that other Asian countries did not. In the begin-

ning the architectural results might seem superficial, as in the
effect the Japanese exhibition of the Chicago Fair of 1893 had
upon Frank Lloyd Wright, or the influence of Japanese houses on
the lesser Pacific Coast architects Bernard Maybeck and the
brothers Greene. But the course of this stream ran deep, surviving
wars and treacheries, and it would appear far more influentially in
American architecture of the mid-twentieth century.

For the long pull the big thing was that American architecture
began to identify itself with international architecture and not
with colonial architecture; that it was anxious to excel, to have
something that could be put before all the world and announced
with pride as American. We found it in the skyscraper. But for
the moment there was a more direct connection with our imperialistic spirit as well. For the individual who commissioned it, the
skyscraper, trying to go higher than any competitor, was the demonstration of a personal imperialism, even if it were that of a ten-
cent-store owner.

10

THE violent emergence of the labor movement in this period ultimately had important and adverse effects upon American building although many were deferred. The bloody and disastrous
strife from the Haymarket bomb incident, the Pinkerton invasion
at Homestead, the guerilla battles at Coeur d'Alene, the stabbing
of Manager Henry Frick, the Danbury Hatters boycott, the jail-
ing of Eugene V. Debs and Samuel Gompers, are fading in our
memories. Still less remembered are the managerial attitudes of
1902, articulated by George F. Baer, President of the Philadelphia
and Reading Coal and Iron Company, "The rights and interest of
the laboring man will be protected and cared for — not by the
labor agitators, but by the Christian men to whom God in His
infinite wisdom has given the control of the property interests of
this country."

But the national temper was not disposed to leave the lot of
labor to the good will of any manager even if he were the benevo-
lent Andrew Carnegie, the paternal George Pullman or the God-
fearing George Baer. The trickles of legislative control of manage-

ment grew in number and in force, mostly in measures governing health, liability, hours of work and minimum wages. Early in Wilson's administration, separate Departments of Commerce and Labor were established. But the period ended as it had begun — with violence. Out of all this turmoil no labor architecture had arisen, but better amenities for plant labor had become inevitable.

The most important architectural effect was' on the building industry itself. Almost all the important craft unions of this industry were established in this time. Bricklayers had been nationally organized in 1865. But between 1881 and 1900 almost every other craft was organized.

The whole sentimental idea of a happy group of building craftsmen, perpetually singing at their work, is one of the legends of architectural reminiscence. The Egyptian and Greek and Roman slaves probably did little singing although an occasional classic sculptor may have. The insistence of the medieval guilds on standards of performance may be overrated. There were fewer "honest bricklayers" in Huxley's day than he imagined. But it is safe to say that there were some in earlier times. The drawings were less complete; more skill and ingenuity were required of the laborer and the buildings were often of a size where his personal contact with the architect could be maintained. All this led to a better human relation and, it is not unreasonable to think, a higher quality of work.

Whatever the views of the medieval guilds may have been, the laborers who organized in America were usually concerned more with maintaining their wage scale than they were with improving their standards of workmanship in building. Not that they were more ignoble than any other labor force, or any other managerial force for that matter. But they met with a particular difficulty not very much of their making though certainly supported by them. This was that the building "industry" was fragmented from top to bottom. It did not have the advantage of bigness. No Vanderbilt or Carnegie ever thought to give it his attention. Even if every building worker had remained exactly as competent as his father, the plain fact is that the makers of materials, the contrivers of methods for assembling buildings, and the architects

themselves were not interested in producing spectacular technological advances in the economy of building based, as it was, entirely on handicraft methods. While on the farm the amount of
produce per man-hour of work went up steadily and in the factory
the rise was dramatic, there was essentially no change in the productivity per man-hour in building on the site. Thus every year
the cost of a unit of building increased with respect to the cost of
any other article subject to machine operations.

Among all these groups, leading contractors seem to have felt
the most elation. Their diaries and articles sing many a paean
to the symphony of the whistles, the jack-hammers, the dynamite,
the caissons, the steel drills eating granite rock, the rivet guns
clinching the white-hot steel, the turning concrete mixers, the
cable hoists and compressed-air lines. They exult in the pressure
of work against the clock. But even this was a kind of romance
akin to Kipling's personalization of a ship on her maiden voyage.
It did not bring the productivity of the building industry in line
with the productivity of the factory.

At some point in this losing battle of relative costs it was inevitable that Americans would have to be content with less space in
their buildings, with inferior housing for those of low income, and
perhaps even with less architectural amenity. If a cubic foot of
enclosed space costs twice as much as it needs to, there may not
be much left for fountains or sculpture or paintings or even grass
or trees — or even for enough space, especially if you want automobiles, air conditioning, television and cosmetics more.

11

SUCH a situation led a few architects to feel common bonds with
urban reformers but they looked at urban reform in poetic terms
not as a pragmatic challenge to organize. Wright was calling attention to the degradation of the city in stentorian tones. In his
1901 address at Hull House in Chicago, he said, "Chicago in its
ugliness today becomes as true an expression of the *life* lived here
as is any center on earth where men come together closely to live
it out or fight it out. . . . We must walk blindfolded through
the streets of this, or any great modern American city, to fail to

see that all this magnificent resource of machine-power and superior material has brought to us, so far, is degradation." When he
revised *The Art and Craft of the Machine* he advised the listener
to go at nightfall to the top of one of the downtown steel giants
and "you may see how in the image of material man, at once his
glory and his menace, is this thing we call a City." Then he provided a prophetic and poetic picture of the skeleton, the muscula-
ture, the blood vessels and the nervous system of this glory and
menace. Although he did not like what he saw, he was not then,
anyway, in despair about the end.

Moreover, though it was an age of enormous reform in many
cities; few of the reformers or their reforms had much direct
effect on the slums or on architecture.

Often the reform movements stemmed not from a desire to
improve the living conditions of the poor or the morals of politics
but just as a way of conquering vice. Thus the reformers made
strange bedfellows like Steffens, Jacob Riis and the Reverend
Charles Parkhurst in New York. To be sure, a model tenement
was built here or there but on the whole the reformers did more
to clean up the police departments than they did to clean up the
slums. But for the few who saw other expedients failing, it
seemed that something at least might be accomplished by regula-
tory acts, preventing the worst abuses of sanitation and safety. In
these crusades a few but not many architects might occasionally
be enlisted.

12

OTHERS who had no desire to apply legal measures or tax-sup-
ported subsidies reasoned that the slums might disappear if the
building industry could only manage to obtain the same increase
in productivity per hour of labor that had been common in the
manufacturing industries. This economic analysis led men of fine
intentions to break their hearts and sometimes their pocketbooks
trying to invent and establish new ways to make housing.

The Hodgson Company had been making prefabricated
wooden houses successfully since 1892 but these were combusti-
ble detached buildings and could not contribute to the supply of

urban dwelling. Thomas Edison and Grosvenor Atterbury labored in vain. All their patents and demonstrations came to
naught. Nobody seemed to know how to invent prefabrication.
Nobody seemed to want to exploit it if it were invented. Some
interest groups were categorically opposed to it; among these, architects usually stood in the front row, arguing that its standardization would impose limitations on their freedom of design.

Reformers who were looking rather for subsidized housing or a
socialized state had no interest in higher productivity — and little
faith that it could be achieved. Moreover the efforts were not convincing. The prefabrication movement was so weak that it was
readily killed by massive indifference.

There were still other ways to alleviate the lot of people in
slums. Octavia Hill had experimented successfully in London
with purchasing, restoring and then personally managing three
verminous and decaying houses in Marylebone, using John Ruskin's capital. Now Octavia Hill Associations were founded in
America, a noteworthy one in Philadelphia in 1896. Even if the
economic principle was sound, which is open to doubt, there were
just not enough Octavia Hills to go around. The effect was like
that of a drop of rain on an endless sand.

Then there were the social settlements designed to bridge the
gap between the life slum dwellers were now living and the lives
they might live later, to bring them together in some kind of
decent community exchange that their home surroundings could
not foster. Toynbee Hall in London in 1884 and the Neighborhood Guild on New York's East Side in 1886 were quickly followed by Hull House in Chicago (1889), Andover House in Boston (1891), and others in New York. Staffed by admirable and
sensitive men and women like Robert A. Woods or Jane Addams,
the settlement house movement, unquestionably a force for good,
did not solve the problem.

Finally there were efforts to reclaim the city altogether and the
beginning of theories about garden cities we. owe to this period.
The important person was Ebenezer Howard. Howard produced
his thesis, *Tomorrow; A Peaceful Path to Real Reform,* at London in 1898. In it he described a garden city set in a large area of
protectable farmland; a complete town would be surrounded by a

wide belt of rural country; the town would be essentially self-sufficient and certainly able to provide housing, farming and industrial employment for all its residents; its extent would be limited; it would not be allowed to encroach on the green belt; it should contain about 30,000 persons, small enough to be personal, big enough to match most of the magnetism of the large city. Groups of such towns could support activities which demanded larger populations. Any rise in land values would be shared by the community which had itself created them. By such devices, Howard suggested, rural depopulation could be arrested; the constant growth of the metropolis into something too big to be managed would stop. Such a garden city must never be confused with a suburb. The autonomy, the profit-sharing and the fact that it was a cross-section of the society all differentiated it both from the company town and the one-class dormitory suburb.

The publication was followed by the Garden Cities Association in 1899 and the first garden city, Letchworth, in 1903. Despite the attractiveness of the notion and the occasional success of an individual town, despite the strong support the movement has had from a number of eloquent voices, it affected little urban development.

Howard was followed at the end of the period by Patrick Geddes, a Scottish-Australian physiologist, zoologist, botanist, sociologist and zealot who started the regional survey movement in Edinburgh and a study of the "organic" relationship between city, country and industrial area, a sort of urban ecology on which he wrote voluminously for thirty years. In 1913 he produced *Cities in Evolution*, a book carrying his persistent slogan about the city as a trinity of place, work and folk, as the rural village had in fact once been. He is more important in the American scene for the impression he made on Lewis Mumford, who subsequently made a comparable impression on many Americans, than for anything he himself wrote. In all of this as in everything else about housing and slum clearance, the period of 1885-1913 simply set the stage for a future performance.

13

INDEED, much of the violence of the debate about reform appeared more in words than in deeds. American writers were now concerned with American problems as they had not been in the earlier day. There was much less escape writing, much less effort to be sentimentally regional. A few writers looked back with nostalgia. Some of these, like Willa Cather or Edith Wharton, resembling the architects in this, were among the best craftsmen. But the vast majority were concerned with but one thing, the decay of the American dream. A subtle thinker like Herman Melville wrote *Billy Budd* (it was not published until 1924). But with the possible exception of Melville, the writers were at bottom optimists. They believed that reform was possible if things as they were could but be exposed to the American view. So the center of American writing was the documentary exposé. It might be as violent and insincere as Jack London's *The Iron Heel* (1908), which described the march of the People of the Abyss, like Carlyle's monsters of the Faubourg St. Antoine and Zola's women of Montsou, but as in most American radical novels marching to slaughter under the Iron Heel of indicted capitalism. Others painted the picture sordidly but with less flaming brushes in the manner of Norris or Upton Sinclair; they dealt with the problem more personally in the way of Dreiser; they produced quasi-fiction in the muck-raking essays of Tarbell or Steffens; they yearned for Wisconsin with Hamlin Garland; or leaned on piety with Edward Sheldon; they couched their criticism in philosophical terms with Veblen; advocated the solution of the strenuous life with Roosevelt, or the technocratic city with Utopian Bellamy, whose *Looking Backward* started abortive Nationalist Clubs off on an attempt to rear a middle-class version of state socialism; they sought with Henry Adams to explain the dynamo by contemplating the Virgin or with John Dewey to turn pragmatism to social ends. But all the time the writing that focused on the industrial and cultural life of America was really cast in optimistic terms. Not a doom-sayer believed in doom.

Henry James, perhaps the greatest American writer of the time, was a partial exception to this general attitude. When he returned to America in 1904 he found it much changed. He did not pretend to like the change but he did sense the grandeur in this world of the office building, "huge constructed and compressed communities, throbbing . . . with a single passion." He could understand how the skyscraper had earned a right to soar above the church. Though he rejected this outcome for himself, he did not deny that it might do for others in the future. So even with James we must conclude that the writers of America continued to believe that the new age was still possible even though it had not yet arrived.

This belief, fostered by the pragmatic philosophy of liberalism, was more evident among the architects of the Mississippi valley than in the work of reform novelists or painters. Men like Wright and Sullivan, Root and Elmslie, shared many tenets of Dewey's instrumentalism, Croly's progressivism, and Veblen's economic theories and especially their appeal to the ultimate authority of experience.

14

FOR such men the painters of the time had less to say, for few painters of Europe or America concerned themselves directly with social protest in paint, although they joined freely enough in verbal manifestoes. But the architects could not go unaffected by the experimental and provocative experiments the painters were making with space and light. It is sometimes easy to forget today how violent the painting revolution was in Europe in this period. The names remind us.

Beginning with Van Gogh and Seurat, it continued with Cézanne, Gauguin, Matisse, Rouault and Braque. It saw the cubist and classic Picasso and the Picasso of the Harlequins; it included the experiments of Fauvism, cubism, futurism. There were new organizations, new manifestoes, the *Salon d'Automne,* the *Deutscher Künstlerbund, die Brücke,* and the first *Blaue Reiter* Exhibition of 1912 revealing the work of Arp, Delaunay, Kandinsky and Klee.

All these men of change did not find a common answer to the

problem of expressing ideas on the flat surface of a canvas. Painters and architects of Europe were able, nonetheless, working on
different problems but contemporaneously, to be satisfied by similar kinds of organization and space. For example there are many
points of resemblance between a painting like Seurat's *Le Di-
manche sur la Grande Jatte* and the interior of the Dufayel Store
at Paris. Some are superficial, like the similarity of bustled, bos-
omy, curving form, bespeaking the ephemeral ways of the haber-
dasher and couturier. But more significant ones lie in the composition of light and form and space. Both architects and painters
silhouetted form against light, flattened it, revealed volumes only
by half-light; both edged the forms with penumbras of shimmering, form-breaking light; both isolated their forms and made
them stand free, in deep voids; both emphasized the structural
elements that made up the forms.

Americans could see the new painting even if they did not
make it. This was due principally to the efforts of Alfred Stieglitz
and his Photo-Secession Group, who opened the 291 *Gallery* at
291 Fifth Avenue in 1906. Through it Picasso and other important European painters paraded their works; 291 was not slow
either to reveal the work of promising young American painters.
Marin's first one-man show was held there in 1910 and the work
of Max Weber and Marsden Hartley appeared there in the same
year.

These young Americans were not yet much admired by their
compatriots. The average citizen hardly knew of and certainly
would not have accepted even the work of the Eight — Henri,
Luks, Glackens, Sloan, Shinn, Prendergast, Lawson and Davies.
The new men painted New York, its East River, its birds, its
children, its ferryboats, its skyline, its cafés, its boxing clubs.

But American architects still esteemed the Sargents, the Ab-
beys, and the La Farges. They were not ready for the Sloans.
They were even less pleased with the work from Europe. In 1913,
when the Armory of the 69th Regiment offered its great exhibition of 1100 works by painters ranging from Ingres and Delacroix
to Duchamp, Matisse and Picasso, it was well attended. But
Nude Descending a Staircase was the most discussed picture,

whether for its manner or its "risqué" title is hard to say. Theodore Roosevelt attended and then wrote about it in *The Outlook*. He was emphatic about the right of "progressive painters" to paint progressively and to have their work examined, but he had many personal reservations. "Probably we err in treating most of these pictures seriously. It is likely that many of them represent in the painters astute appreciation of the power to make folly lucrative which the late P. T. Barnum showed with his faked mermaid." While approving the absence of the commonplace he felt that perhaps any reform movement risked the penalty of being liable to extravagance. "It is vitally necessary to move forward and to shake off the dead hand, often the fossilized dead hands of the reactionaries; and yet we have to face the fact that there is apt to be a lunatic fringe among the votaries of any forward movement. . . . *it is just as easy to be conventional about the fantastic as about the commonplace*." (Italics added.)

On this score Roosevelt, even with his reservations, was far to the left of the American public. The show was coldly received by art viewers in Boston and Chicago and by most American architects. The few experimental American architects of the day did not do well by revolutionary artists. Sullivan commissioned or permitted bovine banalities by an itinerant painter, for his lunettes in the Chicago auditorium and the Owatonna bank; Wright had little taste for any other art than architecture, despite the Japanese screens at Taliesin and the sculpture of the Midway Gardens. More conventional architects like McKim, who did want painters, invariably selected Sargent or Abbey; if they went abroad for their painter they chose the pale and aged Puvis de Chavannes rather than even Derain or Utrillo, not to mention Picasso, Braque or Léger.

15

Nor were American architects of the right or left pleased or influenced by the advanced architectural work of Europe. This was so even when the manner was related to that of the earlier Richardson as in Berlage's Stock Exchange in Amsterdam of 1898-1903;

or could be seen as an imaginative extension of the principles of Jenney as in Victor Horta's splendid glass and iron Maison du Peuple in Brussels in 1897.

By 1900 the lively and varied Art Nouveau movement was a major current in the cities of western Europe. Its representatives worked in highly different styles though most of the work was decorative and floral as in Horta's interiors or biomorphically sculptural as it was when Gaudi began mixing it with symbolism borrowed from world religions for the Sagrada Familia in Barcelona. Exponents of the style offered some major structural innovations, especially the fascinating Gaudi, who seemed to try to escape the tyranny of the classical past; but the group in the mainstream tended to emphasize the structural possibilities of iron and stone, while treating them plastically as in Hector Guimard's Humbert de Romans Building in Paris. Guimard, the architect of many Art Nouveau stations for the Paris Métro, a spokesman for the movement, espoused a triadic philosophy of logic, harmony and sentiment. The movement produced a more angular version in Scotland through the work of Mackintosh and Mackmurdo, and this in turn influenced the Finn, Eliel Saarinen, and through him such later American architects as Goodhue and Magonigle. More directly, some Americans if not many American buildings took notice of the modern French school itself. The *Architectural Record* in 1902 reviewed Guimard's book, published photographs of his work, and an account of the important exhibit of Art Nouveau held at Turin in 1902. The more plastic aspect of the movement greatly influenced the American designer, Louis Comfort Tiffany, whose glass curtain for the National Theater in Mexico and whose studio in New York City owed their curious exoticism to the new art in France. The more rectilinear design of the Scottish group appeared in the buildings of Frederick Scheibler, who worked in Pittsburgh about 1900. His Heidelberg Apartments and Highland Towers Apartments (1911) there are important examples of the modernism springing up in the Middle West soon after the turn of the century. Surely the greatest expositor of Art Nouveau design in America was Louis Sullivan, whose decorative ornament, almost Celtic in its interweaving of form, seems to have developed independently of the Art Nouveau in Europe, though perhaps from the same sources as the iron ornament of the Bon Marché and the Eiffel Tower. But the movement never became widespread in America. It had a long development in France, becoming more cubistic at the time of the 1925 exhibition at Paris, and it was this late decorative version of the Art Nouveau that appeared in America much later in the Barclay-Vesey lobby by Ralph Walker and in many other buildings of the 1920s.

Alongside the fantasies of the Art Nouveau interiors, there were revivalists and realists and modern classicists, all defying any attempt to subsume the ferment of ideas under a single designation. In Liverpool, Giles Scott was beginning his Modern Gothic Liverpool Cathedral, and Voysey was simplifying the picturesque house of Morris and his followers. In Sweden, Ragnar Östberg attempted to develop a modern folk architecture by his arts-and-crafts interpretation of the Town Hall at Stockholm. A vigorous group of men in Austria proposed simple geometrical forms and angular decoration, visible in Otto Wagner's railroad station at Vienna and his chapel at a sanitorium near Vienna. A further insistence upon cubical form, composed asymmetrically and decorated rectilinearly, appeared at Darmstadt in Ölbrich's Habich House of 1906 and also at Brussels in the Stoclet House of 1905. French architects tended to remain under the wing of the classicism associated with the École des Beaux-Arts, but Anatole de Baudot found in the Church a loyal client for his pioneering reinforced concrete frame and his Art Nouveau space and decorative forms, while Auguste Perret broke headlong towards modern architecture in his Theatre des Champs-Elysées of 1911-1914, his apartment on the Rue Franklin and the garage in the Rue Ponthieu.

If there was any one center for the diverse currents of modernism, it surely lay in Berlin and in the office of Peter Behrens, where the important modern architects Le Corbusier, Mies van der Rohe and Walter Gropius were taking their apprenticeship. Behrens's house at the Darmstadt Exposition of 1901 revealed his assimilation of the tendencies towards simplification and unification that gripped all architects at the turn of the century; it seemed a thing of planes, precise but thin. That impression was changed entirely by the buildings coming from Behrens's office after the works of Frank Lloyd Wright were made known in Germany. The Berlin AEG Turbine Factory of 1910, for example, is a building of tremendous power, developed upon masses struck firmly, exposing the nature of brick and glass, and unified by the dominating form of the building. Behrens's pupil, Walter Gropius, revealed his knowledge of the industrial architecture being produced in Chicago in 1914 when he designed the Werkbund Exposition building at Cologne, a model factory which in one jump took the German architects far beyond anything produced for industry in America with the exception of Wright's Larkin Building. His Fagus shoe-last factory at Alfeld-an-Leine was a thoroughgoing modern presentation of the steel and glass architecture being developed for factories in New York and other American cities. It was characteristic that these German architects picked up what was being developed in America in a slipshod and nonarchitectural way — by all save Wright — and made it monumental and architectural.

Americans also seemed uninfluenced by the modern city planning of men like Perret and Tony Garnier. In 1901-1904 Garnier created one of the most far-reaching plans for a modern city ever conceived by any architect. He called it *La Cité Industrielle* and to it Le Corbusier's later proposals are but rich and copious footnotes. Garnier proposed a vast city, with transportation centers, separated residential quarters, circulation patterns adapted to vehicular traffic, industrial centers and business quarters, all given areas compatible with their requirements and buildings functional in form but possessing good scale and silhouette. But this city pattern was not published until 1917, and American city planners paid little attention to it, preferring the grandiose monumental planning of the kind Haussmann had made in Paris.

Suggestive as this all was of the ferment in European architecture, the fact remains that even the most imaginative and sensitive innovators were less surefooted when they attempted to relate their efforts to the largest movements of the times. Thus in 1894 Otto Wagner made a sonorous statement of the kind architects like to make: "Our starting point for artistic creation is to be found only in modern life." But anyone could say that and many would. The question was what the words "modern life" meant. Was it the life of Lorentz and the electrons; was it the Freudian world; was it the life of the space the cubists were uncovering, or the life of the screaming people of Munch; was it a Gare St. Lazare or a haystack of Monet? Was it the life of Marx? Or was it just an immediate life which would use the devices technology offered? The Karlsplatz station of the Vienna subway and the Savings Bank, both by Wagner, with their metal and glass canopies and reminiscences of classicism must have been what Wagner meant by buildings whose starting point was in modern life, but they were still far from coping with the promise of modern science.

If European architects were lagging their own scientists by several decades, what was to be expected from the architects of America where a lag behind adventuresome Europe had always been acceptable? Although they may have discussed art with painters and sculptors, the American architects were not accustomed to the cross-cultural, cross-disciplinary discussions of the European intellectuals and artists. They knew nothing of science, almost nothing of literature, and the history they paraded was more often than not half-studied and ill-remembered. They were interested in the political and social climate. The "gay" discussions between St. Gaudens, McKim and Hunt seldom turned on the gloomy philosophical questions their friend Henry Adams was asking of the atom, or on such social puzzles as the slum. It was more pleasurable for them and more characteristic that they bandied jests about the vulgarity of Chicago, pretended to chase bulls around the amphitheater of Arles, exchanged reminiscences of the boulevards.

The clearest American architectural genius of this day, Frank Lloyd Wright, had little time for such vaporings. But he too seems to have made no effort to comprehend the implications of science or to look for messages in the work of contemporary painters. He was as sensitive to primitive art as Picasso or Braque. Some of the great themes of Mayan architecture leaped from the pages of Catherwood's drawings or the books of other archaeologists and found their new statements in his Wisconsin warehouse or, later, in the patterns of the textile blocks of his

California houses. He was among the first Americans to sense the organic unity of Japanese houses, to glean from the Japanese exhibit at the Columbian Exposition a message of how space could be defined by hovering planes; in this experience he was not led astray by trivia into the idea of copying or modifying the bracket details or the wooden screens as the brothers Greene did in California. He developed his own cubist ornament for the Midway Gardens and here came as close as he ever did to being influenced by the European movement. But Wright was never a great admirer of painting anyway and asserted that he was no admirer of the architectural work of others. How much he really examined, only he could know. In the end he seemed always to find his own nature without the aid of others' eyes. If his work could influence science or art he might regard it as well and good; if not, they might go their separate ways.

Thus practically all American architects of the day stood aloof from the social, aesthetic and intellectual ferments. The most prosperous and worldly of them were still of the middle class, employees of a financial upper class. The more revolutionary like Sullivan and Wright were not so far to the left as the Populists. The indifference of the architects posed problems for architecture which to measure its times needed to pay attention to the factory, to provide symbols for big business, to produce schools and universities that would take account of the new pragmatism; also to use steel and electricity well, to begin to work on the problem of the slum, to prepare at least for the later and almost predictable onslaught of the automobile. The architecture did not manage all of these problems equally well; it was at its worst with the technology and the slum.

16

In retrospect it is easy to see which buildings were most prescient. But it is not extraordinary that the most famous architects and critics, the most influential clients, the best educated public of the day did not see them in that light. They acclaimed Boston's Public Library, New York's Pennsylvania Station, West Point's Chapel, Vanderbilt's Biltmore at Asheville, and Washington's

Pan-American Union, works of imperial quality, executed by admitted and successful leaders of the architectural profession, McKim, Cram, Hunt, and Cret. The idea that many were repelled by the display at the World's Columbian Exposition of 1893 is far-fetched. The frontiersman liked it just as well as the effete Easterner — perhaps better, for he had never seen Rome.

Later historians would praise Sullivan's Wainwright Building in St. Louis, Maybeck's Christian Science Church in Berkeley, Greene and Greene's Gamble House in Pasadena, or Wright's prairie houses, Unity Temple in Oak Park and the Larkin Building in Buffalo; all of these were the voice of the future, but they were not what most men of the day admired.

Although imperialism was making the louder noise and although imperial architecture was making the louder show, the most important motif of the period seems now to have been the drive towards increased industrial productivity. When a comparable drive was occurring in Western religion the great Romanesque churches were born. One might, then, have expected some fine factories and warehouses to reflect the new and great importance of industry. But industry was not yet ready for symbolism. Most industrial buildings remained purposefully utilitarian and incidentally ugly. They grew larger; they cast deeper and longer shadows over the streets they walled; they took more and more green space from the city. But they were given little aesthetic and not much more social consideration. Those still extant reveal the attitudes of the businessmen who built them with small sense of civic obligation.

There was a social program that might have been well expressed still in terms of the engineer's structural aesthetic. Industrialists came to regard good working conditions as synonymous with good business. The Weston Electrical Instrument Company of Newark, New Jersey, noted "how frequently the health of employees, and the requirements of business, are best served by identical conditions." Such statements were typical.

But such a social program focused on health, morals, education and efficiency did not necessarily lead to a fine architecture. Industrialists could provide better washrooms and rest rooms and libraries and gymnasiums without designing beyond utility. They could build more substantial and comfortable housing, such as that of the Colorado Fuel and Iron Company, without creating architecture at all. They could add equipment for ventilation without making shops and lofts less ugly. Design could improve only when the pragmatism of health and education took account also of the pragmatism of aesthetics.

But paternalism did effect some aesthetic improvement. You could see it in a village like Whitinsville, Massachusetts, where the ·Whitins' houses stood opposite the machine factory, surrounded by comfortable houses for the workers. Such arrangements were not unique. They were to be found at the Fairbanks Scale plant in St. Johnsbury, Vermont; at the Kilbourne and Jacobs Manufacturing Company in Columbus, Ohio; at Proctor and Gamble in Cincinnati; at South Manchester, Connecticut, where the Cheneys who owned the silk mills of the town also built their residences. Many of the new industries came to be located in rural settings or in landscaped parks. There had been European examples of this in the '80s when famous English candy manufacturers had moved out of Birmingham and York into the adjacent country. In 1889 Lever Brothers removed their soap works from Warrington to Mersey and established a model village there.

In the United States, we recall, most factories like those of the Merrimack Manufacturing Company at Lowell had expanded on crowded expensive land and had built densely and to great heights. Others, such as the Waltham Watch works, near Boston, were more fortunate. One English visitor, Budgett Meakin, praised "the handsome buildings . . . surrounded by well-kept lawns, overlooking on the one side the river, and on the other a park-like village, inhabited by the employees." The Crane Paper Mills near Pittsfield, Massachusetts; the Bullock Manufacturing Company seven miles outside of Cincinnati; and a number of others sat in rural parks, sometimes not even fettered by fences. Some urban factories like those of the Acme White Lead Works at Detroit, the Cleveland Varnish Company, or the National Cash Register Company at Dayton were provided with landscaping and gardens; the Natural Food Company's plant at Niagara Falls was set in a ten-acre park overlooking the Falls.

Chicago, Illinois, World's Columbian Exposition, 1893

Dayton, Ohio, National Cash
Register Company, ca. 1885

Chicago, Reliance Building, 1890-
1895, Daniel Hudson Burnham and
John Wellborn Root, archs.

Proposal for A.I.A. Building at
New York, 1884,
John Moser, arch.

Berkeley, California, First Church of Christ Scientist, interior, 1912,
Bernard Maybeck, arch.

West Point, New York, U. S. Military Academy, Cadet Chapel, 1908,
Ralph Adams Cram and Bertram Grosvenor Goodhue, archs.

Guthrie, Oklahoma, City Hall, 1902, J. Feucart, arch.

Boston, Massachusetts, Public Library, 1888, McKim, Mead and White, archs.

Asheville, North Carolina, "Biltmore" (Vanderbilt Estate), 1896,
R. M. Hunt, arch.

Buffalo, New York,
Guaranty Building, 1895,
Louis H. Sullivan, arch.

CHICAGO ARCHITECTURAL PHOTOGRAPHING CO.

Owatonna, Minnesota, National Farmers' Bank, 1908,
Louis H. Sullivan, arch.

WAYNE AND

Chicago, Illinois, Schlesinger and Mayer Building, now Carson,
Pirie, Scott & Co., 1899-1904, Louis H. Sullivan, arch.

Chicago, Illinois, Rookery Building, interior, 1886, Daniel Hudson Burnham and
John Wellborn Root, archs.; Staircase, 1906, Frank Lloyd Wright, arch.

Riverside, Illinois, Avery Coonley residence, 1908, Frank Lloyd Wright, arch.

Riverside, Illinois, Avery Coonley residence,
living room, Frank Lloyd Wright, arch.

Pasadena, California, D. B. Gamble residence, 1909,
Charles Sumner Greene and Henry Mather Greene, archs.

Even where there were no gardens there were interior improvements. Many emulated the Weston Company in providing libraries, kitchens, dining rooms, gymnasiums, natatoria, bicycle depots, hospitals and rest areas. Many, like the McCormick Harvester, introduced safety appliances, used vermilion paint on dangerous machinery, took precautions against fire, introduced advanced sanitary or ventilating equipment. Almost all the new factories had extensive areas of glass to obtain better light; the Natural Food Company's "Conservatory" boasted 30,000 panes. Some electrical shops were now lighted through sawtooth roofs, whose glass faces were oriented to the north to keep out direct sun.

Of course this entire social program could be and usually was realized without architectural intervention. As it became more complicated, however, it cried for the work of imaginative minds, trained planners. But even as late as 1909, the *Architectural Record* could still remark: "The American manufacturing plant is a commercial type of structure which the architect has so far played an insignificant part in developing." The editor appealed to industrialists to hire architects, suggesting that a well-planned factory would not only lead to operational economies but that an attractive factory would bring prestige and good workmen.

This argument, most appealing perhaps to those whose business depended most directly on good public relations, seemed confirmed by the successes of such organizations as the Natural Food Company or the National Biscuit Company. A notable plant was owned by the National Cash Register Company at Dayton, Ohio, where buildings were set on well-landscaped sites and arranged to enclose generous courts. The buildings themselves were orderly. Their four stories used bricks in narrow, continuous piers, setting a clear cadence for recessed arched spandrels above wide windows. The owner's concern for moral education was revealed by mottoes prominently lettered on the walls, proclaiming for example that "Labour is a Girdle of Manliness." The owners were justly proud of such buildings. They encouraged visitors who, around 1905, were inspecting the plant each day in groups of fifty to five hundred, enjoying a conducted tour, complete with tea served in the adjoining clubhouse.

One could sense the breath of this new attitude even in cities

G

like Cleveland, whose early industrial history had been so deplorable. There, Robert D. Kohn, always social-minded and progressive, was employed by H. Black and Company, manufacturers of women's wear, in 1909. He provided a picturesque group of basic manufacturing elements set in an open field. The long low skyline was livened by sawtooth roofs. The water tower was a strong vertical accent sculpturally emphatic from a distance, presenting rich patterns of brick and terra cotta. In an article in the *Architectural Record* of 1909 Kohn openly avowed his intention to create attractive as well as useful factory architecture.

Factories and warehouses of some distinction thus began to replace some of the shabby wooden structures and disorderly piles of brick which had so often been acceptable earlier. "Realistic design" became almost a national movement. In Chicago Richardson's Marshall Field Wholesale Warehouse gave the lead to other praiseworthy expressions. Outstanding among these was the Walker Warehouse by Adler and Sullivan. Here Sullivan came as close as he ever did to mimicking Richardson, using a massive arch to frame the lesser parts of the design and developing the whole building as a single unit.

Factories were now sufficiently numerous and impressive to stir critical comment in the leading architectural magazines. One would scarcely have expected Russell Sturgis or any of his Ruskinian friends to admire unornamented, utilitarian buildings. Yet they were recovering from their first love affair with the Gothic. Matured under the tutelage of Viollet-le-Duc, they had found a manly hero in Richardson and were now ready, within limits, to accept a hardheaded philosophy of realism in design. Russell Sturgis led the way. His eye was never so sure, his judgment so dependable, as Montgomery Schuyler's. But like Schuyler, he admired the steel web of the Brooklyn Bridge, preferring it to the stone towers with their Gothic vestiges. Now he went further and championed the new industrial architecture. In 1904 he wrote an account of the buildings designed by Babb, Cook and Willard and some others including the Judge Building by McKim, Mead and White: ". . . one sees in the treatment of these recent and very plain — very utilitarian — structures, a wholesome architectural influence." Sturgis could not bring himself to go the whole

way in asserting the falsity of the prevailing monumental architecture, but he readily admitted that there was something in the
proposal that "designers should be restrained to square masses
and sharp corners and plain windows for twenty years to come —
with sculpture denied them and all the bad architectural forms
tabu."

At Chicago in 1910, Peter Bonnett Wight published his essay
about warehouse architecture, called "Utilitarian Architecture in
Chicago." Like Sturgis, Wight was an ex-Ruskinian, with several
recognized Gothic successes to his credit, including Yale's School
of the Fine Arts and the National Academy of Design at New
York. But in Chicago he abandoned his medieval ways and embraced realistic architecture, praising Richard E. Schmidt's warehouse for Grommes and Ulrich. The warehouse interested Sturgis
too, who once suggested that it showed how professional architects should treat the problem of library design. There had never
been, he thought, a better device for giving light to a building
which needed all the light there was. He suggested applying the
maxim to the fronts of the Carnegie libraries.

It would be wrong to conclude from Wight's and Sturgis's criticism that a new architectural age had arrived in America. Indeed,
the fight had hardly begun. A number of able designers, it is true,
eagerly tackled industrial problems, happily designed buildings
using new materials and structures, successfully developed a new
philosophy of total design. They were not entirely neglected by
critics and they found some business and industrial clients, moti-
vated, at least in part, by a desire to create something beautiful.
But the critics were still hesitant in their praise, the commissions
still relatively few.

No one yet seriously proposed that the new way should be applied outside of industry to buildings intended for monumental
sites or for major civic or cultural purposes. While Huxley's point
of view was acceptable to many industrialists and to a few architects and critics, if it were limited to factories and warehouses, the
same men usually insisted that eclectic design, Gothic or classic,
be used for churches and courthouses at the upper levels of the
cultural hierarchy. Thus criticism and theory worked to a dual
standard.

The dual standard had strange consequences. A supreme example was Albert Kahn, an immigrant who came to America from Germany with his rabbi father at the age of eleven and settled in Detroit. His first factory, made of reinforced concrete and steel sash, was commissioned by the Packard Motor Company in 1903. He inaugurated the all-under-one-roof type of factory and followed this with the even more revolutionary all-on-one-floor design. In such work he was brilliantly innovative and architecturally sure-footed. He designed rigorously and imaginatively planned factories for the Ford Motor Company such as the Highland Avenue Factory in Detroit where the first mass-produced Model T rolled down the wooden ramp in 1913. Buildings such as this commanded great respect in Europe, encouraging men like Gropius and Neutra to develop a consistent theory of modern architectural design. Kahn's achievements in this field were in the end genuinely colossal. But he could not universalize them. Suffering the ambivalence of his colleagues he hardly thought of his best works as architecture at all. He confined realistic design to the lower echelons of the building hierarchy. When he was later asked to design an administrative building for Ford, or the Detroit Public Library, or large office buildings in Detroit for Fisher and General Motors, he and his clients rejected the factory experience and ventured into eclectic dress and ornament.

One must not leap too quickly to a conclusion about which of the Janus heads was the more reliable expression of its day. We think we know which head was looking forward. But a great many Americans of the day were more than happy about the noble Boston Public Library and many fewer cared for or were even aware of the Wainwright Building. Those who made the Boston Public Library and its kind were sincere and upright men, doing competent and sometimes brilliant jobs, given their premises. Our cities would be meaner today without their work. It is as silly to call these men stupid or even "dishonest," as some contemporaries have, as it is to wish to return to their theories as a few contemporaries urge.

17

New York was a confused island of commercial towers, usually tricked out in classical dress, rising from a morass of utilitarian factories, shanties, warehouses and docks but it was not unique in this respect. Realtors boasted of top-story offices that "there was nothing between us and the sun." Since height suggested business distinction all the large cities east of the Mississippi began to develop more or less distinctive profiles depending on the shape of the land. In Chicago the expanse of lake front made the buildings into a wall; on Manhattan the point of the island piled them into a pyramid. The skyline, a word coined about 1897, intrigued New Yorkers. The skyline of Manhattan, changing enormously even in the three years between 1894 and 1897, impressed itself as a symbol. It was a theme that photographers recorded, artists depicted, poets sometimes praised, offered a powerful silhouette but like the Bolshoi Ballet of later date its power lay in the aggregative mass and not in the fine details. Montgomery Schuyler remarked, "It is not an architectural vision."

The sheer immensity and audacity of the new commercial skyline drowned both an appreciation of the tremendous city planning problems it imposed and the enormous architectural possibilities that lay in the component skyscrapers. However the masses might glow from the river, the new form was not so glamorous at the level of the ordinary pedestrian. A walk down Wall Street or Broad Street or Nassau Street by 1905 was a passage through sunless gorges. But the gorges seemed exciting still to illustrators like the one of 1911 who drew a view for *Judge* looking upward from an open street intersection to a sky framed on all sides by the distant roofs of huge buildings that pointed still higher toward weird aircraft. King's *Dream of New York* of 1908 envisioned a future Broadway lined with buildings all of which would be higher than the 612-foot building Ernest Flagg had designed for Singer. At their upper stories, some 500 feet above the ground, the buildings were to be connected by bridges while their roofs were hangars and mooring stations for huge balloons which carried signs indicating that they were departing for the Panama

Canal, Europe, Japan and the North Pole. But all this excitement did not lead architects in New York to discuss the real and mounting urban social problem or even the aesthetic one of compatibility between adjacent buildings of the same generation.

Nor did they usually approach the individual skyscraper as a new problem, requiring first a utilitarian analysis of its structure and function and then an aesthetic expression of them. The Pulitzer Building, for example, rose through many layers of classic ornament to a summit crowned by a Renaissance dome, clownishly proportioned. The Park Row Building, erected in 1897-1898 to be the tallest building in the world, soared from a throne of classic bombast to end near the clouds in silly rabbit's-ear turrets. The cornices of its tall neighbor, the St. Paul Building, turned the corners and stopped, providing a mere starched front to give surface respectability to a dirty brick rear. Bradford Gilbert's Tower Building at 50 Broadway built in 1888-1889, did nothing to reveal that it was the first steel skeleton erected in New York. Its ill-organized tower emerged from a rusticated stone base, fronting a mediocre loft.

The newer cities of the Midwest did better. New York architects had been insulated from the commercial significance of the skyscraper by their background, their professional education and the nature of their work. But after the fire, Chicago attracted a number of young Eastern architects, like Sullivan and Root, who were to become great designers. In Chicago they found competent natives like Jenney, Holabird and Roche who were already struggling to find an aesthetic for the tall building. They found too the pragmatism which called for adaptation to use. It inspired them to seek a way of beginning with the program for a building, developing the forms it required, modifying them in accordance with the materials and the structures, and making the result beautiful.

This almost unconscious search for a modern architecture lay hidden in the theoretical, prophetic writings of the French archeologist Viollet-le-Duc. His studies of medieval structural systems insisted that structural organization lay at the base of any great architecture, including any future one. His own generation saw only the Frenchman's detailed and factual examination of medieval structure; for them it lacked the poetic fire of Ruskin's crusading prose. The new buildings Viollet-le-Duc designed did not reveal his bold prophecies of a future architecture built with an iron structure. His audience at the École des Beaux-Arts, including Richardson, failing to recognize the implications of his thinking, rioted when he was appointed by Napoleon III to teach at that center. Richardson, like most of his contemporaries, brushed aside the challenge offered in the second volume of the *Lectures*. "A practical architect might . . . conceive the idea of erecting a vast edifice whose frame should be entirely of iron . . . and . . . preserving . . . [that frame] by means of casing of stone."

Nevertheless these ideas had been widely broadcast during the '80s. Henry Van Brunt had translated Viollet-le-Duc's *Entretiens sur l'Architecture* for an edition called the *Discourses* and published in Boston in 1875; later, in 1877-1881, it appeared in England with the title, *Lectures*. In 1880 Buffington, the Minneapolis architect sometimes credited with inventing the "cage," read the passage referring to an iron architecture. He began to investigate the possibility of developing such a structural skeleton for skyscrapers, and in 1888, but after Major Jenney's Home Insurance Building had been completed in Chicago, received a patent for a skeleton with laminated steel columns.

18

FAR more important than Buffington's literal and explicit reading of the sentence was Viollet-le-Duc's over-all message to Americans. He insisted upon "truth" in architecture, and by truth he meant adaptation to use and to structure: "There are in architecture . . . two indispensable modes in which truth must be adhered to. We must be true in respect of the program, and true in respect of the constructive processes . . . fulfill exactly, scrupulously, the conditions imposed . . . employ the materials according to their qualities and properties." The program of the "realistic" architects which we have already mentioned called for truth to structure, materials and program. They aimed at "rational building," a term lifted from George Martin Huss's translation in 1895 of Viollet-le-Duc's article "Construction."

The group in Chicago might have applied the idea of rationalism to continue medieval forms as Charles Eliot Norton construed it in Cambridge. Instead the young designers in Chicago came to believe that each building should be regarded as an organism, subject to laws analogous to those of biological growth. Louis Sullivan said of himself: "In Darwin he found much food. The theory of evolution seemed stupendous." What they assumed from evolutionary theory was reinforced by Gottfried Semper, whose writing was translated by Root and frequently quoted by Adler. In 1860, Semper had written: "Every technical product [should be] a resultant of use and material. Style is the conformity of an art object with the circumstance of its origin and the conditions and circumstances of its development." In following Semper, the Chicago architects forged a link relating themselves to Latrobe and Greenough and Emerson. In Whitman they felt an ally, hostile to the survival or revival of historical forms, demanding a new, modern form, expressive of American ambitions. Since the times had changed, it must be that a new idea was required, one related to the qualities of the new times. The Chicagoans, sensing their departure from the past, their difference from the East, determined to emphasize and preserve it, founded the Western Association of Architects. Their publications, *The Western Architect* and *The Inland Architect and Builder*, spoke of a West trying to assert its modernity. They remained in accord, however, with the Sullivan-Wright theory of the identity of democracy with individuality. Each building in such a view was unique.

Wright was the most influential expositor of these confused ideas. By 1908 in the *Architectural Record* he was writing of the new attitude towards building. Businessmen were more likely than the "cultured" to be men of "unspoiled instincts and untainted ideals," capable of judging for themselves, of encouraging the new work. An artist's limitations were his best friends. The machine should not be denied. There was "no more important work before the architect now than to use this normal tool of civilization to the best advantage instead of prostituting it as he has hitherto done in reproducing with murderous ubiquity forms born of other times and other conditions and which it can only serve to destroy."

But neither theories of organism nor those of rational design were enough. Mere adaptation of form to use, materials, structure, environment, would not prevent an ugly result. Great building required more — that the form be adapted to emotional and aesthetic as well as utilitarian needs. Since these were not always consonant with maximum physical utility, each designer was faced with the necessity of resolving a personal conflict between use and beauty. Many, like Jenney, Holabird, Roche, took the rigid course, deciding in favor of the expression of use and materials. Greater men, like Root and Sullivan, took the way of all great designers, starting from pure theory, but modifying the conclusions to their greater ends. In this they were following the basic principles of the Beaux-Arts. This statement seems paradoxical simply because long years of opposition have blinded our eyes to what the Beaux-Arts once was.

Americans, such as Daniel Burnham, who did not attend the École, and some who did, like McKim, tried to legislate a style, an historical one, the classic. That led the Beaux-Arts architecture they perpetrated here to be held in disrepute. But the Parisian Beaux-Arts men had long since attempted to evolve a modern style, and they were not concerned with recreating classical buildings, nor indeed with imposing the classical style upon modern institutions. The École had produced modernists like Tony Garnier, Auguste Perret and Anatole de Baudot at the turn of the century. Many of the Beaux-Arts students might turn out arid and stiff buildings, like the Museum at Grenoble, which obeyed all the superficial formulas, but few European Beaux-Arts men were pedantic. Copying was not the goal of the Beaux-Arts, however much it was the students' device for passing examinations. The École taught general principles of composition, and it is as unwise to judge the École by its worst practitioners as it is to judge Christianity by all its professors.

The Beaux-Arts system in Paris had stood for the designs of Labrouste and Laloux and Sullivan was the greatest American in the genuine Beaux-Arts tradition. This was recognized easily

G*

enough by the French architects who visited Chicago at the time of the 1893 Exposition. They admired Richardson's work. They disapproved of Hunt's. They agreed that Sullivan, alone, had fully understood the principles of the École which would be listed nine years later by Guadet in *Elements and Theory of Architecture*. These include six principles of design. They involve the rationalism of Viollet-le-Duc and also his realism: (1) You must be faithful to your program and see what is the character to be kept in the building; (2) the ground, location or climate can modify the expression of a program; (3) all architectural compositions must be constructible; every inconstructible scheme is absurd; (4) truth is the first requirement of architecture; every architectural untruth is inexcusable; (5) effective strength is not sufficient — it must also be apparent; (6) designs proceed by necessary sacrifices; a design must be good first of all, but it must also be beautiful. "You must compose then with a view both to the utility and the beauty of the building. And, as an element of beauty, you will try to obtain character by variety." That could stand as the credo for Sullivan.

19

THE various components of the new theory developing in Chicago during the '80s began to appear visibly in a series of brilliant designs for office buildings erected during the period after 1890. Gone was the bleak utilitarianism of the Montauk Building of 1882. The structural innovations introduced by the Home Insurance Building were no longer obscured by confused patterns of exterior form. Nor did the designers repeat the unsatisfactory superficial ornamentation of Sullivan's early attempt in the Rothschild Store to find an expression adequate to the modern office building. They had encountered the Marshall Field Wholesale Warehouse, and as Sullivan wrote in *Kindergarten Chats* had seen "stone and mortar, here, spring into life."

The Rookery (1885), at 209 South La Salle Street, was Burnham and Root's first successful office building. Its granite piers and columns support the brick piers and arches of the upper stories within strong horizontal divisions framed by arches, the unifying arcade that Richardson used. But the design is still heavy and granitic and the exterior does not indicate how interesting the interior is. Here one finds a court whose cast-iron columns and wrought-iron spandrel beams display an open skeleton, with airy but vigorous curving iron stairways and the decorations added by Wright in 1906. The interior court was awaiting recognition from a designer who would develop an entire building accordingly.

This transposition of theme was made by Holabird and Roche in their Tacoma Building of 1886-1889. Now they sought lightness throughout the building. The metal columns wore only a minimal covering, while the spaces between them were filled with large areas of glass — a systematic expression of the processes of obtaining light, useful interior space and firm construction.

The Monadnock Building by Burnham and Root of 1889-1891, although of old-fashioned construction, was another triumph of unified design, the last great monument of the wall-bearing age. It is a tremendous unadorned slab, two bays wide and sixteen stories high, built with masonry bearing-walls and an interior iron frame. The narrow slab provides outside exposure for every office but this utility is combined with severe simplicity and fine proportions in a powerful composition of horizontal and vertical lines worked out with a magnificent sweep from the batter of the base to the curve of the cornice. If the Marshall Field Warehouse was the first, the Monadnock was the second great lesson in unified design. Strangely that lesson came, as in the first case, within traditional walls. Yet perhaps it was not strange — all it meant was that the best designers had not yet come to grips with the metal frame while the greatest innovators were not often, unhappily, the best designers.

Even the untalented Major Jenney was led by the new insights to create a bold and vigorous design for the Second Leiter Building (now Sears, Roebuck) in 1889-1890. It is a huge rectangular prism, and its gray granite facing over the columns and spandrels fully reflects the interior skeleton in a large and unified pattern. The interior presents sweeping open areas divided into broad avenues by rows of tall, slender columns which created a dramatic impression of open and airy space, much diminished today even on the upper floors, by the plethoric placards of Sears, Roebuck.

Louis Sullivan took a less literal direction but achieved greater artistic expressions. The tall narrow piers of his Schiller Building of 1891-1892 extend to the sixteenth story where they bend into an arcade. This arcade does not express the shape of the underlying structure but is used to close the composition at the top. Form follows function here but the function is aesthetic, more than structural. He made the same flight from literal engineering in his Wainwright Building at St. Louis, one of the great triumphs of his career. Built in 1890-1891, the building rises from a U-shaped plan in a classical arrangement of masses and voids. The base haṣ a large module at ground story and mezzanine; a smaller module through the shaft; an impressive roof and cornice terminates it at the skyline. The shaft makes no distinction between mullion and pier; only every other vertical element contains a load-carrying steel column; but the failure to express the "honest" structural fact is not aesthetically "dishonest," not a failure of architectural morality. Instead, it follows a higher honesty and a higher morality than that of disclosing the skeleton; it gives the vertical lift and scale that express height and unify the composition. It is an almost perfect outcome of the theoretical and artistic and engineering work in Chicago around 1890.

While each of these buildings had merit, no single style was evolving. Instead each was a highly individual, "democratic" variation of a common theme. This troubled some visitors to Chicago, such as C. H. Blackall, who praised the Rookery Building, but went on to say "that there has been, as yet, no real style developed. Each building is a law unto itself, and no architect seems to feel called upon to follow even his own precedent, either in the choice of design or the character of the detail. There seems to be, throughout, a restless striving after originality; a seeking for striking effects, which . . . is not always good, and generally serves to belittle the character of the architecture." The Chicago work in 1890 included several individually brilliant office buildings, but no convincing demonstration of a national or even regional architecture, and even the brilliance could be negated. Chicago was far from beautiful, and its appearance was not improved by dull exercises like Jenney's Fair Building of 1891, split

absurdly in the middle by an obtrusive horizontal element. Moreover the new theory could spawn monsters like the Fagin Building at St. Louis, built in 1888. In 1893 the *Architectural Record*
gave it the ultimate accolade of being the most discreditable piece
of architecture in the United States. Then the writer labeled it
with the most damning phrase an Easterner could muster; he said
it had all the vices and crudities and vulgarities called "Western."

This was indeed the attitude which pervaded the East at the
time of Chicago's World's Fair of 1893. Sullivan himself often
spoke disparagingly of Chicago's culture as fit only for hogs and
butchers. Once he said that Chicago had been a mudhole fifty
years ago and was one still. McKim's scorn was more superficial
and not born of love. When his agent was trying to buy a piece of
sculpture for the World's Fair, consisting of a bull, a ram and a
boar, he was able to get only the boar and tried to persuade Mc-
Kim to accept the compromise. McKim refused but added that it
would be appropriate enough for Chicago.

Thus, on the eve of the World's Columbian Exposition of
1893, as the New York firms were assembling to advise on its
planning, they were not disposed to take Chicago seriously. They
accepted Burnham and Root, and Adler and Sullivan, and both
firms were in on the ground floor of the planning. Indeed it was
they who had summoned the Easterners to help. And the world
would have thought them right. The West seemed to most to
have produced but little. Of 129 buildings compiled as notable by
the *American Architect and Building News* in 1891, most built
after the Civil War, only ten were from Chicago, only fourteen
from the vast area west of it. Of the ten from Chicago only the
Pullman Building, the Auditorium and the Rookery suggested
that the compiler realized that a new style was developing there.

20

GIVEN such an opinion of the west and its architecture, the classicism of the Columbian Exposition was almost a foregone conclusion. Eastern architects went to Chicago with the firm intention
of providing the Middle West with a dazzling spectacle of the
best; of showing how a national style in the grand classical man-

ner might be modified for modern use even on the prairie. The goal was much like that of a missionary to a "savage" land. The missionaries, like others who seek to convert from without, failed to note that the natives had something of their own to say.

This might have been especially true of Root but on the first day of the first conference of the World's Fair Board Root caught pneumonia; he died before the conference was over. Harriet Monroe, his sister, insisted, "If he had lived, there would have been another battle of Chicago against the East, new methods against old, our own beauty against the past." Perhaps so, perhaps not. Anyway, in Root's absence, his partner Burnham offered no opposition to Hunt, St. Gaudens, and McKim; without Root at his elbow, Sullivan made no headway.

So the Easterners succeeded in putting on their display. Henry Adams blamed the Middle West for regarding art as a stage decoration. He sat down on the steps beneath Hunt's dome at the Fair and pondered, "if . . . the new American world could take this sharp and conscious twist towards ideals, one's personal friends would come in, at last, as winners in the great American chariot-race for fame. If the people of the Northwest actually knew what was good when they saw it, they would someday talk about Hunt and Richardson, La Farge and St. Gaudens, Burnham and McKim, and Stanford White when their politicians and millionaires were otherwise forgotten. The artist and architects who had done the work offered little encouragement to hope it . . . to them the Northwest refused to look artistic. They talked as though they worked only for themselves; as though art, to the Western people, was a stage decoration; a diamond shirt-stud; a paper collar." Adams could not see that it was his Eastern friends who were creating his "shirt-studs."

The fact is, though, that the Western work was not much better. Cobb's Fisheries Building may be assumed to have been the nearest to what Root had in mind, and certainly was the most representative of what Chicago architects had been doing, but it was of no distinction. Sullivan's Transportation Building attracted the most attention. But it too was a shirt stud. As a picture it was marvelous. A great Romanesque arch held five voussoirs, each brilliantly decorated with Sullivan's most exotic ornament. The building had originality and freshness to the extent that it was in opposition to the prevailing classic detail of the Fair. But Sullivan had created no Galérie des Machines, no Crystal Palace, not even a true exemplar of the work of the Chicago school. The building made no statement about the arched iron structure of the shed behind it, no statement about transportation; it made no important prediction for future railroad stations either, although the door details turned up the very next year in the Union Station at St. Louis. Its charm lay in its difference; its quality lay in Sullivan's decorative genius which, great as it was, is not his main claim to fame. Had American buildings of the next fifty years followed its lead, the Transportation Building might well have been as great a barrier to the future as the conquering classic turned out to be.

It has been common to assert that the work of men like McKim was unrelated to the vital contemporary forces of American life. But there can be no doubt that the new classical manner was exactly what the society wanted.

Somewhat later Paul Cret pointed out that "Nobody imposed French architecture on the United States. It was of their own free will that hundreds of Americans went to Paris and that thousands more took their inspiration from the ideas they brought back. Were all these men fools? What were they looking for in France? . . . It was composition and design." Only hindsight could lead Sullivan to assert, and Wright to quote, and those who accept an unusual version of history to believe, that the Fair dealt American architecture a blow from which it would not recover for fifty years. It was fifty years before the new ideas came to fruit; but to blame their lag on a single summer's show and not on the national disposition is to put too much faith in the symbolism of a minor event.

Moreover the greatest buildings of the Chicago style were built *after* the Exposition. Burnham's Reliance Building, one of the finest examples of the steel cage enclosed in terra cotta, was only a small four-story building in 1890, not completed until building was resumed in 1894. The Marquette Building and Beman's Studebaker with its all-glass façade topped inconsistently with Gothic fretwork, all lay in the future. The Fisher Building, the

marvelously simple Gage Building of Sullivan, and the McClurg
Building came at the end of the century. The great Schlesinger-
Mayer Store, later occupied by Carson, Pirie and Scott, was not
built by Sullivan until 1899. Thus the World's Fair did not nip
the Chicago School while it was still in the bud. It had barely
shown what might be done by 1893; it continued to develop long
after the Fair was closed. The Fair did offer American clients a
choice, and most of them, as we now think unwisely, chose the
classic revival. But the Chicago school had its chance to show
competing work off the Fair grounds and American clients were
prepared for a while to support the Chicago school for industrial,
commercial and residential architecture. But the old law of hierarchy of building types still operated to insist that cultural buildings should be in the grand tradition of classical design. The Fair
merely stated the accepted law and possibly revealed and emphasized it to more people. In the end the classic mania overtook the
"non-cultural" buildings too but this was after Sullivan had dissipated his energies, after his break with Adler had deprived him of
strength, after the death of Root had weakened the aesthetic
powers of Burnham's firm, after Purcell and Elmslie had aged
and only Frank Lloyd Wright was left, and he in eclipse.

21

But there was a moment when Sullivan showed the world how a
tall skyscraper ought to be built when his Prudential Building at
Buffalo, completed in 1894-1895, repeated the success of the
Wainwright Building. It expressed Guadet's principles perfectly,
as Sullivan's own explanation reveals. This appeared in an article
he wrote for *Lippincott's Magazine* for March, 1896, "The Tall
Office Building Artistically Considered." They were the same
as in the Wainwright; a clear differentiation of the function of
the five major vertical subdivisions; a determination of the rhythmic module by the size of the standard office room; large functional openings in the base, unimportant ones in the attic.
"Hence it follows inevitably, and in the simplest possible way,
that if we follow our natural instincts without thought of books,
rules, precedents, or any such educational impedimenta to a spon-

taneous and 'sensible' result we will . . . design the exterior of our tall office building." This statement is characteristic of Sullivan's acceptance of the belief that "every problem . . . contains and suggests its own solution," a firm avowal in architecture of the principles of instrumentalism in teaching which John Dewey was developing in Chicago to challenge academic methods of relying on the old process of memorizing facts and rules.

But thus far, Sullivan's results were merely partial and tentative; his form had followed function, but only physical function: "we must seek a fuller justification, a finer sanction. . . . We must now heed the imperative voice of emotion." What is the chief feature of an office building? "And at once we answer, it is lofty. This loftiness is to the artist-nature its thrilling aspect. It is the very open organ-tone in its appeal. It must be in turn the dominant chord in his expression of it, the true excitant of his imagination. It must be tall, every inch of it tall . . . It must be every inch a proud and soaring thing, rising in sheer exultation that from bottom to top it is a unit without a single dissenting line." Now Sullivan prepared his reader to accept the idea, that form must not only be adapted to function, but that it must *express* that function: "All things in nature have a shape . . . that tells us what they are . . . Unfailingly in nature these shapes express the inner life . . . of the animal, tree, bird, fish, that they present to us. . . . Over all the coursing sun, *form ever follows function*, and this is the law. Where function does not change, form does not change. . . . It is the pervading law of all things organic and inorganic." It was that general principle of organic expression, not mechanical functionalism, which led Sullivan "readily, clearly and conclusively" to give the lower stories a character suited to commerce, the tiers of typical offices another, and the attic still another. Each form revealed a different function; but where, as in the offices, function did not change, neither did form. He arrived at a three-part division "naturally, spontaneously, unwittingly . . . not from any theory, symbol, or fancied logic."

Yet Sullivan's interpretation was open to misunderstanding. Years later his word "function" would receive only a mechanistic interpretation, denying that form should be modified for expres-

sive and aesthetic, rather than utilitarian, reasons. Equally misin-
formed were those who ignored the origins of expression in function. For example, Sullivan's desire to express the verticality of the
tall building led him to introduce extra vertical, decorative, non-
structural elements between the structural piers; however from the
exterior no distinction was visible. Expressive form here took
precedence over structural function, with no nonsense about
"honesty." Furthermore, the terra-cotta protection was not self-
supporting. Therefore the casing was treated with delicate ornament. Here form alone scored a triumph unbounded by an
efficiency or economy. The ornament was a great personal accomplishment, but it opened the way to lesser designers to develop
form that was unrelated to structure and function, obeying the
rules of form alone.

The achievement of Sullivan both in the Prudential Building
and in theory was widely recognized and immediately acclaimed.
In the beginning his influence was usually salutary. Many of the
tall buildings erected between 1897 and 1913 expressed the theme
of tall vertical lines, and most were divided into base, shaft and
cornice. The functional mode of design he championed gained
signal triumphs in the field of industrial architecture. Able designers, like Ernest Wilby working with Albert Kahn, achieved a
characteristic expression for American industrial buildings, such
as the Brown-Lipe-Chapin factory at Syracuse of 1908. Frank
Lloyd Wright, Sullivan's most able draughtsman and probably
the designer of some of Sullivan's best ornaments, developed an
idiom of space and form that soon created houses and industrial
architecture more original than any the world had known in
many years.

Even the eclectics gave at least lip service to functionalism and
attempted to respect structure. New Yorkers studied their new
skyscrapers to achieve more unity than the World and the older
Tribune Building had offered. Tortured picturesqueness such as
that of the Wolfe Building in 1895 was quickly outmoded.

But most designers could not resist thinking first of form and in
the end that stopped the clock. It was not long before New
Yorkers reverted to the classical envelopes. The St. Paul Building,
erected by George B. Post in 1898, obeyed Sullivan's formula of

tripartite division and vertical expression, but all the dividing elements and details were derived from the classics. The Metropolitan Life, erected in 1899, became a pile of Renaissance palaces
one atop the other. The Flatiron Building, done by the Chicago
firm of Daniel Burnham Company, was a classic column widened
and imposed on a triangular site. Playing with the forms independently of the structures, some designers soon exacted excessive
freedom from the structural and functional expressions. This
characterized the highly eclectic New York Times Building by
C. L. W. Eidlitz and the pitiful tower added to the Metropolitan
Life Building by Napoleon Le Brun who started the long shaft
with vertical elements and then could not end it without stuttering through successive strata of balconies, cornices, roofs, more
cornices, pavilions and spires. Other designers, recognizing that
such extravagances vitiated their effects, attempted to simplify
classic expression and bring it into accord with the structural facts
of the tall building. Carrère and Hastings essayed such a skyscraper in 1903 when they built the Blair Building, called Beaux-
Arts by contemporaries. In 1905 *The Record* urged New Yorkers
to emulate the modernized, simplified, almost classic expression
Burnham had supplied to such buildings as the Railway Exchange in Chicago, an expression which Holabird and Roche
then broadcast in buildings throughout the West. The critic
wondered whether the Railway Exchange was "not much closer
to a thoroughly sound starting point for the design of a skyscraper
than the more pretentious methods of our school-men."

A distortion of Sullivan's idea that a tall building needed a primarily vertical expression then led eclectic designers to abandon
horizontal Renaissance models for the Gothic. Vertical piers became pseudo-buttresses, ending in Gothic forms at the summit.
The major achievement of this kind was Cass Gilbert's Woolworth Tower, certainly a landmark of the day in 1913 when it was
completed. This 792-foot "Cathedral of Commerce" was the
highest building in the world for almost twenty years. Gleaming
white, it proclaimed its steel frame. Wide piers around the columns and thin mullions between accentuated the verticality by
subdividing the wide spandrels. A tall tower rose from the main
mass to carry the long piers to the summit where they ended as

buttresses, carved into Gothic forms and giving the top a rich silhouette. The envelope of the building had been studied with regard to the setback of form at the top, and the tower, therefore, unlike the Tower Building by Bradford Gilbert and most other skyscrapers, was a finished form on all sides, not a façade masking a brick-walled loft. The scale of the Gothic ornament at the top was impressive enough. It provided labyrinthine spatial sequences. But the intended effect was to create a distinctive commercial building, one whose height readily proclaimed its position in the city. It was a frank avowal of the fact that mere functionalism was inadequate to express the role of business; it showed how the expressive function demanded of a cathedral of commerce might lead an architect to appropriate the Butter Tower at Rouen. Montgomery Schuyler went overboard about it. He praised the plasticity of terra cotta, the successful scale, the sharp outlines, the detail. The gargoyle he thought was the equal of true Gothic. He said that the loss of space caused by the recessions of the upper stories of the tower, to give a more artistic lightening of the mass, commemorated the client's sense of civic obligation.

The Woolworth Building was a major concession to the idea that there should be an historical style, but that the form of a building should also express its structure. Other buildings went straightaway towards formalism, ignoring structure. By 1910 leaders of the formalists like Charles Platt and Charles McKim had relegated the structure to second place and judged it unworthy to appear in the final result. Their tall New York apartments on the east side of Central Park were simply huge masonry Renaissance forms hiding steel. Thus by 1913 the issue of expressing the steel frame and remaining true to structural and functional fact had become dead; "art" had gone in pursuit of varied composition in mass, despite the examples of Sullivan.

The result could not have been otherwise, given the critical reception accorded the pioneers. Even the most progressive critics were intrigued only by the new forms and intellectually stimulated by the new theory; they did not think the results beautiful. Thus the critic writing about the Railway Exchange Building at Chicago in the *Record* of 1905 approved the theory underlying it, but found it "monstrously ugly, a tremendous affair of window sashes." He argued, "It would be a queer eye that would claim beauty for the result. No! the design is not beautiful — it is merely interesting because it is rational."

It seemed still more difficult to accept the early work of Frank Lloyd Wright, capped by his splendid Larkin Building at Buffalo. Some critics, it is true, joined advanced Europeans like Behrens and Gropius in praising Wright's office building. The *Architectural Review* (U.S.), which seldom failed to support Beaux-Arts principles, was nevertheless ecstatic in 1907: "about as fine a piece of original and effective composition as one could expect to find. This sort of thing is absolutely in the line of creative architecture." Not even Russell Sturgis could bring himself to admire the Larkin Building for more than intellectual reasons: "this monument . . . [is] an extremely ugly building. It is, in fact, a monster of awkwardness . . . It is only capable of interesting that student who is quite aware that the architects of the modern world . . . have failed to make anything of . . . following the ancient styles."

Yet the Larkin Building was one of the greatest achievements of the Chicago school. It was planned around an interior court, skylighted from above and surrounded by balconies leading to the offices. The well, itself, had an exultant vitality, relying on the rhythmic statements made by the repeated forms of the several floors. The general idea had appeared earlier in stores such as Eiffel's Bon Marché in Paris. Now it had become a popular and excellent device, used in the Rookery, the Union Trust at Pittsburgh, the Metropolitan Life at Minneapolis, the Brown Place Hotel at Denver, the Bradbury Building at Los Angeles, all of which had deep central wells similar to that of Bunning's Coal Exchange at London. But of these the Larkin Building was easily foremost. Elevators, plainly seen, brought the clerks to the balconies. Four corner towers, ninety feet high, contained the staircases. Many technical features showed great imagination. All furniture was designed by the architect, and much of it was built in. The building was hermetically sealed against the dirty industrial environment. All plumbing was concentrated in stacks. The quarters were light, wholesome and well ventilated. The outside walls

were made smooth and hard to defeat the smoke and dirt of the
locality. There was a restaurant on the fifth floor for employees
opening in turn to a recreation area on the main roof.

But the major accomplishment was to have expressed a magnificent interior space. The massiveness and strength of the exterior forms, their monumental scale, prevented contemporaries
from giving this building universal acclaim. They could appreciate the rationale of the building, but it all seemed too harsh:
"the square corner, the right angle, the straight edge, the sharp
arris, the firm vertical and horizontal lines, unbroken, un-
modified, uncompromising in their geometrical precision . . .
[these] incongruous parts, leading to . . . a hopeless result."
The critic failed to recognize, in a building he knew was important, anything beautiful or prescient. Later, in 1950, the people of
Buffalo hardly knew they were tearing down an historic monument. Wright's own claim was modest enough. "The work may
have the same claim to consideration as a 'work of art' as an ocean
liner, a locomotive or a battleship."

22

But for all progress in design of the skyscraper, the fact was that
it still stood low in the hierarchy of architectural interest. Critics
and architects were far more ready to accept a new style that was
a matter of superficial detail than they were to accept excellent
design based upon structural and functional realities. That was
why it was so easy for McKim to rally an influential group of art
collectors to support his idea for establishing a new academy of
architecture. He felt that the role of this country for some time
should be to catch up rather than prematurely to attempt originality, and he did not sympathize with those who would close the
book and in their impatience start a national art. As Rome went
to Greece, and later France, Spain and England went to Rome, so
must we become students and study, bring back and adapt to
American conditions the splendors of Rome. He believed that
great modern architecture demanded the example of great past
architecture, and that young architects needed contact with originals, much as painters needed to study excellent examples. "No

other city offers . . . an atmosphere so replete with the best precedents."

Such arguments persuaded J. P. Morgan and Henry Frick of New York and H. B. Walters of Baltimore, art collectors all, to help McKim establish the American Academy at Rome, organized in 1894. In this McKim carried the sentiments of most of the profession, except for Gothicists like Ralph Adams Cram. But most architects would have agreed with Burnham, who once offered to send Wright to Paris, and they would have agreed with McKim's letter of advice to Burnham about the kind of candidates to be sent to the new Academy; namely, to stick to classic and ignore any "Yahoo or Hottentot creations." What McKim failed to see was that the Yahoos and Hottentots would exist, Academy or not, and their vigor would breed a style capable of giving form to modern institutions.

In establishing the Academy at Rome, McKim was not making taste, but following it. His scheme was consonant with the national sentiment. Consider, for example, how business reacted to the Schlesinger and Mayer department store in Chicago. Here Sullivan had designed one of the most audacious, far-seeing buildings in America's history. It had no technical innovations; the interior was still of the loft-building type with large floor areas divided by the skeleton. All the innovations were artistic. Along the sidewalks, one saw the relentless precision of piers faced with terra cotta, richly embellished with the elaborate floral ornament characteristic of the architect. Here the show windows drew the pedestrian toward the great corner entrance where the rhythm was climaxed by a protruding rotunda with beautifully molded, bronze-framed bull's-eye windows. Above this base, the building made a strong statement with continuous horizontal spandrels running their long courses over recessed piers. The geometry was perfect in proportion, exact and definite, and the thin metal frames of the windows stated a subordinated theme. This large grid was terminated at the top by a wide-spreading cornice, wrapped around the whole design to bring the eye back to the strong vertical mullions and piers at the corner. No designer in America had more successfully turned a corner on a busy street intersection. It was all a direct consequence of the need for advertisement, for circulation, for light, and yet the whole was animated by great originality in detail and great discipline in the overall composition.

In spite of this triumph, Sullivan was not asked by other Chicago businessmen to attempt anything so wonderful. Instead they tended to support the dreary and monotonous work of Burnham's firm, now bereft of Root. One would hardly suspect that a Burnham building like the Wanamaker Department Store, erected in Philadelphia in 1911, had come out of the Chicago tradition at all. This gargantuan Renaissance palace standing on stilts, monotonous, impersonal, inconsistent with its structure and use, had an exterior envelope which fulfilled all the superficial rules of classical composition, and the underlying principles of structural integrity, but missed the expression of character, conformity to program, and adaptation to cultural environment which all good architecture, including good Beaux-Arts architecture, has followed. The grand court on the interior took the same idea Wright had used in the Larkin Building but turned it into a pusillanimous mockery of a Roman basilica. Burnham willingly created one hall complete with palmetto patterns in the light shades hanging from the ceiling. It was called the Egyptian Hall, and its function was to sell pianos! And this was the usual end. Despite the noteworthy suggestions of Sullivan's Wainwright, Prudential and Schlesinger Buildings, despite the brilliance of Wright's Larkin Building, most commercial buildings were eclectic, and banks especially so.

Meanwhile Sullivan, when he was given the chance, created a few interesting small bank buildings in Iowa and Minnesota, notably the one at Owatonna. There he provided a simple cube, beautifully proportioned, clad in magnificent brick, ornamented with terra cotta and bronze. This Owatonna bank affected the later architecture of the whole town square and made this small farming center a place of international pilgrimage. But it was not the national symbol of a bank, even one in the country, and the classic columns that fronted its neighbors in Minnesota were but weak reflections of the grandeur established by much larger clients, men like the members of the New York Stock Exchange who commissioned George B. Post about 1905 to set up a Roman temple, fronted by a Corinthian colonnade, among the skyscrapers of lower Manhattan.

If commercial buildings were to be so garbed it was not surprising that public buildings should be. A competition held in 1908 for the New York Post Office found no entries appropriate to an age of steam and steel, more or less efficient governmental services, a new culture based on science and technology, the huge transportation and circulation problems imposed by the vast area of the metropolis. The winning design by McKim, Mead and White might, *mutatis mutandis*, have stood in the Forum centuries before. The Customs House at New York, done by Cass Gilbert in 1902-1907, was only less ridiculous than the tall shaft built later for the Customs House at Boston, topped by a mausoleum emitting smoke and suggesting that the whole building was nothing but a vast chimney stack, rising from a Roman temple. The citizens of Nashville voted to erect a plaster copy of the Parthenon in 1897; state legislators in Rhode Island and Minnesota and Missouri supported architects who crowned their Capitols with domes resembling that of the national capitol. Usually this work was composed effectively, the sculpture and murals were executed by artists who had the skills if not the talents of masters. But they remained reminiscent of another civilization unfitted to the habits of the legislators who walked into them from the prairie. Measured against the Larkin Building they were foreign visitors. This admittedly retrospective statement contains its own ideology. Perhaps the citizens of Missouri and Minnesota at that moment needed precisely the symbol they got; and if they did they got good ones. A more original building, say by Wright, might not have served the same purpose.

Once in a great while the government abandoned a strictly classic requirement and encouraged a talented architect to create something more original and appropriate. A noteworthy example of this is the Pan-American Building built in Washington in 1907-1910 and designed by Paul Philippe Cret, the most respected French Beaux-Arts man in any American school. His building revealed how a good Beaux-Arts designer handled problems of siting, planning and expression. Cret reinforced the grandeur of the site by the stately scale of the entrance, in which the central arches were framed by lofty pylons. Through the arches, one caught an intimation of a handsome skylighted courtyard beyond the entrance vestibule. The patio was perhaps the most impressive feature; it was surrounded by an arcade and open galleries. The pavement was of handmade tile with black figures displayed on a field of red. The rough white stucco arches supported a frieze bearing the coats of arms of the twenty-one republics. At the center was an Aztec fountain. Plants grown in the tropics — bananas, palms, coffee, rubber, papaya — as well as the noisy and bizarre macaws in the foliage, combined with the fountain and sculpture to make an interesting blend of classical architecture with the art of Central and South America.

23

THE big town house built for the rich was only a smaller version of the palaces of commerce and government. The individuality characteristic of mansions like the William K. Vanderbilt house, by Hunt, disappeared in favor of formal, uniformly anonymous houses, usually in Renaissance or Roman styles. The New York houses for Henry Villard set the theme in 1885. Characteristic of the best academic work, these houses by Wells, of McKim's firm, were well designed. Their elevation had a planar restraint like that of the Cancelleria Palace at Rome. But they gave, also, an impression of restrained monumentality, much superior to the chaotic and picturesque skylines of earlier houses. They boldly combined several houses into one large palazzo, surrounding a court left open to the street.

Similar houses quickly became fashionable and were freely provided by competent men like Ernest Flagg, Charles Platt, or Carrère and Hastings. They were planned for a luxurious way of life, unsurpassed in the countries from which their style had been imported. Some of the rich people hired architects much as they might hire secretaries, keeping them on a permanent basis, charging them personally with all the family architectural work. This was the way for example of the Wideners with Horace Trumbauer. Such houses were unrelated to American workmen and to any other American resource save money. They were bound to disappear as the economy and the culture matured. But meanwhile this lavish clientele brought in not only foreign styles but foreign architects who provided examples of the full Beaux-Arts version of an elegant town house such as the Clark Mansion in New York, erected in 1901, by Paul Chedanne.

In such an atmosphere, it is not surprising that the old brownstones began to give way to large palace-like apartment buildings, uniformly classic in design, by firms like Delano and Aldrich, Charles Platt and Ernest Flagg. To these classic versions of opulent domesticity architects like McKim added buildings like that for the University Club at New York, of 1900, whose impeccable façade adroitly masks the interior halls with no obvious relation between the two.

24

HOTELS like the St. Regis turned up in formal dress. Hospitals, alas, bowed to the trend. A few, such as the Johns Hopkins Hospital or the early Peter Bent Brigham in Boston, were still able to command sufficient space to be spread out into pavilions. But more often they were consolidated on many floors, as in the Bellevue Hospital of 1908 by McKim, Mead and White. The plan of the Mt. Sinai Hospital of 1905, published by *The Record* of that year as the ideal modern hospital, revealed that advancing technology in the better control over disease had reduced the amount of site planning and architectural planning needed to make the hospital perform well. Consequently, the architects could become much more formalistic.

Indeed, the hospital of 1885-1913 demonstrates how the advancing technology now made it possible for architecture to turn away from rational planning. In earlier times if a building had clearly defined functional needs they could be met only by courting nature. Good and therapeutic light could be brought to the building only from the sun; good ventilation could come only from the prevailing breezes; coolness could be supplied only by shade, by the suspiration of trees or by the surround of non-heat-absorbing surfaces like grass. People had to move about on foot and at the speed of foot travel. They could talk to each other only

by meeting face to face or by writing messages in longhand for
someone else to carry on foot. This meant that a successful building had to take account of nature in the fullest sense even in its
functional planning; and such an account had to have an effect
on the basic composition of areas and masses. Now all these limitations were swept away almost in a stroke. Elevators, telephones,
electricity, heating and ventilating machinery, insulating and
acoustic materials, could be combined to make almost any
scheme work. Thus for a while technology seemed to free the
architect from the excellent and unforgiving discipline of natural
forces; he no longer had to make the design conform to stringent
physical necessity but could manage the necessity within a pre-
conceived and purely visual pattern.

25

IN this a good deal of betrayal and self-deception was possible,
and an architect who turned his back on natural forces was not
likely to face unpleasant social realities any more squarely. He was
aware of the mansions, hotels, and clubs along Fifth Avenue that
provided a fitting background for the funeral cortege of General
Grant in 1885, and the more lavish if less military procession that
moved along Fifth Avenue in 1895 behind the hearse of Ward
McAllister. The kind of life Caroline Schermerhorn Astor saw
from her windows in the mansion at Fifth Avenue and Sixty-fifth
Street revealed no sense of what reporters like the Danish Jacob
Riis were discovering in the Bowery's Tenth Ward where people
were packed 522 to the acre by 1890.

Few architects seem to have been much interested in the dis-
closures of Riis. There were, to be sure, no government or private
agencies for housing reform or urban renewal, to call upon architects to solve the kinds of problem that the social reformers were
uncovering. The magazines addressed particularly to architects,
even the *Architectural Record* under the editorship of the liberal
Herbert Croly, displayed little concern about the slums. Attention was directed to elegant hotels and apartment houses, to lavish private estates, and big churches. Students in architectural
schools would more often be asked to design a fountain or an

orangery or an Explorers' Club than a low-cost housing scheme. The student could readily find an article about the bricks of Siena, the fountains at Tivoli, or the gardens at Versailles. No architectural magazine seems to have reviewed the spate of literature appearing about reform questions.

This revealed the enormous gulf between architecture and a large segment of American society. Concerned with questions of form alone, the architects had lost a social message. They were at their best as interpreters and fashion designers for a small clique of rich Americans oriented towards Europe. Even the radicals like Sullivan and Wright were not radical about the pressing social problem of the slum. Architecture had been in such dangerous waters before, and it would be again.

For architecture gains widest respect when it is allied with important social causes, emotional tones and intellectual ideas. The art of form is at best a narrow section of architecture's spectrum, and those who dally only with this drive architecture further and further from public reality whether they work with classic or "modern" forms. The professional architects of the generation 1885 to 1913 failed to read the future. They created for their profession the reputation of being a luxury, something less than engineering or medicine or law, a reputation it still sometimes has if not enjoys.

The great and powerful architects of the generation seldom lent support to the many institutions being formed for welfare work. Leading architects did not enjoy commissions for frugal institutions such as the Y.M.C.A. or the Y.W.C.A., though these did build enough buildings so that the journals of 1910 carried special articles about them. Charities such as the Henry Street Settlement House in New York or Hull House in Chicago required architects to design new quarters. They hired such firms as Pond and Pond or Henry Ives Cobb to design respectable, modest, non-imperial but still eclectic Colonial or Renaissance buildings. But the architectural leaders of the conservative tradition, the Hunts and McKims, never showed up in these places. Wright went to Hull House in 1904 to deliver his forward-looking lecture about using the machine in future architecture, but this said little for the architecture of the poor of his or another generation.

Wright could at least do this much, but McKim's designer-partner, Stanford White, complete with red mustache and cape, preferred to make a grand and late entrance to the opera. He was not listed as present at the opening of the Henry Street Settlement in 1893 but was very conspicuous at the fashionable ceremony dedicating a temporary wooden and plaster triumphal arch erected on lower Broadway for a trivial pageant.

Architects rarely worked on public recreational buildings but when they did they tended towards dull utilitarianism or a fantastic expression that was not fantasy. They never achieved the serenity and gaiety, for example, of Copenhagen's Tivoli. In the burgeoning urban zoos there was a marvelous opportunity which was largely muffed. In 1905 the American Beaux-Arts society set a competition for an elephant house in a city park and the results were quite indistinguishable from the designs for a library or a school.

26

THE parks and playgrounds offered modest ameliorations at best. Anything more fundamental seemed to require drastic steps, perhaps even moving people bodily to new centers planned upon better lines. Europe had seen many earlier model villages built for and by individual companies, stretched over the fifty years after 1846 when Bessbrook had been built for linen mills near Newry, Ireland; Saltaire; Essen; Bourneville; Noisiel-sur-Marne; Port Sunlight; Creswell; and Earswick, designed by the planners Barry Parker and Raymond Unwin. In the United States, too, employers had offered improved living conditions in an effort to get better and more faithful workmen. Leclaire, near St. Louis, and Berwick, Pennsylvania, had single-family houses set in park-like surroundings. There were others, mainly in the East.

But these were not conceived on the broad lines of Howard's garden cities. They were one-industry, one-company towns, in no sense autonomous; they had no planned relation to other towns; they had no planned limit of growth; they had no protective green belt and bore no particular relation to agriculture; the residents were tenants; the profits from increasing land values fell to the company. Few of them were anything more than business investments by the companies; most of them were only superficially self-governing, and there was almost always some paternalism such as the stipulation that liquor could not be sold on the village property.

There were also several attempts at founding fine parklike residential suburbs. The most famous among these were two built on Long Island, Forest Hills and the so-called Garden City, though neither was a garden city in the sense of Ebenezer Howard. A. T. Stewart who started Garden City frankly intended it for the well-to-do. It had large houses surrounding a cathedral, schools and a public park, and it was well serviced by a railroad. The kinds of control and the kinds of industry that would give any organic character to towns of this kind never matured, and they remained dormitory suburbs serving only the small portion of metropolitan populations who needed service least.

Probably the best-planned was Forest Hills Gardens, Long Island, the work of Olmsted and Atterbury in 1911. Supported by the Russell Sage Foundation, Forest Hills aimed at a lower-income group than it reached. Aside from its curving streets and ample tree-shaded lawns and its concealed prefabrication, Forest Hills, however pleasant, was a romantic reincarnation of Tudor housing; one stepped off the Long Island Railroad into a charming synthetic village square of an England that never was, even in a Rackham drawing. In the distance one could hear not cowbells but the thud of tennis balls on the courts of the West Side Tennis Club.

No doubt this sort of planning might have dug deeper into the social structure had legislation supported zoning and other planning needs, or had the experience with company housing in industrial towns proved more satisfactory. The country was not ready for a more public intervention, much less public subsidy; moreover, the American worker was not ready either. Like other Americans, he hoped to own his own house, even on a scanty margin of equity and even if it were inferior to the one his employer might have supplied. He was suspicious of paternalism; he mistrusted the company store to which historically he had been almost always in debt. On the industrialists' side there was the

sad example of Pullman, Illinois, where President George Pullman had employed architect Solon Spencer Beman to design a
model industrial town.

Many had looked to the Beman-Pullman scheme with great
interest and hope; and by 1892 it was generally agreed that Pullman had a salutary effect on the workers living there, "a training
school for the development of thrifty and thoroughgoing American workmen and mechanics." Attractive as Pullman was, it was
not all cakes and ale for its residents, who found that the amenities of wide streets and lawns, the red brick row houses or the
small private gardens did not fully atone for the loss of private
rights. The company owned the theater and decided what would
be shown, it owned the schools and decided what would be
taught, it owned the public library and decided what books would
be shelved, it owned the church and perhaps decided what would
be preached. The employees could not buy property, could not
acquire real political rights, could not even express opinions in
print. Moreover, on the periphery and outside the boundaries of
company control there was a wasteland supplying any of the
lower human wants that the company denied. At any rate, in
1895 the Supreme Court of Illinois handed down an opinion that
the company must dispose of all its land, homes and buildings not
strictly employed in the manufacturing authorized. Without the
company, the town quickly ran down. After the dissolution the
population waned from the 14,000 of 1895 to 10,000 in 1905, and
by then only 6000 were still company employees. The appearance
and tone of the village deteriorated as the streets and lawns and
buildings got less and less care. In the long run the ten miles
which separated it from the metropolis were built over, and Pullman was engulfed by Chicago.

27

THE imperial aspect of this age dominated the reform aspect and
so it is not surprising that the "City Beautiful" movement was far
more influential than philanthropy in the decisions that were
made about planning. It was this movement with its bias towards
classical architecture that gave to a few American cities a little of

the spaciousness that French designers had achieved in the Rue de Rivoli and the Champs Élysées at Paris.

The movement owes nearly everything to the men who planned the series of great fairs, especially the Columbian Exposition of 1893. Despite modern criticism, it was a dream city of a summer; its axes, wide malls, lagoons, classical façades set on monumental sites, its spaciousness and cleanliness — all these were to last longer as ideas than the brief summer the plaster stayed white and uncracked. Other, later exhibitions were less glorious, but they carried the same message throughout the country in Omaha, in Buffalo, in St. Louis. Even the Alaska-Yukon Pacific Exposition at Seattle in 1909 had a formal plan and was classic except for the California building in Mission style. These fairs gave visitors a taste for architecture in the monumental tradition and a liking for one kind of urban planning.

Certainly the malls of the fairs were seemly compared with the disorderly streets of American industrial cities. An observant architect, Claude Bragdon, blamed *laissez-faire* individualism for the eclectic and licentious nature of our urban growth. "One of our streets made up of buildings of diverse styles and shapes and sizes — like a jaw with some teeth whole, some broken, some rotten, and some gone — is a symbol of our unkempt individualism, now happily becoming curbed and chastened." It was not easy to cut into the living tissue of cities, particularly where tremendous real estate values existed on any downtown piece of property. The absence of any restrictions upon the use of land had inflated values to a level that seemed to justify only the tall office building. But various communities began enacting legislation, zoning for specific uses, requiring, for example, that all buildings in areas like Boston's Back Bay remain lower than a hundred feet, and there were attempts at maintaining architectural homogeneity in towns and historic parts of cities.

But the main renovations within cities stemmed more directly from the Columbian Exhibition itself, especially from the Court of Honor which fixed in the minds of Americans a higher ideal of aggregated architecture than they had previously had. Washington itself offered the best basis for improvement. Its grand plan, it may be recalled, designed by L'Enfant at the end of the eight-

H

eenth century, had never been completed. Indeed many of his planned spaces had been filled by miserably unmonumental buildings during the nineteenth century. The Union Railroad Station had ruined the Mall near the Capitol. Finally, about 1900, protests by many writers and some Congressmen began to bear fruit. Strongly supported by Theodore Roosevelt and Elihu Root, the Washington Park Commission was created to investigate improvement of the city and federal properties. Characteristically, Daniel Burnham was hired to extend and improve the L'Enfant plan. He opened the Mall and placed major buildings on the axes. The president of the Pennsylvania Railroad was persuaded to agree to remove the existing station and Burnham designed a new and monumentally impressive building, the present Union Station, below Capitol Hill. The total result of Burnham's work was to restore Washington to a plan that gave it spaciousness and its buildings a chance for dignity. In many ways it became the most beautiful city in the United States, particularly if you remained within the confines of the major axes and the parks along the Potomac and the creeks leading to it, and if you did not approach it with a disposition to be nauseated by its classicism or its "imperialism." But it was less rewarding if you strayed from the avenues of the northwest quarter. The peripheral areas were still slums and some of these lay in the shadow of the Capitol, while the main avenue from the Capitol to the White House still was unkempt in 1960.

Inspired by this partial success, other American cities tried to carve consolidated space out of the old privately owned urban cores. When they succeeded they erected civic buildings on some sort of mall or square. It was an action of civic reform quite contrary to the attitude that had allowed Cleveland's commercial and industrial growth to destroy her early village green. But it had its own absurdities. When Burnham's firm was called on to design a civic center in the downtown of Cleveland, land was cleared at enormous expense and the city began to build major governmental buildings, all classical, on an open court. But this center lay outside what became the foci of the main activities of the city so its character is not only often missed by visitors but, even for the citizens themselves, it tends to be an empty, lifeless memorial to the City Beautiful idea. Burnham developed similar civic centers as the dominant foci of other large formal plans, for San Francisco, for Manila and in the end for Chicago, itself. The powers of persuasion of this able and energetic man are best summarized by the paragraph his assistant, Willis Polk, the architect, compiled from various passages in his speeches and writings, including the famous lines, "Make no little plans; they have no magic to stir men's blood."

The civic planners addressed a public distressed by the chaos and ugliness of their fast-expanding and uncontrolled cities. Accustomed to legislative curbs on *laissez faire* in business, it conceded the right to enforce conformity on urban development. The planners were so sure of the public support that the Group Plan Commission of Cleveland felt no arguments were needed in 1902 to prove that their new civic center required an architecture "derived from . . . the classic architecture of Rome; . . . one material should be used throughout and . . . a uniform scale . . . should be maintained. . . . The cornice line . . . should be uniform in height." Even buildings to serve radically different functions "should be of the same design and as uniform as possible."

The strengths and shortcomings of the City Beautiful movement are visible today in the civic center at San Francisco. The plan for that impressive complex was made in 1912 by John Galen Howard, Frederick Meyer and John Reid, Jr. They envisioned a long-range development, completed between 1919 and 1933, in which a large open square would be faced on the north by the auditorium, on the south by the State building, while the City Hall, dominating the west, would be the pivot for a large mall stretching eastward for 1800 feet, past the opera and library to terminate at Market Street. The group of buildings was to be balanced and classic, a foil to the earthy ugliness of the "Slot." But, admitting its obvious formal merits, the scheme failed to meet many basic functional requirements; it was hard to expand; it offered badly shaped sites for future buildings; it brought noisy traffic past the buildings and into the square; its classic dignity was soon marred by seas of glistening and unforeseen automobiles. Today it needs to be extended and revised to cope with

traffic problems and new needs. San Francisco would make a sad
mistake if its new plan were merely to follow the fashion of another aesthetic whim, however contemporary.

28

A CITY beautiful demanded monumental buildings to stand as its
gateways. Of these the railroad station became the most important. The railroad was at its zenith, prosperous, luxurious; it demanded an architecture of size and prestige. Some of the early
stations, to be sure, were still large, dark affairs, great train sheds
with skyscraper overlays or machicolated towers such as Frank
Furness's Broad Street Station in Philadelphia of 1893 or the old
Union Depot in Detroit designed by Isaac Taylor in 1889.
Throughout the West picturesque stations had been built by a
number of architects, notably Henry Van Brunt. Romance still
lingers in the Romanesque clock tower of Milwaukee's Northwestern Station by Charles S. Frost (1889), or, at its highest and
fanciest, in the long, complicated, quaint façade that T. C. Link
and E. D. Cameron provided for the great train shed of the St.
Louis Union Station in 1891-1894. Even its individually interesting tower bore no relation to the other masses or to the elegant
Grand Hall whose colossal barrel vault sat at right angles to the
vault of the train shed.

But these medieval reminiscences had all been built before the
turn of the century and most of them antedated the Columbian
Exposition. After that, stations took on a more monumental and
a more Roman appearance. By 1914 the *Architectural Record* recognized that railroad architecture had become the second most
important symbol of the imperial era, next to the skyscraper.

Washington's Union Station of 1904 by Daniel Burnham is
representative of the new classic gateway to the city. The plan is
simple; an enormous Roman waiting room, modeled after the
Imperial baths and penetrated by arched portals, stands parallel
to a functional arched concourse which leads passengers to cano-
pied platforms beside the tracks. The façade facing the Capitol
presents three arched doors of great scale, designed like a triumphal arch with surmounting statues, and corresponding to the

whole length of the vault of the great hall. This central portion is flanked by two long and lower wings in the best manner of the Beaux-Arts classic. Inside, the ceiling of the hall is broken everywhere by impressive coffers. The spaciousness of the hall is not seriously diminished by the absurd statues which loll on the cornice.

Only a little later McKim, Mead and White provided the epitome of an Imperial railroad station when they built the Pennsylvania Station in New York in 1906-1910, now being demolished. Entering from Seventh Avenue through a long, street-level, Roman arcade, past shops and restaurants, the traveler walked towards a grand staircase. Pausing at the top, he looked down into a great hall containing ticket counters and an information booth. This hall, taken straight from the Imperial Roman Bath of Caracalla, did not suggest that the voyager might later detrain at Metuchen, New Jersey, or Altoona, Pennsylvania; its décor derived from the nineteenth-century reconstructions of what might have been in Rome. The scale was colossal, compatible with the throngs who passed through to destinations made clear by the symmetrical plan laid out along the main axis. Passing the hall, the traveler arrived at a wide central corridor, between waiting rooms. Eventually he emerged into a second great space, presented now in terms of modern engineering and not in those of Rome; thought by many people to be more exciting than the great hall. This was the concourse, still one giant level above the train platforms. But however clear the engineering might be aloft, the circulation broke down below amid a confusion of stands and markets and separately beckoning gates.

Pennsylvania Station was not, strictly speaking, great architecture; but its surface effect captured the literary heart of Thomas Wolfe and made Wayne Andrews speak wistfully of an Age of Elegance, now past. Even Claude Bragdon, himself the architect of a splendid space at the station in Rochester, New York, felt the dichotomy between the architect and engineer in Penn Station but had to admire a building that "raised its proud head amid the pushcart architecture of that portion of New York."

One can still see the titanic quality, refined and thereby subdued, in the Grand Central Terminal of 1903-1913, the work of

Reed and Stem in collaboration with Warren and Wetmore.
This building was erected athwart the axis of Park Avenue, which
in turn covered the tracks entering from the north. Traffic past
the building climbs upward on ramps straddling the Terminal,
descends through a building on the other side to flow northward
on the Avenue. The concourse, surrounded by a city of shops and
theaters, galleries and hotels and restaurants, is one of the best-
proportioned spaces in the United States, able to survive, or almost to survive, monumental Kodachromes and inappropriate
three-dimensional advertisements as well as the display automobiles that revolve on its floor. It offers a background fitting for
drama and was suitable thereby as a place for the Bishop of the
Diocese of New York to launch a campaign before hushed thousands to collect donations for building the Cathedral of St. John
the Divine. It is still a space in which Christmas singing sounds
well, and it has a little, though not enough, in common with an
important public square, or the Galleria at Milan. Nor has the
horrendous recently imposed Pan-Am building quite destroyed it.

Neither Pennsylvania Station nor Grand Central reached the
full dignity of a monumental gateway, for they were not fronted
by appropriately scaled plazas. Few stations in America save
Washington ever gained one. Generally they simply sat on the
side of a remote street. The station in St. Louis does have a small
boulevarded park containing an important fountain by Carl
Milles and the later station at Cincinnati is approached by a long
avenue, but neither is typical. Of course, now it no longer matters.

29

THE architectural giants who promoted the Renaissance revival
were capable of a fine sobriety if not of much functionalism. To
modern users, their designs for libraries of American cities seem
to have been completely incompetent. There is no doubt that the
imperial function overcame the function of purveying reading
material. The American architects had some good models from
earlier European building, notably the Bibliothèque Ste.
Geneviève at Paris of 1843, the Bibliothèque Nationale at Paris

of 1854 and less fortunately the British Museum at London, built in 1857. Each frankly segregated a large and often handsome reading room from an enormous utilitarian area where books were stored. But none was really appropriate for American purposes since they were designed for the comfort and peace of the sophisticated scholar and not for the omnivorous reading and browsing habits of a half-literate general public which could hardly be trained to use a card catalogue.

The European system was adopted, and perhaps with justification, for the Library of Congress at Washington when the firm of Smithmeyer, Pelz and Casey prepared a Greek-cross plan for a reading room and placed a stack beneath it, like that in the British Museum; the building erected in 1888-1897 was in full classic panoply with strong touches of the Grand Opera House at Paris.

Among the earlier examples, the Bibliothèque Nationale by Labrouste had solved the problem of furnishing a unified envelope around a large reading room and a utilitarian storage room. It was his solution that McKim modified to solve the difficult problem of the Public Library in Boston's Copley Square which was to be so located as to confront Richardson's Romanesque Trinity Church.

Viewed only as an architectural composition, McKim's design was masterful. The center of the new building, strongly emphasized by three arches, enclosing fine iron gates, was out of line with the center of Trinity Church across the triangle, thereby creating a discontinuity that forced attention on the intervening space. To either side of the Library entrance small rectangular windows admitted light to the stack, and above these the visitor reached the main floor by a grand staircase which rose through the center of the building. This handsome stair was embellished with pleasant, pale murals by Puvis de Chavannes. The great hall on the second floor which formed the reading room was modestly lighted by large, beautifully proportioned windows in an arcade that ran across the whole façade. Arches and columns framed a court on the interior of the building, and this was surrounded by rooms decorated with sculpture and murals, to display exhibits of books and drawings, but also less efficiently to house the public catalogue and the circulation desk. The handsome composition, the elegant choice of elegant materials, the dignity of the court arcade have seldom been surpassed in American architecture. The equally beautiful façade dignifies a civic square near a major residential area.

While Boston's Public Library could hardly be outdone within the premises of Renaissance design, its excellence as a form did not prevent readers from discouragement and librarians from outright criticism. By 1890 the latter had formed a vigorous society with annual meetings where they discussed library administration and the proper planning for library buildings. In 1891, C. C. Soule, writing for the *Library Journal*, stated that the architect was the librarian's natural enemy. After this there were many statements about the utilitarian standards librarians demanded from their buildings. The Boston Public Library achieved few of these. It sounded like Huxley and the Johns Hopkins Hospital all over again. But it was characteristic of the Imperial period that such pleas should be ignored both by the architects and by those who paid for the buildings, or that they countered, with some justification, by looking at librarians as enemies of the arts.

From Bangor to San Francisco classic monumentality overrode all other considerations. In any American city the passerby could identify the library when he saw it, unless he took it for the museum. For museum buildings were also designed more as civic monuments than as places to show pictures and sculpture. This was the program for the new buildings of the Boston Museum of Fine Arts, the Art Institute of Chicago, Buffalo's Albright Art Gallery, the Museum at Cleveland. A wing added to the earlier Romanesque museum at Cincinnati was in the same classic vein. By 1900 even the Gothic Revival Metropolitan in New York had been given a classic face on Fifth Avenue. Few designers asked practical questions as to how heavy works of art were to be moved about; how paintings were to be hung, lighted, best seen or best arranged; they recalled old palaces like the Louvre, later converted to museums, and believed that such palaces were adequate emblems of the European art Americans collected, and indeed they have proved, given modern lighting and imaginative display, to be more versatile and commodious than

Wright's Guggenheim or even the Museum of Modern Art in New York. Generous, even lavish space has its merit.

30

CHURCHES and schools generally remained outside the classic image. But, in 1904, Trumbauer used Palladio's classical Redentore at Venice as his model for the Chapel of St. Catharine at Spring Lake, New Jersey. In 1908, Howells and Stokes installed the First Congregational Church of Danbury, Connecticut, in a Federalist exterior. The Peddie Memorial Church at Newark, in 1890, was Romanesque but with classic details. On the whole it could not be said that any particular architectural expression was widely identified with the aspirations of any faith. So the First Church of Christ Scientist at Boston acquired a classic dome between 1893 and 1906 while another at 96th Street and Central Park West in New York was a Renaissance temple. The early Christian basilica design was adopted by McKim for the Madison Square Presbyterian Church in 1906 and by Maginnis and Walsh for the Roman Catholic Church of St. John at Cambridge in 1905.

Nonetheless the dominant image was Gothic, for which there was a strong prejudice in those churches whose service was vigorously liturgical. Henry Vaughan's chapel at St. Paul's School, Concord, New Hampshire, was a popular type of chapel borrowed from England, including the feature of having pews face each other across an aisle leading to the altar, as was common in English school chapels and choirs of English cathedrals. Even the usually Roman firm of McKim, Mead and White demonstrated their versatility and their tractability (and some would say their lack of conviction) by designing Gothic churches such as St. Peter's at Morristown, New Jersey.

Among the exponents of Gothic churches, the high priest was surely Ralph Adams Cram, another kind of Imperial man. A High Church Anglican, he believed that the heart of religious worship lay in the service at the altar, in the Mass, in the other liturgical elements, not in the sermon. He wished to surround the essential mysteries with all that the art of liturgy, music and ico-

H*

nography could add to their reality, saying, "It is the dogma of the transubstantiation, the cultus of our Lady and the doctrine of the Communion of Saints that made Mediaeval Christianity what it was and gave to . . . Medieval art its supreme beauty and its everlasting appeal." Cram's love of ceremony, his conversion to Anglicanism, his contention that "Luther killed art," show that Christian worship appealed to him on aesthetic grounds. Protestants might build in the Georgian mode, indeed he believed they should, and even designed Georgian meeting houses for Unitarians, such as the Second Church in Boston. But any service in which the Communion served as a major demonstration of theological beliefs should be held in a Gothic building. This latter-day Ruskinism attracted many clients; when Cram's literary force and scholarly understanding of true Gothic were accompanied by the skills of the highly talented designer, Bertram Grosvenor Goodhue, the architectural results were often impressive.

Cram's mission in life was to preach a new Gothic Revival, an archeological one, and to build it reverently and completely, not only as regards materials, plans and structures (though he often suppressed the side aisles, the clerestories and the triforia) but so far as possible to include the iconography as well. He led a few architects toward a "creative" scholarship of the Gothic form by articles such as "Good and Bad Gothic" in the *Architectural Review* (U.S.) of 1899. Meanwhile his partner Goodhue created some masterful churches; St. Thomas's in New York City was perhaps the zenith of this third and latest stage of the Gothic Revival. Its screen and sculptural reliefs rival the stained glass and the structure and space in their harmony of rich effect, quality of execution, and appropriateness to a beautiful ceremonial. Aesthetic environments of this sort fitted in well with the tendency among many church congregations, even among the Protestant, to become increasingly liturgical as their parishioners became more affluent and socially more self-conscious. They were aided in this by the followers of Cram and by the skill of his collaborators of whom none was more skilled than Charles Connick, the designer of stained-glass windows. So, liturgical or not, Gothic architecture now triumphed over acoustics and Protestant reserve, and now many a dissenter's sermon died away in the groined vaults before it reached the ears of the congregation.

The new Gothic Revival swung church architecture from the position in which Richardson had left it with Boston's Trinity Church. The large cathedral of St. John the Divine, in New York, had been begun in Romanesque when Heins and La Farge won the competition in 1892, over Cram's 1889 submission in Gothic. But in the end Cram prevailed. After the arches over the crossing had been erected in Romanesque, the commission was awarded to Cram who warped the whole thing into a Gothic cathedral. A similar building was started in 1907 on Mount St. Alban in Washington where the Protestant Episcopal Church of the United States attired its national Cathedral of St. Peter and St. Paul in fourteenth-century garb. Even the Swedenborgians built a Gothic church at Pitcairn's model village for artists in Bryn Athyn, Pennsylvania. Some architects carried the romance so far as to build entirely by hand, using wooden pegs instead of wire nails, employing artists in residence to work out the iconographical program desired by those who were trying to play the role of modern Abbot Sugers. In 1892, one of these, George W. Shinn, wrote in "The American Cathedral" to praise deliberately slow building, "It would be well for us if more of our . . . buildings were built by degrees and paid for as the work went on . . . on and on, until a stately edifice rises where, under our present way of hurrying, we get a finished but very cheap and flimsy thing." He was thinking more of excellence than of keeping the church budget balanced; and he forgot how rapidly the great parts of the French cathedrals were actually built in the thirteenth century. Indeed in the end it took longer to finish some of the large American cathedrals than it had to achieve their thirteenth-century models. It hardly seems possible that such a piece as Shinn's could have been written in 1892, after the Home Insurance Building and the Reliance Building had already been built in Chicago, and buildings that had formerly taken two years or more were now being assembled in four or five months.

Whatever their style, the churches, like the great classic secular buildings of the period, were designed by men who insisted upon excellent detail, workmanlike construction, and colorful decoration executed by skillful artists. A good example of the high level of performance is Christopher Grant La Farge's St. Matthew's Roman Catholic Church in Washington, begun in 1893. Its cruciform plan carries a large dome over the crossing, recalling the form of north Italian churches. The exterior is a firm mass, imposing and simple, notably courageous for its colorful red brick and stone walls surmounted by the green copper-ribbed dome outlined against the sky. The massive effect of the exterior contrasts well with the interior, where, in the dim light admitted by translucent windows, the piers and arcades supporting an ornate vaulted ceiling carry the eye past bright mosaics to the space under the dome and its octagonal drum; beyond the delicate alabaster rail in the chancel, one sees a gleaming white altar, made more outstanding by its contrast with the delicate arabesques and bronze at the portals. Stanford White's Madison Square Presbyterian Church in New York City (destroyed in 1919) offered excellence of a different kind, and was perhaps the best central-type Renaissance church in America. For Gothic, one would go far to find anything more winning than St. Thomas's. Perhaps at no period in America's history were artists more skillful in working with architects, nor were many periods able to boast of greater sincerity in church design. Churches of this quality fall into their true perspective and lose some of their romance only after one has visited a few European originals from the twelfth and thirteenth centuries.

Against the prevailing medievalism oriented towards handicraft and a worship occurring in the chancel at the high altar, there was a strong opposing force within church organizations and architecture, the growing emphasis on social and educational activities. Ever since the Akron plan had been developed for Sunday School use, churches in the Middle West, especially Protestant ones, had tended to be large auditoria, almost lecture halls, with small rooms arranged on balconies that could be opened to admit a larger audience to the main hall. P. B. Wight had noted in 1880: "The average Western church . . . is a combination of a lecture-hall, a school, and a club-house. It is a congregational home for social as well as didactic purposes." It is "always well heated and ventilated . . . thoroughly comfortable, and even luxurious."

The popular minister Frank Gunsalus made no difficulty of preaching in Sullivan's Chicago Auditorium. Though not one of his best buildings, churches like the one Sullivan designed for Cedar Rapids reveal the inclinations of the Midwest in this matter of planning. The social organization of the church had become as important as the religious purpose; it was a central bureau for charities, diffusion of knowledge, social assembly. One architect who was in favor of designing buildings for such institutions struck a blow at medievalism; it was not, he said, an invective against embellishment but just that too much money is "spent on buttresses that resist no thrust." He went further. Apart from objections to sham he insisted that "these forms . . . were originally born of conditions and necessities that have . . . ceased to exist. The governing requirements . . . today are much the same . . . as a lecture room or concert hall . . . seating capacity, ventilation, heating . . . light, and acoustic properties." It was this point of view that influenced some of the early modern churches that appeared in the West, such as Maybeck's Christian Science Church at Berkeley, California.

In retrospect Maybeck's famous building shows some interesting personal features but was not really so great a departure from prevailing ideas as Wright's distinguished Universalist Church, the Unity Temple at Oak Park, Illinois, of 1906 which was both less romantic and much more noteworthy as a work of art. Long interested in poured concrete, he now had a chance to use it in a moderately important public building. Characteristically he livened its dead surfaces by letting the stones of the aggregate be exposed. The building was a functional dumbbell with the shrine to the left and the social activities to the right. The exterior was quite formal, clearly monolithic, dominated by a projecting roof slab which demanded a large scale in the other parts. Abstract capitals were placed at the top of the piers which framed the clerestory set in panels above a high unfenestrated wall. This was a motif he had used before, for example in his project for the Yahara Boat Club at Madison, Wisconsin, of 1902, and would use again in the Coonley House, the Roberts House, the City National Bank at Mason City, Iowa, but never with greater skill and power and appropriateness.

The inside of the church is more complicated but the remarkable interpenetration of the spaces is apparent at once, as balconies and floors at many levels cross and intersect but never without purpose. The electric fixtures and the wires that connected them were made part of the design. The building was quite as revolutionary and quite as important as the Larkin Building, entirely modern in form and decoration, appropriate for a service based on the sermon and for a considerable number of activities outside the fane. Towards the end of his life Wright sometimes called the Unity Temple his masterpiece and this may well be so.

31

UNIVERSITIES had even more trouble than churches in determining what their image should be and they were becoming self-conscious about it. A few had ancient buildings of dignity such as Nassau Hall at Princeton; some could show, joined to these, distinguished recent work such as Richardson had bestowed on Harvard; more boasted nothing of distinction but their alumni were developing a strange unreasoning affection for their Victorian "Old Mains"; a few like the Gothic University of Chicago were having the bad luck to spring architecturally full-panoplied from the purse of a contemporary Maecenas. None in this moment cared to listen to the messages of contemporary science or technology — or to heed the rational proposals that had been advanced only a few years before at Johns Hopkins. Protestant colleges appeared in the dress of Catholic monasteries, institutes of technology were equipped with Gothic or classic dress; a Texan campus offered a shotgun marriage between Venice and Valladolid.

Major new institutions did appoint architects to develop large and comprehensive master plans. The most impressive of these plans no doubt was the winning design for the University of California at Berkeley, submitted to the Hearst Competition of 1898-1899 by Henri Jean Emile Bénard.

The winner was a Frenchman directly out of the Beaux-Arts and so was his large and expansive site plan. It planted a long and strong axis running straight down the slopes towards the Bay, from an observatory set high on Berkeley Hill. It was a freer plan than the Roman arrangement of the Chicago World's Fair — the minor axes varied in their spacing, and there was room for informal woods and gardens up on the hill and along the lower flanks.

Bénard came, took the prize money and then declined to be supervising architect. A German critic-architect writing for the *San Francisco Bulletin* predicted this, in saying that Bénard's plan was un-American, pretentious and imposing, did not express any deep thought. Bénard, this critic thought, would feel out of place. Whether disturbed by the criticism or simply through lack of interest Bénard did make what seemed to many Californians the incredible choice of Paris over Berkeley.

There was perhaps a moment when attention might have been paid to the *Bulletin*'s plea, "This should be a new University, typically, racially American — not a Chicago World's Fair." But soon the mantle fell to John Galen Howard, also a product of the Beaux-Arts, who moved from New York after 1901 to build the first buildings of the new campus, to be supervising architect, first head of the Department of Architecture, to plant the prevailing Renaissance firmly in California, and to modify the Bénard plan until by 1913 it could hardly be identified with the original except that both had the strong and clear axes of the best Beaux-Arts plates.

California critics, proud of their campus, have been kinder in their estimates of Howard than they have of his opposite and often more talented numbers in the East. The fact remains he was cut from the same cloth. Berkeley has a good campus but by no means one of the finest in the land. The multiplicity of buildings now has destroyed any sense of the master plan for the pedestrian if not for the map-reader.

But the campus is saved from the desolate Imperialism of comparable Columbia by a number of things, if not by its main buildings. The Berkeley hills still seem more pastoral than Morningside Heights, even though the smog and the population are both thickening from Richmond; the eucalyptus trees are big enough to provide a merciful contrast to the architecture; the Howard classic buildings are less congested, less monumental, less Roman, less demanding and pretentious than those of McKim at Columbia; and here and there minor buildings remain that have been built in the warm, vigorous, human mood of what people have liked to overstress as the California style. Buildings like Maybeck's Faculty Club, the Music Building, and the long set of low sheds stepping down the hill that served the School of Architecture so well for so long provide the grace notes of the campus at Berkeley and most of its grace.

Treated as at California, the grand plan yielded some order without becoming formidable; at Columbia the new court of honor by McKim forced library, engineering buildings, and students alike into an unnatural life. Even Harvard had a moment of flirtation with the image of the big classical campus of which the new Widener Library was to head an axial mall stretching to the Charles River. In the end, and mostly because land for the mall was so costly, Harvard escaped these toils, turned the Widener around, presented its small rear entrance to Massachusetts Avenue and pushed its colossal façade with giant columns and enormous and fatiguing steps into the small quadrangle at the north, where it dwarfed its more distinguished neighbors.

During this time many universities held competitions for master site plans, and these provided campuses temporarily more integrated but no more pleasant than the older ones. Carnegie Institute of Technology and the University of Pittsburgh were laid out by Palmer and Hornbostel on large classical lines although the later University buildings became Gothic. Ernest Flagg produced a plan of modern Beaux-Arts classical design for the Naval Academy at Annapolis, whose chapel is similar to that at the Sorbonne. There were also Gothic master plans. Beginning about 1893, Henry Ives Cobb developed Rockefeller's University of Chicago on such lines. But even where the grand plan did not prevail, universities sought order by freezing their architecture at a point in time, usually an ancient time.

Cope and Stewardson confirmed the fashion for this about 1886 when they designed picturesquely composed Gothic buildings for Bryn Mawr College and followed these by similar work at Pennsylvania, Princeton and Washington University at St. Louis. When the plans of establishments such as these are contrasted to vigorously classical campuses like that proposed by Cass Gilbert for the University of Minnesota, one notes greater flexibility of arrangement, more dramatic use of landscaping and land contour, much more human scale and better use of quadrangles and courts; but both stem from the idea that the environment for higher education must be beautiful and ancient and that there must be a controlling master plan in order to get good results. By 1905 even Johns Hopkins University, which had earlier carried the torch for urban *laissez-faire* utilitarianism, held a competition for a new campus to be built outside Baltimore. The campus was ultimately developed there, and it was a highly integrated community of buildings carefully studied as to site, all clothed in Georgian Revival. Thorstein Veblen, followed by Upton Sinclair, inveighed against such dismissals of progressive skyscraper architecture.

The power of strong-minded architects and their academic clients often left an impress that could not soon be effaced. Nowhere was this more evident than in the Graduate College at Princeton.

Princeton acquired the first plant totally devoted to graduate students when her Graduate College, designed by Cram, was erected in 1913. It is a picturesque Gothic mass, perched on the crown of a small hill, dominated by its Cleveland Tower, looking out over a lush golf course and a tree-lined stream, beloved by ducks and geese. The impression is therefore reasonably bucolic. The buildings offer a residential complex providing suites of rooms which originally were elegantly appointed for a comfortable private life. It has a large commons room, a library, a refectory and breakfast rooms all arranged on the perimeter of two seclusive quadrangles. The sculptural and architectural form of these buildings well exemplified Cram's belief that "art . . . as a system of spiritual and psychological influence is perhaps the greatest teaching agency." Today his aversion to modern resources seems peculiar until we learn that it stemmed from his belief that "The liberal arts of age-long human culture have nothing to do with the current seventy-year-old technological civilization (except as a corrective which has thus far failed to work) and consequently the . . . artistic expression of the latter phenomenon can have no part in the manifestation of the older and eternal entity." Hence at the Graduate College this "humanist" used the precedents of English collegiate work of the fifteenth century, especially of the type employed by William of Wykeham at New College, Oxford. Cram wanted an architecture "consistent with . . . that sense of historic and cultural continuity that I am persuaded is fundamental in all educational and ecclesiastical work." Even the bracketing of school and church is significant. He rejected the classicism of the Renaissance and Academic periods in order to return to "our own racial style that was developed while we were yet consistent Christians."

Cram's Presbyterian clients sought exactly that. Long before the architect entered the scene, Andrew Fleming West, Dean of Princeton's Graduate School, had visualized the future college he wanted: "old associations . . . the peace of rural life. Quadrangles enclosing sunny lawns, towers and gateways opening into quiet retreats, ivy-grown walls . . . vistas through avenues of arching elms . . . the exquisite collegiate Gothic . . . of Oxford and Cambridge. Nothing so fully accords in spirit with our desires for Princeton." In such an environment he thought "liberal studies at least find their greatest charm" and the word "charm" reveals the tone of a literary man's architectural standard. We may doubt West's wisdom in so blatantly and arbitrarily trying to return the modern student to his medieval heritage; to many young men of a generation only forty years removed from West, the stained-glass windows in the refectory, portraying the "Light of the World illuminating the Seven Liberal Arts of Christian Learning," seem totally out of place with the science, logic or architecture he is studying. Yet it cannot be denied that some have found solace in the superficial cloisters.

32

As the Gothic and classic forms grew to become national emblems of cultural institutions and as technology tended to destroy regional differences, self-conscious retarding movements developed, aimed at regaining an expression of local and regional character. Ever since the Philadelphia Centennial of 1876 there had been an interest in reviving Georgian architecture. This received further impetus when McKim and White studied the excellent houses that still stood in places like Newburyport, and began to design handsome contemporary houses on Georgian and "Colonial" lines. The fashion for domestic Georgian was so pronounced by the turn of the century that it threatened to become a national style for domestic architecture and for some institutions as well. In 1904, when Wright was designing the Larkin Building, Joy Wheeler Dow published an influential book, *The American Renaissance*, to document the resurgence of good Georgian design throughout the country but especially in New England. Such a formal return to eighteenth-century architecture, if not to eighteenth-century manners or habits, encouraged other sections of the country to resurrect or, if necessary, to invent their own regional heritages. An especially attractive re-creation, made out of whole cloth, was the one that occurred around Philadelphia; side by side with the revival of Pennsylvania Dutch houses, architects built handsome estates that imitated the farm houses and small country houses of rural France and England. The Southwest sought an architecture recalling the missions and churches of Spanish origin, most of which had disappeared or been greatly abused. Now they were copied in residential and ecclesiastical work. Few were really impressive architecturally but they were consistently well designed, well executed and thoroughly charming in the spaces and arrangements for comfortable living. There was less fake about them than in those of the later regional revival of the '20s.

Architecture built in the countryside and at resorts, tended in some instances to show regional characteristics, but more often reflected the monumental character of town houses. McKim, Mead and White provided classic unity such as that of the now destroyed Low House, built at Bristol, Rhode Island, in 1887, one of the finest of the shingle houses. The Renaissance palace dominated many countrysides and resorts. Perhaps none was more lavish than the Breakers at Newport, designed by Richard Morris Hunt for Cornelius Vanderbilt in 1893, unless it was the colossal François I château, Biltmore, built for George Vanderbilt at Asheville, North Carolina, in 1895, also the work of Hunt. There were many others: the Marble House at Newport of 1891 for Wil-

liam K. Vanderbilt by Hunt and the estate of E. T. Stotesbury, a
Versailles raised outside of Philadelphia by the French architect,
Gréber. For clients like these, Hunt became an authority on taste
and made each palace rival the last by its lavish size. At Lake
Forest, Illinois, in 1912, Charles A. Platt completed the house of
Harold F. McCormick; it was a Renaissance villa seeking to rival
the Villa d'Este in its gardens, and it was published in the *Archi-
tectural Record* in 1912 in an article titled "The Renaissance
Villa of Italy Developed into a Complete Residential Type for
Use in America."

Able voices spoke against this kind of adaptation. The strongest
voices were surely those of the giants of the Middle West. But
the men of the Pacific Coast were quietly active, too, and much
later, when California grew more self-conscious, Maybeck, Howard, the brothers Greene, Mullgardt, Polk and Julia Morgan were
given an abnormal amount of publicity. These Californians did
not leave an enormous legacy in the quantity or magnificence of
their buildings but it was an enduring legacy. They did not create
a style. They sensed or analyzed what an informal way of life,
growing out of ranch life, would demand of a house. They loved
native materials. The climate permitted them, indeed invited
them, to minimize the distinction between indoors and outdoors
and they worked at this problem though less boldly than others
would do later. They noticed that almost every site in the San
Francisco region and many around Pasadena had brilliant views
and so they were early to use large panels of glass to frame these
outlooks. They arranged a relatively free flow of interior space.
They loved the aggressive vegetation and their external woodwork
embraced the vines and the gums. It is these things more than
the romantic and pictorial quality of their roofs, the carving of
their screens or rafter ends, the mysterious darkness of their redwood interiors, the occasional flashes of Japanese detail, that
make them of some importance. They offered the best contemporary regionalism of the country, and the finest and most genuine
form California regionalism has achieved.

But the architects were not so distinguished as they have been
made out to be by local patriots. None was consistent. None
avoided the Imperial image in other contexts as Maybeck's Pack-

tivity, to permit no separation between the atmosphere surrounding education and that in the child's home. Gardens were to be important instruments of education, and the main one, lying in front of the house, had a stage where the children acted Greek plays in Greek attire. Other great Wright houses of this time such as the Martin House in Buffalo (1904), the Westcott House in Springfield, Ohio (1907), the Roberts House in River Forest, Illinois (1908), the Baker House in Wilmette, Illinois (1909), and the Robie House on Woodlawn Avenue, Chicago (1909), as well as the first Taliesin at Spring Green, Wisconsin (1911), told the same messages; they are now so firm a part of American understanding that they need no further description, although unhappily not many of them are still to be seen, and fewer still in good repair.

33

But the big clients and the major cities of the Middle West and the Far West were really no more ready than the East to accept the implications of what was being done by Maybeck, Kahn, Sullivan or Wright. One after another each city abandoned any regional distinction it might have had, to become immersed, sometimes drowned, in the monumental City Beautiful idea of the Columbian Exposition. Technology had helped to break through regional differences, carrying the factory and the railroad and their architectures into the West, into places which had formerly had only houses and churches all in some historical style. But more effective even than technology was the steamroller effect of the classical ideology.

When the image of the City Beautiful was at its very best, when McKim or Cret presided over its execution at the top of their bent, we cannot truthfully insist that the results were inelegant or that they did not provide an amenity for the cities that owned them. Insofar as an architecture can express the transient feelings of a people, they were eloquent testimonials to the Imperialism of the day. But the Imperial view was fortunately short-lived in America and the Imperial architecture had no justification or chance of a long career. This is the pathetic oversight in the re-

cent efforts of men like Henry Hope Reed, Jr., to talk America
back into an architecture it never needed very much.

Later on American architects would move towards a goal which
was in part the goal of Sullivan and Wright. But before that
could happen there had to be another interval. In this interim,
belonging to an age of complacency, Sullivan would die in poverty and Wright would go into temporary eclipse. New men
would walk the stage in place of Hunt, McKim, Cram and Cret.
They would be less imperial, more experimental. But they would
also be less certain. Meanwhile, following a gestation in Europe, a
great time was about to begin. Still it was a quarter-century or
more away. And in 1913 if you asked people in the know, men of
certain taste, to tell you who had done the most for current American architecture, they would probably say that Sullivan had made
some imaginative proposals and designed beautiful details, that
Wright had built some interesting houses in the Middle West,
that Cram's Gothic churches were excellent, that Cass Gilbert
had mastered the skyscraper and Paul Cret the problem of a government building, but that if you were looking for giants you had
better first go to New York and seek out the elegant taste and the
highly developed talent of Charles Follen McKim and his partner
Stanford White; they might go further and tell you that the heart
of the whole enterprise lay in Chicago in the resourceful and in-
domitable planner, the real Titan, the emperor of architecture,
"Uncle Dan" Burnham. Because in 1913 it was not apparent to
any of the "right people" that the long-outstanding account with
the past had been so emphatically overpaid. For the moment it
was almost as though Richardson and Sullivan had never lived or
written or built; as though the Unity Temple and the Larkin
Building did not exist.

IV

1913-1933

THE twenty years after the victory of the progressive movement, the Armory Show, and the completion of the Woolworth Building were years of confusion and retreat. Reform at home, idealism abroad, lost their luster. Repression of dissent, begun in war, became commonplace, manifesting itself in the experiment of prohibition, the heresy trial of Scopes in Tennessee, or the symbolic trial and ultimate execution of Sacco and Vanzetti in Massachusetts. The notoriously corrupt Ku Klux Klan now staged its largest and finest public parades.

Technology advanced, little inhibited by the general smug, aloof, prosperous complacency of the American people or the anger and despair of most American novelists and poets. The latter observed the American scene with no great pleasure, but the focus of their attention was on the general disillusion, and the great industrial targets were no longer of interest. Babbitt replaced the Titan.

Though two thousand men virtually controlled American private economic life, they were captains of industry, not buccaneers of heroic mold. Wealthy they might be, but they were not personalities as Peter Cooper, Commodore Vanderbilt and J. P. Morgan had been. Most of them were obscure and preferred it that way.

In the years from 1920 to 1930 this central group of American industrial power showed great skill in applying scientific management to production. It learned how to make all sorts of goods in mammoth quantities and at midget prices. But it did not learn so well how to distribute the produce, or the wealth which would make it possible for the produce to be sold. In the black autumn of 1929 their edifice came crashing down.

Thus Americans of the period began with reform; they knew a high moment of idealistic elation in the crusade to make the world safe for democracy. But quickly they retreated from their contacts with the world, consoled themselves with the lesser fruits of technology, abandoned themselves to an uneasy prosperity, and saw this vanish almost overnight. Though Harding had sounded a popular note in 1920, the same words were hollow in 1932: "America's present need is not heroics but healing; not nostrums but normalcy; not revolution but restoration."

By 1932 America needed a hero and was ready even for nostrums. Posterity might find many a fault in Franklin Roosevelt but it could not honorably divest him of the laurels of a hero. His buoyancy brought confidence to Americans with none; they believed him as they had not believed Hoover; they took his advice not to fear fear. Thus the period ended on a heroic note as it had promised to begin; but between beginning and end there were not many heroes.

There were not many in politics and there were not many in American architecture. By 1925, Sullivan was dead after years of partly deserved neglect, Wright in momentary eclipse. The influence of McKim and Cram was on the wane. The architectural giants were gone or were yet to come. In the same time the most seminal builders of the twentieth century were making crucial architectural statements in Europe. But their works scarcely rippled the bland eclecticism of our leading schools or of our leading offices. They were jeered at by commentators like Mencken, rejected by "humanist" literary critics like Babbitt and More, ignored by architectural historians like Kimball.

What the country wanted for architecture was what it wanted in economics and in politics: normalcy, not nostrums; restoration, not revolution; healing, not heroics. There were numerous architectural Hardings and Coolidges ready to supply what was wanted. Thus except for a few sports like Rockefeller Center, the architectural development in America between 1913 and 1933 is epitomized by the Woolworth Building which began it and the Empire State Building which ended it. The latter was taller and bigger but in no way better; its major achievement was the demonstration of managerial skills involved in coordinating so many tasks into such a large and effortless, if in no other way beautiful, productivity. Big management had moved into architecture as it had into business and like business management it was often anonymous. That it could produce big buildings it demonstrated; whether it could produce fine buildings remained to be shown; whether the new organization implied the death of the artist-architect in an America which had never known many was a question yet to be weighed. But neither the artist nor the businessman could see beyond the bigness of the single building; the bigness of the city escaped him.

It was a twenty years of missed opportunities. American dough-boys who went to France brought few aesthetic aspirations back. The vital force of the automobile and the highway, already noticeable, was neglected. Abundant surpluses of income did not provide good housing and recreation for all or even most of our people. Transportation and motion pictures, reaching pockets of local ignorance and provincialism to tell how others lived, and new technological controls of environment might have promoted the triumph of rational contemporaneity over spurious and sentimental regionalism. Instead pseudo-regionalism sprang up notably around San Diego and Santa Barbara but also in the Southwest and the Midwest and the Northeast. It played hand in hand with eclecticism to create an environment in which serious contemporary architecture, public or domestic, could only mark time.

For American architecture, then, the '20s were timorous, not turbulent; elephantine, not elegant; prosperous, not perceptive. American architectural genius had burned for a moment in Sullivan and Richardson; it was kept alive in Wright; after these years of complacency, stimulated by a small wave of great immigrants, it grew on the power of American technology and the expanding American need. But for all this the '20s were not, save in the technological sense, even a preparation, unless a time of reaction and lassitude, of smugness and mediocrity, is needed by a national culture as a kind of sleep in preparation for a vigorous effort on the morrow.

1

THE American people pursued their westward course. The agrarian Middle West, the Middle Atlantic, the Great Lakes and the

Mountain states grew at about the national rate; the Deep South and New England well below it; while the Pacific region began its fantastic climb.

For the moment and perhaps for a long time to come another movement was more important, the steady, even accelerating flow to the city. Where 45 per cent of Americans had lived in urban places in 1910, 56 per cent were there by 1930. Of the total increase of 31 millions, 27 millions were registered in cities. The larger cities grew the most. The five cities of over a million people accounted for an eighth of all our population. The metropolis had become a national phenomenon to be noted in California, Florida, and Minnesota as well as in the more congested Northeast. The time was near at hand when almost every state in the Union would have a big if not an urbane city.

The concrete highway, it seems in retrospect, might have pricked more imaginations. It was invented as an almost inevitable response to the multiplying internal combustion motors which, emerging from mud and gravel, frayed the macadam, then rutted the asphalt. The concrete road and the automobile multiplied the avenues of escape from the city as the suburban train and the interurban trolley had been unable to do. More and more people found easy exits from the dingy city into the sunshine and open air of the suburb; and the freedom of movement of the automobile made it possible for suburbs to grow up almost anywhere, without roots, without convictions, without permanence. This hegira was only a prophecy between 1913 and 1933, another nascent example of the easy American way of solving problems which was to leave them behind; its terrible toll would not be felt until the middle of the century. But already suburbanites left the city as a home, withdrew their tax support, depleted its finances; withdrawing their political influence as well. Yearning for space, few found as much space as they had dreamed. Hoping for an autonomous and democratic village life, they found the autonomy expensive and the democracy elusive. Accepting the ever longer and more fatiguing trek to and from the city, they ended by finding no stirring amenity at all, in city or in country. By midcentury it would appear to some sociologists that suburbia had so trained its dwellers that they did not want stirring amenities.

There was a fine irony in this. For the most distinctive Americans accomplishment in this time was the conquest of vertical space through brilliant engineering. Yet this was wedded to an abysmal management of horizontal space. More and more Americans found themselves working in the day amid the brilliant verticality, and earthbound at day's beginning and end in a snarl of horizontal traffic. And as the motor commuting increased, the quality of the approach to the city deteriorated. A commuter on the Staten Island Ferry might at least see the miracle of lower Manhattan at every dawn and dusk; but more and more of the millions of commuters to America's centers of culture moved through visual deserts, tunnels and canyons to arrive finally at the office that was their urban home. Many other millions who might call themselves New Yorkers never made the one- or two-hour journey to Manhattan at all. And if they never made the journey they might as well have been living in any other enormous Brooklyn or Bronx, for the urban advantages of the metropolis were not being used; thus cities became anonymous for most of their residents, whatever false fronts they might present to the tourist; and even for the tourist they began to look more and more alike for each coveted the same symbol of prestige, the skyscraper; it was as much wanted on the broadest acres of Texas as on the tightest ground plots of lower Manhattan Island.

The time had long passed when the practical and the aesthetic problems of the city could be solved by mere growth or by individual buildings, no matter how carefully zoned, no matter how elegant, no matter how colossal. Today the self-satisfied '20s offer an object lesson — for they show how clearly the urbanization and suburbanization of America, combined with our vertical skill and our horizontal incompetence, our tendency to solve a problem by leaving it, our zealous maintenance of the wrong kinds of local autonomy have unfavorably conditioned not only American architecture but also American life and to a considerable degree negated the potentials for a better life that lay in the new technology.

2

THE population was changing in other ways. The mammoth immigrations came to an end. Nineteen thirty-one was the first year in our history when the number of American emigrants exceeded the number of immigrants. The ghettos were beginning to change, growing less Italian, Polish, Jewish, more Negroid.

Now only one fifth of the employed, the farmers were getting older as well as fewer; they were older than the national average, for their young people went off to the city and usually never came back.

Although reforms and prosperity had placed the farmer in a fair, even a preferred position, the country still was obsessed by the upsetting ideological concept of the "corrupt" and "immoral" urban mores, the dragons in the fiery wood. But this was changing. Radio turned Chautauqua weeks into losing enterprises. The imitation-Morris craft of the Roycrofters of East Aurora were losing their savor. Mail-order catalogues became increasingly sophisticated and bred sophistication on the farm which in the sequel would own Aalto stools. Through the movies the farmer met the same entertainment as men in the suburban middle class. So the distinctions between the rural and the other middle-class cultures of America grew indecisive.

The immediate outstanding development in the relations between the farmer and his nation was but one of several portents of a future time when the American public would generally accept the view, with an obligato of ineffective grumbling, that the federal government would become a steadily bigger factor in the life of every American individual. From the grain corporations required in the First World War through the inadequate efforts of McNary and Haugen to hold up farm prices; the droughts and the grasshoppers; the erosion of the plow-broken plains; to the situation of 1932 when almost every farmer was a debtor, the hourglass marked only fifteen years, now almost lost in memory. In this the concept of the farmer as independent yeoman inevitably vanished. Unable to survive in a "free" market, he could no longer reasonably declaim against the labor union or the corporate trust, for he had built his own kind of union and his own kind of trust. He could no longer consistently argue against big government, for he was asking big government to help him.

Thus the path was cleared for soil conservation, irrigation, flood control, rural electrification and other projects which would generally bring new technologies to farm operations, make farms more prosperous and American food production more secure. But this could not happen unless many of the farms were much larger than had previously been necessary; so corporate farming got its start.

Out of such crises and such organizations several things happened to rural architecture. Always and everywhere prudent farmers who were even modestly prosperous had maintained farmsteads that had much visual, even architectural, delight and sometimes even a trace of elegance. The village commodity which had been so common in the eighteenth century had long ago deteriorated into the drab mediocrity of places like Abilene, Kansas. Now the farms were to change too and lose their character; more comfortable, better equipped with labor-saving devices, bombarded with news on the radio and style by the movies, the farm establishment soon acquired the aesthetic values of the suburb.

The little red schoolhouse was no longer going to be little or red. It would no longer try to teach all grades in a single shed with a pendant pair of privies. Country children would become used to being driven miles each day in public buses to reach large school buildings and these buildings might often not be Georgian. Indeed you might soon have quite as good a chance of finding Mies van der Rohe on the prairie as in the metropolis. As the city man tried to pretend he was living in the country, so the country man began to act like a city man.

3

JUST as the environment of the farmer was shifting, so was the environment of the laborer. Within the plant his physical task was becoming much more specialized and in most physical ways easier. For the man who had individual skill and pride in it, the new methods of mass production raised serious questions; some of an economic and some of a psychological nature. Would his skill be displaced by that of the machine? If so, how was he to live? If there was a task for him in the new fragmentation of work, would it reduce his role to that of a robot, however essential, and thus remove from him the incentives that rest in pride over a task well done? The new processes were demanding larger factories, more remote management. Could he know the boss any more as he had known him in a simple village factory economy? Whether this knowledge had bred love or hate, and it had bred both, was less important than that the lack of contact on both sides might breed the subtly poisonous hostility of indifference. If management were to be more remote, might not his own union representatives also be so? If big unions were needed to cope with big management, might the laborer as an individual lose any sense of identification with his own agents? Was the unemployment of a specialized worker a more frightening specter than unemployment of an individualistic jack-of-all-trades? These were questions for "theorists"; action concentrated on getting a greater share of the new productivity.

The greatest American achievement in the age of complacency was surely the staggering increase in the productivity of the average American worker, more through scientific management, new machinery and the redesign of products than through his own efforts. But the worker's take-home pay increased only half as much as the productivity and did not make him into an effective consumer of the new goods. We were farther from "the final triumph over poverty" than Herbert Hoover announced in his acceptance speech.

So far as architecture was concerned the slow progress of the labor movement in this time was of little direct consequence. Labor unions in the building trades did not make important contributions to the productivity of the building industry and were seldom if ever interested in building aesthetics. Labor leaders on the broader front did not lead their groups in support of better or regional plans, or even of parks, playgrounds and certainly not of urban beauty. An individual laborer with enough money to spend to build a house at all invariably had conventional tastes and simply tried to make it as much like a middle-class suburban house as possible. Workers rarely built cooperatively as they were frequently doing in Europe; even when they did one cannot point to their projects as important American architecture. Unions did not yet have large enough coffers to build office buildings, nor large enough staffs to fill them; such symbols of the growth of a union would have been neither appropriate nor welcome. The only good architecture for labor was the architecture of the factory and that was supplied by management.

4

WHILE labor was faring meagerly in the complacent years, at least in everything except the fullness of the dinner pail, government actions and public opinion were operating in favor of business. The governmental mobilizations of industry during the First World War, which even put the government into manufacturing for a moment, were abandoned with alacrity after Versailles and scant attention was paid to halfhearted proposals by Glenn E. Plumb that employees should share the ownership and operation of the railroads; or to the suggestion by the United Mine Workers that the coal mines be nationalized. Grumbling about graduated income taxes and muttering about what Joseph Choate had called "a drift towards socialism" and the stifling of initiative, businessmen nonetheless found a way to live with their shackles, especially when, as before FDR, their status was high — certainly higher than that of architects, who, it was thought, were not exactly artists, not exactly professional men, not exactly intellectuals and certainly not good businessmen. As time went on intellectuals, almost to a man, deserted the standpat side while the professionals, like the doctors, seemed to become more and more conservative. This was noticeably true of the engineers and the architects, who could work best in a society which conserved things. Both might always want innovation, engineers more than architects. But both needed clients with funds. These funds had either to be in private hands or in governmental hands; they would not constructively be in revolutionary hands. On the whole the architects and engineers alike had found the bureaucracy of big business far more flexible than the bureaucracy of big government and as believers in conservative change it was not unnatural for them to stay on the side whence such change was most likely to be supported.

The artist in America might feel no such changing status. His position had always been ambiguous. Art was an afterthought for most Americans and the artist of second-rate importance. In a war for survival the poetic stock was expendable as the scientific was not.

It is not at all clear who wanted to be an architect in this situation or why. It does seem clear that few architects of the day came from or joined the angry classes. Few were seeking an economic or social upgrading through successful practice of their profession. Few were burning to rebuild America in some great new image. Architecture was too often regarded as a genteel profession, suitable for the man who had attended an Ivy League college, made the Grand Tour of Europe, caught the lively spirit of the École des Beaux-Arts, knew his wines and brandies and old châteaux, married a suitably wealthy and cultivated wife and could stage grandiose settings for wealthier men whom he knew at social clubs.

It is not surprising that few architects of those days were to be found among the agitators, or in the vanguard of the liberal parades.

Not all architects were like that. A small group of men like Robert Kohn, Clarence Stein, Henry Wright, and Arthur Holden were beginning to press for a different concept of housing and urbanism and men of this stamp stood with the liberals of other professions. But the Henry Wrights and the Clarence Steins in this time of prosperity and self-satisfaction were not conspicuous leaders of the whole profession however many accolades they may have since received. With the New Deal they came for a moment into their own but only for a moment. Even from the New Deal, the neutrals got most of the commissions.

The satisfied architects were undoubtedly more typical of the American consensus than the few professors or ministers or lawyers or novelists or poets who were not so sure that everything was lovely. For the architects, the American dream seemed in no jeopardy. Nor did it for the American people. Moreover, the people had no doubt where the prestige lay. It belonged to business and not to the arts. There was no question of any sort, including that of architectural excellence, on which the opinion of the successful Andrew Mellon would not be taken more seriously than the opinion of the "unsuccessful" Frank Lloyd Wright.

After the early years of the Wilson administration, criticism of businessmen abated. Business leadership was accepted not only in practical matters of economics, politics, and welfare, but in matters of aesthetics, philosophy, or morals as well. People liked Harding's 1920 statement, "What we want in America is less government in business and more business in govenment." They applauded Coolidge's philosophy that "the business of America is business." They agreed with Andrew Mellon that initiative could be associated only with acquisitive opportunity.

But after the crash when nine million savings accounts were wiped out, municipal employees could not draw their pay for months, in cities like Chicago one out of two workers was unemployed, the national birth rate was 17 per cent below that of 1921, and the bread lines and the apple salesmen were real, the businessman looked less infallible.

Even the architectural scepter passed briefly to other hands.

Although the buoyant FDR had himself a vigorous interest in architecture he also had no taste. Nonetheless his inauguration marked the end of a bad period of American architecture and the beginning of a new and better one, even if it cannot be credited to the heroic President. The days of the baronial patrons were gone. The corporate patrons had not yet emerged.

5

AFTER the First World War was over we might try to disentangle ourselves from Europe but we were never to succeed. In many ways the American participation in the first war was fragmentary, romantic, quite uncomprehending of the real dimensions and the real complications of the conflict, as our diplomatic actions during the Russian Revolution remind us. From it we achieved a sense that we could have military power if we wanted it; we learned that we could apply controls to our national life without demoralization, at least in crisis, that we could sustain a national draft of manpower, that government controls could sometimes even promote efficiency. We learned but forgot rapidly enough that no nation was really independent, that a complex modern world might be one of continuous crisis.

But we did not learn as much as we might have. To most of the doughboys, Winchester meant the mud of the base camp at Winnal Down and not the Cathedral, the Round Table or the School. To an American Legionary the symbol of France was a boxcar for forty-and-eight, the culture of France was to be found on the Butte Montmartre, the women of France were the mademoiselles from Armentières. For the architects the coin was a little different though perhaps as spurious. They had a predisposition to like France. Many had studied there; many understood the French cuisine; a few were honest oenophiles. They knew where some of the fine buildings were and managed to see them when on leave. Thus the architects of the AEF did bring something back, a pleasurable nosegay of nostalgia, delightful for the individual, harmless enough for him, damaging to his architecture. For though France offered a wide variety of the finest architectural experiences created over a thousand years, and a few competent contemporary ones, it was the old ones that were visited. These were in themselves seldom eclectic but they could be imitated and adopted eclectically, overromanticized by sketches and etchings and watercolors. The pleasurable encounter with France simply enticed the young American soldier-architect to put on his beret and to try to bring old France to young America.

Our record after Versailles is too well known and too painful to linger over. Perhaps H. L. Mencken was its second-class Socrates in the era of second-class Presidents. Wrong about Le Corbusier, wrong about the genius being always at war with society, wrong about southern culture, he probably hit the nail on the head when he wrote, "In the arts as in the concerns of every day, the American seeks escape from the insoluble by pretending that it is solved. A comfortable phrase is what he craves beyond all things." It was a fair description of the architectural condition of his day and a fair description of some of the make-America-beautiful efforts of our own.

6

DESPITE the general languor of the times the science of 1913-1933 made great strides. A much more elaborate structure was now erected on the foundations of Einstein, Planck, Rutherford and Bohr. In physics the great task was to summarize the properties of matter in terms of electric charges and radiation. It was the time when protons, neutrons and spinning electrons joined the company of familiar words and by its end Enrico Fermi had shown that nearly every element in the periodic table would undergo a nuclear transformation when bombarded by neutrons. The threshold had been laid down for the use of nuclear energy on a big scale.

Meanwhile the quantum theory of Planck was coming to maturity, leading towards the doctrine of kinetic indeterminism. In simple terms it could be stated as Heisenberg's uncertainty principle of 1927 that there was a limit to the precision with which nature could be observed, or more concretely that one could not determine simultaneously the position and the velocity of a particle as accurately as one wished; that the more precise one got about one of these the less precise he would have to be content to be about the other.

Remembering the misinterpretations of Darwinian and other scientific concepts through false analogies to social situations, physicists like Percy Bridgman were alarmed at what laymen might make of the postulates of Heisenberg. In 1929 he wrote, "The immediate effect will be to let loose a veritable spree of licentious and debauched thinking. . . . One group will find in the failure of the physical law of cause and effect the solution of the age-old problem of the freedom of the will, and on the other hand, the atheist will find the justification of his contention that chance rules the universe."

One should not expect to find direct applications of the work of the scientists in the contemporary Empire State Building but one could not expect even an indirect effect if the architects were formally ignorant of everything that was going on in physics, as undoubtedly they were. For a moment the implications of the atomic work for architecture were only philosophical, if they were anything; a little later they would pose concrete questions of location for survival; and still later they might ask architecture what to do for a world in which energy might be essentially free. But at the time they had none of these effects. The architects were then, as now, formally ignorant of science and not anxious to change the situation. Thus even the serious efforts of Sigfried Giedion could not build believable connections between Duchamp's *Nude Descending a Staircase* or Gropius's Werkbund Building at Cologne and the recondite space-time of Einstein. Exactly what architects might have done with the knowledge had they possessed it may be hard to define but that still leaves unanswered the question whether architecture can express its times well while the architects are deaf to some of its most important manifestations. To the physical sciences they seemed quite indifferent though it was from the physical sciences that a new and formidable philosophy was emerging.

If new work in vitamins, hormones and insulin prolonged life, stimulated gerontology and changed the age distribution of the American people, the architects could perhaps defer their interest until this distribution called for new buildings, even new building types. If theories of absorption, concepts of unit operations in the chemical industry, many developments in synthetic chemicals prophesied whole new lines of materials they could perhaps wait until the materials were on the market. But psychology was moving into the architectural backyard. Architects might not enjoy the labor of trying to make a direct connection with the new psychology, behavioristic or Gestalt, or to encounter Jung's efforts to explain the psychology of art, finding it easier to take at second hand through critics like Read and Burke, painters like Miró, Klee, Tanguy, Ernst, Picasso, and Man Ray. The few psychological statements that architects might essay were in the end rationalizations of what they had done intuitively and subjectively to produce work that was satisfying for them. They could seldom adduce experimental evidence to support their views, for exam-

ple, as to what was the right light or the right number of conva-
lescents in a single hospital room, or the effect of color upon the
patient, though they might now begin to "talk pyschology."

There were a few architects like American-born Paul Nelson,
living in France, who pressed the idea of doing what they called
architectural "research," but in terms of true scientific laboratory
techniques and attitudes, the research of those contemporary architects and foundations who worked on architectural problems
seems to have been remarkably primitive, subjective, naïve and in-
conclusive. Thus to praise it with the title "research" is to mag-
nify it beyond its deserts. And it made almost no dent on the
world of the architects in which very few even were interested in
watching the researchers, much less in emulating them.

7

TECHNOLOGY also moved forward in the complacent years and indeed contributed to the complacency. For Americans have always
found it easy to confuse technological change with "progress."
On many counts the material standard of living became higher
although not necessarily on all counts. A high material standard
of transportation was attained, including speed, comfort, flexibility and general availability. But the landscape through which the
Americans traveled did not become finer and the speed at which
they traveled did not improve its visibility; the standardization of
communities might even make the purpose of the travel more dubious. But given such choices Americans have never wavered.
They selected the speed over the amenity and called it a better
way of life. They accepted the scrap heap and the smog as a reasonable price for fast travel and electric appliances in the house.

Now the railroads which had provided the backbone of American passenger transportation began to pass their maturity, although there would continue to be innovations in railroading right
down to 1950. But the once piratical and adventurous railroad
managements had become conservative and unimaginative, unable
to vie with the competition of the air and the highway.

All the red carpets and extra-fare trains, all the stewardesses
and the too few other practices borrowed from the airlines

simply postponed the demise. The passenger railroads were head-
ing towards senescence and no hormones would postpone the
process much. But no one foresaw this at the moment and so the
spate of imperial railroad stations continued until almost every
city had one. Indeed a few of the more interesting ones were built
in this time.

Innovations and improvements in the airplane, on the other
hand, came along at a headlong pace. The airplane needed engineers but it also needed heroes and it found them in the Doolit-
tles, Turners, Alcocks, Posts, Lindberghs, and in women like Amy
Mollison and Amelia Earhart. They launched parachutes from
26,000 feet by 1921; they flew the Atlantic both ways and by 1933
had gone 5650 miles non-stop. They flew higher, faster, and further. They drew away from the competition of the dirigibles. But
after all the heroism and all the excitement of the pioneering
innovations had become common, there remained the drab problem of building a transport system. By 1919 you could fly commercially between London and Paris, between Moscow and Pet-
rograd and a number of other important European cities, but for
a while we concentrated on the mail.

The airplane posed many problems to architecture as it grew.
The most primitive questions would have been simple except for
the rate of change in thought as to what and where an air terminal needed to be. The beginnings were not imaginative as again
we showed that we could solve the difficult problems of dynamics
with more verve and imagination than the simpler static ones of
architecture. It was not yet time to wonder what the airplane said
about the aesthetics of the city; not time even to guess that the
freedom of movement between old civilizations and new might
affect them both profoundly. Hangars might be seen to have an
admissible beauty but it was a beauty that belonged to the engineer and one that seemed to most architects not to have any
transferable suggestions for their less utilitarian needs. So the
effect of the airplane was postponed to the future.

What was squarely in the present was the automobile, although the magnitude of the urban disaster it was preparing was
but vaguely foreshadowed. The mass production started by Ford
in 1913 required the concept of a public need of which the public

was not yet aware. Fourteen years later Henry and Edsel Ford drove their fifteen-millionth car out of the plant and most of the fifteen million had been the sturdy, uncompromising Model T. But at the end of that year Ford showed the new Model A and this reluctantly adopted change broke the ice for the continuous and trivial changes of the present.

The 181,000 cars that were made in 1910 became almost four million by 1930. Truck production increased from 6000 to 571,000. The 458,000 registered passenger cars became 23 million and now there was one car on the road for every five Americans. There were still only 40,000 buses but trucks on the road had increased from 10,000 to 3.5 million. The miles driven in America multiplied by ten.

Of course much of the credit must go to those who improved engines, rubber, alloys, fuel or who developed mass production and distribution. But automobiles were not articles of household use. They needed roads to run on and the early roads were mere remnants of ancient carriage tracks. In old areas and in many new ones they were quite unsuited even to modest speeds. They abounded in sharp curves as they twisted around ancient property lines, steep grades as they assaulted hills head on, short lines of sight that had been perfectly safe for horse drivers. They were narrow, they were replete with blind intersections, their surfaces were uniformly bad.

Indeed, the first problem for the national roadbuilders, aside from providing a system on which even the markings would be consistent and there would be a certainty that one route did lead into the next, was to make surfaces that could be traveled on at all. For a long time after cars began the gentle trickle from the cities it was a real question whether the open road could ever keep up with the national demand. By 1914 it was clear that the prevalent macadam was failing under the increased traffic. Nor could the brick roads of Ohio endure, or the cobblestones of Chicago's North Side. The decade between 1914 and 1924 saw the 2300 miles of concrete increase to 31,000 and by that time concrete roads were being laid at the rate of 6000 miles a year, exceeding everything except the still most common gravel. By 1933 the national road system had been completed as to routes and was

thoroughly obsolete, since it consisted almost entirely of two-lane
highways connecting main settlements but passing through every
congested center and debouching into clotted city squares. The
first rotary grade intersection was provided in 1920 and the first
cloverleaf in 1930, both in New Jersey. The first few miles of an
American superhighway with a grass strip between lanes came in
the same year. The Holland Tunnel became the first to carry automobiles beneath the river in 1927 when it opened a new road
from Jersey to Manhattan. But the builders had no concept of
the dimensions of the oncoming flood and no realization yet that
the critical point might be at the tunnel mouth or the bridge-
head. So the new river crossings simply dumped the traffic onto
conventional city streets quite unprepared to take away the flow.

All this certainly posed immediate problems and a potential
crisis for architecture but the architects seem not to have done
much about it. The trailer, invented in 1929 by Glenn Curtiss,
was displayed in the Hudson showrooms without causing a
tremor in architectural circles. The motel crept in quietly, first as
a mediocre economy for a few travelers or as a source of small
change for a farmer. As the automobile destroyed urbanity and
civilization within the city, muddied the difference between city
and suburb and country, spawned a massive, uniform, banal and
horribly ugly highway culture, the architects did not complain.
Twenty years too late they began to see the damage to the land,
cry outrage among themselves, ultimately join more seriously with
others in an effort to cut out a cancer that had cried for an earlier
diagnosis.

It may be unfair to bang this drum. There is no reason to suppose that city politicians and businessmen would have believed
the architectural alarm had it been sounded. But the architects
were not active even on lesser and more obvious problems. They
might, if asked, design an inadequate storage garage but their interest stopped at the building line and they were quite willing to
let the incoming and outgoing cars pile up on an unchanged
street. For their other buildings they made no pretense at providing off-street parking; for theaters, opera houses and other buildings which many people would approach and leave almost simultaneously they provided no off-street roadways, no entries more

sophisticated and comfortable than the ancient marquees. In all of this there was an irresponsibility that was something less than charming.

8

MEANWHILE electronics, too, was preparing to lay its hands on the American culture. Telephone service became almost foolproof and common. By 1927 the world had been almost girdled with a telephone network.

The use of radio signals for commercial broadcasting was on the verge of developing. In 1910, Lee de Forest had installed a 500-watt transmitter at the Metropolitan Opera House and broadcast a program in which Enrico Caruso took part. After the war evolution was rapid; KDKA began the modern era in Pittsburgh in November 1920 by providing returns from the Harding-Cox election. By the end of 1933 an enormous fraction of the twelve million homes then housing thirteen million sets were tuned in for the first of Roosevelt's fireside chats.

National networks dominated the scene by 1927. The effect of the national and simultaneous distribution of the same music, the same comedy, the same sporting events, the same political speeches, the same news and the same comments about the news, the same advertisements, changed the music, the comedy, the speeches, the interpretations and in many ways standardized them. Depending upon how it was used, national radio might have been able to cultivate or destroy regionalism, elevate or debase national taste.

But meanwhile the engineers were preparing an even more ominous development of electronics. As early as 1884, Nipkow had demonstrated a way to the future television. Practical use had to be deferred until de Forest invented his thermionic amplifier in 1907. On April 7, 1927, Walter S. Gifford, President of the American Telephone and Telegraph Company, conducted a public display of television, showing on New York sets a picture of Secretary Hoover sitting in his Washington office.

Another mass medium was more perceptible for the moment. By 1930, it is estimated, 100 million Americans were going to the movies weekly. The old vaudeville theaters no longer would do. The Strand Theater in New York opened in April 1914 with 3300 seats, a 30-piece orchestra, elegant popcorn-vending machines, glamorously caparisoned ushers who drilled every day and carried magic light wands to speed their work. *The Spoilers* of Rex Beach set a record by playing to 40,000 people in a single week. *The Birth of a Nation*, the first long combination of spectacle and drama, played in theaters which often charged two dollars a ticket. New types of showmen, like Roxy of the radio, had movie theaters built in their honor. The New York Roxy had 6250 seats, a cooling plant, fancy service and stylized courtesies, staged shows based on a permanent *corps de ballet* that moved with the precise impressiveness if not the meaning of the great ballets. All this picture was framed in velvet and introduced with fanfare. The film was approached with something of the awe that befitted a cathedral of the cinema. Given any kind of picture, people would stand in line for hours, would buy so many tickets that the place could gross nearly $150,000 a week.

In this as in almost every other art of the time Americans were showing themselves more adept at massive manufacture and distribution than at imaginative and varied production of more exciting things for a more critical clientele. The list of outstanding American pictures of the day will not stand comparison with the list from Europe. In Europe the makers of movies walked hand in hand with the painters and the writers of higher capacities, sometimes were themselves the painters or the writers. A few Americans were able to see such European productions as Wiene's *Cabinet of Dr. Caligari* or Murnau's *Last Laugh* or Léger's *Ballet Mécanique* but this could be done only in out-of-the-way corners of large cities and not at the Roxy in New York or at the Balaban and Katz palatial and perfumed Chicago Theater in the Loop.

For American architecture the movies posed no direct new problems. The cinematic tycoons had taste only for extravagance and a nose for the kind of delusion the public would take to. Movie theaters, or houses for magnates and stars, all called for the same program, something a little too big, a little too noisy, a kind of building that stopped just short of being a stage set, that was as artificial as the loving and surprised greetings with which the actors accosted each other in public. Nothing contemporary was needed. The new technical requirements were primitive. Almost any style would do that would lend itself to grotesque overornamentation, whether it was the preferred Italian or Spanish Baroque or Moorish, Gothic, Egyptian or Chinese.

At a deeper level the movies, along with the radio, did contain the power to expose large portions of the American people to some common standards of dress, clothing, manners, speech, even architecture. The movies had the advantage that many of these tastes can best be cultivated by vision. As it was they proposed no crusade, contaminated only in a mediocre way, elevated not at all. In the main all they really offered was another version of the steady threat to American individuality or American regionalism that was implied in the mass production of automobiles, of clothing, of soup, of housing, or of ideas. The mass media had the power to create a higher public taste or a lower one, or merely to pander to whatever taste they thought the public had; this is the role most of them chose, most of the time.

Another important operator in the new mass culture appeared when *Time* magazine began to influence American opinion in 1923. Affecting no editorial policy, every piece of news reporting was an editorial or a criticism. Moreover the editorials and the criticisms were anonymous. The criticism seemed to be criticism by committee and therefore to have more authenticity than the writings of an identified individual. *Time* was favorable to change and to much contemporary arts and letters. It struck useful blows (and so did its offshoot *Life*) for the public observation of and even favor for new things in the visual arts. In these respects it was more responsible and more creative than the movies or the radio. In the decades to come new journals of this type influenced general public opinion and taste in architecture and the arts as no earlier journal had ever succeeded in doing. Often it seemed that they were more interested in discovering new talent than in perpetuating old. The role of kingmaker can be too heady. Innovation can seem too newsworthy.

9

THE increase in use of electricity was spectacular by any measure, many times the increase in population. The lamps were larger, brighter, and more durable, and the number of lumens supplied per capita increased by nearly thirty-fold. This great invasion of night, Howard Mumford Jones suggests, had the profoundest effect upon the time sense, the space sense and the color sense of Americans. It also more effectively divorced them from a first hand acquaintance with natural phenomena. They came to make less sharp distinctions between night and day, at least in the cities where most of them lived. They lost some of their seasonal sense.

There were steady improvements in the established building technologies such as that of steel but no great new inventions. Things simply got bigger. When other ways for using steel were suggested in America they were likely to be fanciful like the sus- pended roof of the Transportation Building at Chicago's Century of Progress or R. Buckminster Fuller's demonstrations of tension in his Dymaxion House.

The dramatic uses of concrete were also reserved for a later time. In Europe parabolic arches were used for balloon hangars; Freyssinnet produced amazingly thin reinforced slabs of concrete bent into vaults for some locomotive sheds at Bagneux, France in 1929 but they seemed suitable only for things like locomotive sheds. The Swiss Maillart designed thrilling bridge arches out of concrete but even in tolerant Europe you had to search them out mostly in the remote cantons. In America there was nothing to suggest that architects found them fine, if they had found them at all.

There were of course many little contributions to efficiency: bulldozers, polishing machines, jets, cranes, scaffoldings, eleva- tors, chutes, paint sprayers, cement guns, caissons, salamanders, and other ways to help winter building, and unless these had been used intelligently and to the hilt a monumental structure like the Empire State would have been quite impossible. There were im- provements in the quality and consistency of cement, aggregate and the resultant concrete. Glassmakers were learning to draw larger and purer sheets, to make them more consistently, to temper the glass against shock, to make it resistant to heat, translucent to some ultra violet, to tint it. They were developing industrially what was historically one of the oldest forms of glass, the thread. From this came new textiles and insulating blankets. Other insulating materials were being invented too, heat absorbents, sound absorbents, ways to reduce the reverberation in a chamber, to keep the sound from reaching another room. A science of auditorium acoustics was being born in the work of pioneers like Sabine and Watson; and of the proper physiological environment for the human body, especially the thermal environment, in the work of C. E. A. Winslow, sponsored by the John B. Pierce Foundation. Air-conditioning and ventilating systems were being invented or refined and thus engineers and scientists were creating a situation in which a sharper definition might be made as to what human bodies needed from a given room and more satisfactory ways of providing for that need. These artificial environmental controls would become almost a standard element in the architect's kit bag later although the actual performance of air conditioning, of insulation, and even of acoustic design might remain tricky and not quite predictable for a long time. They would relieve the architect of any regional limitation but at the same time they would encumber him with the demand for a great deal of space for the ducts and other things that the environmental services demanded. But in 1933 all this was merely a promise.

There were a few who felt that architects must somehow come seriously to grips with the new techniques of mass production which were obviously changing the economy of so many things other than building. Michael A. Mikkelsen summed it up in 1929, saying that the outstanding problems of architectural practice were how to adjust design to the conditions created by mass production and how to adjust the practice of architecture to the conditions which tended to segregate architects into groups of specialists — on hospitals, schools, banks, and so on.

Both problems commanded special attention in the field of housing. It was clear that there would be an enormous market for a good and inexpensive detached house, that good dwellings might be more important to the national welfare than good automo-

K

biles, that good houses obviously cost too much, that it should be possible to design them for mass production and that not enough was being done about it. Some large companies like Johns-Manville and the United States Steel Corporation carried on desultory, modestly financed, almost entirely empirical investigations. The American Radiator Company maintained its captive John B. Pierce Foundation which was ineffective in its construction research. Sears Roebuck relied mostly upon attractive financing and found itself in the curious position of being a national manufacturer and distributor which had no real control over the quality of the houses it sold, since so much depended on the local arrangements. Many individual inventors including several architects tried out their dreams for a mass-produced house, almost universally with no success.

Lawrence Kocher and Albert Frey proposed an *Aluminaire* House supported on six Duralumin columns standing inside the walls, thus offering a hung construction such as would be common in big buildings later. They put up a full-scale model in Grand Central Palace for the New York Architectural League Exhibition of April 1931 and later re-erected it as a permanent summer house for architect Wallace Harrison at Syosset. Robert W. McLaughlin, Jr., another architect, designed the Motohome, based on a frame and asbestos-cement panels plus a lot of equipment. Assisted substantially by Gerard Swope and other important industrialists, he organized a corporation, American Houses, Inc., which stayed in business for years and sold a good many houses filled with gear but never became a real industrial giant although for several years it showed substantial profits. American Rolling Mill tried to find ways to use more strip steel in housing by designing what was essentially an all-metal chassis. Grosvenor Atterbury continued his experiments with concrete and finally invented a nailing concrete which he formed into blocks. The American Car and Foundry Company became interested in this by 1919 but by 1921 work at the demonstration plant stopped. At that point the inventor concluded that a proper method had been found, that one method of production applicable to successful commercial use had been developed, but then drew the other highly important and disappointing conclusion "that no commer-

cial concern could be expected to solve these problems scientifi-
cally, economically, and rapidly with the sole object of creating a
new basic industry devoted to the production of minimum-cost
housing; that such work could be done satisfactorily only by some
non-profit agency." Such a confession was a retreat from the
whole notion of successful pre-fabrication and the history of
American private enterprise as it had been conceived up to then.
Only the minor successes of American Houses and National
Homes have suggested that Atterbury was wrong and no large
company seems ever to have gone at the problem wholeheartedly.

Steelmakers all too often simply sought, by prefabrication, to
put more steel into a house, even where it served no useful or
economic function; other designs relied on precut wooden frames
and panels; or concrete precast into all sorts of interlocking shapes
or poured on the job in all sorts of standardized forms. Among all
the experimenters, none was more devoted or more prolific of a
variety of ideas than Albert Farwell Bemis of Boston and none
spent more personal time and fortune on the experiments.

But in the end all of them really came to naught. Although
some of the companies remain, although a few may have made
small profits, the fact is that their history bore no resemblance to
that of the motor industry; even today the factory-built house
accounts for but a minuscule part of all the housing production in
the country.

World-famous inventors like Thomas A. Edison and Simon
Lake tried and failed. Elaborate schemes of financing, imitating
those which had been used by Electric Bond and Share, were
brought in and did not succeed. Howard T. Fisher in his proposals for General Houses had a scheme for integrating existing producers like the Pullman Company into a cooperative productive
and distributional effort. If you believed the right issue of *Fortune* you would have thought that this show was really on the
road.

The high point of the movement was no doubt reached when
each of many producers and inventors actually erected single
demonstration houses at Chicago's Century of Progress Exposition in 1933. The houses attracted few sales and many of the
producers could not have made sales if asked to; the main effect

in the long run was to acclimatize many Americans to some trivial changes in interior design and decoration and one or two other features, of which the parade was unfortunately led by the corner window. When the New Deal entered upon its housing program and sought to put every American resource to work, none of the great exhibitors at Chicago was really ready to make a major contribution. There was no magic in Foster Gunnison's Magic Homes.

More quietly, mass production was moving in on the details of architecture. Individual parts — windows, radiators, ducts, panes of glass — were becoming standardized in shape and sizes. For a full realization of the potential benefits, architects needed to discipline themselves in a way to which they were unused and of which most of them were suspicious. Standardized parts did not necessitate standardized buildings as Bemis was constantly asserting about his modular proposals. Walter Gropius praised the standardized part on both ideological and aesthetic grounds. But large buildings used so much of everything that they could really establish their own plant standards and make their own module independent of any national norm. Little buildings were usually in the hands of little men and such men feared the "menace to design" of any standardization. Thus the profession was unable and unwilling to take any concerted action although it did set up committees. Buildings were partly standardized and partly not. A few of the benefits of mass production were reflected almost accidentally while many potentials went quite unrealized. Buildings were moving to an over-all standardization while preserving costly independence, even anarchy of dimensions. So the editor of a leading American architectural journal could still truthfully write in a private communication in 1956, "Having just gone through a hospital, a high school, and a housing project under construction, I cannot testify to any influence from objective technological improvements, such as the use of the module, prefabrication, or whatever. Tile is still cut and fitted around door frames, flooring is still laid by craftsmen on hands and knees."

This was surely one of the great recent failures of American technology and industry. Probably everybody was to blame; not enough imaginative men found themselves drawn to the techno-

logical problem as they were to the problems of flight; no entre-
preneur of enough stability and power was interested enough, resourceful enough and determined enough. The organization of
labor, of the politics of business supervision, of the whole process
of making a building was almost certainly in opposition. And
what of the architects? Not solely culpable, can they escape blame
on the grounds that it was somebody else's business?

On balance it seems we must say that the architects of 1913-
1933 in America failed their times. They were able to use modern
industry efficiently to make the Empire State Building but could
not harness themselves or the building industry to housing, or
even to mass production in general. Buildings, therefore, suffered
some of the limitations of the new production without reaching
to grasp its potential benefits. The craft disappeared but the machine was not put to work. In all this the architects were naïve
when they were even interested. They were incredibly innocent as
inventors. They played with specialization but hastened to disclaim it in the same breath. In these matters they were, to be
sure, acting with less ignorance than they were in acting about
science; with less indifference than they were in acting about the
automobile and the movie and the electric light or about the social problems of the millions of ill-housed. But even in matters
very close to their own business they seem to have been both
surprisingly ignorant and surprisingly indifferent, following if you
like the example in another sphere by President Coolidge. The
charge cannot be defended merely by saying that architecture is
not an intellectual business. The successful American architects,
with a few exceptions, were simply not full of the spirit of experiment that moved many of the painters, the spirit of compassion
or angry repudiation that was common among the novelists and
poets, the spirit of dedication to search that marked the scientists.

10

In such a climate it is not surprising that they ignored or deprecated the important buildings and writings that were appearing in
Europe. American architects might read Sullivan's *Autobiography
of an Idea* now that he was dead but they gave shorter shrift to Le

Corbusier's essays or to Paul Nelson's project for a City Hospital at Lille. The Chicago Century of Progress revealed its half-baked, halfhearted ideas in the same year that the Nazis were dissolving the Bauhaus. The native Buckminster Fuller was laughed at or ignored. A civilization may provide its architectural symbols without intending to. The admired American buildings were appropriate to an age of complacency. The successful American architects of this day were complacent too.

This was not true of all the American artists. It was not true, for example, of composers like Piston, Sessions, Thomson and Copland who were entering upon a very experimental age following the two great Europeans, Stravinsky and Schönberg. Such composers were trying, as the European architects were trying, to find out how they could break up the long-standing relations between the various traditional elements and recombine them in greater freedom.

Also, the best writers, European and American, could not be accused of complacency about their times and their world although their standards of criticism and the things they chose to criticize were different. In France, for example, there was a towering group of novelists and poets headed by Proust, Valéry, Mauriac, Gide and Claudel. Among all of them there was a great uneasiness about the world, a questioning of the human condition itself. Joyce, D. H. Lawrence, Aldous Huxley, Mann and Hesse were asking comparable questions. They did not have a monolithic point of view except on one point — that the individual in Western society was having a bad time and we needed to take a new and unparochial look.

American writers paid more attention to the details of American life, more materialistically, less symbolically, with less style and, although angry, really with less pessimism as well. Most of the American writers, indeed, continued to use methods that no longer seemed appropriate to Europe which welcomed only Dos Passos, Hemingway and Faulkner as important.

But Americans seemed to be generally prosperous, dressing up to go on what Scott Fitzgerald called "the gaudiest spree in history." To be sure, Communist writers like Michael Gold proclaimed that "The new artists of the people . . . will learn what Life is from their solidarity with the eternal, yea-saying masses." The American people would now be ready to "put forth those huge-hewn poets, those striding out-doors philosophers and horny-handed creators of whom he [Whitman] prophesied." But the great roughhewn poets and the horny-handed creators did not stride forth from the nonexistent proletarian faubourgs.

This does not mean that the intellectuals and the writers of America were content. Indeed they shared an excitement to which the architects were immune. In 1913 they had been happy about the future. They thought a new America was on the march. John Butler Yeats announced, "The fiddles are tuning as it were all over America." Ezra Pound, acting as first foreign editor of Harriet Monroe's magazine *Poetry*, proclaimed an American Risorgimento that would make "the Italian Renaissance look like a tempest in a teapot."

The optimism faded away with the war, with the repudiation of the League of Nations, with the peccadilloes of Harding, the indifference of Coolidge and the ultra-conservatism of Hoover. The intellectuals found themselves again forced into revolt but the taste for proletarianism had dulled too and other ways had to be found.

The novelists continued to berate America in a quasi-naturalistic manner but now the butts of attack were not the great cities and the great tycoons but the little towns of Winesburg, Ohio, or Gopher Prairie, Minnesota; the targets were middle-class men and women like Carol Kennicott or George Babbitt. The revolt was not, as Kazin notes, concerned with great questions but with "the sights and sounds of common life." In opposition to them stood the Baltimorean sage H. L. Mencken with the blunderbuss leveling shafts at all middle-class morality, and his disciples Nathan, Hergesheimer, and Cabell. Each in his way tried (and failed) to outdo the Mencken pronunciamento, "If I am convinced of anything it is that Doing Good is in bad taste."

In a more responsible vein, Frost hinted at the tragic aspects of American existence while T. S. Eliot was the "laureate of nostalgia, of dwindling hope." *The Waste Land* of 1922 expressed the feeling of many Americans towards their times by examining many failures and disintegrations in an arid world that had once been green.

Who were the architectural counterparts in America of Eliot, Faulkner, Dos Passos, Fitzgerald and Hemingway? The answer is no one, really. Nearest were the less famous people who clustered around the housing movement: Arthur Holden with his early studies of the economics of mid-Manhattan; Clarence Stein with his planned communities, often done with the help of Henry Wright; Frederick Ackerman and Robert Kohn; all oriented in the general direction of Sir Raymond Unwin. But these men were not then regarded as very important architects and none of them was really ever an artist. The only great architectural artist, Frank Lloyd Wright, could hardly have been less interested in the social problem.

But artistic or not, the leadership of Stein and his associates did become important for the country when the New Deal offered them a chance to work at the vital center.

Before this happened most of the architectural attitudes had to be expressed by critics or by architects turned critics. It was the words and not the buildings that had to do the speaking. This is always unfortunate for architecture is not, finally, a matter of words. But in such a time it was inevitable that the leaders should be writer-architects like Clarence Stein or Henry Wright, historical critics and social philosophers like Lewis Mumford, then at the height of his powers and influence though not of his acclaim which came later, or sociologists like the young and ardent Catherine Bauer. Few of them were then identified nearly so closely with architectural reform as with political and economic housing reform and they worked more for social change than for a change in architecture — which is perhaps just as well. But Mumford wrote penetrating and important criticism of individual buildings while also preaching persuasively the theories of his idol Patrick Geddes, improving and fortifying them as he did so. When the right moment came the work for which Stein and Henry Wright were responsible, and which Mumford and Bauer publicized, had a benign if brief effect upon the American scene, regrettably partial, regrettably transitory.

11

AMERICAN sculpture and painting of the moment stood somewhere between the architecture and the literature but again was
less experimental than the painting and sculpture abroad, and
much less clearly connected to architecture.

In Europe a certain tranquillity hovered over the arts for a few
years after 1915. Cubism had worked itself out. The new movements had not clearly emerged. Léger was trying to examine the
importance of the machine but more and more abstractly.
Amadée Ozenfant and Jeanneret issued their purist manifesto,
Après le Cubisme, in 1918. This said in effect that cubism had
become purely decorative and that it had adopted elements of
impressionism from which it ought to be purged. This effort to
"reconquer the plane surface" was an essential element in the
new architectural thinking. So were the architectonic studies of
the constructivist Malewitsch. But the most concrete architectural stimuli came from the movement of the neo-plasticists
called *De Stijl,* founded in 1917 by Theo van Doesburg, including
Mondriaan, Oud and van Eesteren. Best remembered through
the early constructions of van Doesburg and the late flat, linear
and usually rectangular abstractions of Mondriaan, it obviously,
almost too obviously, suggested the inner space and even the façades of buildings that were to come; but it also repeated messages that had been stated in Frank Lloyd Wright's Unity Temple more than a decade before. The abiding principle insisted
that "the universal is simple and through that abundant." The
application forced concentration on the purity of planes and
color.

The disciples of this movement were direct and forthright and
reveal that even fellow soldiers in a movement can have differences. Today we recall the Bauhaus as one of the most influential
forces in the modern movement up to the time when Hitler destroyed it. Certainly its subsequent influence on American architectural education was more than substantial. But van Doesburg
went to the Bauhaus in 1921 and announced that it was romantic,
that it permitted and even encouraged a contradiction between

theory and practice, between the functional theories of its architects and expressionistic abstractions of some of its artists like
Klee and Kandinsky. In other words, it did not have an adequate
theory, it was too permissive. It was a great compliment to
Gropius though not so intended.

A new idea was offered to architecture in 1925 when Léger
tried to let color define his objects. This provided a new concept
of mural space but more importantly suggested that interior space
might be less rigid, emulating the "elastic rectangle." This was
hardly noticed in America where architects did not look to
painters for suggestions.

One of the great European movements included the many
efforts to exploit the Freudian undertones of surrealism proclaimed by André Breton in the surrealist manifesto of 1924. Arp
worked sometimes with the surrealistic and sometimes with the
abstract, relying equally on chance and intention, producing in
either case ameba-like forms. Miró combined spermatozoa,
breasts, wombs, telephones and a humorous outlook on life which
may have meant much or nothing; Klee painted sophisticated
fantasies like *Um den Fisch* which were pitiless if often mystical
satires.

This work, too, can be regarded as suggestive to and anticipa-
tory of the later architectural interest in "free forms," but the rest
of the great painters like Rouault, Picasso, Braque, Schlemmer
and Kandinsky, though experimental, skillful and sincere, though
much admired by their European architectural contemporaries,
were obviously pursuing their very personal and very different
lines. This occasioned some bewilderment. How could it all be
called modern painting and have the term mean anything? But
the bewilderment was not limited to the enemies of the experimenters who might have been expected to pretend bewilderment.
It arose because if you believed there were some truth about the
world, and if all the painters were really trying to express truth,
then if some of them were right the others were wrong, unless the
world was, after all, chaos. The messages of the painters were too
many and too contradictory. All they could agree upon was the
inviolability of the personal expression. And this very determina-

tion to defend the personal expression at all hazard was a sharper indictment of man's twentieth-century condition than anything that the writers had prepared, since it seemed to be a thorough-going denunciation of the idea that there was any profit in or even chance for commonalty. If it was the last mad dance before chaos the painting nonetheless provided an exciting ballet.

A comparable atomization of architecture was to be delayed for a quarter-century.

As in painting, so in sculpture. Lehmbruck, Maillol, Picasso, Arp, Brancusi, Moore, Gabo ranged from primitivism to supersophistication, from exaggerated naturalism to complete abstraction, from three dimensional amebas, flying surfaces, eggs, to perforated forms and very architectonic space constructions. Here was a shower of suggestions quite explicitly transferable to architecture.

By 1929 Americans had had a chance to see a great deal of this work at the exhibition with which the Museum of Modern Art opened its doors. But its effects had to come later, for in American painting the stir was much less vigorous and so far as the American architects with commissions were concerned there was no contact whatsoever between them and an even pallid follower of Arp or Picasso.

They found no stimulus to new forms in the suggestions of the painters and the sculptors; moreover they had so little sympathy with the work that the art they occasionally commissioned for their buildings was not in the vein of the leading contemporary artists. To the Americans of the day even Milles seemed too advanced. Nor would the innovative work have been appropriate in the buildings Americans were making. But it was the architects who were too far behind, not the artists who were too far ahead.

Occasionally there were summonses for modestly modern murals but these were almost always disastrous. Orozco, Rivera, Curry were commissioned at Dartmouth, Rockefeller Center, Kansas State Capitol. Benton was commissioned by the State of Indiana for the Chicago World's Fair and his murals were later placed in Indiana University. The American works were trivial; the Mexicans were too pungent; all were in uncongenial surroundings. But for the most part the architect-clients had no intention of using painters or sculptors at the center of the creative process, even in a collaboration such as that of Goodhue and Lee Lawrie.

They were perhaps right not to want the work of Prendergast, Marin, Demuth, Sheeler, Max Weber, Stella, Stuart Davis, Grant Wood, Hopper, Marsh as an addition to their architecture; and none of these painters was suggesting a new adventure in space.

Yet if American architects did not read the kicks to their complacency in the writing of their own land or suggestions for new ways in the work of local painters, they might have found plenty of both abroad. Unfortunately the local journals were not at this moment leading taste. Thus *The American Architect* was more likely to carry an article by Edward Pearce Casey to denounce the awkward appearance of parabolic arches, or one by Lorado Taft on recent tendencies in sculpture which would ignore everyone after Rodin. The readers of this journal might find favorable comments about Letchworth or the Rogers model dwellings on West Forty-fourth Street but they were given much more information on the dimensions of the Temple Antoninus and Faustina or the Arch of Constantine. They would also be told a great deal about the properties of such "interesting woods" as Demerara mahogany, the bullet wood of British Guiana, or Himalayan deodar.

Yet there would have been much to publish. As early as 1911, Gropius had used glass as a screen for iron-framed walls and joined the glass cleanly at the corners in his Fagus Works. In 1914, Behrens, Hoffman, and Van der Velde had shown precedents for the '50s at the Deutsche Werkbund Exhibition in Cologne. Here too Bruno Taut had exhibited a glass house and Gropius his design for an office building. This *"Fabrik"* had an abundance of glass, covered terraces, projecting horizontally planar roofs and at the ends pavilions reminiscent of Wright. By 1921 Mies van der Rohe had published his sketch for a glass tower. Gropius built the Bauhaus at Dessau.in 1926. Again there were the glass curtains, the balcony slabs jutting into space. If the reinforced concrete skeleton was heavy it was because of German law. But the glass curtain was ubiquitous, meeting the horizontal white ribbons of opaque wall only at top and bottom and then only as a matter of closure. Here as at Fagus the columns were set inside. Here were many of Wright's principles, the regrouped planes, the many levels of reference, the glass curtains lacking only the solid anchorage to the ground which Wright never forgot.

And there was the work of Le Corbusier starting with that simple and revolutionary drawing of 1915 that showed nothing but four concrete posts, three horizontal concrete slabs and a connecting concrete stair. His major principles had already been enunciated as Sigfried Giedion so clearly shows — the pillar, the functional independence of skeleton and wall, the free plan, the free façade, and the roof garden — all mightily obvious in this drawing but not obvious to man before. His Villa Savoye at Poissy of 1928-1930 demonstrated these in very pure form. Here the isolated lot had afforded him the freedom to build above the swell of the valley of the Seine. Where Wright would have hugged the rocks, Le Corbusier threw his platform skyward on triumphant *pilotis*. There was his design for the Competition for the League of Nations Palace of 1927, so near to winning but for the surprising defection of juror Victor Horta. Here acoustical and traffic problems had found masterful technical solutions, but, and more important, these limitations of the practical had been used to enhance the design. One could see also his Geneva apartment house of 1932, the Maison de Verre, a late extension of Jenney's Leiter Building and Sullivan's Carson, Pirie and Scott, especially as to the properties of the skeleton now boldy used for residential instead of commercial purposes. There were the powerful *pilotis* of the Swiss Pavilion at University City of Paris in 1931-1933. On the city planning side the skyscrapers-cum-greenspace of the proposal of Buenos Aires were ready for study.

In Switzerland many of Maillart's bridges were long completed, including the dramatic leap from cliff to cliff of the Salginatobel and the refined thin slabs of the marvelous Schwandback bridge. Karl Moser, too, had completed his magnificent, bald, concreteribbed church of St. Antonius in Basel. The CIAM had been organized at La Sarraz in 1928. In Barcelona after 1929 there was

Mies van der Rohe's German Pavilion whose walls were thin planes of light materials easily rearranged for different spatial effects.

In Amsterdam there was Oud's Café de Unié, in Brno the Tugendhat House of Mies, in Viipuri Aalto's library; in housing there were Siemensstadt, Sundahl, Neubühl.

But when they did see the new European ideas, the leaders of American architecture and the A.I.A. sniffed. They read with approval Mencken's attack of 1931: "If I were building a house tomorrow it would certainly not follow the lines of a dynamo or a steam shovel." Of Le Corbusier's suburb he said that if it were to be built in America it would appropriately be laughed at. "When men really begin to build churches like the Bush Terminal there will be no religion any more, but only Rotary. And when they begin to live in houses as coldly structural as step-ladders they will cease to be men, and become mere rats in cages. . . . To say that the florid chicken-coops of Le Corbusier and company are closer to nature [than the 18th century] is as absurd as to say that tar-paper shacks behind the railroad tracks are closer to nature."

Comparable pronouncements were being made from the lecture platforms of nearly every American architectural school. At M.I.T. a thoroughly mediocre critic-architect compared works of Le Corbusier with a Pacific-class locomotive much to the favor of the latter and then announced that neither was, of course, architecture. But more often the European work was not mentioned at all. Fortunately not all the students were hypnotized. Many had seen or would see Europe with their own eyes. They did not all follow their predecessors to the fountains of Rome. Some went to Viipuri, some to Stockholm, some to Zurich, some to Helsinki. When they came back they listened with less interest to the comments of reactionary critics and were preparing to arouse American architecture from its thirty-year sleep which had dreamed of the importance of business in America but had not imagined an architecture for American life.

12

INDUSTRIAL buildings now re-emphasized the belief that better architecture might promote better business. Some factory designs consciously tried to nurture the team spirit which the Hawthorne Experiment and the work of the industrial sociologist, Elton Mayo, suggested might help to raise output. In 1918 George C. Nimmons, a prominent industrial architect from Chicago, argued that the heads of industry should use improved architecture to keep labor happy. He cited Eastman Kodak, National Cash Register, United Shoe Machinery, Armour, the Shredded Wheat Company, and did not leave out Sears, Roebuck and Company for whom he and his partner, Will Fellows, had designed a plant that year. In this plant the plan had been influenced quite as much by the welfare program as by the production flow diagram.

An even earlier example was the "campus" built for the National Electric Lamp Association at Cleveland in 1914. Abandoning inefficient buildings in downtown Cleveland, the company located its new plant twelve miles east of the city center on forty acres of wooded, hilly land, readily accessible by trolley or automobile. There the architects, Wallis and Goodwillie, laid out what was called "a university of industry." It contained two quadrangles formed by two-and four-storied buildings devoted to administration and research for the plants, scattered all over the country. The architecture was in true imitation of the university, an inappropriate late Georgian, sufficiently pleasing to prompt Montgomery Schuyler to write that it added to the character of the institution but was yet businesslike in its convenience, concluding from this scene of cooperative industry that " 'big business' may be not only a very big, but a very beneficent thing." The *Architectural Record* of 1914 thought that Nela Park represented a new era that "Business men are beginning to recognize the financial value of good architecture."

The efficiency studies of Taylor and the traffic diagrams and flow sheets that were the trademark of the industrial engineer made an even more convincing case. In 1914 George M. Price published his influential book, *The Modern Factory*. It suggested standards for lighting, acoustics and ventilation, proposed standard layouts for various production schemes. But such studies tended to glorify the engineer. Matters of aesthetic form were either ignored or discussed only as products of functionalism. Following such theory the Austin Company and other engineering firms such as Stone and Webster built efficient factories whose functional approach occasionally yielded handsome forms like that of the Conowingo Dam and Hydro-Electric Plant on the Susquehanna River of 1926-1928.

This dominance of the engineer was not overlooked by industrial architects, who lost no time in exhorting their fellows to wake up. In the *Architectural Review* (U.S.) for October 1915, Frank E. Wallis asked, "Is architecture a live art or only a pedantic profession?" He reviewed a list of important industrial buildings in Berlin, Strasbourg, Bremen, and Dresden; their merits persuaded him that American architects were backward: "If we had . . . made our architecture publicly *accepted* as a live art, the dickie fronts, the raw and unsightly brick back-sides and the tank sky-lines of New York would never have been perpetrated." Wallis contrasted pairs of buildings to show that the engineers' solutions had been inferior to the architects'. He praised the Storehouse for the Hoyt Company at Chicago by Nimmons and Fellows and the Continental Motor Car Factory at Detroit by Albert Kahn and Ernest Wilby: "To-day America is a great manufacturing nation . . . The use of Fine Arts in the market-place, in the slaughter-houses, and in the shoe factories, where steel beams are rolled and where vegetables are canned, is necessary and financially important."

The field of industrial architecture now enlisted a number of able men who continued to be led by Albert Kahn. They created buildings like Frank D. Chase's Wilder Tanning Company at Waukegan, Illinois, a simple and open expression of reinforced concrete construction. Kahn produced a handsome and expressive modification of this structural system by recessing the spandrels and carrying the piers upwards to support low arches in the Burroughs Adding Machine Building. These American builders seldom used concrete plastically, seldom realized the continuous curves that the contemporary Maillart was molding. There was

some development of the rigid bent frame in automobile factories
and reinforced concrete mushroom columns were sometimes used
to support continuous concrete floor slabs as in the Metropolitan
Printing Plant of 1922 at Long Island City. But Americans felt
more at home with linear structures based on grid frames whether
the frames were of wood, steel or concrete. The modules of such
frames yielded rhythms that they liked, such as those of Kahn's
Woolen Mills at Mishawaka, Indiana; and they liked the effect of
clothing the frames in brick to provide a foil of color and texture
against the mullioned glass, as in the Lakeside Press Building
(later R. R. Donnelley and Sons) in Chicago.

The American industrial architect was at his best when he
worked with steel, gaining relief by the forms of the columns and
girders as Alfred S. Alschuler did in Chicago's A. Stein and Company Building. One of the best examples was a building of about
1930 designed by Joseph Leland for the Pressed Steel Company at
Worcester, Massachusetts. It was a prism of steel and glass,
strong and clean, bent to form courtyards. The laminated steel
columns were enriched only by their flanges and the exposed
rivets; the girders carrying the second floor were marked by spandrels containing a floral pattern in iron. Large panels of glass set
into the structural frame revealed the floor levels, staircases, and
radiators with a directness quite as modern as the Bauhaus of
1926. Many years later Leland confessed that he had not thought
of this fine building as architecture.

"Top" architects seldom undertook industrial architecture and
were still less often successful. One exception was achieved by
Cass Gilbert, the architect of the Woolworth Building and the
United States Supreme Court Building at Washington, when he
designed the United States Army Supply Base at Brooklyn. The
Supply Base showed how sensitive this man could be when he was
working without historical presuppositions. The buildings were
great gray masses, all one color, all one tone, yet the concrete was
modulated by sun and shade, and the simple outlines and surfaces
were broken by salients of fire towers, elevator shafts and utilitarian openings. The texture was simple, lacking, as Gilbert once
wrote, any "trickets and gegaws and patterns and . . . fictitious corbels. . . . The logic forbids such intrusions." He was

justifiably proud of this work but could not imagine a comparable approach to the architectural problem of the Supreme Court or the Minnesota State Capitol.

Albert Kahn was now at the height of his powers, world-famous, commissioned for work in many parts of the world including an enormous task in the Soviet Union. His various small plants like the one for the Ford Motor Company at St. Paul were exemplary arrangements of elements needed for production or display. The main plant at River Rouge, Michigan, begun in 1917, masterfully assembled complex production facilities, grouped so effectively that it enticed photographers like Margaret Bourke-White and painters like Charles Sheeler to record the dramatic vistas of cranes, drive wheels, walls and chimneys. Kahn carried some of this directness and vigor into the administration buildings and research laboratories at Dearborn, Michigan, although the tendency for display here overcame his engineering skill, and he fell victim to the prevailing commercial habit of clothing the industrial firm in classic dress as soon as it was to meet the public. And the minute he tried what he felt to be "more important buildings," he remained a victim of the notion of hierarchy expressed through style and his skill fell away.

Some concerns began attempts to develop an individually identifying corporate iconography. The Richfield Oil Company built a series of gasoline stations basically similar in form and color, each flanked by a tall steel pylon, as a kind of line of beacons guiding men across the deserts of the West. Sears, Roebuck, using its own architects, Nimmons and Fellows, strove for telling and identifiable silhouettes to characterize their buildings throughout the land. So did Montgomery-Ward. Such iconographic architecture was a new application in advertising terms of the notion of appropriateness which had so long affected church and college architecture. Later it played a part in gaining acceptance for the cubistic architecture of the late '20s and early '30s, when it was adopted by such national companies as those of the Bell Telephone System. Thus throughout the land corporate architecture was tending to transcend regional considerations.

Still the tall office building mounted to its zenith. It seemed to

offer the most exciting problem on the American architect's draft-
ing board, the telling sign of a society whose business was business. Solutions changed over the twenty-year period, moving all
the way from McKim's classicism to the relative modernism of
Raymond Hood's McGraw-Hill Building and Rockefeller Center.
All designers felt excitement in the skyline of New York, all were
able to reconcile their aesthetic sentiments with business. You
will not find in their writing any doubts about the efficiency or
the necessity for the concentrations. You will find no deeper philosophy underlying design than that our constructions would
demonstrate Americans to have been "a people of wonderful engineering knowledge and commercial enterprise." Even the ablest
of these designers, Raymond Hood, moved from one traditionalist style to another and so on to traditional modern without for-
mulating a personal philosophy of design that could be compared
with Sullivan's or Wright's. In 1927 he admitted he was as much
in the air about style as everything else and that if he had been
interested in Chinese pagodas at the time he was designing the
Chicago Tribune Tower or the American Radiator Building they
might perfectly well have come out as horizontal compositions.

One does not have to search far to see that big business offered
architects a compelling objective. The skyscraper architects proclaimed their clients' prestige through height, through peculiari-
ties of form, through color, by dramatic night illumination.
Searchlights hidden in the setbacks of the tall towers dramatized
the buildings at night, maintaining the drama of the evening in
April 1913 when President Wilson threw a switch in the White
House to turn on 80,000 lamps in the gleaming new Woolworth
Tower in New York.

"A style is developed," as Hood said, "by copying and repetition, both destructive to creation and maximum usefulness,
which is essential to building." It also depends upon slow refinement through experience. The demands for advertising originality
deterred the architects from working out a consistent "classic"
form for the skyscraper. As long as each building was supposed to
have a unique shape, as long as its usefulness was identified with
display and prestige, novelty would have a higher value than re-

finement; commerce was placed above art with almost the same reverence as that with which the builder of Chartres placed God above his own aesthetic impulses, if they were in conflict.

By 1913 Sullivan's structural realism was almost forgotten; when he died in 1924 Fiske Kimball had to recall for readers of the *Architectural Record* the contribution "the old master" had made. Only an occasional work like Severance and Van Alen's Bainbridge Building of 1924 remained true to the structural frame. A much more common treatment provided a column arranged with base, plinth, and capital. McKim's Municipal Building set the fashion for classic appliqué; Le Brun's Metropolitan Building of 1913 had shown how to stack a ladder of Renaissance loggias. Charles Platt tried to obtain a massive and unified business block by inflating the Renaissance Strozzi Palace to create the "princely" Hanna and Leader News Buildings at Cleveland in 1922. Benjamin Morris's Cunard Building of 1921 was another classic column; while in 1924 for New York's American Telephone and Telegraph Building, Welles Bosworth piled eight tiers of Ionic upon a Doric hypostyle hall complete with a frieze of triglyphs and metopes carried on thirty-foot Doric columns!

The classic formula for the skyscraper was ridiculous when sequences of twenty or more plain stories were capped by cornices, temples or domes. Nevertheless its only serious rival was also archeological, emphasizing the verticality of the tall buildings and capping the towers with Gothic buttresses and Gothic ornament. The Woolworth Tower had set this fashion; it was succeeded in 1917 by the equally interesing and simpler Bush Terminal Tower Building, in midtown Manhattan, designed by Harvey Wiley Corbett. This tower gained impressiveness through its isolated position and its vertical expression of the frame. Piers were distinguished from mullions, while the general character of the detail was late Gothic. Since the tower could not be protected from future buildings that might be raised alongside it, the side elevations did not contain the shadow-producing voids and ornamental relief of the front and back. Instead the ornamental work was simulated in brick most of which was buff with white used for highlights and black for shadows. The device revealed the growing concern that the tower should be seen as a whole and from all sides, not merely as a facing for a loft building. It rose steadily without breaks until the top receded in several slight setbacks, suggesting a small chapel, the plinth being modified first to a large octagon and then to a small one terminated by copper finials. The setback was used here merely as a means for achieving a positive termination and perhaps for effective night lighting.

A different envelope appeared in a striking but isolated building at San Francisco, the Hallidie Building of 1918. There Willis Polk produced a fine if uncharacteristic façade extending the theme of Beman's Studebaker Building in Chicago and with more restraint and skill. The frame of the building carried cantilever floors so there were no columns at the exterior wall; this permitted him to hang an entire glass façade divided into well-scaled panels against which he played brilliantly detailed balconies and fire escapes. A few other glass-walled buildings, such as the more capricious Boley Building built in Kansas City in 1909 by Louis Curtis, had explored this motif of a transparent glass wall enclosing an entire structure, but it had never been done before with such finish. The interesting lead was largely ignored by American architects of the period, however, as were the contemporary examples in Europe, and the message of the Hallidie Building was not really heeded until the middle of the twentieth century when a large photograph of it adorned the halls of Harvard's Graduate School of Design and appeared also in many other schools, now wrapped in the mantle of prophecy.

Whatever possibilities lay in transparency and a revealed frame were overwhelmed by the much-heralded Chicago Tribune Competition of 1922. Drawings came from all over the world and they remain interesting on many counts, including the light they throw on what foreigners thought skyscrapers and Americans were like. A few of the submissions did not take the competition seriously. Some submitted lampoons such as one of an elongated Doric column, or another a skyscraper grown into the form of an Indian wearing a full ceremonial war bonnet. And of the 281 drawings which reached the final jury the majority were still unintentionally ridiculous by any architectural standard. The Italians and the British seem entirely to have missed the point. Their elaborately festooned drawings were filled with heavy classic and baroque detail; one even took the *Tribune* publicity seriously and multiplied the Doge's Palace indefinitely. The entry submitted by Gropius and Meyer from Germany was a stiff and logical expression of the tall frame. It showed much of what Gropius had done earlier at Fagus and would do later at Dessau. The basic skeleton was clear, the fenestration orderly, using the "Chicago" window as a kind of vertically-disposed reminiscence of Carson, Pirie and Scott. The occasional projecting slabs seemed less orderly, the project was quite clearly unfinished and even insensitive, a misreading of America. But even if it had been in the best vein of the matured master, it could hardly have prevailed in McCormick's Chicago of 1922. The resemblance to Chicago of the '90s would have been repudiated, if noticed, since anything less romantic, less Gothic, than Eliel Saarinen's tower could not be entertained by the prevailing taste.

Of all the collective foreign entries, those from Holland offered most promise; one entered by Bijvoet and Duiker from Zandvoort was a highly advanced composition of long thin planes cantilevered the whole length of ladder-like bays. American architects did not present anything as good. Sullivan and Wright did not enter; their absence was only faintly compensated for by the entry submitted by Walter Burley Griffin, a former pupil of Wright. In the first two stages of the competition the chauvinistic jury awarded all three top prizes to Americans, and the newspaper proudly boasted that the judgment acknowledged the undisputed superiority of American design. Meanwhile an entry from Finland, the work of Eliel Saarinen, belatedly cleared customs and was rushed into the final stage of the competition. In the last vote, that entry stood beside the design of Hood and Howells, and the jury awarded the Americans the first and the Finn the second prize.

The winning design was built in Chicago by 1925; until diminished by the proximity of other buildings it was the ephemerally impressive landmark of the *Tribune*, though totally retrogressive as a work of architecture. Wright and Sullivan and Root and Jenney might as well have never lived and worked in Chicago. Despite its vertical emphasis, despite its search for light offices, the whole thing was a fraudulent stage set. The unnecessary Gothic tracery ended in colossal and meaningless flying buttresses. The door was the portal to a cathedral. Hood was as pleased as the owners; in 1929 he wrote to praise his buttresses, and the architectural effect of the whole, and insisted that the whole structure "soared magnificently into space."

Others were far less sure about the forty-foot decorative buttresses. They criticized the Gothicism as totally alien to American soil and having less than nothing to do with the structure it covered, much less the activities of the newspaper it housed. They preferred the second-prize Finnish design by Eliel Saarinen, whose tower played freely with the steel skeleton beneath the piers and spandrels; the whole envelope rose with discreet setbacks, each terminated by the jagged silhouette of pier tops, bracketing the sculpture carved above the spandrels, an elaboration of a manner he had learned from the Scottish architect Mackintosh and developed on the railroad station at Helsinki. Perceptive American critics openly suggested that the jury had erred in not awarding the first prize to Saarinen. The most fervid admirer was Louis Sullivan who wanted to reverse the verdict of the jury: "confronted by the limpid eye of analysis, the first prize trembles and falls, self-confessed, crumbling to the ground. Visibly it is not architecture . . . Its formula is literary . . . It could be but as a foundling at the doorstep of the Finn." Architectural students in the schools of the day generally agreed. Saarinen's losing design drew so much attention to his talent that he was soon brought to Detroit to build the Cranbrook School, to direct it and to live out his life as an American architect who added much to the texture of the American scene, through his own buildings and especially through the young men trained at his school such as Harry Weese, Charles Eames, Edward Bacon and his own son and later partner, Eero.

The prize winner in the Chicago competition at least set one standard; the classic formula for skyscraper design would be discarded. Leon Solon, writing in 1924, recorded its passing, "We are about to bid a glad farewell to the standard formula for the skyscraper design, with its Graeco-Roman or Byzantine feet, its geometrically punctured torso, and its Renaissance topgear." But the replacement was a spate of minor Woolworths and Tribunes as the tall building took its motif from the perpendicular pier; Cross and Cross designed a Gothic tower fifty stories high for 570 Lexington Avenue, New York, in 1930; Day and Klauder appropriated the commercial form for the Cathedral of Learning at the University of Pittsburgh in 1924-1925.

Meanwhile leading architects, having abandoned the classic formula as well as the earlier Chicago functionalism, set out on a search for cubistic masses handled simply. It led them to the tower of setback blocks, the "ziggurats" that Wright scorned. The form was the result of a marriage of aesthetic style and legal restrictions, of cubism and zoning. Painters like the early Georgia O'Keeffe and John Marin and Charles Sheeler began to represent the towers of Manhattan as large soaring masses, boldly simple in silhouette, a vision Hugh Ferriss often published in Sunday supplements. Somewhat later these imagined multi-blocks appeared in actual buildings.

But the form was also a response to legal restrictions. Before 1916 John M. Carrère had drawn a scheme in which New York buildings would be held within the limits of a plane passed from the opposite sidewalk at an angle of twenty degrees from the vertical. The New York law of 1916 zoned skyscrapers to maximum envelopes that were supposed to let light down into the streets. By 1922, a series of studies had revealed that it would be possible to have rentable well-lighted offices on the top floors only by reducing the width of the building at the upper levels where banks of elevators had been dropped off and the central core correspondingly diminished. This relationship between the elevator system and the setback tower, existing even in free-standing buildings, reinforced the aesthetic origins of such designs as that of the Heckscher Building created by Warren and Wetmore on upper Fifth Avenue in 1921. Setbacks frankly acknowledged the prevailing opinion that offices more than thirty feet deep were unrentable; the offices clung to the perimeter of the elevator core.

This new tower form was proposed in a number of graphic studies. Of these the most influential were published by Corbett in *Pencil Points* of 1923. He visualized a tall tower, of indefinite verticality, with tall pyramids clustered about its base. This preliminary diagram was uneconomic since the pyramids dropped some floor area at each story. More advanced diagrams grouped the fall-offs in packages, leaving a central tower that rose inside lower, cliff-like blocks. Corbett himself failed to recognize the aesthetic power of his block diagrams but decorated the envelope with rectangular and circular temples of Greek and Roman origin.

Corbett's study might have attracted less attention had it not included a drawing by Hugh Ferriss. This showed a city of cliff-like towers. Cut off sharply at each setback, the buildings were cubical shapes, with grids of windows placed flush with the piers and spandrels. Ferriss's towering black mass made the skyscraper better and it made the skyscraper city seem not only plausible but exciting. The drawing became the touchstone for a new vision of the commercial skyscraper.

For a while the idea remained only a sketch while architects decorated the setback forms with colorful detail. A good example of the tendency was Hood's American Radiator Building of 1924-1925, a soft black mass with windows blended into the walls, beveled corners and vertical piers crowned by golden decoration. It was described as "one huge cinder, incandescent at the terminals." A retrogression from the simplicity of form predicted in Ferriss's sketch, it was the natural consequence of an advertiser's insistence that the skyscraper be readily identified by the florid character of its summit. Seen from Bryant Park in New York, Hood's example is still effective but the same doctrine led unerringly to monstrosities in less competent hands, the cluttered Paramount Building in New York with its capping glass sphere, the ribbed crest of Sloan and Robertson's Chanin Building.

The commercial spirit led architects to crown their setback towers with distinctive forms often inspired by the ornament and furnishings which had been shown at the Paris Exposition of 1925. Some were curvilinear simplifications of the Art Nouveau work of Horta and Guimard, made suave by machined precision, as in the stainless steel spire on the 1030-foot Chrysler Building at New York designed by Van Alen. The RCA Building by Cross and Cross was a surrealist stage set of cubistic forms intertwined with tracery, pyramids and lightning-shaped spires. A more rectilinear version of Art Nouveau appeared in the zigzags, chevrons, and cubistic forms of the Union Guardian Building at Detroit. One of the best of such efforts was the Barclay-Vesey or Telephone Building at 140 West Street in New York, completed in 1926, for which Ralph Walker received a Gold Medal from the Architectural League of New York and praise from Lewis Mumford. The decoration was no less superficially applied to the structure than the older Gothic and classic details had been, but it bore the imprint of a non-archeological search for an ornament compatible with the tall building's cubistic form.

By 1926 everyone in America except Wright agreed that the tall building should have a setback silhouette, but there was little further agreement. Some architects continued to insist that the towers carry the mausoleum of Halicarnassus as they did on the Los Angeles City Hall, or a Roman temple such as sat on top of the National City Bank at New York. Some labored for regional interpretations of ornament like the curiously contrived San Francisco Telephone Building of 1926 where Miller, Pflueger and Cantin ended the tiers of spandrels with ornaments based on campaniform flowers and made the entrance an effulgence of Chinese bracketing systems, moldings and screens. Still others carried forward the suggestions of anthropomorphically terminated pilasters that Saarinen had made in the Chicago *Tribune* competition. One of the best of these was Holabird and Root's building at 333 North Michigan Avenue, whose tower, set on a thick slab, had vertical piers capped by figures at the edges and terminals of the setbacks, and this idea, culminating in Goodhue's Nebraska State Capitol, was particularly popular in the West.

It is paradoxical that the search for archeological ornament led in the end to an elimination of all ornament. About 1925 Alfred C. Bossom, an English engineer who was working in the United States, advocated the pyramidal form for New York's skyscrapers, as others had before him. He called the 230-foot pyramid at Tikal, Guatemala, "the original American Skyscraper," and he proposed a 35-story modern building with a similar form and decoration. The idea was reinforced by current Mayan archeology and it intrigued many. Robert Stacy-Judd, writing in the *Architect and Engineer* in 1933, saw in it the long-awaited "All-Ameri-

can Architecture with Ancient Maya Motifs as a background."
Mayan forms had long impressed other American architects, notably Wright whose warehouse at Richland Center, Wisconsin,
and handsome textile-block houses in Pasadena looked as though
they owed something to Mayan inspiration. But the new grasp on
Mayan was directed to the details and not to the forms as Bossom
had suggested. The Sears Roebuck Store at Los Angeles of 1926
and the Telephone Office at Houston, Texas, carried Mayan ornament. An important building of the "Mayan Revival" was the
one at 450 Sutter Street, San Francisco, built in 1929-1930 by
Timothy L. Pflueger. It was a massive shaft twenty-five stories
tall, with rounded corners and vertical piers. It loomed above the
business district. It had modern notes, a thousand-car garage,
broad windows flush with the walls to give a decidedly horizontal
effect; but the ornament at the entrance and on the tower, convincing as it is, was Mayan and Aztec.

Designers soon looked beyond the decorative side of Central
American architecture into its massive contours. The interest in
cubistic forms led them to revalue the Pueblo architecture of the
Southwest. Even modernists described Pueblo buildings as America's first examples of cubism; the comparison impressed the
Austrian modernist Richard J. Neutra and in his book *Amerika*,
published at Vienna in 1930, he displayed photographs of Pueblo
architecture placed adjacent to modern skyscrapers, factories, and
industrial products. Thus an interest in eclecticism and archeology joined momentarily with a modern taste for cubism.

About 1927 the office building became a cliff-like block of cubistic forms, massive, almost monolithic, the windows alone giving relief to wall surfaces. Even the windows were played down,
the piers were broad vertical bands, and solid stone covered much
of the space which the Tacoma and other early skyscrapers had
given to glass. There were no belt courses; all divisions were accomplished by major setbacks and projections; decorative elaboration was left to movie houses and cheap theaters. The new fashion appeared in Chicago's Palmolive Building and the Daily
News Building of 1928, both the work of Holabird and Root, and
New York saw a cubistic form at 120 Wall Street, the work of Ely
Jacques Kahn, who wrote, "The beauty of a plain surface, re-

lieved in whatever way the artist may desire, is the ideal." The
mood prevailed even among traditionalists like Coolidge, Shepley,
Bulfinch and Abbott when they designed the cliff-like New York
Hospital. Ralph Walker's Irving Trust at 1 Wall Street was a
clear reflection of the new fashion. The same spirit moved the
facile Raymond Hood and, as always, Hood created one of the
best examples of the new mode, the Daily News Building in New
York City. There a great mass was reduced to what then seemed
an ultimate simplicity. A bold silhouette of setbacks and piers,
shaped as tall thin slabs, emphasized the verticality. But at night
it was noticed that the lighted offices revealed horizontal stripes.

Beginning about 1931 the horizontal dimension became dominant, a clear reversal of Sullivan's verticality, partly derived from
European design. Functionally it was equally defensible. It appeared in New York at the hands of men like Joseph Urban,
whose New School for Social Research had a façade made entirely of horizontal spandrels alternating with continuous strip
windows, a device Wright had used earlier but which had then
been ignored. The façade emphasized the structural function of
the beams, played down the columns. Furthermore the façade
was no longer a solid mass. The broad horizontal windows divided the building into long continuous planes of transparency
and reflection alternating with planes that were opaque. The new
spatial and formal effects led Hood to his handsome McGraw-
Hill Building of 1932. The sheer unornamented prismatic tower
was enriched by the transparency and reflectiveness of the glass
walls and by olive-green bands which alternated with bands of
dark blue in the glazed terra-cotta surfaces. Only a step beyond
this building lay the possibility of an entire curtain wall of glass
carried upon floors cantilevered outward from the columns as had
been suggested by the façade of Polk's Hallidie Building of 1918
(illustrated in the *Architectural Record* of 1931) or by Mies's
charcoal sketch for a glass tower of 1921. About 1930 Hugh Ferriss, too, imagined a skyscraper tower in which glass alone enclosed a series of horizontal planes, the floors. The essential structural and aesthetic principles imagined by all these pioneers
finally found partial realization in the bank and office building of
the Philadelphia Saving Fund Society of 1931. Here the American

George Howe joined the Swiss William Lescaze to create a fine tier of continuous spandrels and continuous windows all cantilevered from the columns which he set well in from the wall.

Now the new characteristic form of the skyscraper became the slab, a term applied to the buildings erected at Rockefeller Center beginning about 1930. The slab form had appeared briefly in the early history of the skyscraper, notably in the Monadnock Building and in Wright's unexecuted design for the San Francisco Press Building. The form did not become at all popular until the late '20s, although Albert Kahn's group of classical office buildings for General Motors Corporation at Detroit suggested it. It remained isolated in works of the late '20s such as the Lincoln Building near Grand Central in New York and the Chicago Daily News Building of 1928. It remained for the architects of Rockefeller Center, notably Harrison, Hood and Fouilhoux, to modernize the slab, to make it thinner in relation to its height, to simplify it and to treat it with characteristic but underemphasized setbacks. The Center's buildings, taken individually, were retrogressive as contrasted to the McGraw-Hill Building; but their form contained a new aesthetic property, the horizontal direction emphasized by the axis of the slab, which became the important element in the grouping of tall buildings around open plazas.

The great slabs of Rockefeller Center paved the way to an important future, offered a new approach to urban planning, seemed to end all the flirtations of the skyscraper with classic, Gothic, Mayan, with elaborate theories of horizontal or vertical structure, with pyramids and setbacks. They opened a gate and it may not be surprising that they caused some dismay although they were not that revolutionary. The New York papers printed angry letters and *Pencil Points* for May 1931 published an article, "The Functionalist Design for Radio City Has Aroused Public Indignation." After Rockefeller Center, American tall buildings would never be the same again. There was a fair chance they would be better.

13

THE urban scene was filled with other large structures. New hotels rose in districts filled with offices, stores, and transportation terminals, hotels like the Commodore at Grand Central Terminal or the 1931 Waldorf-Astoria. Despite their creature comforts, none was distinguished; few were in good taste; some, unfortunately, were monstrously ornate, like the Traymore at Atlantic City of 1918, with its assorted domes, buttresses, vaults, and towers. The Los Angeles Biltmore was characteristic, with its four-story lobby beneath a gambrel roof vaulted and coffered in gold; a huge and ornate balcony stood upon a pair of curved stairs that led to a baroque entrance portico; the building realized the slogans of hotel designers: "Fine motor cars stop at fine entrances," and "Social functions need impressive settings." It was a design exactly like those that were currently winning the best prizes in American architectural schools.

Large town houses were disappearing under the pressures of economics and social change. Herbert Croly noted this in 1925: "New York society has changed much since the days of the old Mrs. Astor. It is no longer necessary for its queens and duchesses to build houses in which four hundred guests can be sumptuously entertained. . . . The only new buildings now being constructed on upper Fifth Avenue are apartment houses."

Whether by Charles Platt or Cross and Cross, the big apartments were reduced to a formula — a stone base with quoined corners, an arched entrance, a brick façade, string courses, and banks of double-hung windows.

John Taylor Boyd actively promoted the garden apartment about 1920, while Clarence Stein and Henry Wright made extensive studies of it in the early '30s, but the tower type enjoyed greater favor because it reserved more land for tennis courts, playgrounds, landscaped areas, gardens and promenades. America's best sample of European apartment modernism was New York's Beaux-Arts Apartments designed by Murchison, Hood, Godley, and Fouilhoux. These modern, glass-filled buildings contained suites of studios and bedrooms arranged on long corridors. The ground floors provided cafeterias and other common or public spaces. The modernity of the buildings was here coupled with retrograde site planning, for they filled the site as tightly as earlier buildings had. Thus they showed that modernism could be as much a cliché of style as any other if it were dissociated from its planning principles.

While the apartment houses and tall commercial structures supported larger urban populations, transportation facilities abetted decentralization. The fringes of all major cities burst the previous boundaries. Roads and bridges were extensively overhauled or created, facilitating automobile transportation, breeding larger bridges like Philadelphia's over the Delaware or New York's George Washington of 1931. Commuting railroads added cars and buildings including important commuters' stations such as Philadelphia's at 30th Street and substantial parts of Chicago's Union Station of 1925 or Cincinnati's of 1933. These usually reflected the classical glory of the railroads' heydays though like those in Chicago and Cleveland by Burnham's successors they were sterile ghostly versions of the greater days. Only the functional plan and dramatic arched form of Cincinnati's Union Station of 1933 by Fellheimer and Wagner suggested that railways might still claim the right to provide the gateway to the city.

By 1929 competitive designs for airports were appearing in the magazines and exploratory building-type studies were published in 1930. But the development was embryonic and the problems were not yet really understood, as the details of air transportation service were also in a state of rapid evolution.

The automobile now began to call for its buildings too and not only garages and bus terminals. During the '20s and '30s Ford and Packard dealers enlisted architects to design impressive showrooms such as Maybeck's grandiose Pompeiian affairs for Packard at Los Angeles and San Francisco. Gasoline companies began building service stations in cities and along highways. These stations started the ill-formed ribbon developments along rural roads and they were quickly followed by tourist camps, wayside refreshment stands, drive-in movies and modest stores. At the end of the period in 1933 architectural magazines had published drawings for suburban shopping centers, and the model town Radburn was being advertised as the town for the motor age.

Even as early as 1924-1925 the problem of urban transportation and congestion was looming large. It had not been solved by the City Beautiful, except in isolated grand boulevards which connected public monuments and squares. Better theoretical schemes had been proposed in Europe from Garnier's *Une Cité Industrielle* of 1901 to the exhibitions at Stuttgart where Le Corbusier, Oud, Gropius and Mies showed apartment houses. Under these proposals high buildings covered only a small portion of available land, large open areas were preserved. Of all the architects who worked on such proposals, Le Corbusier was the most imaginative. In 1920 he proposed an ideal project of tower apartments sixty stories tall, rising to a height of 700 feet, separated by 250 to 300 yards of landscaped parks. A drawing of 1923 showed the towers placed among gardens and playing fields, shielded from main arteries which were freed for rapid traffic. As early as 1915 he had proposed to raise all buildings one story above the ground which would be free for vehicular traffic while pedestrians moved on bridges at a higher level. In 1922 he advanced a plan for a whole park-like city of these tall free-standing business and apartment towers, and he contrasted the city of New York to the city model he proposed. Much of his thinking was broadcast in an important book, *Vers une Architecture*, originally published at Paris in 1923, followed by a translation published in England in 1927. The basic ideas proposed by Le Corbusier gained theoretical acceptance in Europe, and they began to appear in America soon afterward.

In 1923, following the Chicago *Tribune* Competition, Eliel Saarinen made his design for the Chicago lake front embodying some of the new principles of planning; this plan was followed by the Detroit River Project of 1924. His Memorial Plaza set tall buildings in open areas from which traffic was excluded by subways, underground garages, multi-level streets, and walkways. The chief plaza avoided the geometric alignment characteristic of Le Corbusier's city plans, and symmetrically placed buildings afforded dynamic vistas. Those features Saarinen had learned

Washington, D. C., Pan American Union, 1910,
Paul P. Cret and Albert Kelsey, archs.

Washington, D. C., Pan American Union, interior, 1910,
Paul P. Cret and Albert Kelsey, archs.

Worcester, Massachusetts, Worcester
Pressed Steel Company, 1930,
Joseph Leland and Niels Larsen, archs.

PAUL J.

San Francisco, California,
Hallidie Building, 1918,
Willis Jefferson Polk, arch.

MOULIN STUDIOS, S. F.

Washington, D. C., Lincoln Memorial, 1922, Henry Bacon, arch.

GOTTSCHO-SC

New York, St. Thomas' Episcopal Church, 1913,
Bertram Grosvenor Goodhue, arch.

Spring Green, Wisconsin, Taliesin East I, 1911, Frank Lloyd Wright, arch.

Lincoln, Nebraska, Plymouth Congregational Church, 1931, Henry Van Buren Magonigle, with Robert McLaughlin, archs.

Lincoln, Nebraska, State Capitol, buttresses, 1922, Bertram Grosvenor Goodhue, arch., Lee Lawrie, sculptor

Study for Maximum Mass permitted
by 1916 Zoning Law,
by Hugh Ferriss, 1922

FERRISS

New York, McGraw Hill Building,
1931, Raymond Hood, arch.

Chicago, Chicago Tribune Building, 1923-1925, Raymond M. Hood and
John Mead Howells, archs.

from Camillo Sitte's important *Der Städtebau nach seinen Kunstlerischen Grundsatzen* of 1889, and from Hegemann and Peets's *The American Vitruvius: An Architects' Handbook of Civic Art,* published at New York in 1922. Both books described the rich conformations of famous squares developed in Europe over long periods of time, and the authors favored an aesthetically pleasing city, filled with controlled variety, not one standard, not chaos.

Leading designers now began to study the skyscraper as it might be built under ideal conditions. In 1924, Corbett, always an advocate of building tall buildings in dense surroundings, turned out a fairly serious study of traffic flow in relation to skyscrapers. In the *Architectural Forum* of 1927, he proposed that different kinds of transportation be separated on different levels, the rail traffic underground or carried in the air, vehicles on streets, and pedestrians on an elevated level. In this he built upon some of the ideas proposed by Saarinen in his work for Detroit, and he saw in Saarinen's plan "a very modernized Venice, a city of arcades, piazzas and bridges, with canals for streets, only the canals will not be filled with water but with freely flowing motor traffic, the sun glittering on the black tops of the cars and the buildings reflected in this waving flood of rapidly rolling vehicles."

The new scheme for cities appeared in Hugh Ferriss's *The Metropolis of Tomorrow,* published at New York in 1929. The book opened with a dramatic description of the early morning fog lifting from the skyscrapers of New York. A second section of the book offered suggestions about set-back envelopes and overhead traffic ways. The third and final section displayed an imaginary metropolis of free-standing towers: a government center, an art center, a business center, with large intervals between them. In the Science Zone of this metropolis there would be: "Buildings like crystals. Wall of translucent glass. Sheer glass blocks sheathing a steel grill. No Gothic branch: no Acanthus leaf: no recollection of the plant world. A mineral kingdom. Gleaming stalagmites. Forms as cold as ice. Mathematics. Night in the Science Zone."

But even such a singular success as the less spectacular Rocke-

L

feller Center did not stimulate enough practical action in the cities. The plans may not have been well enough known by the electorate and in the centers of decision; perhaps the problem the plans were intended to solve were not yet excruciatingly painful or harmful to the prosperity of business and cities; they would have to become more than unbearable before any individual private interest would be prepared to make any sacrifice in the common good and the common good required sacrifice from all; perhaps the solutions did not really seem more attractive to the users than what they found elsewhere in the city. Until the designs were better understood and the pressures more insistent there could be no legal or economic instruments for guiding cities towards a better form. In their absence the commerial components of cities simply became larger and more centralized, while the arteries leading to them were further congested by *laissez faire*. Despite the disaster that we now know was being prepared it is idle to scold our predecessors. Any different arrangement would have required enormous changes in commercial and commuter habits. Workers *might* be brought to live at their places of business but Continental urban mores had never caught on in America; business might change its attitudes towards land ownership and use; both might in time accept more governmental assistance and control. But most American architects of the day realistically avoided socialistic or dictatorial answers.

The problem remained then one of improving transportation and finding new sites for large apartment buildings. Consequently in 1924 Hood proposed that skyscraper apartments be built upon bridges surrounding Manhattan, an idea recorded in a sketch by Hugh Ferriss which appeared in *Metropolis of Tomorrow*. In 1929 Hood turned up again with an even more radical remedy, a 45-story building covering three city blocks and containing stores, theaters, offices, clubs, hotels, restaurants, and in the floors above the 35th, apartments for workers. He hoped that many such buildings might unite whole industries, housing "a city under a single roof," as he said in *Nation's Business*. But the American businessman preferred his daily jaunt to the city and his wife certainly preferred the country or seemed to. The automobile bridged the distance and the architects, more concerned with aesthetics than with social implications, did not press their ideas to the point of trying to get them executed. True, Lewis Mumford had begun about 1927 to ask whether the skyscraper was tolerable and to suggest that legislation was required to make it respond to social needs, but the architects Hood and Corbett did not seem disposed to share such liberal social beliefs, while Mumford's writing was more effective as criticism than as suggesting workable remedies. Moreover, most of the discussion centered on the urban residential problems of families of high income.

Nevertheless the period saw a few noteworthy advances in low-cost housing and community planning, including Goodyear Heights at Akron, Ohio, a garden city built by a private company. The war promoted industrial housing, and Lawrence Veiller, an authority on housing legislation, prepared the framework for governmental standards. The principal achievement was to set some low-cost houses in healthy surroundings. George B. Post and Sons planned Eclipse Park at Beloit, Wisconsin, while Sawyer Park at Williamsport, Pennsylvania, and a colony at Erwin, Tennessee, were also the work of architects. One of the best was Indian Hill, an industrial village at Worcester, Massachusetts, designed by Grosvenor Atterbury.

Development slackened after the war but now American architectural magazines began to publish German and Scandinavian work, notably the Danish housing schemes by Kay Fisker. The American designers Kocher and Ziegler proposed sunlight towers, and Duhrie, Okie and Ziegler developed a neighborhood of ingeniously planned quadruple houses at Chestnut Hill, Philadelphia. At Sunnyside Gardens, Long Island, in 1929 Clarence Stein and Henry Wright provided *cul-de-sac* groups of houses running through from street to street but facing toward the restricted part of the community. Their work culminated in Radburn, New Jersey, a town laid out by the City Housing Corporation, where *cul-de-sac* streets were separated from pedestrian ways on which the houses faced. Here Stein and Wright went far in the direction of providing a new social pattern for their town but the architect of the houses, Frederick Lee Ackerman, designed traditional buildings. At that point the social objectives of the planners had not yet been associated with modern architectural form.

It was a strange dichotomy. Architects like Hood and Howe who brought something of the modern European style into American work ignored the social ideas that had been associated with the style in Europe, did not change their social orientation when they changed their architectural costume. Indeed they probably enjoyed the superficial aspects of the new forms while deploring the social and economic penumbra that European theorists like Le Corbusier and Gropius cast around the new architecture. There were too many overtones of collectivism in the writings of men like Bruno Taut, for example, and those ideas, however necessary to the new European city planning, must have been anathema to most American architects of the day. Thus Taut's book, *Modern Architecture*, published at London in 1929, could not fail to raise hackles on those architects who glorified *laissez-faire* prosperity even if its obvious Marxism was less distressing to men of 1929 than it was to men of 1959. Taut was an avid proponent of functional architecture. "Everything that functions well," he said, "*looks* well." From aesthetics he moved to morality: "If everything is founded on sound efficiency . . . its utility will form its own aesthetic law . . . The architect who achieves this task becomes a creator of an ethical and social character . . . Thus architecture becomes the creator of new social observances." Unlike Hood, Taut strained to ally the new aesthetic with a social mission.

He applauded the communal organization he saw in city planning in Holland: "the miracle actually did come to pass, i.e., the creation of a collective architecture, in which it was no longer the individual house that was of special importance but the whole long row of houses in a series of streets." He thought comprehensive unity was possible, under such collectivism, even when the buildings were made by different architects.

Such social theories, held by many other influential European architects of the day, implied a responsibility to society and to the architectural profession and perhaps a view of the economic order to which American designers did not often subscribe. It was not merely that Corbett or Hood used their facile pens in praise of commercial advertising. It was a more profound question of philosophy. Underlying the eclecticism, for example, of Ely Jacques

Kahn and most others was the belief that style was no more than a superficial coating, intended to please without any relation to social objectives, and that modern designs could be adopted quite as readily as Greek or medieval or Renaissance. Such formalism was confirmed by Geoffrey Scott's *Architecture of Humanism* of 1914 which asserted that the aim of architecture has nothing whatever to do with expression of structure, use, function or morality. Its aim was solely to create pleasing forms and it was valuable only because the forms were pleasing. Scott totally disavowed the idea that social objectives were fundamental to style. His perfect formulation of art-for-art's-sake in design appealed enormously to most of the leading American designers of the day.

Indeed men who liked to build great suburban houses and skyscrapers were unlikely to heed any socialist attacks on individualism. Harrie T. Lindeberg, the famous maker of suburban villas, would have thought Taut was silly to say: "The small individual house, built in accordance with the wishes of an individual man or woman is . . . indicative of . . . the delirium of individualism . . . Only by its collection in a co-operative sense can it avoid the dreary schematism of international trash." Goodhue could hardly quicken upon learning from Taut that "Neither the Church, nor Autocracy, nor Feudalism can be regarded as style-forming factors . . . Neither cathedrals nor castles lead the building profession to-day. The fact that such edifices are still being built cannot disprove the fact that they have relinquished leadership." Nor could Corbett, Hood, Gilbert, or Wright accept the equalitarian dogma of Taut: "Leadership has been transferred to other hands. To the hands of those who erect buildings, produce building materials, manufacturing them from raw materials, extracting them from pit or mine, and working them up in factories; to the hands of those responsible for installation and transport, to those who can, in short, produce everything that everybody needs." At this particular point in their history the thoughts of Gropius and Le Corbusier were not different although Taut went farthest and wrote the most. Reading him and seeing the housing in Europe, industrialists and their architects could hardly escape the conclusion that modernists might be harboring treasonable thoughts and thinking of other revolutions than architectural revolution; so modernism came into some bad odor. Wright labeled the "International Style," "socialistic." Others used even more damaging adjectives.

Similar social theories became more pointed after the depression. Meanwhile city planning remained formal without regard to centralization, traffic congestion, or legal, economic and social bases for better city plans. In 1929 American cities had 377 skyscrapers more than twenty stories high. Of that number 188 were in New York City and fifteen of them were over 500 feet tall. Yet until Rockefeller Center was built no city had provided an example of how a skyscraper might be made to define handsome sequences of urban space, nor was there any significant development of new patterns for pedestrian traffic or shopping centers.

14

THE new fairs had nothing new to contribute either. The Panama-Pacific Exposition at San Francisco in 1915 clearly elaborated the City Beautiful plan with its long axis leading to the Court of the Universe, terminated by the Art Palace and Machinery Palace, both classical; bordered by domed buildings and confusedly eclectic offerings like Mullgardt's Tower in the Court of Abundance. Maybeck's Fine Arts Palace was fatuous Piranesi in full color, and, like the fair, offered nothing to the knowledge of urban forms. San Diego was if anything even less instructive. It attempted to embody the romance of a high Spanish civilization that had never been, "to build such a city as would have fulfilled the visions of Fray Junipero Serra as he toiled and dreamed while he planted missions from San Diego to Monterey." Such a theory ignored the historical fact of Serra's modesty but it appealed to Cram and Ferguson as they stated it in the California State Building's torrid Spanish baroque entrance and towers. Bertram Grosvenor Goodhue, the supervisory architect for the Exposition, outdid even the exuberant Balvanera Chapel in Mexico City in his Commerce and Industries Building, and he covered the grounds with polychrome domes which he took with him to most of the permanent architecture he built thereafter. Most of these buildings have been preserved and they contribute today the attractive fairy tale of Balboa Park, sitting above San Diego, but the buildings taught architects nothing valuable, nor did the grounds make any suggestions as to how a city might solve its modern problems.

Thus the City Beautiful movement persisted even though it had become a formal abstraction quite unrelated to the political and social problems of the cities to which it was applied. San Francisco and Philadelphia and Cleveland continued to work on their civic and cultural centers. Their monumental schemes inspired Denver to a reawakened interest in the inappropriate improvement scheme Charles Mulford Robinson, the City Beautiful exponent, had made about 1904.

In Cleveland hopes were high for developing the first natural American cultural grouping but rivalries among the institutions and failures to relate the new scheme to a comprehensive economic and social plan for the whole neighborhood and city led only to chaos. By 1938 University Circle was a seriously blighted area.

Realistic city planning barely appeared in this time. Planners needed first to know more about society and its operation. The knowledge was long in coming. In 1929 Pitirim Sorokin's *Principles of Rural-Urban Sociology* still described a clear-cut distinction between city and country that was nullified by the intrusions of city into suburb. Adna F. Weber's classic *The Growth of Cities in the Nineteenth Century*, published in 1899, had looked towards rapid transit and the rise of suburbs as the amelioration of city evils resulting from overcrowding. The process was actually going on in the period 1913-1933, but the transportation system and the suburb somehow never managed to lessen overcrowding in the cities themselves. It was obvious that the planners were working with an unrealistic social unit. About 1920, two new units were defined on the basis of economics, geography and sociology. One was the comprehensive unit, the region, which grew out of studies by geographers, introduced into sociology by Warren H. Wilson about 1920. One real experiment in operative regionalism, the TVA, was established by Congress in 1933. The second unit was the neighborhood, which Clarence A. Perry made the basis for city planning in a study published in 1929. The neighborhood was not an aesthetic purely formal unit, as it had been with the City Beautiful planners. It was a cohesive pattern determined by business habits, topography, physical barriers, street plans, transportation systems, locations of schools, churches, community organizations, social clubs and political districts. The determinants frequently existed within well-defined physical boundaries, as was shown by a study of neighborhoods in Chicago of 1929, which reached the conclusion that "In the planning of a neighborhood unit . . . boundaries . . . physical limits enable the public to see a local community as . . . a distinct entity."

The new determinants provided planners with sociological, economic and legal tools for guiding the growth of cities. Many designers still ignored them for the purely formal schemes of Ferriss or Hood or Corbett. But Lawrence Veiller and the National Housing Association attempted to place sociological foundations under their work. Robert Moses in New York City organized powerful administrative and legal means for public works projects and for preparing vast recreation areas like Jones Beach. Men like Mumford insisted that *laissez-faire* skyscraper development, suburb and City Beautiful movements would not alone produce healthy and happy urban environments. The most effective new planners, Henry Wright and Clarence Stein, followed Sunnyside and Radburn with the still distinguished Chatham Village at Pittsburgh. But these were not the areas where many architects had any interest, nor did many of the leaders find it interesting to provide architecture for social settlement houses or YMCAs.

15

THE suburban house commanded more attention. Upper-class suburbs, on winding tree-shaded drives leading outward from nuclei of stores and churches, schools and municipal buildings, contained few if any industries or businesses; each was essentially an expensive dormitory. It protected its appearance with legislation aimed at preserving conformity in building height, land use, architectural style, and racial use. The Georgian house set on a broad lawn became the characteristic image of residential Amer-

ica and the lawn was as important as the building. It was in this
period 1913-1933 that many of the famous and fancy American
upper-middle-class suburbs were developed: Shaker Heights, Lake
Forest, the Main Line, Glen Head, Chestnut Hill, Tuxedo,
Grosse Pointe.

The emblematic building of the upper-class suburb became the
country club, to which the *Architectural Forum* devoted whole
issues in 1925 and 1930. The architecture often resembled that of
a stately country house of the ante-bellum South, like Guy Lowell's Piping Rock Country Club at Locust Valley, Long Island.
Such buildings were seldom imaginative or significant architecturally, and while Albert Kahn might design the Detroit Golf
Club and Robert Kohn the Sunningdale at Scarsdale, the country
club set seldom had any desire to employ an artist like Wright.

Behind the country club, comfortable, even pretty houses were
produced in French classic, in picturesque Gothic, in half-
timbered English, in Cotswold stone, in Williamsburg Georgian.
Some architects like Frank Forster specialized in a particular style
such as Tudor, but others could summon at will any costume to
fit a client-customer.

Of all the protean designers Harrie T. Lindeberg was the most
popular and versatile. At Lake Minnetonka, Minnesota, he provided an Elizabethan house for John S. Pillsbury; Duncan Harris's house at South Norwalk, Connecticut, was rustic rural; H. L.
Batterman at Locust Valley, Long Island, wanted Roman Doric,
while a slate-roofed Tudor housed Eugene du Pont at Greenville,
Delaware; the dwelling for Nelson Doubleday at Oyster Bay,
Long Island, was red-tiled Spanish Colonial, and Clyde Carr had
a half-timbered dovecote at Lake Forest, Illinois. No two designs
were alike, and though he tended to favor picturesque thatched-
shingled roofs, Lindeberg was accurately praised for his "freedom
from formula." He even put many of these together in the new
Houston suburb of River Oaks.

For smaller houses domestic regionalism was durable, even self-
consciously defiant against the universalizing technology, mass
production, communication, and advertising. By 1927 A. Lawrence Kocher, editor of the *Architectural Record*, thought he had
discerned three principal regional styles, the adobe house of the

L*

Southwest, the California ranch house and the Pennsylvania farm-house. There were actually many more: for example, the Mediterranean Renaissance which was locally popular in Florida. There Addison Mizner built the J. S. Phipps house at Palm Beach in 1922, a lesser version of the greatest Florida villa, Vizcaya, the estate of James Deering, which had been designed by J. Burall Hoffman and Paul Chalfin in 1916. Vizcaya was a Spanish-Italian Renaissance-baroque ensemble of terraces, fountains, parterres and perspectives, combined into a fortress overlooking the Bay of Biscayne, and drawn from the Rezzonico Villa at Bassano. Boat landings, Venetian mooring poles, gondolas, a bridge of sighs, a teahouse, cascades, sculpture by A. Stirling Calder, obelisks, potted trees and an Empire bedroom from Malmaison completed the jumble of resort elegance. Taste of this sort was abetted by historians like Rexford Newcomb whose book *The Spanish House for America*, published at Philadelphia in 1927, offered illustrations of many houses of Spanish flavor to be seen in California, Florida, New Mexico and Arizona.

Meanwhile the Southwest was spawning a regional architecture derived from rural buildings of Mediterranean countries. Winsor Soule's book, *Spanish Farmhouses and Minor Public Buildings* of 1924, provided the architects with plans of simple establishments built around patios, surrounded by loggias and arcades that led to living and dining rooms. The houses were low, of one or two stories, with abundant porches; the floor levels and the roof lines could be varied picturesquely. A few tended mildly towards modern forms, by following and modifying the suggestions of the Spanish style. William Wilson Wurster opened his office at San Francisco in 1926 and his early ranch houses stemmed from the historical tradition of revivalism. The one-story grouping he did in the simplest vernacular for Mrs. Gregory in 1927, set in the Santa Cruz mountains, showed how fine such work might be when approached simply. But the romance was still there.

New Mexico recovered the adobe remains of the pueblos, and Texas's Governor's Palace at San Antonio was restored in 1931, concrete and wood replacing the mud walls. A writer in the *Architectural Record* of 1923, Rose Henderson, suggested "The Indians were the first cubists in this country," and she praised the

modern cubist revival work of Carlos Vierra whose house at Santa
Fé of 1922 was an imitation of the old pueblo buildings. Sante
Fé's hotel La Fonda of 1925, the Museum of Art of 1917, and the
Light and Water Company of 1920, all by Rapp and Rapp, were
Indian pueblos. In 1926 the *Record* willingly went along with the
joke by a full article entitled "The Southwest Develops Native
Architecture." That joke was less funny in 1929 when it encour-
aged Albert Chase McArthur to build a pueblo village for the
Arizona-Biltmore Hotel at Phoenix.

Except for the California work, the regional stylists most capable of outstanding performance worked in the vicinity of Philadelphia. Built in ledge stone, their houses were picturesque compositions, elementary in geometric form, based on rural French
farm groups or the Cotswold cottages of England. Such compositions were not localized, as the Van Schweringen estate at Cleveland shows, but Philadelphia was their chief center. It had many
French "villages" inspired by the farmhouses of Normandy that
withstood scrutiny independent of the historical details because
the brick and stone cylinders, conical roofs, high dormers, and
long walls were admirably composed by such firms as Mellor,
Meigs and Howe.

Most wealthy clients of a sentimental turn of mind, and this
meant most wealthy clients, demanded historical copying and architects abounded to supply the copies. When Mrs. O. H. P. Belmont decided to plant a teahouse overlooking the ocean on her
estate at Newport she readily enticed R. H. Hunt, a descendant
of the famous Hunt, to design a green-tiled, wood-bracketed Japanese temple, and the *Architectural Record* of 1916 gave over
thirteen pages to illustrate the sketches Hunt supplied. In an environment of that kind the creative artist had no place. Nor was
he much better off in California where Packard dealer Anthony
had Bernard Maybeck do a Spanish castle complete with moat
and portcullis, and William Randolph Hearst employed Julia
Morgan to create at San Simeon a castle filled with rooms and
furnishings brought over from Europe.

In all this America's greatest architect and his tradition were
not quite forgotten. But it was generally asserted that Frank
Lloyd Wright was finished. Even Henry-Russell Hitchcock

tended to regard Wright's more ornamental work of the '20s as an unfortunate atavism. Paul Cret took the view that Wright and Sullivan had "struggled to open a trail to a barren country" and had survived their own influence. Fiske Kimball said they had been great masters "of a school which is now a thing of the past." Wright was moved to write Kimball: "I have been reading my obituaries to a considerable extent the past year or two, and think, with Mark Twain, the reports of my death greatly exaggerated."

There was no doubt that Wright was striking his own course in a nation that did not worship the artist-architect who worked poetically upon small residential problems, fitting each to his client, the site, the materials, the structure and the program. Many of Wright's projects of the '20s remained in sketch form. Some were baroque fantasies like the project for the Doheny ranch in California of 1921. Others were progressive technically like the project for National Life Insurance Company of 1920-1925. His apartment projects of the late '20s were incredible accordions of concrete and glass forms, richly detailed, and planned to accommodate residents humanely. One of these, the St. Mark's Tower Project at New York, of 1929, was to be a tall tower carried upon a spine and four reinforced concrete vertical fins from which the floors and mezzanine inner floors would all be cantilevered. But none was built then and it was unfortunate for his ultimate reputation that when they were built they were in the wrong places, for the wrong purposes, and too late.

Yet in this period Wright did build some of his best works. The Japanese called him to Tokyo to build the Imperial Hotel, unjustly more famous for its excessively low ceilings or for having withstood the great earthquake of 1924 than for its innovative plan and decoration. It was in reality one of his best combinations of interpenetrated spaces. Upon his return he created important houses, especially in Southern California and Oklahoma. Vertical and horizontal compositions were sympathetically related to the particular terrain, enriched with patterns molded in structural cement blocks. The Millards and Ennises and Barnsdalls of California resisted the prevailing fashion for Spanish Colonial and gave Wright a few commissions that carried him through this time.

But largely he was ignored and he turned inward at Taliesin East, Wisconsin, creating there a beautiful house and farm, where he surrounded himself, feudally, with young disciples, mostly from abroad where his reputation never faltered. It was a time for reflection, partly self-enforced by rebellion against society, prolonged by the rampant social urge toward standardization and advertising and extended still longer by the depression. But this does not mean that Wright's voice did not continue to be heard. The *Architectural Record* published a series of articles by him in 1927-1928 and there he proclaimed that the architect should be master of the machine and use it creatively, rather than falling victim to "standardization — the soul of the machine." He insisted that architecture begin with the "logic of the plan," and he fought against eclecticism, historical or modern. He insisted further that form develop solely from the personality of the designer, the materials, the site, the structure. To a generation dazzled by the gleaming products of machinery, he recalled the riches that were still latent in the quarry, the kiln, the sawmill. But this was not a message that looked backwards. He was foresighted about the possibilities of glass, concrete, and sheet metal. At Princeton in 1930 he delivered a set of lectures later published as *Modern Architecture*. He seemed then a man out of his time, against the modern style that was appearing in Europe, against almost everything except his own work. No one had an inkling that he, an acknowledged master, would live to see his dreams of the '20s appear in great buildings of the late '30s like Falling Water or the Johnson Wax Building. Certainly no one expected that the St. Mark's Tower project of 1929 would in the end be realized in 1955 as the Price Tower in Bartlesville, Oklahoma.

Wright's followers, unfortunately, failed to grow. Most of them modeled their work on his Prairie architecture of the first decade of the century, never creating anything so fine as the Robie House of 1908. The group was large enough so that it was written about and the world heard of Tallmadge and Watson, George W. Maher, Walter Burley Griffin, and William Drummond. Perhaps the best were Purcell and Elmslie, draftsmen under Louis Sullivan. Their work in Minneapolis was Sullivanesque. After the firm dissolved each designer became increasingly indebted to Wright, as we can see in the house Elmslie did for Bradley at Wood's Hole, Massachusetts, or in Purcell's own house at Rose Valley, Pennsylvania. Although the group emphasized horizontal lines and cubistic bracketing systems, it urged also careful adaptation of form to rural landscape. William Drummond's house in Chicago embraced the old trees on the site: "Because I love trees I bought this lot and snuggled my house among them, so that three big trees are growing through the front porch. I cut a hole in the eaves to make room for one."

Not all of Wright's apprentices stayed in the Middle West. One of them, R. M. Schindler, moved to California, where he built some interesting houses at La Jolla and Los Angeles, notably the Kings Road House of 1922. But the general attitude was against regional modernism. Both Schindler and Richard Neutra spent time with Wright at Taliesin East. Schindler had studied at Vienna under Otto Wagner and worked for Wright at Spring Green in 1918-1921. F supervised the Barnsdall House at Los Angeles and then remained there. In 1923 Neutra came to the United States and in 1925 formed a partnership with Schindler. Their designs showed more careful adaptation to rugged sites than the buildings of the international style, but it was no less mechanized. Schindler's house for Dr. Philip Lovell at Newport Beach of 1926 was a constructivist project in concrete, while Neutra's Lovell House in Griffith Park, Los Angeles, of 1927 was a white-ribboned, glass solarium, cubistic in inspiration. Their work picked up the cubism Irving Gill had used in the Los Angeles house of Mary Banning of 1911, which excited interest when it was belatedly published in the *Record* of 1929 and 1930, but still they received few commissions and these were minor.

The *Architectural Forum* of 1929 showed what was happening on the East Coast when it published a simplified, traditional house by Julius Gregory with the note, "We are gradually becoming accustomed to 'modern' architecture." The house was a plain version of Lindeberg's French eighteenth-century style and not modern at all but the remark was an admission that the public was being bombarded by modern design. In 1929-1930 *The Record* drew its readers' attention to the Europeans, Oud, Dudok, Brinckmann and Van der Vlugt in Holland, Le Corbusier, Perret, Bonnier, Roux-Spitz and Mallet-Stevens in France, Gropius, Neutra and Mies van der Rohe in Germany. At the same time the Museum of Modern Art rapidly became the propaganda center for the modern movement. The exhibition held there in 1929 and broadcast by Henry-Russell Hitchcock in a book *Modern Architecture, Romanticism and Reintegration* was succeeded by a second exhibition of 1932. Now Hitchcock and Philip Johnson wrote the descriptive and analytical text, *The International Style: Architecture Since 1922* which supplied a new and unfortunate tag to the movement, from which it has never quite been able to escape. The catalogue contained a foreword by Albert Barr. The new aesthetic, he asserted, was based on structure, materials and planning, in which volume was defined by planes as opposed to being enclosed by solids; regularity of repeated parts produced order in compositions that disregarded symmetry and tripartite division; compositions had the flexibility of asymmetrical balance; and the forms gained aesthetic worth through the technically perfect use of materials, without any ornament. The exhibition emphasized four founders of the international style: Gropius, Le Corbusier, Oud, and Mies van der Rohe, and it included Wright as the original inspiration. This was more important than the few East Coast houses which appeared at the end of the period by immigrant architects such as Kem Weber, Joseph Urban or William Lescaze and the American George Howe. Such work was hardly representative of residential work in America nor was the dream by R. Buckminster Fuller of a central-master Dymaxion House.

16

NONE of these little efforts at modernism or the number of essays about them seemed to offer much of a threat to the Old Guard. The books gave the impression that Americans were enormously addicted to utilitarianism but covered it up with gross borrowing from old Europe. That was the impression Jacques Gréber brought with him about 1918 when he came to Philadelphia with plans for the Parkway made in his Paris office. One of his teachers had told him that America was nothing but a forest

of skyscrapers and factories, that Americans with all their money
multiplied the copies of the beautiful French monuments and
tried to do with money what time alone had permitted the
French to accomplish: "Tell us about their machines, but not
about their works of art." Gréber was delighted to find his
teacher's opinion mistaken and remained to give the Laird lectures at the University of Pennsylvania though he never stayed
away from Paris long. His book *L'Architecture aux États-Unis,
Preuve de la Force d'Expansion du Génie Français* of 1920 reveals the source of his pleasure. He had found an architecture
derived from France in Cass Gilbert's Customs House, McKim's
Penn Station, Burnham's Union Station at Washington, the
Cunard docks, M.I.T.'s new buildings, the Morgan Library, the
New York Public Library, the Widener Library at Harvard, the
Cleveland Museum, the Pan-American Building, the Harvard
Club at New York, and large estates like the Rockefeller estate at
Pocantico Hills designed by Welles Bosworth. The little modern
houses in Philadelphia and Connecticut he could ignore as Hunt
had ignored the Gare de l'Est long ago.

Gréber's tribute to French architectural imperialism truthfully
described the image of America desired by the majority of American architects. Few would have disagreed with his selection of
masterpieces nor with those published by Edward Warren Hoak
and Willis Humphry Church in a folio edition of plates in 1930.
All the buildings were in the classical tradition derived from
France. Paul Cret's introduction to this book was "an Apology for
Imitation." In it he suggested that the Parthenon and Amiens
represented "not the new but the perfected, not the promise but
the fulfillment." The emphasis on imitation was in striking contrast to Guadet, who in his book of 1902 had insisted upon functional composition. But the generation of the '20s tended to ignore the necessity to evolve differences in exterior forms, and
were bent on imitation of examples they considered perfect. It
was at this point that the Beaux-Arts camp followers became increasingly sterile, giving precedence to form over logic and structure and function while relying on historical paragons over which
no improvement might be expected.

"The study of design — of proportion — " one teacher wrote

in 1927, "resolves itself into a study of tradition." Books and foreign travel, museum collections and drawings were the tools and objects of an architect's study; he examined history not to understand the society and the emotions that had called for the buildings but to indenture him to a library of forms evolved for past problems of societies long dead.

Systematic quarrying brought Georgian tradition to the surface and handsome books of plates described *The Great Georgian Houses of America*, while after 1916 the Association of Northern Pine Manufacturers published a series of twenty-six volumes of photographs, descriptions, plans, details and measured drawings of early American buildings; their *White Pine Series of Architectural Monographs* sired many Georgian houses in the suburbs. There were many other fine examples that a skillful copyist could now find to imitate.

No doubt the Beaux-Arts education had encouraged an enormous proficiency in drawing, audacity in composition, exact knowledge of materials, form and details and a keen sense of space and finish. In all this the Beaux-Arts had supplied discipline. In none of it was there any implication of a sterile reliance on literal and established solutions. But in the '20s, absolute standards for good design were rigidly established by contemporary books written by teachers in American schools.

The most thorough work was written by a much-beloved teacher at the University of Pennsylvania, John F. Harbeson; his book, *The Study of Architectural Design,* had special reference to the program of the Beaux-Arts Institute of Design, a national organization founded in 1916 at New York in misshapen memory of the great school in Paris which issued programs for the separate architectural schools. The level of proficiency expected of drawings was announced by the frontispiece, a skillful watercolor of the Tarpeian Rock at Rome by Jacques Carlu. The architectural student was advised to follow a disciplined procedure: first, learning the grammar of architecture, taught through the *analytique,* a study in proportion and in the elements of architectures. All studies were initiated by *esquisses,* preliminary sketches done in a fixed time, usually nine hours spent *"en loge,"* that is, isolated in a box or booth. Proportions of the *esquisse* might later be varied, but the elements shown in the sketch had to appear in the final *analytique*. All drawing should be done "by the axes," the vertical planes separating the halves of symmetrical structures, and proportions of big masses were studied at small scale before they were enlarged to the proper size. It was at this introductory stage that the architectural student mastered the orders and the great monuments recorded in books. Next he learned how to make an effective and clear composition on the sheet that would present his final drawings. Those would be drawn in pencil before the architect "passed to ink," Chinese ink laboriously ground, strained through a wick, and etched into the hot-pressed paper with ruling pens. Last came rendering, which modeled the forms by showing shadows cast by a sun conventionally indicated at an angle of forty-five degrees to the horizontal and which was achieved by building up a series of washes. Armories and prisons were fortresses to be built in Romanesque or Gothic style; banks should reveal their strength but also be inviting through Roman character. Everywhere the strong hand of tradition developed a reliance upon precedent and discouraged questions about the requirements of a building which were stipulated. This shackle was coupled with another: an interest in geometry of form regardless of use or cost. There was a tendency to award prizes to the design that showed the most developed garnishing of form through the mosaic of moldings, steps, furnishings, reticulated walls, and elaborate landscape entourage, including terraces, gardens, fountains and loggias. Such encouragement led students to create prize plans that looked like magnifications of snowflake crystals, and it was this unrealistic version of paper architecture that marked the worst of the American Beaux-Arts work.

The Beaux-Arts student could ignore social reform, slum problems, traffic problems; he could turn his back on all industrial problems. He fancied himself enormously audacious if his school, in a moment of academic adventuresomeness, permitted him to try his hand at an airport, skyscraper or gasoline station. The coming building types were factories and office buildings and public schools. Meanwhile the architectural student studied the central motif for a garden wall, a fountain to end a vista, a temple of love, a municipal art gallery, an establishment at a mineral springs, a casino for the Mediterranean, a French embassy in the Far East, the palace of a president in the capital of a great republic.

At no time was American architectural thought more dominated by a foreign school. Francophilism ran to inordinate devotion, and no architectural school thought itself complete without its *patron*. In the importation M.I.T., the oldest school, had led the way when its founder, William R. Ware, had brought Eugène Létang from France; he was succeeded in 1892 by Désiré Despradelle who stayed there for twenty years and was succeeded in turn by a parade of Frenchmen, Duquesne, Le Monnier, Ferrand and Jacques Carlu. Paul Cret came to the United States in 1903 and taught at Pennsylvania from that time until 1937, where Arnal and Hébrard joined him briefly. Carnegie Institute of Technology had Ferrand and Grapin; Columbia, Prévot and Arnal; Cornell, Hébrard, Manxion and Prévot; Harvard, Duquesne and Haffner; Princeton drew Jean Labatut in 1928. Michigan had Albert Rousseau; Washington University, Abella and Ferrand; and Minnesota had Hébrard and Arnal. Many of these men were serious teachers; a few like Cret and Despradelle were excellent designers; but one and all were oriented towards classical architecture built on the grand axis; they understood very little about the social and intellectual ferment in America and they cared less. Their prescription for the ills of the city was the City Beautiful; their idea for a cultural institution was the grandiose classical monument, and America happily bought their ideas, in one last fling.

At its worst, what America bought was dreadful. There was, for example, John Russell Pope's ugly Temple of the Scottish Rite at Washington, built in 1916. The headquarters for the Supreme Council of the Scottish Rite of Freemasonry of the South, its ceremonial chambers and temple room were encased within a reconstruction of the mausoleum built by Queen Artemisia at Halicarnassus for the tomb of King Mausolus. Nor were the Beaux-Arts men successful in inventing a new style. Few buildings have been so abortively contrived as the Báhai Temple of Peace on the shore of Lake Michigan north of Chicago. Louis Bourgeois, its designer, spotted nine piers upon a star-plan radiating to nine towers from which concave buttresses rose to a dome. In spite of its structural chaos and flagrant mishandling of materials, it caught the eye of juror Henry Van Buren Magonigle who said, "It is the first new idea in architecture since the thirteenth century; I want to see it erected." It was novel enough, but its structure violated its plan and its ornament violated its structure, and the circle of violations had nothing whatever to do with architecture. Aberrations of that kind were excoriated by the good Beaux-Arts critics in France; but their formulas for good design could not summon genius, and few designers avoided Pope's commonplace or Bourgeois's fantasy.

17

THE conservative tradition was at its best in the City Beautiful movement, particularly in the commemorative monument. Even here good taste did not intervene against having the mausoleum of Halicarnassus erected again as a War Memorial at Indianapolis in 1923-1933. There was no magic either in the Memorial Amphitheatre for Washington's Arlington National Cemetery. Yet that magic did appear in Henry Bacon's Lincoln Memorial at Washington. A physical description fails to convey any sense of majesty. It is a Greek temple with a Roman attic. The temple contains four features: the statue of a man; two halls, one a memorial to the Gettysburg Address, the second to the Second Inaugural Address; and the naos itself. Thirty-six columns represent the number of states at the time of the Civil War; the frieze has wreaths with the names of forty-eight states and the dates of their entry into the Union. Not everything is successful. The iconography of columns and frieze is contrived. The two halls screened by Ionic colonnades are not memorable; Jules Guérin's allegorical paintings fail to convey the symbolism they intended. These must be dismissed, and they *are* in a flash when we confront the majestic statue of Lincoln, the work of Daniel Chester French, which in scale, in bearing, in expression, brings to life the real and mythical meaning of Lincoln's statesmanship. Here, building remains subservient to sculpture, but appropriately provides a resonating void for the statue, a platform for illuminating it, a colonnade that crowns it as laurel. The setting adds to the effectiveness as the great axis leads from the Capitol over a mile to the Washington obelisk and then past a long reflecting pool to the Memorial at the bank of the Potomac. The monumentality of the Lincoln Memorial is a matter of composition, refinement and sculptural art, not of Greek and Roman forms, and, alas for architecture, it may owe most of its final quality to the text of the Gettysburg Address cooperating with the statue. But this may be a compliment to Bacon's architecture if he sensed, as architects never do today, that sometimes architecture should act mostly in a supporting role.

In spite of a few such successes, including Magonigle's fine Liberty Memorial at Kansas City, the most finicky classicism prevailed in city, state and federal architecture. Most cities acquired additional post offices, courthouses, office buildings and federal banks. Denver looked like a Western province of Washington. White, pilastered and domed buildings stood on axes at the perimeter of great malls, like those developed at Harrisburg, Pennsylvania. Guy Lowell's New York County Court House of 1926 was typical: hexagonal in plan with a central rotunda and fronted by a Roman temple portico. State capitols were similar, whether for Washington, or Wisconsin, Minnesota or West Virginia. The domed capitol was increasingly a *tour de force;* the enlarged number of offices required a block larger than the legislative chambers; but symbolism overrode function, and the classical designers simply increased the base for offices and enlarged the domes for the legislature. They were a far cry in their liveliness from Shryock's gem at Frankfort, Kentucky, seeming to suggest that even democracy had become bloated and ritualized.

Yet even in the conservative camp, there was a movement towards modernized classical government buildings. Goodhue's first study for the Capitol at Lincoln, Nebraska, was entirely classical. His design of 1919 was a skyscraper, but it was later made more vertical, better organized and simpler in form when, in 1920, he studied the work of Eliel Saarinen, particularly his Finnish Parliament House at Helsinki of 1908. Goodhue's later design of 1920 solved the problem of the offices by spreading them out horizontally with one story under the terrace and one above it. Four interior courts, open to the sky, admitted light to four blocks of offices and provided natural ventilation. The Senate and House occupied large, beautifully paneled chambers right and left of a central hall. Out of the center of the terrace, Goodhue shot his tower skyward, and it rose in a series of strong steps to support a small polychromed dome on which the figure of The Sower was mounted and under which the suitably remote library was located. Thick corner piers rose to buttresses capped by human figures carved by Lee Lawrie. All decorative sculpture was carved into the structural form and made integral with them; so were the capitals of corn, wheat and sunflowers on the interior columns. The plan coordinated varied spaces upon axes, a triumphant demonstration of Beaux-Arts skill, and the elevations were progressive modern developments, only occasionally reminiscent of historical architecture.

Goodhue's building seemed at the time to indicate the possibilities of a new American style, one that harmonized well with sculpture and painting, one that was in the great tradition of classic monumentality. He had abandoned his Gothicism after he broke away from Cram in 1914 at the end of a medieval brotherhood that had lasted twenty years. He felt that the Nebraska State Capitol was a sort of classic. With time America might develop its own version of that tradition, Goodhue thought, much as Jefferson and Latrobe had thought earlier. The State Capitol at Lincoln might have contained the seed of a modestly new national idiom but if so it fell on stony ground although Paul Cret cultivated it handsomely in one last example, the Folger Shakespeare Library at Washington of 1929-1932. Imitations of the Nebraska Capitol, often enriched by Lee Lawrie's sculptured buttresses, appeared over and over again in post offices, banks, and regional government agencies; it was seldom ugly but it was often pedestrian and insipid. Goodhue himself strayed to the Spanish baroque in his California work.

Meanwhile the Beaux-Arts architects continued to case their libraries and museums in the monumental classic envelope, emphasizing grand staircases and overly large public spaces, shunting functional areas to the side. But the spirit or quality of the Boston Public Library was seldom recaptured by Trumbauer, Gilbert,

Hunt, Goodhue as they built for Philadelphia, Detroit, Pasadena, or Los Angeles. Even Paul Cret's Indianapolis Public Library of 1917 was scarcely an exception although often called the best classic building in America. Its axial plan was dramatic but not serviceable. Greater attention was paid to the exteriors. Two tall pavilions terminate the Doric colonnade, a fine scheme for a scenic building to head a civic square. The difficult problem of arranging a single envelope to unify the vast spaces of reading rooms and the multiple smaller spaces was solved masterfully by changes in elevations which ranged from one story at the south to two on the east and west and to five on the north where a new rhythm and scale marked the fenestration of the bookstacks. But it seemed to have nothing to do with Indianapolis, which, in turn, had little in common with Paris.

18

CHURCHES continued to remain outside the classical tradition and to look away from modern suggestions. The triumph of the Gothic was clear by 1917 when Goodhue wrote an article in the *Architectural Review* (U.S.) in which he complained about the increasing absence of achitectural, liturgical and ideological differences among churches.

Even Unitarians adopted the liturgical Episcopal architecture to which Presbyterians had previously succumbed. Princeton's Chapel was a striking indication of how architecture had betrayed the presbytery. Many of the buildings by men like Goodhue and Cram were pleasant enough, as Goodhue's St. Bartholomew's or St. Vincent Ferrer in New York reveal; in minor ways they were steps from archeological and academic Gothic; but they were not giant steps, any more than was the colorful bell tower which Magonigle and MacLaughlin provided for the First Plymouth Congregational Church at Lincoln, Nebraska. They were cheerful, comfortable, pretty, sentimental, appropriate for the grudging religion of Father Day or the confused acceptance of his wife Vinnie. They were not more important when they were gargantuan like the major cathedrals at Washington and New York which, undaunted by modern commerce and industry, attempted

to rival Amiens and Bourges, not only in form and size but in
their slow handicraft construction. For anyone who knew the real
thing they were as pale as old Quebec is compared to a real
French city, or today's religion to that of the Middle Ages.

If few church architects and clients followed the mild leads of
Goodhue or Magonigle, almost none encouraged greater change.
They were quite uninterested in the modern church movement in
Germany and Switzerland where an encyclical broadcast by Pope
Pius X had encouraged Catholic architects to move toward a vigorously modern church architecture. In the United States even
Catholics like the lively Charles D. Maginnis, the architect of
many less lively Catholic churches, remained arch-conservative.
In 1929 he wrote, "The self-conscious persuasion of such an architecture [modern] to the secular thought of the day would be
impertinent and incalculably mischievous." Joseph Hudnut, writing in the *American Architect* of 1932, commented favorably
about the modern spirit of church architecture in Europe; but his
praise did not shake the general love for the Gothic. "Probably
the safest method," wrote architect Hobart Upjohn in 1929, "is
the following of established styles."

Educational institutions were as usual even less curious or courageous. The Harvard Business School Competition of 1925 resulted in an emasculated campus of red-brick Georgian buildings.
Harvard's excellent system of undergraduate residence elicited no
architecture to match it. If anything the situation was worse at
Yale where the Gothic colleges by James Gamble Rogers affected
Oxonian diversity inside a modern city and university; picturesqueness forfeited land and use. The form of one quadrangle
was warped to include a tower based on one at Wrexham, Wales,
a town where a president of Yale had died during a summer holiday; its Welsh Gothic, barbaric though it sounds, was not worse
than the architecture of another quad which boasted an inner
court of Georgian while the street façade was Gothic, a lesson of
some sort to Yale undergraduates who would work on Madison
Avenue.

Money poured forth for the Fogg Museum at Harvard with its
inner court derived from an Italian palace; but scientific departments remained in poorly appointed quarters constructed during

the '50s and '80s of the preceding century and the humanists of today might remember how much better off they seemed to be only a quarter-century ago. Institutes of technology like the Carnegie Institute were comprehensively planned by Beaux-Arts men like Henry Hornbostel. Of these the new Massachusetts Institute of Technology revealed the best application of the City Beautiful movement to campus planning. Following the lead of Jefferson at the University of Virginia, Welles Bosworth placed a library in a rotunda at the summit of the plan, while a great lawn open to Boston across the wide Charles River Basin was framed by blocks of court-lighted buildings all connected by interior passageways. The plan itself offered flexibilities which were uncommon on traditional campuses whose individually separated buildings served to constrict the growth of the departments they housed while assisting to maintain departmental barriers. In the new M.I.T. all space was essentially interchangeable as to function (classroom, office, laboratory, library) and casual interdepartmental exchanges of ideas were common. If the neo-classic envelope belied the brilliance of Bosworth's plan, developed on strictly Beaux-Arts lines, the building was nevertheless ahead of its day, following industrial practice more than that of the universities.

At the University of Colorado, Day and Klauder avoided the Roman classic, Georgian and Gothic by developing a modest version of rural Spanish architecture. The result was far more successful than a more delicate example of dependence upon Spain like Myron Hunt's Occidental College at Los Angeles of 1914 or than Cram and Ferguson's pitiful variation upon Spanish Renaissance at Rice Institute in Houston. Architects· could not long forego trying the skyscraper form for urban universities, but those who did usually forgot that greater building height should free more ground area, a mistake James Gamble Rogers made at Chicago's Northwestern University; and the skyscraper solution could not be shaken free of Gothic detail, as Klauder unfortunately proved in the Cathedral of Learning at Pittsburgh of 1933. The tower blatantly confused education, advertisement, religion; and its Gothic crypt was no palliative — with the changing patterns of college life it housed student activities and its absurdity in the service of student newspapers, quizzes, and booths, or in the pres-

ence of modern American student attire showed how little
Gothic sentimentality accorded with the realities of American
undergraduate life, while the elevators failed dismally to get their
students to the class on time.

Under the leadership of Howard Myers, the *Architectural
Forum* stumped for modern design. There is now, it said, "an
opportunity for the newer colleges to erect thoroughly modern
buildings, but few have availed themselves of this opportunity."
A student at Yale in 1931 thought that "colleges are likely to
become museums of gilt and glory rather than workplaces of simplicity and directness." Nowhere was architectural taste more
banal, architectural daring more restrained, than in America's
seats of learning in the age of Coolidge.

19

YET little criticism was in the air so long as prosperity continued
to mount. Nowhere was there more prosperity than in Chicago.
In 1928 no American city felt more secure in her attainments. So
she looked forward to celebrating the city's Centennial with an
expenditure of twelve million dollars. She had much to celebrate
and, with her traditional vitality, and despite the deep depression
that followed 1929, she carried through and in 1933 opened her
Century of Progress Exhibition which was intended to look towards the future.

On the shores of Lake Michigan south of the Art Institute, 424
acres of land attempted to give the visitor a glimpse into the progress of science and industry. The major buildings were boldly angular, with planes of asbestos and gypsum board and plywood on
light steel frames, standing on a lagoon bisected by the irrelevant
Skyride, an aerial railway carried on cables suspended from two
steel towers. "Modernism" prevailed. "It would be incongruous
to house exhibits showing man's progress in the past century in a
Greek temple of the age of Pericles, or a Roman villa of the time
of Hadrian," said members of the architectural commission. "We
are trying to show the world not what has happened in the past,
because that has already been effectively done, but what is being
done in the present, and what may happen in the future." The

display of what was possible architecturally was as feeble as the display of what was to come in science.

The buildings assured people of advances in interior lighting and filtered ventilation; gaily colored, they were "ultra-modern" in intention but did not add a single idea for the future; it was not predicted by Cret's circle of pylons, Holabird's suspended dome or George Fred Keck's circular glass house. By the time of national recovery there was little to remember about the Century of Progress, except, perhaps, that Louis Skidmore, its architectural director had emerged there. It was in any event an appropriate architectural end to the period of complacency.

The depression hit no professional group harder than architects who knew only how to serve private colossi, who had cared more for country clubs than for housing, who were themselves victims of the advertising fashions they promoted. Four thousand firms failed to survive; the average annual volume among the surviving five thousand was less than $100,000, a fourth of the 1928 figure; the total cost of all buildings directed by architects plunged from three and a half billion dollars to half a billion.

These men had lived to see the end of an era of unquestioning plenty and might now be forced to reflect upon a wider social basis for architecture. The tower, the suburb, the monument, the country house had been the symbols of superlatively prosperous times. Between them lay acres of busy factories and hours of stop-and-go traffic. The electric light shortened the night; the telephone compressed time and distance; the automobile beguiled the observer of congestion into the belief that the whole nation could take to the woods on wheels. What the factory produced, the tower sold. Some of the proceeds went to the monument; but more went into the great general spectacle of luxury. What the tower distributed, the suburb bought. The outward form of each was a testimonial to advertising.

The works of Wright, the Philadelphia Saving Fund Society by George Howe, Rockefeller Center and the McGraw-Hill Building by Raymond Hood, and a scattering of modern houses showed the way to the future. But they were neither typical nor much desired. The buildings that American architects liked to build in these years and the buildings that the informed American public most admired were Lindeberg's houses, Bacon's Lincoln Memorial, Goodhue's Nebraska State Capitol. These at least were buildings whose architects were competent if not contemporary; their taste good, if not forward-looking. To even more people the Paramount Building, the Chrysler and Empire State towers, the United States Supreme Court, the Minnesota Capitol and the phony Spanish revival of Santa Barbara seemed marvelous.

American architecture rested in complacency unable to justify itself by espousing a liberal social objective or by making a vigorous aesthetic statement. The Beaux-Arts had nothing more to say to modern America; most of the American modernists were merely dabblers playing with another foreign style; the regionalists could not long withstand the assaults of a universal technology or escape their own romantic historicism; Frank Lloyd Wright worked alone. Where other times had yielded Latrobe, Hunt and Richardson, McKim and Sullivan, these could yield only Goodhue and Hood.

V

1933-1960

BETWEEN 1930 and 1960 it became obvious that the details and perhaps even the principles of the American world had undergone a major change. American architectural attitudes went through a similar, if transient, shift. It was now agreed that the architect could not be cavalier about his social responsibility. There seemed to be no place for a vestigial Stanford White. In the cause of a new and "functional" aesthetic, an important junta of American designers and critics, reinforced by powerful immigrants from Europe, set out to convert the majority of Americans to a modern architecture, "expressive of the times," which that majority was perfectly sure it did not want.

This small body of ardent protagonists arrayed themselves in active opposition to the taste of men placed in the highest quarters of finance, government, education, criticism, religion and the organized architectural profession. They assumed a polemical role; their aesthetic and social protests were rebellious, bitter, and (as must be the case with all successful revolutionaries) much exaggerated. In the end the aesthetic, if not the civic, victory was complete. By 1960 there were hardly even enclaves of the old eclecticism. The early European leaders of the revolution, with the exception of Henry Van der Velde all still living, were now enshrined as demigods in the new architectural Parnassus. So was the American, Frank Lloyd Wright. A new crop of young modernists was pressing them for laurels, and this group had never known rebellion or failure. Even the eclectics worked with modern motifs. The painful question now was whether "modern motifs" did "express the times." A new generation of Stanford Whites might even be developing at New Haven.

1

IT is hardly necessary in 1965 to recall the impulsive and gigantic inventions of the New Deal, the rise of the dictators, and the uneasy peace that followed the total war, threatened both by the mutual antagonisms of America, Russia and China and by the drive of all the old colonial peoples to achieve a sometimes premature and always uncertain autonomy. We must continue to remember that Belsen and Dachau shook Western optimism about civilized progress. We must never forget the razor's edge of atomic disaster on which we have walked every day since the early '50s.

But beyond the crevasses of the present troubles it was hard to perceive a terrain of greater safety and repose, however exciting and adventuresome it might be. Modern science and technology were expanding at such a rate as to pose majestic questions, not to be answered by crude and unenforceable measures such as moratoria on science. How were men to understand science, how were they to control technology lest it control them? Where were men who needed belief to sustain them against the events of life to find it as the works of the intellect steadily gnawed away at the foundations of their old belief? Much as it might have disturbed and still does disturb fundamentalists, Darwinism had been an optimistic doctrine. It could be read as the irreversible story of progress from ape, through man to superman, perfectly master of his environment, his destiny, perhaps even of himself. It had accepted as self-evident that progress was a meaningful word — and that its rate was roughly linear, so that human accommodation was possible.

But the new science, whether or not denying Darwinism, offered no such optimistic interpretations. The advances in knowledge, it turned out, were going to be geometric rather than linear. What Henry Adams had foreboded in isolation in 1905 was apparent to many in public in 1960. The new science provided no Spencer, offered no easy analogies to social Darwinism, either in relativity or in uncertainty. But along with it went a sort of geometric doubt among those who were not scientists or engineers as to whether all this necessarily meant progress at all, save in the most literal senses that the pool of knowledge in technical matters was obviously increasing, and that ever more daring and incredible machines could be designed and put to work.

For all human beings able to sense it, including the scientists as much as any, this situation engendered the deepest apprehensions. Some scientists could dismiss theirs in the pursuit of their science. Humanistic scholars struck out blindly and usually wildly. Artists became aware that their antennae, hitherto always thought to be the most sensitive of men's predictors, were not well tuned to modern science which it was easier to reject than to understand. Theologians wriggled to adjust their theology to more and more obdurate facts and hypotheses of science. Historians found themselves in a position of cultural relativism. This, in the end, might lead to the conclusion that there is no objective pattern in history and hence that history might no longer be worth studying at all! Philosophers saw much of their ancient domain occupied by linguists and social scientists. In all this intellectual turmoil, could architects go unmoved, no matter how little they, themselves, were disposed to be intellectual?

2

THE architecture of America, if it were to reflect the life of America, had somehow to respond to all these changes, and this in a time when an aesthetic conflict was being waged almost on independent terms. Even a slight examination of the theories of the conflict will reveal how erratically they were related to the truths of the times.

The genesis of the modern movement in architecture rested on theories of Le Corbusier, Mies van der Rohe, Gropius and Wright who all recognized that the machine was here to stay and that architecture must seek to use it affirmatively, not to deny it. But this was almost their only point of agreement, basic as it might be. From it Wright deduced his theory of individuality, and Gropius his theory of group-work and these notions were not the same thing, but, in fact, antipodal. From the same premise Mies worked to his continuous refinement of parts and Le Corbusier to his primitivism. These conclusions were again antipodal. The refinement of machine-made parts was naturally plausible to American industrial technology so that the greatest examples of Miesiana are in the United States; the primitive theory was implausible to Americans who were late in accepting Le Corbusier,

M

even at second hand as José Luis Sert and Paul Rudolph, followed by others, composed their variations on his themes in the sixties.

Neither a common philosophy about the machine nor a common philosophy about society led the four great pioneers to common conclusions about aesthetic solutions. They were no more in agreement about aesthetics than they were about the logical use of the machine. Thus the road from a belief in the "organic," through the elevation of structure and mechanism, to worship of the primitive was perhaps both straight and circular but it was never communal. From all of the premises, some of the actual expressions seemed to derive a common validity. It was perhaps only about 1955 that architects and critics alike began to see that their common banner only concealed their fundamental differences. It had been that of toppling the traditional and the eclectic from the seats of power. As soon as this triumph had been won, the four leaders emerged, each really on a separate altar. Acolytes surrounded each. While a new eclecticism was being prepared in those schools which sat admittedly at the foot of a single leader, a new catholicity of innovation was being brewed in the rest.

Thus in the success of "modern architecture" of 1960 there was a massive irony. The public now accepted modern architecture but the modern architects were not quite sure what modern architecture was, and even those who seemed sure did not agree. It had been born as one evidence of social reform but the new modern architects were not often individually identified with social reform. Nor was it really possible for anyone but a self-convinced zealot to insist that a geometrical design for a housing project à la Mies, or a romantic "human" design à la Wurster struck the greater blow in the cause of reform. Indeed, to the idea of reform, most of the great buildings were neutral.

Again, modern architecture had been born in the study of structure and in the felt necessity that this structure should be clearly, "honestly" revealed; it had moved to a classical expression of this necessity in the works of Mies van der Rohe and Pier Luigi Nervi but this necessity now seemed less universally urgent; on the one hand it was being concealed by the integuments of the neo-classicism of Philip Johnson, Minoru Yamasaki and Edward Stone; on the other hand it was being stretched into structural *tours de force,* structure for structure's sake, by Eero Saarinen, Victor Lundy and all the younger men who were now fascinated by the form if not the analysis of conic sections. Between these and in all sorts of costumes were such talents as those of Ieoh Ming Pei, Gordon Bunshaft, The Architects Collaborative and Louis Kahn.

Modern architecture had never been unconscious of aesthetics. But in its infancy it had played down aesthetic necessity, had seldom talked of art for art's sake, had defended its arbitrary aesthetic conclusions with appeals to the rationale of social need and structural necessity, rationally advanced even when garbed in explosively irrational polemic. But, with success, most of the architectural discussion became frankly aesthetic. Now in 1958, an artist-architect, Minoru Yamasaki, said, "The social function of the architect is to create a work of art." Nobody protested much.

Perhaps we can perceive the ultimate ironies only dimly. What is clear is that the impact of New Deal reform and social unrest conditioned the pattern of American architectural thought. It joined with the aesthetic revolution to make our contemporary approaches to architecture possible. The war then extended American architectural horizons, increased the influence of exotic forms on American thinking, greatly widened the area of the world into which American designs would obtrude themselves. To all of these influences the direct responses were, on the whole, favorable.

At this level one could say that the struggle had availed; that the architectural appearance of America had been improved. There were many notable new buildings, if fewer than the occasion had provided and demanded. The postwar atmosphere was one of an apparently abundant prosperity with increasing inflation. The world was engaged in an unprecedented building boom, demanding more architectural attention than all the architects, brilliant and dull, sound and unsound, impulsive and reflective, could possibly provide, so that even reflective men were tempted to design without enough reflection. You were as likely to meet Gropius in Baghdad, or on an airstrip in the Pacific, as in the Harvard Yard; and so it went for all men of reputation. It was embarrassing for any American architect of any pretensions not to have at least one job in Hong Kong, Manila or Nairobi. Throughout the world exciting buildings were good for but a moment's discussion on a local street corner, almost never slated for reflective reconsideration.

But when one turned from the individual building to the city it was at once clear that things were out of hand. The city was falling apart in many ways, socially, politically, economically. All this was so trite that it was almost embarrassing to repeat it. But the city was falling apart aesthetically too for all its brave new architectural ornaments. Engineering czars like Robert Moses, aesthetic czars as brilliant as Le Corbusier at Chandigarh or Niemeyer at Brasilia left important questions unanswered; collections of stars on teams such as were assembled for New York's Lincoln Center obviously were not the answer. Great urban redevelopment schemes seemed either not to get under way or to end as sterile aesthetic, even human achievements. Many were led to wonder whether architects could learn, in time, to deal with the new and enormous scales, and time was pressing. It was not clear that they would have the chance even if they could learn. It was by no means certain that all the brilliant gains in personal architectural aesthetics of the past twenty-five years would not now be negated by the crushing, irresistible and insensitive Juggernaut of economic and political forces generated by urban expansion.

Behind this, for a few to ponder, lay the much larger philosophical questions of what the world of 1960 was really like, and whether anyone could understand it by the intellect or by the intuition or by both. Could anyone who did understand it begin to interpret it in architectural terms? The confusion of the painters in these matters was painfully apparent to anyone who sampled the modern galleries. Was there perhaps the same confusion among the architects?

At the most elementary levels there was cause for comfort. The society *had* at long last reached some agreements as to what was architecturally important. Commerce and manufacturing *were* valuable and could now, and without remorse, be provided with dignified and beautiful architectural domiciles. Business could be a legitimate patron of the arts, perhaps might even become the most important patron. Social architecture, especially housing, *was* to be recognized as essential and important. The more ancient subjects of design, museums, libraries, universities and churches, were still to have as good architecture as they could get, often very good, but they must at least share the bench in the sun and probably give way even more than that. As to the private house, it remained interesting only as a point of relief from conformity and a starting point for young architects. Although Americans clung to the idea of the private dwelling it was no longer quite such an important architectural problem; indeed few leading architects could afford to design private dwellings any more, not even their own, unless like Neutra they chose to do one occasionally as an Antaean stimulus.

3

THE New Deal stopped the flood of failure, abated the financial crisis, repaired the financial and commercial machinery. The President and his ebullient advisers experimented with youth, with farming, with the ecology of a valley; they provided greater security for buyers of stocks, for borrowers and len `'ers, for old and young. Relief, recovery and reform danced together in a complicated but exuberant ballet in which laborers and farmers often made the spectacular leaps.

The labor measures of the New Deal had only indirect effects on American architecture. The long-range improvement of labor's purchasing power brought a larger market for private houses, but the market was largely preëmpted by real-estate developers and building contractors, though many architects attempted to supply designs for better houses at comparable costs. If the site planning that the best architects insisted upon had been allowed to govern the speculative developments, the resulting communities, even those with amateur-designed and traditional houses, would have made American residences the boast of the world, but unfortunately the developers and builders took the course that gave immediate financial ease, ignoring the long-term benefits of sound design. The absence of a single building union and archaic craft policies continued to make it impossible to launch a full attack on new ways of fabricating buildings. In the end trivial economies were effected by eliminating ornament, by some modular standardization and by improvements in on-site machinery. But the principal brake on the rising cost of the house was the steady shrinkage of the amount of space it offered.

The farm measures bore more directly on architecture, stimulating some model towns and farm workers' housing, creating a few new communities through rural electrification and power projects, even new types of community. The Farm Security Administration provided suggestive if financially unsuccessful demonstrations with its three Greenbelt towns. On another front, Yuba City, California, offered an example of a well-planned housing scheme for 284 migrant families and 84 farm families. Firebaugh and Woodville in California, and Chandler Farms in Arizona, offered notable chances to study low-cost housing, perhaps to make fruitful experiments in inexpensive amenity. At Chandler, Vernon DeMars provided houses whose site planning was imaginative although their architectural quality was minimal. Indeed, this was the general description of all the architecture supported by the depression agencies.

It is easy enough to caricature the WPA projects — the inevitable waste and folly, given a hastily invented task, and direction by a strange mixture of theorists, idealists, and hardheaded ward politicians.

But the WPA did temporarily end the disasters of unemployment and has even something to its credit in the arts, the 1935 WPA painting project. Whether the feeble quality of most of the WPA murals in federal post offices and banks was because of the conditions of the work, or because the artists were not competent, or because murals were no longer actually resonant with the times may not matter now. The murals were sentimental about national or local history, sentimental about regions, sentimental about underdogs. They tried for pointed social criticism and were usually only funny; they tried to be contemporary, aping what seemed to them the principal determinant of "contemporary" art, to wit, bad drawing. Even the murals by the best-known were not often good and perhaps never represented their best work. It can be said, though, for the "creative" side of the WPA program that it bridged a bad time for many painters who have since become well known. But it is an open question whether it would not have been better simply to buy whatever the painters wanted to paint than to go in for this mass-produced mural moralizing. Unfortunately, the directors wanted employment and social messages, not art. The Society of Abstract Artists, founded at New York in 1936, could hardly be a part of WPA, which from Roosevelt through Mrs. Roosevelt to Hopkins to Cahill was suffused with sentiment about rural America and the affirmations of Archibald MacLeish, "Democracy is a thing never done"; the promoters of the WPA were better fitted by taste and training to admire Grandma Moses than John Marin, Thomas Hart Benton than Lyonel Feininger, John Steuart Curry than Stuart Davis.

The housing efforts of the New Deal mixed pump-priming with reform.

Each agency scored some success. The HOLC, conceived at a time when there were a thousand house foreclosures a day, purchased more than a million mortgages and by 1950 was certain that it could liquidate its investment of three and a half billion dollars without loss to the government. FHA's home loan insurance yielded a few exemplary projects, such as Baldwin Hills Village, Los Angeles, by Clarence Stein and Robert Alexander. By 1949 the USHA had succeeded in working in forty-three states and at the end of the war had accounted for 191,000 low-rent public housing units.

PWA produced 21,800 dwelling units in fifty-one low-rental developments spanning thirty-seven cities. Architect Robert Kohn was director, Architect Frederick L. Ackerman was in charge of slum clearance; both had high ideals and fair experience in housing. But neither had the aesthetic imagination or talent of the Europeans who were building dwellings in Europe. Kohn surrounded himself with a staff of young Americans possessed of enormous enthusiasm and considerable critical judgment, but inexperienced, better with words than with bricks and mortar. PWA produced no better project than its first one, Lakewood in Cleveland, designed by Walter McCornack. Its three-story apartments covered only 32 per cent of the slum-cleared land; there were many playgrounds and some variety in the groupings. Despite readily available and notable European examples, the New

Deal seldom did much better. The general level of its architecture
was almost as low as the level of its painting, and considerably less
amusing.

In quantity all the public-housing efforts together did not
scratch the surface if, as the housers consistently alleged, one
third of the nation had been ill-housed. As soon as there were
harbingers of prosperity they dispelled the vision of extensive well-
ordered American public housing comparable to the communities
of Sweden, Denmark, Holland, Switzerland or Germany. When
it was all over it was clear that the American people did not covet
the planned way of life, was unwilling to make its own plans and
did not trust anybody else with them either. Left to themselves,
the private builders soon forgot Baldwin Hills Village. The housing effort did not add much to the elegance of the American architectural scene. But it did create some sense of habit under
which the citizens would no longer repudiate any and all public
aid to housing, as private industry continued to fail to find a good
antidote to subsidy.

In the absence of industrial advance, architects experimented
with house construction though with less élan than they had displayed in the '20s. George Fred Keck advocated a solar house.
Konrad Wachsmann, Gropius and Mies van der Rohe worked on
problems of mass-produced standards with no really important
results. Many of these efforts were possibly frustrated by the fact
that the shell of the house, on which the architect does so much
of his work, costs but a small fraction of the whole and that
changes made in the shell do not materially affect the cost of the
land or the basic equipment. When good houses were designed
they were never purchased on a suitably large scale. There were
again exceptions like Skidmore's houses at Oak Ridge, Tennessee,
or the TVA demountable houses of 1944. The best of these may
have been the Acorn House of 1950 and the Techbuilt House of
1952, each a prefabricated shed designed with considerable imagination by architect Carl Koch who collaborated with John Bemis.
But even in 1960 America had not really applied factory production methods of mass housing. The largest single producer of
houses made and sold the trivial number of 25,000 houses a year;
its houses, practical enough, were banal even in their convention-

ality; and this isolated success really had no important industrial competitor. The field of the small individual house remained in the hands of speculative builders whose towns degraded even the occasional good house plan by their bad site planning and their mediocre architecture. Factory-made housing to be successful had to come from mobilized industrial power, not from the dreams of architects. The industrial power never chose to mobilize for this purpose. At best it geared up to produce elaborate trailers which by 1960 were almost as big as a small house, were becoming less mobile, were housing many other Americans besides the few gypsies and the many Florida-bound gaffers who first took to them. Trailer parks might some day develop the amenities of a well-planned residential area but this was more a possibility than a likelihood. If trailers were to be the total answer of industry, it had to be admitted that the New Deal housing had at least sought something better.

To the record of architectural mediocrity, the New Deal offered one distinguished exception, in the valley of the Tennessee. We do not speak here of the politico-economic triumphs over private power interests or the merit of the controversy. Cheap electricity, flood control and soil improvement brought to 40,000 square miles in seven Southern states marked the beginning of the South's recovery. Great dams stimulated the growth of industries and towns and the improvement of farms; artificial lakes served recreation. TVA architects and engineers under the direction of Roland Wank set up a model organization for coordinated architectural-engineering work. Their powerhouse at Pickwick Landing housed giant turbines in beautiful elemental forms that were triumphs of functional design. Their Watts Bar steam plant of 1942 provided an elegant display of a few balanced elements. Kenneth Reid, writing in *Pencil Points* in 1939, said that the TVA had demonstrated how beautiful works of engineering might be. The "engineering" demonstration had been made by architects like Wank and his able designer, Mario Bianculli. No other landmark could stand so well as the architectural monument to the New Deal. None was so often visited by foreigners.

The New Deal's tax schedules did not destroy the rich, or turn

M*

America, as is sometimes alleged, into one vast middle class. The private enterprise whose corporation felt a public responsibility continued to promise a fine industrial and commercial architecture. If more of architecture were to be built in America by government instead of by individuals, it was important that there be great changes from earlier cautious and bad expressions of the public taste. There was not much indication that the changes were being prepared. Moreover no record of history suggested that a vast middle class bereft of really wealthy patrons, operating on the decisions of a middle-class bureaucratic central government, was likely to encourage or produce any important art at all. Most great art seems to come from the poles of a society, not from its equator. It is unrelated to other kinds of eminence; nothing guarantees that Eisenhower or Stevenson, Reuther or Wilson, King or Wallace, Goldwater or Johnson will be an enlightened client — or the progressive more imaginative than the mossback.

The ultimate disappointment of the New Deal to an architectural or art historian must be that its aesthetic aspirations were muffled in its social ideals. New Dealers were quite as content with shoddy aesthetics as Coolidge or Hoover might have been. Social reformers need not, of course, be identified with architectural reform; when they were so identified, they did not always fight for architecture with the same vigor as they fought for legislation. Nor need we blame them for this. One can tilt at too many windmills at the same time. Among the legions of reform there were surely many aesthetically conservative or even ignorant troops. Not one could safely be alienated for the sake of art. But beyond that it is regrettably clear that few of the leading New Dealers cared about the arts at all. Roosevelt himself may have cared as much as anyone. He was interested in architecture and even liked to design it on the back of envelopes. But he had an impulsive, dogmatic, sentimental if impeccably mediocre judgment in aesthetic matters.

4

WAR may stop the course of building briefly. It may damage or destroy some admirable historical monuments. It may change the balance of world power and thus send a new colonial architecture coursing through the world. It may modify the taste of the winners or losers. It is too early to speak of the long-term effects of World War II on the architecture of the West or of the East. What, for example, does a memory of Hiroshima say to an architect when he is designing unless it suggests he should not design at all?

Any war tends to establish a hiatus in arts which are not directly useful for fighting it, or serve it well as propaganda or escape. Modern war is less lenient about this than the war of the ancients. Whatever the Athenians may have accomplished on their Acropolis during the Peloponnesian War, our Seabees built no Parthenons in the Pacific during the years from 1940 to 1945, nor were important palaces erected at home. At the war's end the deficit in needed building was large, so that architecture not only recovered quickly but gained by the delay the war had imposed. The eclectic conservatives were five years older and wearier; new leaders had come to industry and the universities, and these men feared the new architecture less.

At the highest level of response, architecture could find no fitting answer to the times. Men with a doom sense might have declined to build at all, on the thesis that to build was meaningless; they might have built fantasies and luxuries in one grand final fling, a sort of architectural dance of death; they might have frantically sought to build underground cities for survival and this would not have been above their powers had they really believed that demolition was near or survival important; or they might have tried, as the Byzantines had tried unsuccessfully, to create new shrines and to mob them with feverish appeals to God to spare them from all the consequences of their inconsequence. In the event they did none of these things. Instead, for the most part they went about their ordinary ways.

Historians trying to generalize from our buildings may develop elaborate hypotheses to explain the metal and glass cages as an expression of the feeling of a society with a sense of death, "ephemera, ephemera, all is ephemera," in which building for permanence was obviously futile and for which there was something symbolic in using fragile and transitory materials; or as the desire of the same society to catch all the physical light there was since so much of the spiritual world was dark. These would be no more far-fetched than interpretations that have sometimes been proposed for older architectures by people who like to read into works of art more than is there.

The scars laid on the conscience of the West, the uncertainty as to whether man had really become human during the long centuries of his alleged rise; all such philosophical questionings, heavy as they might lie on the hearts of individual architects, could find no outlet in the symbols of a society which, no doubt rightly, set out to try to get along with the daily act of living. There was little or nothing in the words or the lives of the people who were making the buildings of 1950 or 1960 to indicate any morbidity, conscious or subconscious. Unless the symbolism were clearer one was prone to conclude that the architectural results depended upon far more immediate and practical situations arising in an attitude of "let us do the best we can, so long as we can."

For each nation this posed a different problem. For those countries of Europe which had borne the brunt of the bombing and the shelling and the fires, and for equally devastated Japan, it meant an opportunity like that of the phoenix, a new day of chance to replace obsolete buildings, to revivify the city plan. But like the phoenix most of the reborn cities looked much like the old, save for some details of the plumage. The story of opportunities gloriously grasped, as in Berlin, or at least partially enjoyed, as at Osaka and Coventry, was outweighed by the story of opportunities muffed as at London and Tokyo. It is an important story of contemporary architecture but not this story, for the demolition passed America by until the days of urban redevelopment. The problem was different for the newly developing nations, often building from scratch, having little worth saving, but this too varied from culturally mature India or aggressive Brazil to the newest and most naïve and most artificially constructed African tribal nation, seeking to create architectural symbols of status overnight. This too is an important story yet to be told, but again it is not our story.

If America gained no chances to rebuild by the destruction of war, its soldier-architects did voyage afar and were influenced by what they saw, notably in Japan and Korea. The rise of the dictators forced a flow of brilliant architects from Europe to America and these were a major force both in the controversy and the subsequent victory. America's new world position asked her to do much more building abroad so that American architects were now called upon to design for foreign sites; while in a sort of unofficial reciprocity many foreigners designed buildings or parts of buildings for America. It was a world in which, by 1960, and with the notable exception of the Soviet Union and Red China, architectural ideas were a free item of international exchange.

From the war construction only a handful of buildings were of more than passing interest: the Main Reception Building at the Great Lakes Naval Training Station, by Skidmore, Owings and Merrill, the United States Merchant Marine Cadet Basic School at San Mateo, California, by Gardner Dailey. A few aircraft hangars gave the engineers, Ammann and Whitney, some experience with concrete vaults but the Fascists had done more exciting things at Orvieto.

War housing, military or civilian, generally yielded a dreary array of two-story row houses and apartment buildings, crowding too many people on small sites even when the specifications of the USHA were observed. There were notable exceptions, to emphasize what might have been, by the Saarinens at Center Line, Michigan; by Gropius and Breuer at New Kensington, Pennsylvania; by Oscar Stonorov at Carver Court in Coatesville, Pennsylvania; by Wurster at Valencia Gardens, San Francisco. An outstanding example was provided by Neutra for the Channel Heights project at San Pedro, California. Here pairs of low-cost, one-story houses were built on *cul-de-sac* access roads, well sited on landscaped terraces. All these showed was what might have been. Mostly the war defaced a great deal of American land with "temporary" buildings which have turned out to be remarkably permanent even in the heart of the capital city. The Quonset hut was its symbolic residue.

5

ALWAYS the center of population continued to move relentlessly westwards, clinging firmly to the 39th parallel, now crossing the Indiana line into Illinois. The West Coast became as culturally important as it had long wished to be. The great power still rested in the Middle Atlantic states and the industrial Middle West. Each of these regions held a fifth of the population and a vastly bigger fraction of the national productive capacity and wealth. The South seemed to be beginning a renascence if it could abandon its racial prejudices and its ignorance. The agrarian Middle West was declining slightly. The prairie was still culturally cold and dry. The Mountain and Desert states were beginning to open up. But it was still true that most of the best education and the innovation came from New England or nearby; most of the lively arts and the ancient ones as well were centered around New York; there was still a preponderance of money in the East despite the claims of Texas; the Middle West was still the heartland whence came the new battalions of ambitious young men. But the Pacific Coast and Texas were roaring ahead, developing their enigmatic cultures. That there was more than one could be learned from even the briefest visit, say, to Portland, San Francisco, Los Angeles and Houston. But the anthropologists were not speaking of San Francisco when they said that the new West contained the inevitable future culture of America. To much of the rest of the country, it might have seemed interesting to be recast in the mold of the Golden Gate but there might be less aspiration to emerge in the costume of Los Angeles, yet the latter had more to propose than the former.

While the cultural dominance of New York was still felt in the world of publishing, the theater and painting, New York no longer had even a semblance of a monopoly on first-class architects. In 1960 if you set out to stick pins in a map of the country to indicate the place of business of notable and imaginative architects, you would notice no heavy concentration anywhere.

The small but influential immigration of the artistic and intellectual refugees of the '30s had been fully assimilated into a society that, except for the stretching color tension, was culturally pluralistic.

It was a population blessed with an enormous increase in the energy at its disposal. In 1930 Americans had had 24 thousand trillion BTU's to use, while by 1950 this had increased a half, to 36 thousand trillion; meantime the population had grown only a fifth. Water still supplied only a few per cent of the energy but coal which had furnished two thirds of it in 1930 yielded only one third in 1955. Petroleum was king.

Though all might wonder what the nucleus would ultimately do to challenge the older sources of energy, even the change from coal to petroleum had many implications for architecture. It established new centers of wealth, often on virgin land and among culturally virgin people, and it offered to the people of Texas, Oklahoma and Louisiana or the Williston Basin an opportunity to forego the mistakes of their ancestors and to build a finer urban environment. This was just a chance and not a promise, and by 1960 it looked as though it might not be taken up.

Decentralization of plants became easier because oil, gas and electricity could be conveyed easily; railroad locations became less significant for industries whose primary problem was fuel. Petroleum combustion offered the opportunity for cleaner cities although these had been technically possible with coal and were not automatic with petroleum as smog-laden urban airs were demonstrating.

Consumers now used much more electricity in their homes. The per capita consumption of 550 kilowatt hours in 1930 was stretched five times by 1955. The total electric power used throughout the country was tripled.

The energies available merely increased the size of the problems of urban transportation without introducing new modes. The demands of transportation were positive and clear, but still they were not taken seriously until almost too late. Meanwhile the architects cultivated the gardens of their individual buildings. Individual residents abandoned public transportation for their private cars and drove in long lines to work, one rider per car; then public transportation abandoned them. And thus it was that the new buildings thrust their sharp and elegant faces among the burdock and thistles of the highways and the streets, ignoring the life they would have to live among the exhausts and klaxons of a desecrated city, the lines of motors, more deadly to urban aesthetic when parked than when moving, asking whether man was not really the servant of this machine rather than its master.

After the peak of activity, in 1944, the decline of railway passenger traffic was precipitate. Despite the fantastic improvement in the speed, safety and comfort of air travel, which by 1960 had helped to obliterate comfortable and convenient rail travel, the big losses suffered by the rails were not to the air lanes but to the highways. Three million passenger cars were made in 1930; eight million were produced in 1955. The 24 million registered autos became 52 million; and each one averaged more than 10,000 miles in 1955. The trucks and buses grew bigger as well as more numerous. Despite frenetic road construction, which widened the highways and increased the safe speed on which they could be coursed, no important measures were taken to improve the conditions at the termini. Practically nothing was done to take account of the changes the highways were imposing on the cities themselves and in 1958 President Eisenhower characteristically encouraged a highway building program conceived in a vacuum and in which those few in the federal government responsible for the future of the American cities were scarcely consulted.

A few superhighways were built, a few new expressways were cut through the cities with as little concern for what they did as the railways and the rapid transit lines had previously shown. New lines of blight were gleefully created. Buildings continued to rise to increase the traffic densities without being required to contribute anything to reduce the mounting deficit of parking facilities. As the rails had once split cities and left devastation along their routes, now the great expressways were allowed to provide new and greater channels for erosion. The flight to the unfinished suburb which had only houses and none of the other requirements of a sound community accelerated while the centers of the cities continued to dwindle and to decay. In all this rush to the new desolation there were voices of protest, none stronger than that of Lewis Mumford. But they had as little influence as the ill-starred Cassandra. Even those contemporary architects who were most aware of the problem and most vociferous about the misdeeds of others were prone to forget when they themselves had interesting buildings to create, as irresponsible in their way as the City Beautiful men had been before them. For the city of 1960, public indifference and the automobile were greater enemies than the H-bomb. As between slow decay and demolition there was no significant choice. Though not solely responsible, the automobile became the symbol of the fall of the city.

6

CHANGES in techniques burgeoned everywhere after the war. In 1950, eight million television sets and forty-five million radio receivers raised their all too visible antennae over American roofs. The telephone became commonplace, its extraordinary technical advances taken for granted. Electricity served so many functions in a building as to go uncounted. Electric lights were so common and current so cheap that many were allowed to burn night and day. The "neon" lights had an important visual impact, as their use in advertising changed the nocturnal aspect of cities, whether on Broadway, Ginza, or Boston's Charles River Basin. Neon was not a trivial potential factor in urban design but no one knew how to control it.

Other inventions changed the living habits of the typical American family. By 1960 a plethora of electric appliances was a standard element of American domestic life and an important determinant of the layout and the cost of residential units. Space could be constricted, architectural amenity could be absent in the mind of the typical family if only the kitchen and the bathroom were efficient and well-stocked with modern domestic machinery.

The great European architects had long vaunted the opportunities that were present for architects who would use technology to the hilt. American architects were a little slower in rallying to this gonfalon but by the end of the war they were more than ready. Some of the older architects had scorned technology, admitting that it was a necessary evil but seeking to conceal it through art. They of course could not get along without their copies of *Sweet's Catalog*, the compendium of building equipment that was begun in 1906. But the standardized hardware, plumbing and woodwork they could find there would go unspecified if money were available for tailoring a gold bathtub, forging a wrought-iron hinge, or carving a mantelpiece. On the other hand *Sweet's* enchanted the immigrant architects. To them American industrial products offered a stockpile of inexpensive parts and their ideology insisted that the stockpile was charming. *"Sweet's Catalogue,"* the Viennese Neutra wrote in 1937, "looked to me . . . as inspiring as a healthy forest to a Norwegian carpenter."

Further contact with industrial products excited more general interest in mechanical equipment and its possibilities in architecture although the ancient concern with structure was still dominant. Rigid frames of steel were conceived. There were new ideas about wind-bracing to reduce vibration and eliminate distortion, particularly in towers. Continuous glass sash could be pivoted vertically or horizontally. The covering for steel frames was drawn thinner as veneers of metal and glass replaced brick and stone. Better floor finishes were found, better ways of concealing duct systems. More parts came prefabricated to the big buildings. Thin concrete shells began to be used, timidly at first, for the successes of Albert Kahn had firmly entrenched the light steel frame. The timber industry sought new markets with its new timber connectors, glued laminates, lamellar diamond-trussed roofs, all of which opened up wide spans to timber. These and other technical innovations occupied the thought of architects and engineers, as much as design and history had occupied the man of the Beaux-Arts. Engineering became almost a fetish and the interest was inevitably reflected in the appearance as well as the working of the architecture.

The greatest lag was in the exploitation of the structural, plastic and textural potentials of reinforced concrete. It was not that American engineers were intellectually incapable of designing in the ways of Freyssinet, Maillart or Nervi but rather that their clients were more accustomed to steel. American building economies *seemed* adverse to brilliant use of concrete, and the role of the engineer in America was clearly limited by the architects if he essayed to be an artist. Moreover the coarse textures that Le Corbusier and his Japanese disciples cultivated did not seem refined enough to the always polishing Americans, so when concrete structures were made they were often overrefined. The leadership that America had shown in the days of Roebling and Eads had moved to Italy and Spain and Mexico and Japan and it had not returned by 1960, though there were harbingers of change, stimulated more by new techniques in pre-stressing and pre-casting of modular units than in the freer forms permitted by concrete cast-in-situ, though each had its advocates.

Beyond the novelty of materials and the experiments with structure lay the rules set down by the demands of equipment. Not only did the equipment require more and more of the volumetric space of a building but it began to ask for strategic location as well. Air-conditioning plants could not push the air efficiently more than a few stories and intermediate units sometimes needed to be placed in high buildings. For almost all buildings the penthouse was a technical necessity which most architects continued to deal with as an afterthought. No one seemed to realize the potentials inherent in the cities' flat roofs either for good living or for the display of horizontal sculpture. On the far horizon might loom the computing machines. For if these were to come to play the role in business operations that many predicted, they too might become conditioners of design; they might for example lead to a re-evaluation of the masses of an urban commercial building, ask for a return to the old broad blocks which had been abandoned for thin-slab buildings when it seemed that every office worker needed a chance for a daily look at the sun while sitting at his desk. The computers would have no such necessity. They might not even need to be downtown.

But if this forecast of the implications of technological development were far-fetched, it was evident that many other effects were not. New ways of doing things, such as air travel, called for new ideas of terminals and the ideas had difficulty keeping pace with the changes in the transport. Urban decentralization by the automobile reopened the discussion of the relative advantages of horizontal and vertical buildings. Incessant movement of peoples changed the rate at which an innovation here would be learned about there. Indeed the whole admiration of change, in knowledge, in speed, in space, reinforced established American philosophy, now applied to the arts as well as to technology, even perhaps to economics and politics. This held that change was, in itself, a good; that innovation was desirable for its own sake; it helped to build a feeling in architect and client alike that each building must offer a new and dramatic adventure in which the newness was the most important thing. Thus each designer and each client was tempted to seek his own moment of euphoric collaboration to provide a building, poised like a butterfly, on the edge of the ephemeral.

7

THE other arts, as they were being practiced in America, seemed to have little to say to the art of architecture. American literature was no doubt providing a true response to the times. Directly, or suggestively, it was expressing concern about twentieth-century life, even a rejection of it; sometimes the rejection was only of the secular development, sometimes of the very philosophical underpinning. Many of the writers chose still to try to communicate, troubled themselves about perfecting their craft, developed their symbols out of ancient and well-recognized forms or used their invented new ones often enough so that they too became recognizable. The beatniks had no more to propose to architecture than any other form of anarchy ever has had.

Not many of the painters offered more hope; and if they did it might be hard to make it out in the obscure messages of men like de Kooning, Pollock, Baziotes, Callahan, Rothko, Tobey and Motherwell. Whether obscure or clarion, the message echoed endlessly in what they wrote to explain their painting. The age or at least the painter was sick, sick of mechanization, sick of human degeneracy, sick of "progress," sick of order, sick of old values, sick of science.

Many of the earlier realists had loved the American scene, even the ugly parts. Charles Burchfield found things to love in the small Midwestern towns that Mencken had found so depressing; Stuart Davis incorporated barns, gas pumps, booms, masts, coal elevators, excursion steamers, fish piers and floodlights into semi-abstractions which were not flights from reality, denials of America or even bitter criticism; Edward Hopper worked with the ordinary, never glamorizing it, never prettifying it, but never satirizing it or wallowing in its meanness either unless the reality was satire enough.

By 1933 social-satiric painting was also direct and common. Reginald Marsh showed it in his Hogarthian girls; Philip Evergood in *My Forebears Were Pioneers* (1940) exclaimed as some of the novelists did against the betrayal of the American dream. But by 1954 in *American Shrimp Girl* Evergood, like others of the fiery WPA days, had said farewell to satire and to protest which was either no longer necessary or no longer any use. The same thing happened to the still more critical Ben Shahn. In the end there was more love than hate although there was still an abhorrence of sentimentality. As Shahn said, "All the wheels of business and advertising are turning night and day to prove the colossal falsehood that America is smiling. And they want me to add my two per cent. Hell, no!"

But if Evergood, Shahn and the bitterly satiric Jack Levine were in the way of being painters of distinction and not quite like anybody in Europe, they were unlikely to be of much direct service to the cause of architecture. Their methods of composition, their concepts of space were not calculated to provoke a new or better architectural understanding. Their choice of subject matter was not calculated, either, to appeal as murals, for it was too often revolutionary, critical, sardonic, sinister, or at best somber.

It would have been silly to expect that the most powerful protests in paint should have come from America. Here, despite all difficulties, the protests were minor, at least until "the long hot summer" of the civil rights movement; and in the face of the Kremlin, the Brown Shirts, the Spanish Civil War, the difficulties of America seemed actually trivial. Thus it is not surprising that the Spanish Picasso, working in France, should produce the great monument of protest in *Guernica*, where fractured planes of black, white and gray held the macabre finale of a bullfight, in which the triumphant brute surveyed his slaughter by the light from one naked, shimmering bulb. If made to condemn the atrocities of the Spanish Civil War, it managed somehow to expand into a bitter and universal indictment of man's inhumanity.

We found no painter to deal as forcefully with Alabama and Mississippi. But neither *Guernica* or the nonexistent *Birmingham* could contain suggestions for architecture, though they might for architects as mere humans. Architecture cannot feed on pain, anger, discontent, anarchy, or the inarticulate.

Where painting could affect architecture in this time it seemed to do so from the works of the serious abstractionists. There had been notable immigrants in the '30s and many of them, though not all, were abstractionists. Now there was a spate of American abstraction typified at its best by de Kooning, Pollock and Kline. But it was the older Mondriaan and Doesburg or the meticulous Albers more than Motherwell who had anything to say to the new American architecture; and it was the constructivist Gabo rather than Calder the maker of mobiles who furnished useful architectural suggestions, at least for the moment, though the work of the latter was among the gayest and most original of all the American efforts of the time, and well fitted to cooperate with architecture. But even the ideas of Doesburg and Mondriaan and Gabo found their way to American architecture indirectly through the influence they may have first had on the European proposals of the great elder statesmen of the modern architectural movement.

The abstract expressionists often supplied their own criticism even if unconsciously. What was one to think of painting which consisted of an "unknown adventure into an unknown space"? Rothko assembled his brushes, pails, spoons, toothpaste tubes and brooms and insisted that people find expressions of emotions in the movements of the painting. But what movement? And whose emotions? The emotions of the individual painters, of course. It had to be taken for granted that the emotions of every dauber were by some mysterious process important to someone besides himself; it had to be accepted that de Kooning was saying something profound and not something silly when he declared that the world of the atoms was beginning to bore him. As time went on, the vanguard of the school seemed to depart further and further from any will to craftsmanship or communication. At best, many were producing only intricate and colorful or bold and rough ornaments for the large blank walls and empty spaces of neutral office buildings.

In the same time there were potential new stimuli from Europe. American architects were well enough aware of Mondriaan, Miro, Picasso, Léger, Arp, Brancusi and Moore in a general sense and, if they were modern, architects tended to accept them all quite indiscriminately as fellow revolutionaries who were also "progressive" and "men of our time." But who were the men of the time? The range took you from Dali to Siqueiros, from Matisse through Rouault to the geometrical abstractionists and the "action" painters. This range was so great that no one architect followed the lines of many while at the same time he tended to esteem them all collectively since they, like himself, were "modern" even though they beckoned down altogether too many mutually contradictory roads.

8

IF the established and serious arts of America seemed to have little to say that might influence architecture, it was still possible that the new "lively" mass arts might have something to offer. The question might have been shouted into the void but few echoes came back. The Broadway theater was a mass art on Manhattan at least, pandering to the low taste of expense-account men from all over America. It often provided dramatic excitement, particularly in ballet, sometimes a social message, but little visual imagination which might have influenced architecture.

Television was generally inept when it came to the visual arts. It tried no significant experiments in vision. When it approached the arts descriptively or critically it was on tiptoe and with hushed voice. Even in 1960 NBC's hour program about architecture was both dull and misinformative. In 1965 it did no better with *The City*. It was not often different with the movies and Hollywood.

Music, painting, architecture, sculpture had found some assistance in technology, much new subject matter, and architecture at least had found new problems, but for all the ancient so-called "fine arts" the role of technology as a helper was marginal. The new arts of the movies and television owed their existence to technology. They had had a long chance to justify this existence, to develop their own unities. In this they seemed to have failed. That they were a powerful cultural force could not be denied; that they were a good one could not be asserted. For architecture neither really had anything to say though there were a few anxious years when it seemed as though American domestic taste might be formed by the taste of the Hollywood stars; then we learned that the stars were just American bumpkins whose taste was as shoddy as our own. Perhaps we may be thankful that the movies and television felt no need to conduct an architectural crusade. What architectural taste might have been like in America had it been ministered to by Sam Goldwyn, Cecil B. De Mille, John Gunther, Lowell Thomas, Gabriel Heatter, Bishop Fulton J. Sheen, Arthur Godfrey, and Frank Sinatra is something better not to contemplate.

Things were occasionally more promising on the industrial front. Industrial advertising sometimes approached a level of communication appealing even to sophisticated taste. Designers at Chicago's Institute of Design made a mark with their layouts for posters, advertising, photo-montages and photography. In adopting these, progressive businessmen like Walter Paepcke, Chairman of the Container Corporation of America, led the way, employing artists like Herbert Bayer, Herbert Matter, Leo Lionni and Gyorgy Kepes to design advertisements. Some of their work was put together in a folder; more appeared in Kepes's study of visual communication, *The Language of Vision*, published in 1944. Here he tried to apply Gestalt psychology to optical communication. His first sentence revealed the social objectives of these visual studies: "Today we experience chaos . . . our common life has lost its coherency." His examples of new typography and paintings, his analyses of texture, focus and spatial patterns revealed an open desire to relate manifold discrete aspects of modern thought. Still in 1960 the problem of communicating ideas visually was not as near solution as it had been in the Middle Ages or the Renaissance. The old common symbols had been discarded but there were no new and common ones. The real and lasting symbols earn meaning only through much use and nothing was used long enough in commerce to gain much meaning.

In advertising there lay another commentary on the American architectural scene. European architectural magazines were consistently gay with advertisements of building products, designed by good artists, laid before architect-readers in an abstract way but quite in keeping with the art manners the architects were known to approve. The advertising pages were thereby quite as interesting as the text. No such nonsense reached the pages of the American architectural magazines, whose advertisers regularly advanced dreary sets of facts or claims aimed at the most pedestrian instincts of the profession. Of course it is also true that no industrial Olivetti (other than Paepcke) arose to subsidize architectural and art magazines so that they could afford to be bold, critical and gay. It was almost inevitable that advanced American architects and especially architectural students should seek their stimulus in magazines of Italy, England, Switzerland and Japan and not in those of their own country. Here was a curious American attitude which seemed to say that if advertising art did appeal to the sophisticated it was bound to repel the unsophisticated mass buyer, despite evidence to the contrary from all over Europe.

Developments in industrial design had a more direct and not often benign effect, at least upon the public taste. To this day, architects and probably people in general have not been able to establish clear-cut and logical attitudes about the role of industrial design in an industrial society. Primitive societies do not entertain such doubts. The maker of the utensil, the craftsman, and the maker of magic, the artist, have different roles but the question of status does not arise. Eastern societies generally do not make the distinction between the minor arts or "crafts" and the major arts such as we make in the West; particularly they do not assign to useful things a necessarily lower status.

But sometime in Western history, a persistent schism occurred. We think there is something nobler about the useless arts (or theoretical physics) than is to be found in useful tools (or engineering). Time and again from William Morris, through the

German Bauhaus, to the Institute of Design in Chicago, first-class talents have asserted that the problems of industrial design are genuine problems of contemporary art, deserving first-class attention. Time and again but with varying success they have applied that attention. New York's Museum of Modern Art has made notable displays of the products of industrial design. The chances are that the ordinary objects in daily use in a conventional contemporary American house have never been more efficient or more lovely in any other time; and it is ten to one that they are more lovely than any objects of art the same household has collected. Yet the stigma remains.

No leading architectural school in America is willing to house a school of industrial design despite the brilliant example in Dessau. We need not attempt here to follow all the implications of this curious position. Industrial design may have deserved its lowly status because industrial designers have not consistently been incorruptible. The hucksters perhaps call too many of their tunes. For every fine bowl, mixer or gas stove in an American kitchen there is a vulgar automobile in an American garage. Industrial designers have, it is true, usually turned out to be meretricious architects.

Industrial design at its highest seeks to improve both the performance of the product and the attractiveness of the package. In this it has some similarity to architecture. Like architecture it becomes corrupt if it is concerned only with the package.

Industrial products became "streamlined" about 1934. The 1933 Ford, blocky, with large useful square windshield, was changed to a V-motif in 1937 mainly for reasons of style quite divorced from the aerodynamic reasons which had caused the clumsy strut-winger Condor biplane also of 1933 to give way to the Boeing Clipper of 1938.

Now Raymond Loewy's Pennsylvania locomotive, his familiar Greyhound buses, and his Coca-Cola bottle became national emblems. The styling and packaging were similar, no matter what the object. Thus Walter Dorwin Teague's Ford Exposition Building at San Diego bore a family resemblance to his Brownie camera, dynamos, and Texaco gas stations, all emanating from a standard solution with trade-mark value in a variety of geo-

graphic, social, operating and competitive conditions. As Edgar
Kaufmann, Jr., pointed out in the London *Architectural Review*
of 1948 in an article called "Borax, or the Chromium-Plated
Calf," form followed sales.

The most popular form in the '30s, the teardrop, became a
symbol of machine production. It perverted functional design
and became a selling trick applied indiscriminately. Now vivid
colors, shiny textures and horizontal or vertical stripes culminated
in the ubiquitous cult of "three little lines." This was not the
kind of modern display any good architect wanted. By 1950 it was
difficult to purchase anything else, while the obscenities of the
rear fenders were yet to come. For a moment in Dessau it had
seemed that architecture and industrial design might achieve a
common destiny but this hope was blown away by the men of
sales and advertising who were less dangerous when they knew
they had no taste than when they all began to aspire to it. The
momentary influence on architecture of a few industrially inspired shapes did not last. The useful residue lay, on the one
hand, in chairs, lamps, and other items of furniture or fabrics
with whose design leading architects liked to play from time to
time; or in utensils with which the architect had seldom anything
to do professionally save when, and rarely, he involved himself in
the liturgical properties of a church. The great threat that industrial design might ruin architecture went away; the great hope
that it might ally itself with architecture went away as well.

9

THUS, out of all the messages the other arts of America might be
sending to its architects, only the message of the painters had
meaning. But their rebellious and accusing roads could not lead
directly to a new rebellious and accusing architecture. The com-
munistic and revolutionary ideology of much of the bitterest European and Mexican painting was not entrancing to the American
architect and he was unlikely to have a chance to lay down an
indictment comparable to Rivera's much less to want to. But, in
less radical form, and for a short time, the most striking fact
about the new generation of architects was their social idealism.

This generation would not listen seriously to Cram's orisons for a return to the Middle Ages. Even Geoffrey Scott's apostrophe to the Renaissance seemed to be a useless delight in form enjoyed independently of social purpose. There were new gods: the sociologists, men like Lewis Mumford, women like Catherine Bauer, who kept the architect mindful of his practical, social mission. Established and well-connected architects like Wallace Harrison concurred with social liberalism: "As a builder . . . [the architect] must take his place as the originator of both better buildings and a better society to control those buildings." No one seemed very sure about how the architect would acquire such controls or handle them once he got them. Yet the architect was to be the emergent leader, as Mumford spurred him to "organize the forces of society, discipline them for humane ends" and "express them in plastic-utilitarian building." A similar faith in the pedagogical magic of architecture excited educators like Joseph Hudnut, Harvard's Dean of Architecture, who renounced for a time the poetry of his Georgian Revival youth and brought Walter Gropius and Marcel Breuer to his faculty: "The young architect must leave our halls . . . resolute to use his technology for the reconstruction of our human environment."

His social awakening prompted the young architect of the '30s and '40s to swallow whole all that Sullivan and Wright had spoken about the architect as the man of faith, of emotion, the individual, the hero, the genius. He longed to become the great architect who would reconstruct the world along Utopian lines, fighting the bankers, the industrialists, the politicians, the conservative architects as he went. It was a potion, rich with nineteenth-century faith in the morality of art, made stronger by the twentieth-century statement of a social ideal.

The new books, too, tended to discuss buildings primarily in relation to their technology and their social history. Talbot Hamlin's *Architecture Through the Ages* (1940) attempted hazily to relate design to general psychology. Students no longer took out texts on composition or books of theory such as Guadet's *Elements*, as the library circulation cards reveal, preferring Le Corbusier's *Towards a New Architecture*, and books by sociologists, even confused and amateurish ones like Buckminster Fuller's chaotic *Nine Chains to the Moon*. As in architecture itself, social analysis was often one-sided and naïve; valued any form, however inept, mediocre or ugly, provided that it expressed social ideals or claimed to.

Ironically, the architects who were inclined towards new forms as well as social liberalism received little support from liberal governments here or abroad. There was little difference between Fascist taste, Communist taste, and democratic taste at least as expressed through official channels. It was abnormal that Niemeyer, admittedly a Communist, and extreme in the freedom of his designs, remained influential in Brazilian governmental circles; that Le Corbusier, with strong ideas for collective social action, was able to build in Marseilles, even admitting that the city had always been a notorious breeder of revolution.

But the Russian experience was no doubt the most traumatic. Here Bruno Taut, Oud, Mendelsohn, Le Corbusier and others had hoped to work freely. After a decade of supporting modern work, including city planning which was praised by Wright on his visit of 1937, the Soviet climate changed and the modern artists were expelled. The competition for the Palace of the Soviets at Moscow, open to international architects, had included Le Corbusier, Gropius and Mendelsohn, who were invited to make submissions. None of the principal modern architects won a prize. The highest awards went to two Russians, including Iofan, and to G. O. Hamilton of New Jersey, who submitted a building wrapped in Paul Cret's version of classic. The publication of all the entries announced Russia's intention to favor an eclectic architecture springing particularly from Greece and Rome. Maxim Gorki was quoted in his paraphrase of Cicero to the effect that he who does not know about the past cannot work in the future. Zorach's commentary was pungent; he called it a "reactionary form of architecture wholly unsuited to revolutionary ideas . . . It goes back to the most decadent pseudo-Roman development." Things had not changed in the USSR by 1953 when Rudnev designed the monstrous caricature of the Wrigley Building for Lomonosov State University which quickly became the pride of Moscow.

But even the New Deal liberals, notably Roosevelt, preferred

John Russell Pope's classic for the Jefferson Memorial and National Gallery of Art or the Georgian of Hyde Park to any modern architecture, and the new American embassy in Moscow was
built in a "truly American style," American Colonial, by Harrie
Lindeberg, while Australian Canberra's Californian terrain and
climate received a pathetic recollection of Williamsburg.

Indeed, the progressive architect could not look to any governmental or cultural institution for a sponsor in 1933. Industrial
corporations became increasingly dominant, while privately supported churches and colleges followed their lead. The architect
saw a nation of increasingly similar people whose dominant locale
was the managerial office, the salesroom, the secretarial room —
no longer the vividly individual farmer or mechanic, seldom
Maecenas. He saw a nation responding almost unanimously to
similar advertisements and sharing the uniform products of
nation-wide technology and communication. Despite revolts from
the consequences of this change, decisions were national and this
called for an architecture that reflected a nation-wide technology.

In these conditions it was not surprising that the large architectural firm practicing on a national basis was a unique American
development. Leading architects of the rest of the world had always worked in small and highly personalized groups, and this
was particularly true of the leading modernists. It was also generally true of the men who were leading the revolution in America.
Most of the large firms doing large work were conservative by the
very nature of their responsibilities and their clientele. From this
it was an easy jump to the *non sequitur* that no large firm could
ever do much in the way of innovation, could ever be capable of
distinction even in its imitations. For many of America's largest
firms the allegations were true, for some the further allegation
that they were better salesmen than artists may have been valid,
but for at least one, Skidmore, Owings and Merrill, the evidence
was that the generalization would not stick. Skidmore, who recognized the importance of research and organization in the handling of large commissions for the growing corporate clientele, together with design partners like Gordon Bunshaft and Walter
Netsch, seized upon the Miesian idiom and employed it skillfully.
Like other big firms, this one did not often aim in its early years

to produce innovations but it did expect to undertake major commissions, and give them thorough and honest study. Moreover such firms were not necessarily monolithic. The Chicago office of Skidmore, Owings and Merrill seemed more interested in experiment; the New York office in perfection; and as time went on sophisticated observers could note the difference.

European-born architects largely remained outside the new arrangement. Like Wright, they preferred to keep small offices, gaining their reputation on the basis of innovation and quality and preserving in their work the sense of an individual who can make mistakes. The European attitude toward the big firm was expressed by Giedion in 1951: "in the hands of huge architectural firms with hundreds of employees . . . the backbone and the creative impulse of the young architect are effectively crushed." The statement was not only overdrawn but it also ignored the fact that by 1952 some though not all of the big firms were often doing the most professional work while amateurish failures in performance and aesthetics were being eliminated. It also ignored the new kind of corporate client, frequently a steward of other people's money, who thought it had to place commissions in firms that were tested and reliable, that could meet production schedules, that had the staff to design and supervise the building and guarantee work. Finally, it ignored the great volume of work that was coming to new men like Eero Saarinen, who soon developed large offices themselves.

The sheer size and institutionalism of the new American business and industrial client insisted upon having a type of firm that, by its very nature, would perfect types of building but not be expected to make radical innovations in design. At their best, as in the case of Skidmore, Owings and Merrill, such firms might do some of the finest architecture of the day. Some other big firms did some of the worst. It was perhaps no worse than some of the small work but it was unfortunately more noticeable. And bigness had other perils. There were firms whose commercial instincts exceeded their architectural desires and from their boards came little but blight. Architecture is not something to be sold like cosmetics over a counter, and Wright was one of the first to declaim this axiom. If supersalesmanship were to overcome con-

science then the fear of the big firm might prove more than justified. By 1960 it was not clear what the outcome would be. There
were good small firms and mediocre small firms and a few, hardly
firms at all, who nurtured a single genius. There were brilliant
large firms but not many and most large firms were stodgy or
worse. Large and small alike, they were all much too busy; a designer can do only a few things at a time well, and very little while
airborne or between planes at Orly.

10

BIG firm or little, the course of the American development was
changed drastically by the European architects who came to the
United States in the late '30s. Without them one suspects American architecture might have tried to remain eclectic, taking off
from the classic of Cret and Goodhue, taking note of the functional work of Albert Kahn, following perhaps the modified
"modern" of Ralph Walker or the cautious work of Pietro Belluschi of the Portland Museum, influenced certainly by the elder
Saarinen and Dudok but by no one more drastic, rediscovering
perhaps the ways of Magonigle and Myron Hunt.

But whether, in the end, American architecture could have resisted a world movement of which, as things turned out, it became a leader, it is certain that the immigration accelerated the
American acceptance. The immigrants had the advantage of coming to America after there had been a wave of critical preparation;
and of having been principals in establishing the gospel which
they were now to preach to a new audience.

They readily won favor among a generation which believed
that art might, indeed ought to have important social consequences. The new belief typified earlier by Bruno Taut was also
advocated by the English critic Herbert Read, whose early books
Art Now and *Art and Industry*, had passionately advocated modernism. In *Art and Society*, in 1937, Read drew so close to the
notion of art as propaganda that he took special pains to point
out the crimes Nazi Germany and Soviet Russia had perpetrated:
"in certain ages society has made the artisan an exponent
of the moral and ideal emanations of the super-ego, and art has

Tennessee Valley Authority, Pickwick Landing Dam, 1935-1938

Chicago, Illinois Institute of Technology, Crown Hall, 1955,
Ludwig Mies van der Rohe, arch.

Fort Worth, Texas, model showing the city of 1970,
Victor Gruen Associates, archs., 1956

Colorado Springs, Colorado, U. S. Air Force Academy, Academic Building,
Cadet Library, Cadet Quarters and Social Hall, 1957-1960,
Skidmore, Owings and Merrill, archs.

Wellesley, Massachusetts, Wellesley College, Jewett Art Center, 1959,
Paul Rudolph, with Anderson, Beckwith and Haible, archs.

EZRA STOLLER

New York, Lever House, 1952, court, Skidmore, Owings and Merrill, archs.

New York, Lever House, 19
Skidmore, Owings and
Merrill, archs.

EZRA

Palo Alto, California, Center for Advanced Study in the Behavioral Sciences, 1955, Wurster, Bernardi and Emmons, archs.

Cottage Grove, Oregon, First Presbyterian Church, 1951, Pietro Belluschi, arch.

Detroit, Michigan, General Motors Technical Center, Styling Buildings, 1955,
Eero Saarinen, arch.

Detroit, Michigan, General Motors Technical Center, Research Laboratories
Administration Building, lobby, 1955, Eero Saarinen, arch.

Bear Run, Pennsylvania, "Falling Water,"
residence of E. J. Kaufmann, 1936,
Frank Lloyd Wright, arch.

...cine, Wisconsin, S. C. Johnson Company,
Administration Building, lobby, 1939,
Frank Lloyd Wright, arch.

Bartlesville, Oklahoma, H. C. Price
Tower, 1954, Frank Lloyd Wright, arch.

Detroit, Michigan,
Reynolds Aluminum Building,
1959, Minoru Yamasaki, arch.

thus become the handmaid of religion or morality or social ideology. In that further process art, as art, has always suffered." This was a strange and untenable generalization in the face of the Virgin of Chartres, but for a generation concerned about having indigenous art and alarmed about Rivera's Communist murals in Rockefeller Center, Read performed the service of insisting that the expressive content of art be a spontaneous, almost subconscious thing.

In his earlier book, *Art Now*, published in 1933, Read had not been so careful. He regretted that modern artists "are singularly devoid of ideological motivation." But neither Bruno Taut nor Gropius disagreed with social utilitarianism. Gropius had been influenced by the ideas of William Morris and John Ruskin and some of the themes of Marx and Kropotkin and could not help but have ideological motivation. "The Bauhaus," Gropius later wrote to D. D. Egbert "was more than an art institute. We were seeking to find a new way of life. The main tendency with which everyone was imbued was to stress the point that in this world of economic expediency the human being should be again the focus. That is to say, that all the economical and industrial issues are to be subordinated to the life requirements of men." As the stars of McCarthy, Jenner and Dondero ascended, liberals had to step carefully, moderating the social convictions they had so readily and safely voiced in the '30s. Thus Gropius felt impelled to add: "In consequence of this many of the members of the Bauhaus were interested in social improvements but the main tendency was very much anti-Marxist." Such a qualification was seldom made in the '30s and there was no reason to make it. Then the staff of the Bauhaus had particularly wanted to find a way to make industry serve humanitarian problems like adequate housing for the masses. Their interest was drawn to the most pressing social problems of the day, and theirs became the increasingly dominant social orientation of American architectural schools after the depression. This had nothing to do with Communism.

Such a social objective implied a relationship between art and society that now became the arena of scholarship. Geoffrey Scott's amoral interpretation of Renaissance architecture was no longer so popular. Mumford's trilogy, *Technics and Civilization*,

N

The Culture of Cities, and *The Conduct of Life,* considered art
not as form but as expressions of social, political and technical
accomplishments. That had been the thesis of European historians, beginning with Max Dvorak and Jacob Burckhardt, whom
Sigfried Giedion brilliantly followed in *Space, Time and Architecture* and *Mechanization Takes Command.* Following their
lead, John P. Coolidge made a pioneering study of the related rise
and decline of industry and architecture in the town of Lowell,
Massachusetts. Nationalism was no longer the dominant social
question in America; Greenough, Sullivan and Whitman engaged
new interest, and especially the work of the Chicago School, fostered by books like Hugh Morrison's *Louis Sullivan: Prophet of
Functionalism.* This interest was much intensified by the publication in 1941 of Sigfried Giedion's *Space, Time and Architecture*
which stressed America's development of functional forms like
Windsor chairs and the balloon frame, culminating in the functionalism of the Chicago school in the '80s and '90s. This important book grew out of lectures which Giedion had delivered in
1938-1939 when, with unintentional irony, he was appointed
Charles Eliot Norton lecturer at Harvard University. Periodically
reissued with addenda, it remains a modern classic setting forth a
number of important theses. Most durable, perhaps, is the insistence that the modern movement will attain no stature until it
aims at monumental expression based on modern concepts of
space. This idea became an important inspiration for much of the
work done after 1952.

The work was weakest in its failure to give any credit to the not
always malign contributions of French academic architecture and
its purblindness about living American architects other than
Wright. But its shortcomings do not really diminish the luster of
the work or destroy its long-range significance. They may even
have enhanced its appeal to progressive architects. Over all it did
well to counteract the notion that the best American work was a
testimonial to French genius, a thesis that had been argued
strongly in the '20s by men like Gréber, Réau, Hegemann and
Peets and widely accepted, too.

Another influential source was the earlier thesis of Lewis Mumford, published as *Sticks and Stones* in 1924. This held that

America, despite much blindness, *was* developing an architecture
in the tradition of Greenough, Richardson, Sullivan and Wright.
Mumford was no victim of any of the arguments of CIAM. He
did not really admire science and the machine as Le Corbusier
seemed to; perhaps he did not really accept the automobile and
certainly he rejected the automobile-centered cities of the Swiss
theorist. Moreover his social commitment to planning caused him
to waver in the extent of his interest in aesthetic quality; in this
he was unlike Montgomery Schuyler, the critic of the '90s whom
he admired.

11

BUT in the end the victory owed only modest thanks to the preparation by the writers, to the propaganda of CIAM and the Bauhaus, to the brilliant theoretical and polemical writing of Le Corbusier, or to the later acclaim of the American tastemakers
bringing up the rear. All of these influences helped, may even have
been necessary, but the central influence was the solid architectural accomplishment on the European scene, beginning to be
clearly evident, as we have noted before, as early as 1923.

Concurrently with the new statements about space there were
experiments with materials. The traditionally dominant ones
were replaced by white stucco, glass and fine metals and stones,
emphasizing the quality of surface rather than mass. Construction was exposed or featured. Transparency and interpenetration
of spaces (what came to be called "the flow of space") were confined largely to rectilinear compositions, and the continuous
spaces were shaped by discontinuous rectilinear planes. There was
some cultism in the direction of sparseness and austerity, sun and
light worship, and the machined qualities of materials. Thus all
ornament was banished as being unsuited to machine production,
which was presumed to produce precise edges and machine-
smooth surfaces. It was good doctrine to repeat uniform, factory-
made parts, but not with much solicitude for the phrasing of
older architecture. Composition, satisfied often by a brutal silhouette, was derived from programmatic planning and frank,
even forced, exhibition of functions. Envelopes for buildings were

the forms needed to enclose distinct spaces containing distinct functions. There was a rational, even an irrational, attention to problems of function and construction and insistence that these be expressed in design, even if it were necessary to exaggerate them. It was this kind of architecture that some Americans began to see in the '20s, as the Austrian Neutra brought it when he arrived in 1923, and as it was exhibited at the Museum of Modern Art in 1932. It was only a beginning, less sophisticated than it would become, and it shocked most American architects and observers who only looked at it without repeating or accepting the accompanying credo, both aesthetic and social.

The credo was based on mechanism, the belief that the world is best understood as a machine that operates efficiently in accordance with strict laws ultimately expressible in mathematical terms. Such a metaphysics placed high priority on natural science and on its extrapolations, even on false analogies drawn from it, on statistical analysis, on physical efficiency, and on finding objective and durable laws underlying human behavior. Carefully balanced rectilinear compositions proclaimed new forms, new materials and new construction, and architects addressed new problems with the sense that modernity alone was compatible with mechanism. They admired industrial buildings, pure, funicular engineering, and those objects like airplanes and ships and bascule bridges whose clean lines, sheer planes, and simple surfaces were the results of careful adjustment of form to performance.

Consequently the new group espoused an extreme functionalism; Moholy-Nagy wrote in *The New Vision:* "the artist pioneers . . . dared to proclaim the conception of 'functional rightness' even as applied to machine products." With this idealized functionalism went an aesthetic envelope related to the geometric art seen in paintings by Mondriaan and van Doesburg. It was a healthy and moderately tough-minded point of view; given the hypothesis, it was objective and teachable. There was no Wrightian glorification of the individual, nothing personal or anarchic, none of the elfishness of Alvar Aalto. Though Le Corbusier's Villa Savoye contained a roof terrace of forms that would later be developed into the most personal of buildings, Ronchamp, his theory during the '20s broadcast the functional house, *la machine à habiter*, which, as a product of technology, could operate in any place, regardless of terrain. It seemed then as if design might be analyzed and described and as if even the zeniths of architecture might be aspired to by teams, as Gropius insisted. "Not the single piece of work, nor the individual, highest attainment, has to be emphasized," Moholy-Nagy wrote, "but the creation of the commonly usable type, the development of the standard." Thus the objective was to have efficient planning and strictly geometric form and to realize these with mass-produced materials that could be economically assembled by modern industry.

Gropius consistently advocated mechanism. "We want to create a clear, organic architecture, whose inner logic will be radiant and naked unencumbered by lying façades and trickeries. . . . We want an architecture adapted to our world of machines, radios, and fast motor cars," he wrote in *Bauhaus*. Since fully functional architecture would require it to be adaptable to new uses, it must be flexible, even temporary, he thought, and proceeded to the questionable conclusion that nothing permanent, nothing merely ornamental or monumental, is truly useful: "The old monument was a symbol for a static conception of the world now overruled. I believe, therefore, that the equivalent for monumental expression is developing in the direction of a new physical pattern for a higher form of civil life, a pattern characterized by *flexibility for continuous growth and change*." But this belief, reminiscent of the scientists in America during the '70s, notably Charles William Eliot, save that it was not very clear about science, failed to recognize the facts of economics, tradition, and beauty, even of evolution, or that sentiment and affection are as often noble as foolish.

Intransigent mechanism had other strange consequences. If change were to be the pervasive mood of American society, as Gropius suggested, then there could be no immutable architectural laws, whether of composition or style. Rather than aiming at static and absolute values, Gropius sought an architecture that served the needs of current society, "for modern man has made the important discovery that there is no such thing as finality or eternal truth." Consequently, Gropius tried to explore architectural problems as if there had been no previously satisfactory solutions: "If the emphasis today is on the plain human being, not on the Caesars, we have to study man's biological way of life, his way of seeing, his perception of distance, in order to grasp what scale will fit him." To the great detriment of architecture, history had little part in his program: the goals of education are to "stimulate the student's mind towards his own creative thinking *according to laws of nature*." Those laws were objective principles derived from mechanics and psychology: "a special language of shape . . . a scientific knowledge of objectively valid optical facts." What those facts were, Gropius never announced. None of the great men seems seriously to have studied psychology. Gropius's glorification of science seemed strained to a later generation which deplored his failure to make *space* the chief objective of architecture or to those who knew he knew no science. They regarded the functional road as a probable blind alley which the Bauhaus had carefully dug through the steep grade of structures and the beautiful landscape of formal design. It had been useful as an educational discipline, but Eduardo Catalano and Paul Rudolph, both taught by Gropius, later found it an empty way, failing to lead towards total architecture, or so they thought.

The modern buildings of America that will probably hold a place on history's scene were seldom monuments to such extreme functionalism. To be sure, the awe-inspiring grandeur of the dams at Boulder, the Grand Coulee or the TVA, could be sensed at once; to be sure, much of Albert Kahn's mastery was obviously functional as it was revealed, for example, in the Dodge truck plant at Detroit. But the important buildings, though not unfunctional, were something more. They depended quite as much upon their sympathetic understanding of materials, their environment, their details as upon their functionalism. Perhaps they depended more. This was quite apparent in such different buildings as Neutra's Bell Experimental School at Los Angeles, Eliel Saarinen's Lutheran Church at Minneapolis, Mies's 860 Lake Shore Drive, or Eero Saarinen's Dulles National Airport. Modern world or not, science or not, architecture was still not a matter of the intellect alone. Great buildings continued to transcend their functional requirements.

12

UNIVERSALLY valid or not, the work and writing of the great men had an irresistible impact. It is dangerous to try to write history of one's own times and about men whom one knows in life, and history can easily change to personal criticism. But with this much apology let us say that it now seems safe to conclude that in all the galaxy, the star of Le Corbusier was brightest. Of all the Europeans, he might most beneficially have influenced America by his presence. He had the best grasp of space and the most fertile imagination of any of the Europeans. His city plans were the most influential urban proposals known to modern architects. But he remained in Europe, staying there even through the war. His book, *Vers une Architecture*, translated into English in 1927, contained important sections about American factories, sky-scrapers and machinery. He made a trip to New York in 1935, sponsored by the Museum of Modern Art; he came again after the war to engage in what turned out to be an unhappy experi-ment in playing on the team, captained by Wallace Harrison, which produced the United Nations buildings, in an emasculated version of what seems clearly to have been his original idea. His impressions are recorded in his book, *When the Cathedrals Were White*. It bears the telling subtitle, *A Journey to the Country of Timid People*. He was at once fascinated by the drive and the opportunity of America and appalled by the American failure to exploit the opportunity to the hilt.

The influence of this Swiss on America was thus largely indirect and in print. It was enormous even upon those who professed to deny his teaching, even among the few who had the temerity to assert that their ideas had predated his. No young designer in-vited to prepare a scheme for a new urban complex could avoid the suggestions Le Corbusier had made as early as 1922 when he set tall sheer towers and lower functionally shaped buildings in large pedestrian plazas and parks; but sometimes his followers forgot that adequate space between the towers was a *sine qua non* of his proposals. Suggestions of the '50s by Ieoh Ming Pei for Philadelphia and Denver, of Gropius for Boston's Back Bay, of

Ralph Walker for Chicago's Lake Meadows, and of Skidmore, Owings and Merrill for the later Fort Dearborn project, all owed their origin to Le Corbusier, whose ideas were most maturely expressed in the end in his unexecuted plan for reconstructing the war-leveled city of St. Dié in 1945.

On another front his Unité d'Habitation, a colossal apartment house for the workers of Marseille, 1952, was a modular slab in which two-story apartments and communal rooms, including a central floor devoted to shops and markets, were supported on sculptural *pilotis* and crowned by a roof-terrace of plastically modeled concrete "play sculpture." This again was an extension of ideas he had been proposing since the '20s.

Such sculptural freedom showed still more clearly in his planning for the new town of Chandigarh in India, beginning in 1952; it emerged to shape the space of the most original of all modern churches, Notre Dame du Haut at Ronchamp (1957), whose silhouette offers ever-changing lyrics as the three towers and the rolling overhanging roof present themselves in various combinations of architectural sculpture. The linearity of Marseille and the freedom of Ronchamp were combined in the brilliantly honeycombed cell-block and the sinuous ambulatory of the Dominican convent of La Tourette at Eveux-sur-Arbresle of 1959. Here too his theory of proportion, the modular, was brought fully and obviously into play in the spacing of the columns of the cloister.

As Le Corbusier's ideas developed he become more of a complete artist, less of an architect as usually conceived; he needed no crutch, whether it was provided by his universal module, his universal geometry, or the resources of modern technology which, as a matter of fact, he very often did not or could not apply. His leap into poetry automatically released him from the prose written by too many commercial firms in America or by the sober functionalism of less commercial moderns. At the same time a general interest in the total city advanced along lines he had forecast in his exhibition at the Salon d'Automne of 1922.

It was the freedom and power that Le Corbusier exploited in concrete which most escaped Americans, whose ultra-refined desire to polish tended always to reject its honest coarseness of form and texture which was well recognized not only by the Swiss but by talented disciples in Italy and Japan. It was a gospel which could be found brilliantly displayed in almost every other part of the world from Brasilia to Ahmedabad to Tokyo and Kyoto and at the hands of men of quite different births who had either passed through the atelier on the Rue de Sévres or admired him from afar, knowing him only through his buildings and his works. Indeed, his ultimate modesty and retiring nature, concealed beneath a formidable masquerade of ego, and sharp comment, made him quite difficult to know on other terms. Between his executed and unexecuted projects he proposed most of the important individual ideas of modern architecture, including a great many of the most important details; to this he added the most thorough theory of the city. Lesser men rejoiced at the many times he lost commissions but could not take much comfort in the patent fact that even his unexecuted proposals were more influential than their completed work.

This great man was never very happy in America, flitted through briefly, and it remained for others to try to work out American versions of his urban proposals; in this working out there was almost no reflection of the plasticity of architectural space that he had created beginning in the '30s. At the end of 1959 it was announced that he would design a new building for the fine arts at Harvard University — a bold and wise decision by this ancient seat of learning, but for America as a whole, and no matter how it came out, this was much too little and no doubt too late as well. Large-scale adaptations of his concrete designs were made by American architects only on the eve of his death in 1965.

But in 1960 most Americans were not at ease with the work of Le Corbusier. They hoped for something less disturbing. They found it in a thoroughgoing, uncapricious philosophy of design, tied to a social program, capable of being institutionalized so as to be partly independent of genius, achievable by groups who could assault problems collaboratively relying on a few mutually accepted axioms. Although the most American demonstration of this has to be attached to the work of Mies van der Rohe and his acolytes, the revolutionary point of view of the Deutsches Bauhaus was at first the most influential.

Gropius was a figure to command respect. He had great natural dignity, restraint, modesty. He had unshakable convictions and steadfastness, even stubbornness of purpose. If Le Corbusier was a scalpel, Gropius was a rock. He honestly believed in the social mission of architecture, in the beneficial potentials of the machine for all the arts, in the blessings to come from true standardization, in the genuine creative productivity of teams in which personal glories would be submerged.

It is perhaps even harder to assess Gropius than it is Le Corbusier, for the very reason that Gropius has been easier to know. The facts of his life seem clear enough although they may have been confused by over-adulatory biographers. From 1907 to 1914 he was primarily a promising young architect; from 1919 to 1928 at the Bauhaus he was primarily an educator; in 1934-1937 as an exile he practiced in England; from 1937 to 1952 he was again an educator, this time at Harvard. In this period he was surely the most influential single man in planting modern architecture firmly in America. At the end of this long and distinguished career he retired from the university in 1952, surrounded himself with younger associates and under the name of The Architects Collaborative (TAC) had more important commissions than had come to him in all the rest of his life.

In the beginning Gropius provided some of the best and most influential buildings of the early modern movement, notably the Fagus Works of 1911, the office buildings of the Cologne Workbund Exhibition of 1914 (with Adolf Meyer) and of course the Bauhaus itself. Although in the long verdict of history he will not stand as one of the great artists of the modern development, and surely not as its greatest theorist, his contributions always had elements of distinction, even of innovation, while there can be no doubt that he was the greatest teacher of the day.

The early German Bauhaus may have witnessed Gropius's finest days. Of the ideas then followed, he now says he would change only details. He held that the machine was the modern executant of design; its terms could not be avoided. All designers had to recognize this and this meant that new aesthetic criteria would have to be established. He asserted a "common citizenship of all forms of creative work and their logical interdependence on one another." To him the scale and complexity of the modern world made the necessity for collaboration self-evident; and so was the need for manual training of a very practical sort coupled with theoretical instruction in the laws of design. It was in the manual exercises that the transplantation to Harvard was least effective — for American universities, of which Harvard was the archetype, have for a long time had scant affection for any work save that of the mind. Were these theories of Gropius silly or romantic? Are they obsolete? Does any current architectural school face its problems as squarely as the Bauhaus did? These were questions which James Marston Fitch asked rhetorically in the *Architectural Forum* in May of 1960. The answer was almost certainly No.

Under Gropius's direction, the early German Bauhaus became the leading school of modern architectural design in the whole world. In the halcyon years, first at Weimar but mostly at Dessau, the Bauhaus steadily stretched its influence. Its scope included all the visual arts; urban planning, architecture, furniture, painting, sculpture, typography, photography, industrial design, ballet, theater, film. It insisted that these should originate in a common modern understanding, including an acceptance of the machine as a tool for modern artists. It aimed at perfecting an elastic method of working that would produce a total environment, untrammeled by traditions of style. It stimulated designers to be mindful of industrial processes and of the social consequences of design. It sought for quality in quantity production. It brought together more artists of eminent talent than any other art school of the day. Its building at Dessau of 1925-1926 was the most forward-looking building on any campus. It grappled with real social problems such as that of low-cost housing. Its spokesmen were strong and persuasive. They had a flair for dramatizing their ideas throughout the world. And they had courage. But a number of the individuals were Jews; a number were inclined to the political left; their designs could not possibly appeal to the ideological purposes or the low-bourgeois taste of the Nazi leaders. As the latter grew powerful they first put shackles on the Bauhaus, then truncated it and moved it to Berlin, and finally abolished it altogether. After that the hegira was inevitable. It was America's good fortune that the hegira went westwards, beginning about 1937.

Despite all its doctrine the Bauhaus was less rigid than might be imagined. It could not be hospitable to an artist who rejected the machine or who sought to see nature in a nineteenth-century romantic light. It could not have been indiscriminately palatable to all leaders of modernism and it is hard to imagine that Wright, Le Corbusier, Aalto or Léger could have thrived there. But it could accommodate people of such different purposes and tastes as Albers, Bayer, Breuer, Kandinsky, Klee, Feininger and Schlemmer, to say nothing of Moholy-Nagy. As Mies van der Rohe said at a Chicago dinner in honor of Gropius in 1953: "The Bauhaus was not an institution with a clear program — it was an idea, and Gropius formulated this idea with great precision. . . . The fact that it was an idea, I think, is the cause of this enormous influence the Bauhaus has had on every progressive school around the globe. You cannot do that with organization, you cannot do that with propaganda. Only an idea spreads so far."

After the first buildings of the pre-Bauhaus day, Gropius's own architectural work was less influential than the work of others — less influential than his theories, his writing, his teaching. It is not easy to see any very enormous development from Fagus of 1911 to Harvard Graduate Center of 1950. Many of his late buildings — the Berlin apartments, the embassy at Athens, the buildings at Brandeis University, the Baghdad University project — cannot be simply attributed to him since they were the product of his "anonymous" team, The Architects Collaborative.

But Gropius also gave his students an example of character, and this may be the thing that students least often see. Unlike Wright or Mies he was driven always to consider the social setting, just as Le Corbusier was so driven. He was not always sophisticated about social problems; but at least he chose what he deemed the principled, not the expedient position. He was certainly Utopian, even Transcendental. These traits were endearing to Americans, as the sharp wit of Le Corbusier was not. To Americans he was and will remain the great Puritan of the modern movement.

Other Europeans, also men of major talents, had their influence on American thinking. Mies van der Rohe continued to move inexorably towards universal space, always simpler, thoroughly interchangeable, subdivided by admittedly temporary partitions, urging the paradox, "Less is more." In the end he had an enormous effect on at least one aspect of American architecture. But this effect did not become strong until he moved to the United States in 1939.

In his glass-skyscraper project of the '20s he had made an important statement to the effect that it was not light and shade that mattered but the play of reflections on the wall. In his 1923 project for a country house he had mixed the planes of Doesburg with a free-standing wall. This, Philip Johnson discovered, broke "the traditional box by sliding out from beneath the roof and extending into the landscape." From that point to the masterpieces of 860 Lake Shore Drive in Chicago, or Seagram's in New York, was nothing but a steady, undeviating, long evolution of strongly contrasted forms, precisely articulated structures and decisive details. For many architects it had the advantage over the work of Le Corbusier or Wright that the Miesian order was one that could be learned and then repeated. This was shown in good time by such talented followers as Gordon Bunshaft, Ieoh Ming Pei, Philip Johnson, and Eero Saarinen. Saarinen was the first to move away and by 1960 Bunshaft, Johnson and Pei were also trying to erase the debt. Meanwhile as the *Architectural Record* justly said in its tribute of April 1960, "some less able architects have been released from the imperatives of originality and architecture is the better for it."

But as early as 1960 Mies, himself, rejected so easy an imitation when he reminded an audience at the Illinois Institute of Technology, "I hope you will understand that architecture has nothing to do with the invention of forms. It is not a playground for children, young or old." The great influence of Mies in America, which probably reached its peak a little before 1960, also owed much to the fact that the results seemed clear to American clients, a reasonable expression of the American machine and of American organization in a way that the freedoms and even primitivisms of Le Corbusier and Wright never could.

There were others, less influential. The great humanity and the poetic manipulations of brick and wood by Alvar Aalto were much admired though not much emulated save perhaps now and again by Eero Saarinen. The muscular concrete engineering of the Italian Pier Luigi Nervi was also much admired but even less often emulated. In the end the big influences remain those of Le Corbusier and Gropius and Mies, and of these Gropius and Le Corbusier will in the end be seen to have cast the longest shadows. There was, of course, one other — the American Wright.

For a while it was not apparent to most observers that Wright's architecture was actually quite different from the Europeans' both in theory and in realization. His early exhibitions in Europe had moved the European revolutionaries and they had adopted him, though he proved to be an unwilling foster-member of the family. His Larkin Building at Buffalo and the Robie House of 1908 at Chicago seemed to be progenitors of European modernism of the Saarinen-Dudok persuasion. But this was not the line of the Germans, and his course was in fact set against the functional and mechanized forms and materials Gropius and Mies employed and the "houses on stilts" of Le Corbusier. His diatribes against the other leaders of the modern movement which became more virulent as he aged were not mere perverse exhibitions of displeasure that some other architect had a place in the sun.

Wright's buildings found their geometric themes in the contours of the land; his space was plastic; his lighting was soft and chiaroscuro; he preferred natural rough textures; his colors were autumnal, not primary. His architecture grew like an organism by adaptation to specific sites, materials, structures. When Henry-Russell Hitchcock published his important monograph on Wright's work, *In the Nature of Materials,* in 1942, he awakened renewed interest in our native titan.

But even if Wright had been generally recognized as the author of an American architecture (and he was not), it is doubtful that any other designer could have attained his inimitable personal style. Some tried but even the best of them, Alden Dow, Harris Armstrong, Paul Schweikher and Bruce Goff, somehow failed fully to capture his spirit. Others who by the '50s had come to accept him were often, like Ralph Walker, perhaps a little more sympathetic to his forms than they were to the European forms

which they castigated; but principally, one suspects, they liked the
doctrine of individuality which Wright proclaimed for himself
and presumably extended to others even if he did not admire
their talents. Wright's statements could not be otherwise than
personal. They did not conform to a national technology or to
any classifiable national sentiment.

In 1948 a portfolio of the *Architectural Forum* showed a decade of his work. His imagination bounded like a lamb in spring.
His exhibition held at Gimbel's in Philadelphia in 1950 was taken
later to Europe where it had almost as great an effect as his earlier
show of 1910. Now many new buildings showed his unsurpassable
skill in handling volumes and especially planes. This appeared in
great variety at "Eaglefeather" in the hills of Santa Monica, in a
Sports Club for Hollywood Hills, in some of the buildings at
Florida Southern College, in the Johnson Wax Administration
Building, in the Pauson House, in Falling Water. Moreover his
long career was reaching an epitome in his thinking about the
city.

His book, *The Disappearing City*, of 1932, had announced an
agrarian, almost Populist, denunciation of contemporary urban
life, and it set him upon the problem of developing a new form
for communities. That emerged in Broadacre City, a plan first
exhibited at Rockefeller Center in 1935 and again at the Museum
of Modern Art in 1940. The model of Broadacre City showed
how four square miles of land might be developed as a country
seat with residences, civic buildings, cultural buildings, industries
and farms. Here we find quotations from a lifetime of work: the
Gordon Strong Planetarium of 1925, the Steel Cathedral of 1926,
apartment houses like St. Mark's Tower and another for Eliza-
beth Noble of 1929; the gasoline and service stations of 1928;
farm units and market units of 1932; there were many types of
house, large and expensive houses like the House on the Mesa, as
well as minimal dwellings like the Usonian houses Wright invented. Each was to stand on a large lot of landscaped ground,
connected with special highways and bridges for automobiles. It
was obvious that Wright here anticipated the tremendous exodus
from the city and prepared a plan for suburbia and the rural communities, facing a problem which was largely ignored at the most

crucial time by planners, American and European alike. Broad-acre City was more a compilation of Wrightiana, to be sure, than a great and serious solution of the urban problem. It did not have the same complete logic and understanding of the automobile that Le Corbusier had shown in his earlier proposals. Wright's solutions were at once less efficient and more humane. Taken literally they could set no pattern for the future as the ideas of Le Corbusier did. But they had in them a consideration for personal life that was most missing in Le Corbusier when he was most logical.

It is hard to realize now that, in 1933, there was still a question whether the American public would recognize the messages of modern architecture coming from abroad and the few harbingers built here; whether it would accept them without further architectural miscarriages such as the Jefferson Memorial in Washington. Indeed, there was every reason for apprehension that the infant American modern movement might die in a backwater built around the enthusiasm which had greeted Eliel Saarinen when he came from Finland to head the new Cranbrook Academy at Bloomfield Hills, Michigan. Saarinen had done notable modern work in Finland. But now the modern movement somehow began to pass him by. His new school buildings at Cranbrook, accompanied by the whimsical sculptures of Milles, were backward looking and eclectic in a special Scandinavian way, enjoying ornamental reminiscence and rich materials. They showed the kind of empathy that suffused Ragnar Östberg's Town Hall on the canals of Stockholm. This building was much more to American taste than the projects of Le Corbusier, Gropius or Mies. It was prominently displayed in America and won for Östberg the gold medal from the A.I.A. in 1934, long before it was conferred on Gropius or Mies, to say nothing of Le Corbusier who got the honor only in 1961, while Mies received his award in 1960. The work of Dudok at Hilversum, Holland, also gained enough popularity to win him an early medal as a modernist.

The early A.I.A. awards may now seem to have been applauding mostly the laggards of the modern movement. This simply reflected general American taste which hoped that the American architectural revolution could be gentle, even unnoticeable.

The work that was most easily accepted sought to develop a modern idiom in ornament and shape without ignoring or discarding ancient principles of composition. It exposed a desire for rich craftsmanship in architectural accessories such as tiles, lamps, and textiles, not inevitably products of the machine. The question was whether this was enough or whether America needed the wholesale shock of a revolution. Would Americans adopt the revolutionary notions that had already been so clearly set forth in Europe? Would they develop something comparable of their own? Would they ignore the new altogether? Or would they follow their traditional course of a reluctant cultural importation? If that were to be the way, American modern might have to wait a long time, for the modern movement was not really firmly established in the European seats of power.

But, as the *Architectural Review* pointed out in 1960, Wright, Mies, Le Corbusier and Gropius had each to fashion a modern world in terms they could build. Each cast the world in his own image, one organic, one structural, one primitive, one mechanistic. Together they offered the generations to come both ideas and choice and this would have been enough. In fact, a major share of what they contributed was to make "the gift of their worlds."

13

IN the beginning some of these gifts needed further exposition. Ready at hand was the Congrès Internationaux d'Architecture Moderne (CIAM) which propagated the faith from its founding at Sarraz in Switzerland in 1928 to its official demise at Dubrovnik in 1956 and the failure to resuscitate it at Otterloo in 1959. CIAM was for a long time the most effective spokesman for modern principles, notably those of Le Corbusier and the Bauhaus, but also of Wright. The Europeans accepted its support with as much enthusiasm as Wright repudiated it. The first congress at Sarraz was succeeded by eight others at Frankfurt, Brussels, Bergamo, Heddesdon, Aix-en-Provence, Bridgewater, Paris, and Athens between 1929 and 1953, before the Congress of Dubrovnik in 1956 when the leaders of CIAM officially declared its mission accomplished. But a few of those who owed much to CIAM and

who had faith in the continuing vitality of its principles including the Italian, Ernesto Rogers, were determined to revive it at
the 1959 meeting, held symbolically at Otterloo, the site of Henry
van der Velde's greatest work. Rogers provided a personal farewell in his magazine, *Casabella*: "The CIAM represents the moment of greatest commitment and solidarity in modern architecture; a commitment still more valid today and more and more
necessary if we are not to abandon the debate and our hope for a
progressive architecture."

But the young English, who by 1960 were finding themselves
powerful propagandists and critics, if not interesting architects,
mustered the strength of other Europeans who felt as they did.
John Voelcker drew the significant contrasts which supported the
coup de grâce of CIAM. In 1930 CIAM, he said, espoused a
frame-building and multi-level high-rise urban image containing a
complete urban system, but by 1950 its image was random, drawn
from many sources, made up of single ideas, which one by one
contributed to change and extended the experience of space. The
prototype buildings and master plans of 1930 were didactically
charged with a full international program while by 1950 the
buildings related to unique situations. How could there longer be
a program for such an organization? The critics were no doubt
right but were they aware that their picture of CIAM was really a
portrait of the whole modern movement, old or new?

CIAM had never been a group which one could join at will. It
was self-selecting and in the beginning most of the selections were
brilliantly made. Its architects came together for a purpose expressed by Le Corbusier: "In CIAM we do only what the individual can't do alone." It was, in a way, an effort to establish a
common vocabulary for a group of very individual individualists.
It was not a group which could be expected to march indefinitely
in harness — the poetic and mercurial Aalto, the poetic and polemical Le Corbusier, the patient, stubborn and prosy Gropius
and Markelius. There were other threats to ultimate unity such as
the mounting menace of closed borders and contradictory national ideologies. But for a time and very likely under the relentless prodding of the distinguished Swiss historian-critic Sigfried
Giedion, this group of Pegasuses did act as a team. They prepared

presentations to a common theme sometimes even with standard-ized format and symbols. They discussed the presentations in their congresses, agreed upon resolutions which are more a part of European than of American habit, published several of the con-gresses in temporarily influential books.

The CIAM broadcast the modern movement influentially for many years but outlived its maximum effectiveness and by the mid-'50s it was saddening to see some of the members poking in the embers, as indeed they also did about the Bauhaus, hoping for a phoenix in Berlin in 1957, which seemed unlikely. The individ-uals remained friends long after their personal successes and the differences of their temperaments had no longer seemed to make it desirable for many of them to continue to try to work in care-fully structured group efforts. These men had found a common bond in CIAM in their difficult years and had hoed together a row which isolated individual Americans were trying to hoe alone. Thus they had forged a durable bond. So, as the point of CIAM grew duller, the peripheral men still did not resign, did not with-draw in a display of acrimonious pyrotechnics aimed at each other, but simply kept their names on the roster without participating. But before that CIAM had burned with a brilliant flame and everyone who had helped to stoke it could be proud of his part.

Many national action groups sprang from CIAM, such as GATEPAC in Spain and MARS in England, but the ways of CIAM and the dogmatic approach of Giedion were not calcu-lated to make it appealing to Americans. In 1939 Giedion tried to organize a more effective American wing of CIAM, with no great success. Americans were characteristically unenchanted by joint theoretical projects, characteristically uninterested in writing manifestoes or passing resolutions, characteristically unwilling to regard K. Lönberg-Holm and Serge Chermayeff as typifying American attitudes. CIAM's leadership in America had to be of a different sort, principally through its publications.

But even in its best days there were disturbing things about the CIAM line. The opinions of an individual critic may be admired or detested, accepted or rejected, in whole or in part. When these are expressed as organizational doctrine the color is different.

There seems to have been in the organization or among its leaders
a penchant for the doctrinaire which tolerated only its own here-
sies. Stringent adaptation to function was applauded and the cult
of sparse austerity dominated its aesthetic canons. Thus the work
of Markelius in Sweden was denounced in 1951 when Giedion
published *CIAM: A Decade of New Architecture:* the new em-
piricism "under cover of 'humanising' architecture leads it
only into another cul-de-sac." Though the book contained the
work of such Americans as Eames, Lescaze, Schweikher, Wurster,
Harris, Soriano and Catalano, many of whom were not members
of CIAM, America was generally castigated with very little sensitivity as to what America was really like. CIAM remained a club
of aging fighters meeting after the fight was over; and somehow it
never found a new Theseus or a new cause for him to lead.

14

ANOTHER push was needed, one that had to come from a group of
tough-minded aggressive designers located in America, men who
would be spokesmen for the technological, universal architecture,
who would ask all to take sides for or against their buildings, who
would be stubbornly, even passionately, dedicated to radical design.

R. M. Schindler, an Austrian immigrant, thought that his
Beach House of 1926 in California with *pilotis* of concrete was
the earliest fully modern house in the United States. As early as
1922 he had built his own house, one story high, cellarless, with a
full-height wall of glass and sliding doors that opened to a patio;
but in spite of his prescience Schindler was neither a top-flight
designer nor a convincing protagonist.

Richard J. Neutra, another Austrian, was a stronger character
but he never managed to gain the point of vantage in governmental or educational circles where he might have been fully influential until the victory was won and he was clearly an elder
statesman. William Lescaze, like Eliel Saarinen, had little revolutionary impetus. Erich Mendelsohn quickly became identified with
Jewish communities but his American work displayed a tendency
to compromise that had not been so clearly forecast when he was

in Europe. Thus though his Maimonides Hospital in San Francisco and his much less refined synagogues at Cleveland, St. Louis and St. Paul gave some life to Jewish architecture, he was not prepared to affect the national scene. The influence of Antonin Raymond was felt more in Japan than in America, while Oskar Stonorov's was localized in Philadelphia. Far too many of the European architects were too extreme to be given jobs even at educational institutions. Typical was Frederick Kiesler, who came to the United States in 1926 after a European career that had begun in the office of Adolf Loos. His Space House of 1934 was of continuous shell construction with continuous windows opening upon a single space tenuously subdivided into fourteen living areas. In 1942 he opened the Peggy Guggenheim Gallery with paintings at different eye levels and without benefit of frames, floating upon unseen supports from a curved wooden background; other paintings, suspended on strings stretched between floor and ceiling, floated in space. This supplied spectacular staging. So did his sets for the Juilliard School of Music, but neither his talents nor his personality was directed toward those agencies that could effect a major change in American environment.

Thus no positive turning point, no indigenous movement can be clearly perceived. If there was a turning point, it came at about 1937 when the great Germans and Central Europeans came to the United States, generally after a sojourn in England. Walter Gropius and Marcel Breuer joined the faculty of design at Harvard, headed by Joseph Hudnut. Lazlo Moholy-Nagy went to Chicago, where he established the New Bauhaus in 1937. This attracted other Bauhaus men like Gyorgy Kepes. In 1939 Mies van der Rohe, Gropius's successor in Germany, accepted appointment as head of the architectural school at the Armour Institute, later joined with the Lewis Institute to become the Illinois Institute of Technology. Josef and Anni Albers joined the faculty at Black Mountain College in North Carolina. Those who started a new life at experimental and progressive institutions such as Black Mountain had years of uncertainty, turmoil, internal dissensions and financial difficulties. Despite some staunch support from industrialists of Chicago, the New Bauhaus was launched and maintained only with the greatest difficulty and self-sacrifice on the part of Moholy, his wife and the staff. Their commitment to modern art was not casual; it was a religion, all-demanding and all-consuming. Life was easier at older institutions like IIT where Mies, almost from the first, became king. But at Harvard there was steady friction, even though Gropius prevailed, and his fifteen years as chairman of the School of Design ended in a clash between urgency and patience and an unhappy dispute between Hudnut and him which helped neither. But by then the heroic, historic, role of Gropius and the solid acceptance of his cause made this more a matter for personal regret than of any deeper significance. In the end, the appointment of José Luis Sert as Gropius's successor guaranteed that Harvard would see a continuity of principle, if not of detail. Moreover the modern cause was so thoroughly accepted throughout America that a reaction at Harvard would have done more harm to the University than to architecture.

Much the same thing could be said of the dénouement at IIT Here the instruction was very rigorously laid out by Mies and brooked no deviation from the principles he was espousing in his own work as he went inexorably towards universal space. Whenever it was inconvenient to attend the functional efficiency of space he disregarded it. Though he worked on proportions and on the details of materials with the greatest care and refinement even his structure might be symbolic. This was clearly admitted in the steel beams he set vertically outside the skeleton of 860 Lake Shore Drive of 1951, which he carefully terminated above the ground so no one could imagine they were columns. The German Pavilion at Barcelona of 1929 had not been functional in any purely utilitarian sense and, in the end, this is what you had to say of 860 Lake Shore Drive, nearly a quarter-century later.

But such freedom from function was delayed by the depression. In the meantime, and until after the war, Mies worked out his proportions with great care and refinement which came to fruition in such buildings as Crown Hall at IIT of 1955 or the Seagram's Building at New York City in 1957.

Such refined study of proportions and of scale controlled both the design of the buildings he made for IIT and the training he gave its students. But when his retirement came in 1958 there was another unhappy crisis. The rumor that he would not continue to do the buildings for IIT proved true and was the occasion for a good deal of acrimonious comment. But in the end everyone realized that IIT had valued good working arrangements more than the privilege of being wholly designed by one of the great men of the twentieth century. The decision could not seriously arrest the course of modern architecture. The impress of Gropius and Mies had been laid ineradicably on their times.

But in the years between 1937 and 1960 the outcome was not always so predictable.

15

DURING the struggles for acceptance, Mies van der Rohe was refused permission to practice alone in New York and Aalto had to be joined with another and lesser man in Boston. Even when a modern firm, the Saarinens, won a competition to design the new Smithsonian Gallery of Art at Washington, the best effort of Joseph Hudnut and his hand-picked jury could not persuade the sponsors of the competition to have the winner built; though years later a new director of the Smithsonian, Leonard Carmichael, was quick to approve the building of a banal design for his new Museum of History and Technology.

Even the social aims of the Bauhaus group and other modernists were disliked. Gropius's appointment to Harvard in 1937 excited derision among many older architects, such as Charles Killam, Professor of Architecture Emeritus at Harvard, who wrote bitterly against the appointment of "social reformers," "mere critics," "specialists in domestic work of low-cost housing," "extreme modernists." Others were suspicious of what Gropius called "a new way of life." Conservative communities such as Lexington, Massachusetts, thought that all the modernists who were settling on Six Moon Hill or in nearby Lincoln in modern houses must be liberals, even radicals, probably intent on violent reform.

The most outspoken critic was Ralph Adams Cram. His autobiography, *My Life in Architecture*, of 1936, bristled with Gothic fury against the sacrileges of modernism. If industry and com-

merce were modern, they might have a new architecture, he
thought, but only because they were ephemeral and culturally unimportant. Functionalism was, for him "the Pentecost of ugliness." "The cubist, 'dimaxion,' 'functional' house . . . the work
of M. Le Corbusier . . . or the new type of apartment house
. . . seem to me to be a betrayal of trust, a vicious though unintentional assault on the basic principles of a sane and wholesome
society." Of modern religious sculpture he said, "while they have
their place in the New York Museum of Modern Art or in the
showrooms of the Carnegie Institute in Pittsburgh, they adapt
themselves with scant sympathy to the purposes of any religion
other than that of Voodooism, fetishism, and similar psycho-
pathic manifestations." There was much folly that Cram could
point to in the modern movement. Dadaism, surrealism, futurism, each had its lunatic fringe. An exhibitionist like Salvador
Dali did not help matters when, on his arrival in New York in
1936, he announced his desire to live in a "fur-lined uterus."

Essentially a Ruskinian, Cram did not object to the social purposes of architecture, but he did disagree with Gropius's relativism and attacked the anti-individual and irreligious positions of
the mechanistic functionalists: "For my own part," he wrote, "I
cannot conceive of an adequate training in art which does not
involve the element of worship . . . All good art in the past has
developed from organized religion." His religious beliefs buttressed his notion of aristocracy. He disliked the current "perilous
condition of fictitious social equality."

Others who were not conservatives still had strong reservations
about the new European architecture. The most eminent of these
was Wright. He argued that the art of architecture has many
sides for which function and economy are no measure. He always
insisted that the architect makes the image of his age, is not
merely a reflector for it. He called the modern European housing
"the slum of the future." Still others, like Edward Stone, converted by the immigrant architects, came late to mechanistic architecture, only to have another change of heart later. Other late-
comers, like William Wurster, never succumbed to the Bauhaus,
and kept their designs sensitive to regional landscape, materials,
history and institutions.

As in other times, many architects escaped the challenges altogether. There were lingering classicists, like Cass Gilbert, John
Russell Pope and Otto Eggers, who kept on grinding out classic
monuments at Washington; the Supreme Court and the National Gallery of Art — buildings of a hollow and pompous cast,
despite materials so rich that any modernist envied them the opportunity. There were tattered remnants of medieval piety, still
visible in the unfinished Episcopal Cathedral at New York and
the Episcopal and Roman Catholic Cathedrals at Washington,
which kept to their handicraft, pseudo-Gothic ways. Nor was
Georgian languishing: heavy, elephantine and clumsy, badly
sited, feebly composed, it appeared in public schools and town
halls and churches throughout the nation, and it received official
sanction from Franklin Roosevelt when he designed his own library at Hyde Park. Sometimes a New England architect like
Robert Dean, once a devotee of Williamsburg and then of Dudok's Town Hall, combined the incompatible two in an extraordinary if not otherwise notable high school, as at Wellesley, or in
a downtown department store for Boston.

Courageous men of an earlier day, such as Ralph Walker, tried
to make their own personal compromise between the old and
the new, "*sans dogme, sans monotonie*," but, unable to concede
anything to the new prophets, were unable to learn anything
either. Some of these men might have played majestic roles in an
earlier American day. It was their misfortune to live in a different
age; and though many of them continued to have many clients,
they had to reconcile themselves in the privacy of their libraries to
the fact that their buildings would seldom be published, seldom
praised by any knowing critic and that their position as middle of
the roaders was no better than that of the "black reactionaries."
By the '50s no competent revivalists remained. When the wistful
Henry Hope Reed, Jr., the lonesome piping voice of the Renaissance revival, needed to find a designer for propaganda purposes
for San Francisco, he had to turn to an obscure friend "over the
bay in Berkeley" who was ready to come forward if called. No call
was heard.

One might have expected the traditionalists to fall under the
demands for functional and economical performance during the

depression. But aesthetics really remained the crucial issue. "Modern" came to be identified in the popular mind with something unusual, blatant, ugly. When the public spoke scathingly of modern designs it thought of the extreme, even the experimental ones. Those who disliked flat roofs and "chicken coops" in the landscape had little that was good to say for architectural experimentation, on the ground that architecture needed no further study or research. Soleri's glass dome for a desert house in California seemed to be a flagrant defiance of nature. There were obvious shortcomings in Buckminster Fuller's Dymaxion House and in Bruce Goff's Umbrella House at Aurora, Illinois, of 1950. But even those who did not perceive these criticized the structural exhibitionism and the seemingly capricious subdivision of internal space. Philip Johnson's early house on Ash Street in Cambridge, with its solid plywood wall around the front garden, provoked the curious to kneel on the sidewalk to peer through the small crack beneath the front door to see how a privacy-loving bachelor lived. Polevitzky's Bird Cage house built in Florida in 1950 seemed to be nothing but the work of *flâneur*, despite the sophistication of its spaces; Charles Eames's experiment in assembling standard materials for his case-study house in California of 1950 suggested to the conventional a box kite, filled arbitrarily with a clutter of materials. Few laymen were able to see past Paul Nelson's hung stairs and rooms and ramps to appreciate the graceful spaces and stately rhythms for the model of the Suspended House he showed in 1939.

The critics were not always wrong. Some of the modern buildings were atrocious. Some were cheaply commercial, or belligerently harsh and crude. More were boringly monotonous, with flat roofs, crude juxtapositions of planes of glass and masonry; many were ruled by an inexorable and unimaginative geometry that was insistently rectilinear in plan, elevation and section. The new clichés were turned out endlessly. Many designers flunked the problems of transition as others had before them but the failure was perhaps more nakedly apparent. Intent upon the grail of functionalism, many forgot the determinants of great design. Hypnotized by the mysteries of the right angle, some ignored the exciting spaces that might have been created with modern materials and structures. Clichés like the tapered corridor, the corner window, the shed roof, the open house-stair were seized avidly, consumed voraciously.

But if the first phase of the modern movement was troubled by the rigors of doctrinaire and uncouth rectangularity, it was succeeded by the even more destructive notion that the cliché must be avoided at all costs. Now many architects, and not always only the younger ones with the lesser names, became obsessed with the ambition to be original. They thought they must always create startling forms, even new religious symbols out of whole cloth. You could see this in Arthur Brown's First Lutheran Church at Tucson, or Lloyd Wright's Swedenborgian crystal at Palos Verdes, California. Even the master Wright succumbed at times. Abandoning the poetic integration of space and structure he had achieved in the much earlier Unity Temple of 1901, he provided the Unitarian Church at Madison, Wisconsin, with an attention-getting roof in 1950. It pitched towards a steeple that rose obliquely from the ground. Harrison and Abramovitz scored some kind of high mark in this direction when they lunged into the eye-catching First Presbyterian Church at Stamford, Connecticut, erected in 1958, while the genius of Eero Saarinen seemed to be fighting itself on this issue all through the last part of the '50s.

This aim to be unique was a strange bedfellow for functionalism. Innovation tended to stop any effort to perfect interesting types of structure, plans, elevations. In 1938-1940 many architects were critical of Anderson and Beckwith's elegant design for the Alumni Swimming Pool at M.I.T. because it leaned on an excellent Swedish precedent; yet its performance and the improvements the architects introduced clearly justified the study. They had improved greatly upon a good precedent. But individuality seemed to be more highly valued than perfection among the *avant garde* and until they learned to produce at least some charming spaces and forms the public could easily rest its antagonism toward change on the most bizarre products of the cult of originality.

Those who resented even modest and thoroughly legitimate experiments in space and structure were delighted when they could find functional inadequacies in the modern buildings. This was often easy to do. Suddenly all the Colonial gutters whose paint was peeling were forgotten and so were the tiring stairs and the dark reading-rooms of the public libraries. The opposition gloated when it learned that a hurricane had caused some difficulties for Neutra's glass-enclosed house for John Nicholas Brown on Fisher's Island, New York. It never forgot that Frank Lloyd Wright's roofs leaked or that one of Gropius's clients had not been given the book-lined living room she had expressly demanded of her "functional architect." Far too many modern buildings were cheap and looked it. Their artificial materials soon became shabby, their flimsy construction fell apart. Wright had never been secure against physical failure. The houses of younger modernists, eager to try their wings even in the face of lean budgets, were no match for the excellent construction and careful detailing that Goodhue, Magonigle or Lindeberg provided for their usually wealthier clients. Too much of the modern work was amateurish. There were strong suggestions that the houses of Mies were notoriously awkward to live in; they were far from cheap, their white walls and pristine furnishings responded badly to grimy-fingered children or to disorder. They were unsuitable for a mother with three children, "one girl in bed, one girl in school" and a recalcitrant boy pounding his way into the Czerny exercises; she might pray for the return of partitions that were now so old hat. It was said that the students living in Gropius's Graduate Center at Harvard could not study for the corridor noise and that they cared little about using its common rooms. The plate glass in the main cafeteria at Eero Saarinen's General Motors Technical Center was so strongly affected by wind that post-construction bracing had to be added even though it marred the proportions of the building; and there were anxious days at his Kresge Auditorium at M.I.T. when the concrete shell refused to stop creeping as soon as it was supposed to. James Johnson Sweeney, director of the Guggenheim Museum, introduced strenuous alterations into Wright's wonderful new space in order to hang pictures at all and thereby launched another international controversy on art versus use. There was enough truth in all such accusations, or most of them, so that the public, already suspicious about the aesthetics of modern design, doubted also its claims to economy and performance, even when penitents of the modern movement, examining more conservative buildings, showed that they, too, seldom stood the same tests.

These demurrers had some justification as long as the members of the new movement acted like *enfants terribles* suddenly discovering architecture for the good of the world. The modernists undoubtedly claimed too much for their social and functional achievements and underplayed their aesthetics. No one could question their sincerity, but their work was still often ungainly, awkward, contrived, and filled with an infantile urgency.

The vigor may have suffused the work and sustained it against any merely aesthetic or practical judgment. But however expressive such vigor might be, expression alone could not constitute great architecture and the public sensed what the younger modernists later had to discover. It was a point which had been impressively made by Geoffrey Scott in 1914. To an entire generation befuddled by Ruskin's desire for moral expression, Scott had declared that the basic value of architecture lay solely in its capacity to give pleasurable sensuous experience, quite independent of any ethical or social undertones. This formalism buttressed the inclinations of architects of the '20s like Hood, Corbett and Goodhue who cheerfully ignored or denied social and moral programs. But in the revolt the new generation could not accept the art-for-art's-sake mentality as anything but an irresponsible anachronism. In the face of housing problems and those of war production Henri Focillon's romanticism of 1942 seemed incredible: "form, guided by the play and interplay of metamorphoses, go[es] forever forward, by its own necessity, toward its own liberty." Formalism could not weather the storms of demand that architecture be bound to social purpose; and it was only at the end of the '50s that modern architects began to read Scott again and to suggest that art might be first and foremost a matter of visible spaces and physical forms, not social beliefs.

Meanwhile the opponents of the new movement had almost everything on their side; the schools suppressed it and sneered at it even while the students sought it; the bankers denied it in their loans and the realtors in their projects; journalists tried to kill it with bitter ridicule; the public did not understand it, did not

really like it, were more content with things to which they were
accustomed; the public wish, if this were represented by the opinions of legislators and governors and presidents, would have none
of it in public buildings; university trustees were assiduous in
keeping it off the campus and were fully supported by the few
alumni who were observant and articulate about the architecture
of Alma Mater which they inevitably venerated more for its
memories than for its distinction. Even in 1958 most Bostonians
who wrote to the newspapers hoped that their new city center
would be 22-story Georgian, or at least theirs were the letters the
editors cared to print. People who had never gone near Beacon
Hill now feared its degradation.

16

SLOWLY conservatism modified the modern movement. During
the '50s, younger architects like Rudolph, Yamasaki and Nowicki
sought solutions undominated by the stringent original mechanical aims of the Bauhaus group. Older converts like Howe and
Wurster reserved their admiration for Le Corbusier's imagination, Wright's masterly sensitivity, and Mies's patiently studied
proportions. The resulting humanization of modern architecture
was most apparent first on the West Coast where the Bauhaus
group had never planted one of its dogged pioneers. It appeared
in a number of houses by Wurster, Soriano, Henry Hill, Neutra,
Harwell Harris, and Mario Corbett. Each respected its terrain,
used natural materials so as to emphasize their textures and colors, and seemed to be free of clichés in their windows, plans, roof
lines or compositions. Planned picturesquely, they achieved unity
through balance, often occult, and the counterpoise of masses
and spaces. Above all, these Western houses seemed to stand in a
long line of development out of the Spanish ranch houses and not
to owe so much to the inventions of a few European innovators. It
was even possible to imagine that they were in the line of the
earlier Maybeck, and the brothers Gill and Greene. Many a client
who would have recoiled at the thought of commissioning Breuer
or Lescaze now became a client of one of these exponents of a
more gentle modernism.

For some time, modern architecture was not publicized in the United States with a thorough and convincing attack, such as the Chicago Fair of 1893 had led for classicism, but after the '30s, exhibitions began to spearhead the modern propaganda. In 1931 the New York Architectural League staged a show organized by men who had designed New York's skyscrapers with an eye to the decoration they had seen at the Paris Exposition of Decorative Arts in 1925; they excluded all truly modern work, and so the show was picketed by the progressives. In 1940 the League reversed itself in a new show. Called *Versus*, it led visitors past a simple and conventional display of old buildings like the Boston Public Library and Harvard's Lowell House, while upstairs all the tricks of contemporary display technique helped to glamorize modern work.

Expositions also turned modern. The International Exposition at Paris in 1937 showed modernized classical buildings. Le Corbusier and his followers, excluded from the exhibition, created their own tent at the Porte Maillot where they exhibited a convincing model of an ideal city. This caught the favor of some American architects who had already essayed the tepid and misconceived modernism of Chicago's 1933 Fair.

Thus the major expositions at New York and San Francisco in 1939 were filled with efforts at modern design. California had buildings by Pflueger, Born, and Wurster; New York's trylon and perisphere were the work of Harrison and Fouilhoux, while Albert Kahn, Lescaze, Howe, Teague, and Stonorov designed some of the buildings. Most of them derived from European work of the '20s in the manner of Loos and Hoffman; long planes of white plaster, incised by strip windows, frequently at the corners, were topped by flat roofs and terraces.

But among this conventional unconventionality, two small and winning exhibits were more important than all the display of established modernism. Both were from Scandinavia, the Swedish Pavilion by Sven Markelius and the Finnish Pavilion by Alvar Aalto. There, modern architects learned from Markelius the strength of continuous space, from Aalto the interest of sinuosity and that old materials like wood could be handled freshly and beautifully. They were reminded that the articulation of small structural parts might offer a way to give scale to buildings. Over-all, Markelius and Aalto taught a lesson in the plastic manipula-tion of form and space, offering American architects the first clear path away from the rigid plans and the hard materials of the Bauhaus. No American, Russian, British, French or Italian build-ing at the fair was memorable for its architecture even though the evening scene was enlivened by the fountains and fireworks of Jean Labatut. In the end, and except for the magnificent gastron-omy possible on Flushing Meadows, only the Swede and the Finn prevailed.

It was possible to look to few museums for leadership in the new taste, though gradually some contemporary paintings began to creep into the older museums, despite the hostility of their directors and most of their trustees. A few communities were more fortunate. In Pittsburgh the Carnegie Institute held impor-tant shows and began to praise modern artists; at Hartford, Con-necticut, the Avery Memorial of the Wadsworth Athenaeum acquired a new building with modern galleries for modern paint-ings; at Boston the Institute of Contemporary Art became a mod-estly important center, as the Boston Museum of Fine Arts con-tinued to suggest up to 1956 that art had stopped with Monet. But the outstanding center was in New York. The Metropolitan Museum tried to show the quality of the modern furnishings. Farther to the left, the Whitney and Guggenheim collections, very well selected, very specialized, stimulated a limited but scarcely a popular audience.

But the story of American introduction to modern design is almost completely the story of New York's Museum of Modern Art. In 1929, when the Museum opened, an important exhibition was organized by Philip Johnson. It gave Americans their first large look at the work of Le Corbusier, Mies, Gropius, Oud, even of Frank Lloyd Wright. This exhibition spawned an important book, *Modern Architecture*, published in 1929, with essays by Henry-Russell Hitchcock, Johnson, Mumford and Alfred Barr. In 1931, Johnson and Hitchcock began to collect photographs of modern architecture, and in 1932 there was a second major exhi-bition, held in the Museum's quarters in the Heckscher Building. This show gave the modern European movement the inappropriate name "International Style," widely broadcast by the book of the same title, written largely by Hitchcock.

In 1935, the Museum brought Le Corbusier to the United States and organized an extensive lecture tour for him. The preceding year had seen Johnson's Machine Art Exhibition, which showed furnishings designed by modern architects, such as a desk lamp, inkstand and calendar by Howe and Lescaze; these were placed alongside industrial products: a flush valve, a caliper, a propeller, the section of a wire rope, self-aligning ball-bearings, a burglar-proof chest and a brass plumb bob. The first choice of the judges was the section of a steel spring, a product of the American Steel and Wire Company. Such awards and exhibits attempted to end the old fight between art and the machine, and tried to improve the state of industrial design.

Meanwhile the Museum acquired its present building, the design of Goodwin and Stone, erected in 1939. Refusing to concede anything to its inconspicuous site and the nearby St. Thomas's Church, the building had a glass-enclosed lobby that invited the public to visit the galleries behind the grid of its bold façade. Dramatic exhibition techniques, notably René d'Harnoncourt's open vista grouping, pioneered in the South Seas exhibit, lured the public to study paintings in the Museum's growing collection as well as special shows such as that of the engineering of Robert Maillart in 1947, the sculpture of Henry Moore in 1946 or of Gabo and Pevsner in 1948. Lively discussions about modern art and architecture, notably one held in 1948 to address the question "What's Happening in Modern Architecture?" kept the Museum in the forefront as a promoter of modern design. Against this skillful and insistent presentation of work that was gaining in stature, the protesting books of Robsjohn-Gibbings or the more scholarly ones of Francis Henry Taylor had no real chance. The battle was long and tiring but it did not have many ups and downs. The Museum really paved the way for the advent of Gropius.

Now architectural magazines joined in the taste-making. None aimed consistently at a sophisticated audience and none boasted a critic comparable to the earlier Montgomery Schuyler. For some time they essayed their own catholicity, publishing the architec-

o

ture they thought best, regardless of style. For example in January, 1934, the *Architectural Forum* spent many pages on two houses. One was in Regency style; the other was a very modern design by Frederick Kiesler: "both are excellent examples of their respective kinds," said the *Forum*. A typical issue of that day contained William Templeton Johnson's Music Auditorium at Claremont College, California, which was North Italian Renaissance; a group of Philadelphia houses by McCaskey which were in the regional style that had been popularized locally by Mellor, Meigs and Howe; a Master Detail Series showing a Georgian Colonial house by Philip Goodwin and a Regency house by Verna Cook Salomonsky; and eight unfortunate model houses designed by New York's skyscraper architects, Walker, Hood, Corbett, Van Alen, Kahn, Harmon, White and Schultze, all of whom were attempting to be modern in a halfhearted way.

In defense of this weak and catholic editorial policy we must recall that there was little modern architecture of any quality to publish and that the older experienced anti-moderns were often producing better buildings than the modernists. Thus, the *Forum* devoted an issue of Master Design Series of 1934 to California Spanish architecture as it was being designed by Wallace Neff, Reginald Johnson, Gordon B. Kaufmann and H. Roy Kelley. The houses were charming and much more than competent. Beginning with their cool and comfortable patios, filled with moist air and rich plants, they were consistently graceful and comfortable. Simple exterior façades were formed by broad white stucco walls, covered by low-pitched tile roofs. Wrought-iron balconies, sequestered views, varied vistas and luxuriant foliage created a wealth of textures, color, patterns of light and shade, and a gracious ease of movement through space; the buildings were professionally finished, yet never dull, as delightful quirks and unexpected deviations from a rigorous scheme featured a statue, a potted shrub, a pool, a fireplace or window. In 1934, outside of Wright's work, which the editors generally championed, no other American architecture had comparable warmth.

The problem faced by the editors was a knotty one; namely how to encourage modern design and its adventurous advocates while being mindful of their faults. Unfortunately the educational problem became mired in questions of how to maintain circulation and advertising copy. For a time magazines like the *Architectural Record* seemed to ignore this question as they followed the direction of Mumford and Stein and others who had a liberal social mission, freely praising the fine planning of towns like Radburn, New Jersey, while conveniently neglecting to criticize their undistinguished architecture.

But as modern work became better and more acceptable, the editorial direction of magazines followed the leaders. After the war traditional work found little sympathy even when it was praiseworthy. The hinterlands and the architectural centers were still full of traditionalists, but their work reached the eye of the magazine reader only when it came in for abusive attack such as was properly leveled at Pope's National Gallery of Art. There were fewer and fewer philosophical articles in the magazines. No strong stands were taken on major questions of research, social philosophy or design. Criticism almost disappeared. A student seeking aid in distinguishing between good and bad designs in 1950 received scant help from editors or publishers. In part this was a reflection of the uncritical basis for modern design which tended to favor innovation rather than excellence; in part it stemmed from fear that modernism was so tender a plant that it might wither if abused; in part it was a result of increased reliance on advertising which inexorably forced each magazine to seek a headline, an exclusive masterpiece of the month, a scoop. Naturally there were not enough scoops to go around, especially when the more influential popular news magazines joined in the competition.

But illustrations in magazines did offer a noncommittal, reportorial, apparently objective way to help modern design to gain ground. Long before any advertisements were showing modern buildings, the *Architectural Forum* and the *Architectural Record* occasionally devoted sections to architecture done abroad. Factory buildings at Avellaneda, Argentina, by Luciano Chersanaz, and the work of Pier Luigi Nervi and Ernesto Rogers in Italy were suddenly presented about 1941. They dazzled architects and engineers who had thought that Albert Kahn had placed America permanently in the forefront of industrial architecture.

There was naturally still a great deal of noisy opposition from influential traditionalists. But the temper of the times had set against them as early as 1937. What the young wanted was clearly shown at the Princeton Architectural Round Table of that June. A. Lawrence Kocher, editor of the *Architectural Record* and himself a modern designer, stood firmly for functionalism. Clarence Stein exhorted the Princeton graduate students to believe that architecture should start "with the social life in which we live."

Such ideas left no place for the vacillations of Ely Jacques Kahn, whose style was only skin-deep. "Is not the ultimate function of the architect to please the client?" he seemed to ask. "Why go into all this frenzy of cantilevered buildings and insist on doing something stunty . . . ? Why can't we take it for granted that we are different people, liking different things?" At one point he made the error of asking the group assembled in Cram's Gothic college whether, if Princeton were destroyed overnight, they would like to see it rebuilt by Le Corbusier; the students' "yeas" were overwhelming. But university trustees and especially Princeton trustees were the last to agree with the students. They have not really agreed yet.

Few of them had any aesthetic convictions. By 1960 the magazines, newspapers, museums, and all other sources of influence had so unanimously mounted the bandwagon that if there were to be a Salon des Refusés it would have to be for any architects who tried to design in the older ways. Institutional buying of something that could at least be called contemporary design was so confirmed that the institution which bought conventionally bought modern, while the one which tried to buy Georgian or Gothic seemed only eccentric. But the progression to this dénouement was not without travail; the beginnings were tentative and meager.

17

INDIVIDUAL clients followed convictions about the new ideas long before anybody else did. But still they moved slowly. In 1939, the *Architectural Forum* was disappointed to note that thirty years after Wright's Coonley House and fourteen after Le Corbusier's

Pavillon d'Esprit Nouveau and Mies's Tugendhat House the new houses in the 1939 landscape were still predominantly traditional. But this was not surprising. Individuals continued to have leanings towards sentimentally rustic primitivism. These were nurtured by charming books about old New England village life such as Samuel Chamberlain's beautifully sympathetic drawings and photographs of Old Sturbridge or Deerfield, which seemed to reflect the American longing for a past that seemed less vexatious than the present was known to be. This was fortified in 1933 when the Historic American Building Survey was inaugurated in an effort to provide useful relief for unemployed architects and draftsmen. In the summer of 1938 architects and art historians began to plan a Society of Architectural Historians which made its debut in 1940. Their *Journal* frequently dealt with the Colonial and Georgian scene, and for a long time it published less and less about ancient and medieval architecture, or foreign buildings generally, while it also contained few pieces about modern American building or city planning. In this the editors reflected the mood of many Americans.

The mood was pampered by the restoration of Colonial Williamsburg, a village that could not possibly suggest any solutions to modern problems, even in its reconstruction, which began in 1927. Some applauded the idea on the ground that America should own a few choice restorations as documents of civic art. This was the defensible position of city planners like Kevin Lynch. Others like Gropius questioned whether the expenditures of the Rockefellers were justified in such projects in view of the social needs of the American people — a far-fetched view. A more serious criticism came from historians who knew how often the restoration ignored historical evidence and this is what bothered men like Lawrence Kocher and Marcus Whiffen. Others like Frank Lloyd Wright never ceased to ridicule the "Williamsburg Wigs" and the "Codfish Colonial" sentimentalists for fear of the damage they might do to American taste. Their fears were justified. The American public listened to no intellectual explanations, cared for no carping criticism. One and all, they were charmed by the gardens, houses and costumed guides, quite as much as by the buildings Perry, Shaw and Hepburn invented or restored. Since 1937, when Williamsburg acquired an Inn, invented out of whole cloth, the annual pilgrimage has been heavy. The question of motor cars among the Colonial precincts, of streets paved whose traces had once been deep in mud, of overelaborate collections of furniture, all this paled beside the sense of pilgrimage Americans felt while journeying to an ancient provincial capital whose minor significance in American history they understood but faintly if at all. What they could understand was the privilege of photographing their children in the stocks.

Such pilgrimages stimulated support for preserving other villages. Money poured in for Colonial, Georgian and Federalist buildings, for the Rappite colony at Economy, Pennsylvania; for ghost towns of the Gold Rush and Spanish missions; and later for a few Victorian arks. Meanwhile, the Larkin Building and the Marshall Field Wholesale Warehouse fell to the wrecker's bar and swinging ball. Wright's Robie House was threatened with demolition in 1958 at a moment when Congress willingly prepared to spend vast moneys for adding a completely useless and dome-diminishing classic façade to the National Capitol in Washington. Such a view was not of course exclusively American. At the same time Horta's work in Belgium and some of Le Corbusier's in France were equally threatened by time and "progress." On the other hand even at the end of our history, San Franciscans who said they could not afford the cost of a major master plan subscribed seven million dollars to rebuild Maybeck's trivial confection for the Panama Pacific Exposition, the Piranesian Palace of Fine Arts.

But even when the choice of what to preserve was, as in the case of Williamsburg, a reasonable one, the effect was to slow down the acceptance of modern designs. In 1939, the architectural magazines of America could show a few white-stuccoed cubist boxes such as Howe, Lescaze and Kenneth Day occasionally built around Philadelphia, or a little, still European work by Gropius and Breuer around Boston. Edward Stone's vigorous house for A. Conger Goodyear in Old Westbury, Long Island, was a rarity in 1940. After the war, however, acceptance was rapid. By 1952, the F. W. Dodge Corporation could publish a book displaying eighty-two modern houses.

At this point there was, perhaps, not much originality. The work followed the style of one or another major man. Among these the influence of Mies van der Rohe was strong though few emulated his perfection; no one handled volumes, for example, as austerely as he had in his Barcelona Pavilion. But still many aspired to the Miesian brilliance with materials, with hovering planes, with modulated space. They were given a striking example of ultimate purity in 1950 when the Farnsworth House was completed at Plano, Illinois. It was limited to the most basic elements: two rectangular floor and roof planes suspended on eight steel columns, walled solely by glass, and interrupted only by a utility core of kitchen, bathrooms, heating unit and fireplace near one end of the single room. A year earlier Philip Johnson completed a similar house for himself at New Canaan, Connecticut. The ultimate in purist, even self-conscious simplicity, it contained a single space defined by the brick floor, the roof, steel columns, and glazed walls. The space was subdivided only by furniture, a painting, plants and a brick cylinder containing the bathroom.

Another inspiration for house design was the work of Gropius and Breuer. Somewhat angular and awkward in their early attempts at fitting houses into the landscape of Lincoln, Massachusetts — although from the beginning impressed with the quality of New England's characteristic white-painted wood siding — they became increasingly less addicted to unblended machined parts, like the Lally columns in Gropius's own house. Their house for Henry G. Chamberlain at Wayland, Massachusetts, of 1940, notwithstanding some awkward moments in the disposition of doors and windows, showed a greater appreciation of native materials like rough fieldstone and wooden siding, and its rectangular module admitted their greater concern for proportion.

In California, Neutra's style was changing rapidly in the direction of greater sympathy with the landscape. The Tremaine House at Montecito of 1949 was a series of planes interrupted by wide windows. The center of the plan was devoted to living and dining and the remainder branched outward like the spokes of a pinwheel, with a wing for the servants' quarters, another for family bedrooms, another for guests and a fourth for the outdoor terrace. The whole still contrasted its precise lines to the rocky slope

and gnarled trees, but its openness created an informality sympathetic to the site.

The architect who displayed the most remarkable genius for
America's broad terrain continued to be Wright, whose houses
consistently developed themes compatible to their sites. Boulders
and hills near the Friedman house at Pleasantville, New York,
suggested the great disks covering the house and carport. A huge
rock near a lake in Quasqueton, Iowa, became the theme for the
massive oblongs of a boathouse, while the bluff above demanded
the stroke of the long, low-lying silhouette of the Walter House,
with its unexpected quirk in the roof. Cacti and desert rock suggested the battered walls and angular cantilevers of the Pauson
House at Phoenix, Arizona, while the bunker of a hillside shaped
a modern sod-house in Wisconsin. Each of these was Wright's
original creation, quoting no one, not even his own prairie houses.
Falling Water, the country lodge at Bear Run, Pennsylvania, belonging to Edgar Kaufmann, became the most celebrated of the
houses. Inseparably related to its unique site, the house took its
theme from the waterfall, where a massive rock was the spillway
for a brook. Cantilevered balconies repeated the theme, as the
upper balcony overlapped the space created by the lower one and
the pools seemed to run in and out of the building. Sun terraces
and masonry walls echoed the stratified split ledge stone in the
hillside. Diffused light within the interlocking spaces of the interior reflected the foliage around the brook. The theme appeared
also in the bastion of the small bridge, but now in stone, where
space was enclosed by intermeshed L-shaped masses like those of
the balconies, but no longer cantilevered since stone, unlike reinforced concrete, is brittle. Falling Water, built in 1936, never
failed to look fresh and intriguing; its breath-taking leap over
water and ground excited admiration, and its dark, penetrated
spaces provided recesses that seemed inviting, comfortable and
harmonious with their purpose, as a weekend retreat in a Pennsylvania woodland.

This quality of site expression extrapolated to a regional level
was sought by many architects especially in the Western states. In
California, William Wurster's houses, like the Clark House at
Aptos and the early house for the Gregorys in the Santa Cruz

Mountains, used native wood and made prominent use of enclosed courtyards. Mario Corbett tended towards classical elegance, as in his house for Moritz Thomsen at Vina, in 1952; but Harwell Harris seemed to have studied the Japanese villas and the romantic work of earlier architects like Greene and Greene always leaning to the purer austerity of Nippon. His Johnson House at Los Angeles of 1951 and his earlier house at Fellowship Park, Los Angeles, of 1935, masterfully adapted pitched roofs, wooden structure and open plans to romantic topography. Around San Francisco, there was so much of that kind of design that it seemed briefly as though a new style had emerged. The *Architectural Record* published a series of articles in 1949 on the question, "Is there a Bay Area Style?"

The Californians were sure they had something different. Even as late as 1960 Wurster wrote about it in *Casabella*. Their attitude, he said, was relaxed and undogmatic, not bound to accede to a machine aesthetic but also not bound by tradition, genuinely bound however by the regional conditions. Socially he thought the houses reflected two conditions, the taste for outdoor activities and the natural landscape and the lack of domestic servants. The California architects wanted to achieve their results simply and did not care about labels. Of this northern California architecture he concluded, "It is therefore a truly popular architecture, in a sense that much of the internationalists' work is not, it is an architecture of *everyday use* rather than form or intellectual theory. Viewed as sculpture, it may disappoint, but if in a democratic society architecture is a social art, it may have some validity."

Others appropriate to their terrain could be found in Florida, Massachusetts and Oregon. Houses of this kind were major influences in producing a general appreciation of modern design. They were neither bizarre nor austere. They did not require a change in a way of life; they did not lug the machine or the washbasin into the living room; they were comfortable for children as well as adults; they could tolerate a little mess; and they needed neither manifestoes nor exhibitions to explain themselves.

Modern furniture and decoration did much to provide general acceptance. Many people who could not build new houses or who might have built conventional ones if they could, nonetheless

o*

were attracted by the new utensils, the new fabrics, the new chairs. Of these, most found the Scandinavian work of Wegner, the Dane, Mathsson, the Swede, and Aalto, the Finn, more ingratiating than Le Corbusier's severe structural logic or his witty reclining chairs. Not very many could afford the opulent steel-and-leather Barcelona chair by Mies van der Rohe. But there were American designers too such as Eero Saarinen, Charles Eames, and George Nelson. Altogether one could find many a modern interior in a house whose façade was reminiscent only of the cartoons of Charles Addams. Much of the acceptance was, of course, based on fashion rather than on merit, but regardless of motive it paved the way to familiarity with modern interiors and thence to acceptance of the full range of modern design.

Similar influences were imposed by the new gardens, which abandoned formal parterres and meandering English Romantic types in favor of outdoor spaces intended to serve as centers for recreation, shaped by informal architectural elements, using new types of perennials and shrubs that were both hardy and easily tended but also provided some sense of the exotic. In California and the Far West during the '40s and '50s, Thomas Church and Garrett Eckbo invented exciting ways to compose the new shapes, colors and textures. In all these changes the formal informality and the subtle restraint of Japanese gardens were clearly influential, notably in layouts by such men as Isamo Noguchi and Hideo Sasaki. All of these had too much sense, most of the time, to import Japanese treatments of the most abstruse type such as the Zen stone garden at Ryoanji. Such treatments would have been most appropriate to the austere designs of the housebuilders, but would also have been mannered and inappropriate in America. The gardens were therefore things that could be appreciated at once and by many and they, too, helped modern architecture in its struggle for acceptance.

18

It is not surprising that the first inroads should have been made in the domestic field, for here all that was needed was to convince a single human being or at most a couple, especially if they had enough money so that a banker, too, need not be convinced. It is not surprising either that the first committee-accepted architecture to come into the modern tent was industrial. Industry had new problems as it moved from ancient sites to new ones, on the periphery of the old cities or even into new regions; it had a chance to try a new horizontality. The plants on the great highways offered a chance for architecture to serve public relations. Industrialists like General Robert Johnson became advocates of beautiful factory architecture. The Ligature Building of his Johnson and Johnson Company on Route 1, near New Brunswick, New Jersey, offered one of the earliest displays of the new factory symbol. Designed by R. W. Cory, it took full advantage of its highway location. From their cars, speeding motorists saw the long white planes, ribbon windows and clear signs. These were twenty-four-hour advertisements, lighted by searchlights at night. The whole effect was a convincing suggestion of the integrity of the firm's products.

In some instances functional design produced strong and telling if unintentional forms. The Hortonspheroids on the shores of Texas and Louisiana and the refineries at Baton Rouge or Bayonne with their intricate diagrams of steel lighted by flaming gas, were near to being wonderful if unconscious sculpture. The Willow Run Bomber Plant spoke clearly of the traffic of personnel and materials, the assembly lines, traveling cranes, bridge cranes and chain conveyors it housed. The solid glass-block walls of a rayon factory at Painesville, Ohio, of 1939, told of the need for thoroughly controlled environment in the manufacturing of synthetic fibers. A new throwing mill at Winston-Salem, North Carolina, dipped and rose over the vats and racks where the nylon was processed. At the Pulp Mill of the Weyerhaeuser Timber Company at Everett, Washington, designed by Schoenwerk, an engineer, the concrete tanks and acid vats were powerful cylinders. They stood in rhythmic array against the sulphur storage bins. Conveyors leading to the chipping room dramatically brought the eye to climactic steel digesters turning timber to pulp.

Paul Rudolph's extensions of these ideas in the late '50s for CIBA and others seemed self-conscious when compared with functional architecture for the mass-production industries such as the buildings of Albert Kahn, to whom the *Architectural Forum* devoted an entire issue in 1938 which showed over and over again that architectural quality might be evoked by industrial necessity.

We did not learn of a more beautiful architecture created out of reinforced concrete until after the war, when Nervi's work in Italy was generally discovered by American architects. The initial work of Freyssinet had been ignored by Kahn. The usual explanation, that high labor costs and low steel costs prevented our exercises in concrete, ignores the fact that Americans have purchased anything they really wanted; the truth is that until recently Americans did not understand concrete well enough to design in it and did not want the forms enough to wish to study the methods. Until the war's restrictions upon steel, neither Ammann and Whitney, nor Roberts and Schaefer gained many commissions for thin-shell designs, and American industry remained content with the steel buildings the Kahns erected.

Satisfaction with the works of Kahn encouraged industries to employ architects for industrial buildings. There were early successes like the B. B. Chemical Company at Cambridge, Massachusetts, of 1939, a surprising display of modernism on the part of the then traditionalist firm, Coolidge, Shepley, Bulfinch and Abbott. The Forest Products Laboratory at Madison, Wisconsin, by Holabird and Root in 1933, used fins of cypress and vertical mullions to advantage. In 1950 Ford planned to build a huge administrative center, and hired Skidmore, Owings and Merrill to make the design. The Corning Glass Works employed Harrison and Abramovitz to design a new plant and exhibition gallery expressive of its sophisticated products. Lever Brothers hired the Bechtel Corporation and Welton Becket to lay out a factory in Los Angeles with strong industrial forms, tanks and piping systems all displayed as architectural elements. At Corpus Christi, Texas, in 1949 the Bluebonnet Plant of the Corn Products Refining Company, designed by Frank J. Whitney of H. K. Ferguson Company, brilliantly exposed the manufacturing processes in its Mill House and Steep House, covering them only with platforms, a roof, and some sunshades. Alden Dow created distinguished

work for his family's Chemical Company at Midland, Michigan,
while William Lescaze designed the new Kimball Glass Company
at Vineland, New Jersey.

But the most ambitious and successful was the General Motors
Technical Center on which the Saarinens began work in 1945,
though it was not completed until 1956. The Center, a vast project, was conceived by Alfred Sloan as a long-term reminder to his
successor executives of General Motors that their successes were
founded not on law, but on merchandising, not on financial plans
or super-service but on technology. In the end Eero Saarinen contrived one of his finest groupings to provide the symbol. The
buildings were low, of great simplicity and dignity, skillfully
placed on a technological campus, embracing reflecting pools,
fountains, plazas and modern sculpture by Alexander Calder.
Colored glazed bricks were used on the end walls. The design
building contained a handsome open stair hung on wires of stainless steel, hovering over a graceful pool. A punctuation was provided by the circular display conference room, which served as the
secret kiva in which the design executives would first see the new
car models. All this excellence, even that serving the mumbo-
jumbo of design secrecy, might have influenced the designers to
make better designs, but the hope that architecture may improve
society escaped the promoters of swept-finned automobiles and
these·same "designers" finally corrupted many of Saarinen's interiors at General Motors.

By 1960 there was even more provocative industrial architecture to ponder. The architecture of General Motors was refined,
acceptable, and a great improvement even though it contained
little of experiment. It was quite otherwise when O'Neil Ford set
out to provide a plant near Dallas, Texas, for Texas Instruments,
Incorporated, in 1958. This company, manufacturing transistors,
was growing rapidly in a business where freedom to change was
fundamental. The management was adventurous in every direction and naturally demanded efficient flexibility. In particular, it
needed enormous areas of unencumbered floor space, while at the
same time it needed a complex of water or gas pipes, electric
tables and other manufacturing resources, which might be required on any square foot of the building, at any time, and on

short notice. To solve the problem, Ford provided an intermediate service story which acted as skeleton, circulatory and nervous system for the working floors above and below it. This story consisted of one great space frame of precast concrete struts and tension members running along the edges of what would have been pyramids had they been solid. Between the tetrahedal arches thus formed, stretching in both directions, supporting the ceiling of the story below and the floor of the story above, electricians, plumbers, steam-fitters and other bringers-of-service could walk and work at ease, channel their wires and pipes at will, drop them through the ceiling or push them up through the floor to any desired point. To permit unencumbered floor space at the top, the roof of the building was a set of hyperbolic paraboloid concrete shells. The structure itself was novel and daring; but it was even more daring that the architects should have decided to let the intermediate structure show through glass walls. As they saw the possibilities in this, so they saw the Léger-like nature of the great machinery room which they emphasized in the use of various colors of paint on variously functioning units.

This building was done hastily and with élan. It had many mistakes of detail that were not to be found in the refined works of Bunshaft or Saarinen when either was in his Miesian phase. The lighting problems were not fully solved; the fire escapes, which made a good part of the daylight architecture, cast ugly shadows at night; most of all the enormous parking lots destroyed much of the dignity of the ensemble. But this they were doing on every other important decentralized factory lot in the country, denying, for example, the purity of the buildings Bunshaft had erected for the Connecticut General in Hartford. Nevertheless the principles of Ford's design were valuable, the results exciting; given more projects and more time, the refinement into a great design might easily come.

19

NEW office buildings seldom lived up to the new factories in the early days of the modern movement. With few exceptions their designers ignored the lessons of the McGraw-Hill and PSFS buildings, following, instead, the older Metropolitan Tower; even when they were more adventurous, they tended to produce downright dull exhibits of functional clothing on skeletal structures. Supplied with an overabundance of office space, the new clients did not vie for height and no building reached toward the Empire State Building. Some of the new buildings like Philadelphia's Penn Mutual Life Building of 1934 mocked the style of nearby Independence Hall, disregarding the great difference in scale which made the contemporary application ludicrous. The New England Mutual Life Building at Boston by Cram and Ferguson would have been equally laughable had it not been the first flagrant vandalism of the distinguished and discreet low Boston skyline. The building was a Roman temple between two wings flanking a tall tower that supported a ridiculous lantern, a far cry from the competence of the departed Gothic man whose reputation the firm still wore by title. The equally absurd Provident Mutual Life Insurance building at Philadelphia borrowed its façade from Bulfinch's State House at Boston but added a tower and lantern for good measure. Such thinking led to the climactic John Hancock Building in Boston of 1947.

Removing the ornament from such buildings or changing their sheathing to expose a grid of windows did not improve the architectural quality. The boom in office and commercial construction that followed the war produced monotonous bores like the Mellon Bank and United States Steel Building in Pittsburgh; 477 Madison Avenue in New York belabored the standard clichés: the first story, set on posts, supported nine stories of vertical mullions over recessed spandrels, then six stories of ungainly setbacks turned horizontal — without any reason for the changes. These proved that architecture is never a matter of style, for the horrors appeared in all styles; sometimes the worst were modern, as many of the office buildings erected around St. Thomas's in New York later revealed.

There were interesting experiments such as Lescaze's balconied Longfellow Building at Washington (1941) or Wurster's rural office building for the Schuckl Canning Company at Sunnyvale, California (1942). But the most interesting project of this moment was the group Administration Building and Research

Tower for the Johnson Wax Company of 1936-1938 and 1950.
These buildings in Racine, Wisconsin, revealed Frank Lloyd
Wright's undisputed mastery over new materials like plexiglass
tubing and new engineering forms. The beautiful dendriform columns made of concrete reinforced with wire mesh turned the
heavy and utilitarian mushroom column into a thing of grace.
They were America's first major architectural demonstration of
concrete used plastically, not as wood or steel or as chunky cantilevered slabs like those in Wright's early Unity Temple. Wright's
drawing of the column labeled the major parts "stem," "calyx"
and "petal." He had developed his column upon the analogy of a
plant, much as Paxton had used the Victoria Regia when he invented the structure for the Crystal Palace.

This organic theme exfoliated in the sculptural masses and
spaces of the two buildings at Racine. The Research Tower of
1950 was a tall stack in which the floors were slabs, branched off a
single reinforced concrete trunk. Alternate cantilevers were narrow mezzanines that increased the laboratory space within and
enabled Wright to treat the tower with a larger sequence of bays
to give it greater apparent scale, though there were those who
thought the organization might not be favorable for research. The
theme of the cathedral-like main office space in the Administration Building was similar; dendriform columns were clustered to
form a forested canopy over the secretaries' desks. It was pedantic
to carp about the fact that these powerful and beautiful columns
actually supported only a light roof and glass tubing. Their function was to be beautiful, and that function was magnificently performed and brought an environment of rare loveliness to people
who were involved in routine tasks. The balconies and walls surrounding the space and the red brick walls of the foyer and exterior flowed in curves that further developed the theme of the columns. In the foyer one felt that Wright no longer worked with
palpable concrete and brick, but rather with space itself, kneading
it, grasping it, letting it go, pinching it down here, releasing it
there.

Ignoring the spatial lessons Wright offered, other architects
moved towards the planar aesthetics of rectilinear grid walls pat-
terned in Mondriaanesque ways. The search was on for an elegant

covering for the steel or concrete structural frame. The Woolworth's terra cotta had to give way to less expensive materials like porcelain enamel, glass and metal. Bulk alone made millions of bricks impossible, and increased costs for labor made any kind of masonry uneconomical. The ideal sheathing, as Robert McLaughlin defined it, would be a curtain wall pre-assembled in panels capable of lasting a hundred years, no more than two inches thick, light, insulating, fire-resistant, withstanding winds up to 150 miles per hour, weatherproof and vaporproof, ventilated and drained, and allowing flexibility of application. Such a hung wall would have to be made of glass and metal or possibly of new materials like plastics. It would be the ideal envelope architects had aimed at in earlier buildings like Polk's Hallidie, Gropius's Fagus Factory and Bauhaus, Despradelle's Berkeley Building and Mies's unexecuted project for a glass skyscraper.

The United Nations Secretariat of 1950 by Wallace Harrison was the first of the stronger statements of the new office building form. Its thirty-nine stories were wrapped with green-tinted glass subdivided by thin aluminum mullions and spandrels to create a non-directional geometric grid. Three bands of aluminum screens marked the floors devoted to mechanical equipment; an aluminum grille, enclosing the equipment on the roof, effectively brought the rhythm of glass and mullion to a stop against the sky. A narrow southern wall entirely of marble protected that side against the sun although the north wall was a concession to formalism with a juncture at the glazed sides that was ill considered. The great glass walls of the east and west façades were exciting. One photographed brilliantly from across the East River; the other was a magnificent mirror catching the clouds and the sunsets and transforming the skyscrapers of Manhattan into pictures for those outside the building; meanwhile the people inside shrank from the trying western sun.

The advertising value of such walls caught on quickly. Lever Brothers, the manufacturer of soap and edible oils, commissioned Skidmore, Owings and Merrill to design their new office building on Park Avenue, New York, in 1950-1952 and out of this commission Gordon Bunshaft, a designing partner, created one of the important buildings of our day, a great advance over the United

Nations Building. On a low box of glass supported on pilotis he
threw a sheer shaft of glass reaching heavenward. The curtain
wall contained mullion, panel frame and spandrel all in one unit.
Its green-colored glass offered a new note to austere Park Avenue
while it helped a little to reduce the effects of insolation on the
occupants. For the first time since Rockefeller Center, New
Yorkers found a little building space given to them as they wandered in and out among the plants that adorned the outdoor
space that the firm had left open on the ground floor. Even the
window-washing trolley was skillfully incorporated into the design. Until Mies van der Rohe built the Seagram Building on an
adjacent corner, Lever House was the finest new building in New
York.

Different curtains were less successful. One such was attempted
by Harrison and Abramovitz in their Alcoa Building, Pittsburg,
1952. Made up of small railroad-like windows set in aluminum
frames and inflated tubular rubber gaskets, it appeared almost
windowless as the aluminum panels were deformed to add rigid-
ity, create shadows and attempt to produce scale. Despite a pleasant lobby and some good interior spaces, the dull mass of the
building and the superficiality of its metal panels displeased most
architectural critics.

Then Mies van der Rohe and his temporary acolyte Philip
Johnson achieved the purest of the new buildings in 1957-1958,
the House of Seagram on Park Avenue, whose amber glass and
dark sheathing rose sheer from a portion of its large platform.
Skidmore, Owings and Merrill followed their success in Lever
House with a new building for the H. J. Heinz Company, and a
glass bowl for the Manufacturers Trust Company at New York.
By now the curtain wall was a formula, and Skidmore, Owings
and Merrill employed landscaped gardens and sculpture to enhance it. A more sculptural effect within the building itself was
achieved by the Chicago office of the same firm whose designers,
Walter Netsch and Bruce Graham, completed the Inland Steel
Building at the corner of Dearborn and Monroe Streets, in Chicago, in 1958. Here interior space unencumbered by columns was
obtained by putting the columns outside the exterior wall and
putting all elevators and service elements in a blank-walled an-

cillary shaft, adjacent to the office building. The massive columns of the main structure, clad in stainless steel, rose outside the floors and the cage of glass and thinner mullions which they supported. The entrance lobby was inadequate, without doubt, but otherwise the whole building was one magnificent and chaste icicle and the executive offices on the nineteenth floor and the lounge on the thirteenth were among the finest sustained modern interiors, just as the building as a whole found few peers anywhere.

Meanwhile Frank Lloyd Wright was enabled by the H. C. Price Company, manufacturers of oil-well pipe, to consummate in Bartlesville, Oklahoma, the design he had conceived for the St. Mark's Tower twenty-five years before. The Price Tower, built in 1953-1956, consolidated offices and apartments within a multi-faceted concrete-and-copper-sheathed building. Angular living spaces were cantilevered from a central stem or core in a composition of amazing visual charm. It is kinder not to speak of the multitude of practical defects which take it out of the main stream of American development.

The best among these office buildings, such as Seagram's or the Inland Steel, firmly established modern design as the emblem of national business concerns. America had finally achieved an architecture compatible with her industrial might. The successes scored with such architecture after 1952, particularly as it became more refined, even more classic, confirmed the achievment; the only pity was that so many of the copies were crude and insensitive.

20

THE new was gradually accepted even for churches, which in the beginning resisted modern design in this country. Neither Gropius nor Breuer built a church before 1957. Mies's chapel for IIT in Chicago was a hollow box which seemed to most observers to be cold and uninspired; devotionally uninspiring. It only reinforced the idea that modern architecture had little range and could produce no church that did not resemble a shoebox. Meanwhile Georgian and Gothic chapels were built in Atlanta, Philadelphia, Boston and Chicago throughout the '30s and '40s. Most were ob-

viously dull; they lacked any spiritual quality beyond that lent to
them by literary symbolism.

Writing in 1940, Talbot Hamlin discussed the causes of the
poor state of church architecture. He had to turn to Europe for
noteworthy contemporary examples. America offered little except
an occasional piece by Paul Schweikher or O'Neil Ford such as
the former's brick and wood Third Unitarian church at Chicago
and the latter's brick-vaulted church at the Texas State College
for Women. These, outstanding for their rarity, were mere glim-
merings of the vigorous modern church acrhitecture then being
produced in Germany, Finland, France, Switzerland, the Scandinavian countries, and even in Japan where Antonin Raymond
erected his Church of St. Paul at Karuizaw in 1936. The European churches awakened Roman Catholics to the possibility of
realizing the encyclical letter Pope Pius X had written about the
necessity of developing an art form compatible with the modern
period and the Catholic service. An American Catholic magazine,
The Liturgical Arts Quarterly, under its intelligent editor, Maurice Lavanoux, became a strong advocate of good contemporary
design in the furnishings, art and architecture of American
churches. In the end, great Protestant theologians like Paul Til-
lich took up the same cudgels. Only the Mormons and the Christian Scientists seemed to stand immune.

The most successful American churches started on modest
premises. They tried to offer spaces that had repose and quiet
dignity rather than awe. This was no doubt a commentary on the
religious psychology of the time that sought security and serenity
and comradeship. It did not take long to learn that such spaces
would not arise from designing with fixed symbols in mind. Barry
Byrne's St. Francis Xavier Church at Kansas City, which had a
plan abstracted from the shape of a fish, as a symbol for Christ,
was an artifice in which the imposed form gave no very distinguished architectural results. It was better to start with the requirements for a beautiful auditorium or liturgical space. This
approach resulted in the strikingly handsome though perhaps
melodramatic Corpus Christi Roman Catholic Church at San
Francisco by Mario Ciampi where raw colored glass squares were
dominant. Eliel Saarinen's Tabernacle Church of Christ at Co-

lumbus, Indiana, spread out in several wings, its offices in the south, the Sunday Schools at the southwest; its main block contained the auditorium and stately nave which were beautifully related to the ground by reflections in the large pool on the west, while the whole was held together by a dignified and simple rectangular tower. Saarinen followed this by one of his finest works at Christ Lutheran Church in Minneapolis (1949) whose brick and wood interior never fails to move the visitor. In the Northwest, Pietro Belluschi used brick and wood to make simple churches, with atria that suggested Japanese courts, and with modest experiments in small light sources. Such buildings as his First Presbyterian at Cottage Grove, Oregon, won many more people to "modern" church architecture.

Thus the period saw a steady improvement in American church design which can best be epitomized by the serene and modest interiors of Belluschi. These were fine enough in terms of their aspiration. Were the aspirations too low or was it explanatory of America that more vigorous efforts, whether made by Harrison or Lloyd Wright or Joseph Murphy in Stamford, at Palos Verdes or in St. Louis were either vulgar or weak? Except for Marcel Breuer's powerful Abbey Church at Collegeville, Minnesota, the notable experiments in modern church architecture had to be sought elsewhere — at Assy, Vence, Ronchamp, Baccarat, Milan, Blumenau in Brazil, Francavilla-a-Mare, Helsinki, Cologne, Berlin or Zurich, and the architects were Swiss, French, Italian, German or Finnish — not American.

21

THOUGH the churches were modest and found their way quickly to small communities many of the littler places got their first taste of modern design with their school buildings. The oppressive multi-story barracks of brick, filled with box-like classrooms that WPA had fostered in the '30s now gave way to the new demands for project-type teaching, laboratories, exhibitions. Under John Dewey's influence, Dwight Perkins, Reginald Johnson and Myron Hunt had essayed early designs that aimed to facilitate object-teaching and problem-solving. Now this was good official doctrine. Howe and Lescaze designed low, one-story buildings filled with sunlight and flexible classrooms for the Oak Lane Country Day School at Philadelphia and Hessian Hills at Croton-on-Hudson; Lescaze followed this with another model in his High School for Ansonia, Connecticut. Neutra's experimental school on Bell Avenue, Los Angeles, of 1935-1937 was outstanding. A covered passageway on the east ran past five one-story classrooms with sliding doors on the west, opening to outdoor classrooms. A light wood-framed building, the structure, with its movable partitions, allowed flexibility and permitted quick alteration of rooms for classes. The long glass walls were protected by deeply overhung roofs and canvas blinds supplied good lighting. In 1940 the Midwest achieved its exemplary modern school when the younger Dwight Perkins with Philip Will built the Crow Island School at Winnetka, Illinois. Here different age-groups were separated in four wings, each with its outdoor play area. The one-story wings were composed of model classroom units. Each unit was L-shaped with a work area in the short side and well-lighted classroom with movable furniture on the long. Though some of the detail was heavy, bright colors created a gay atmosphere, and the flat chimney-clock tower at the entrance later became an emblem of many modern schools.

The new buildings hugged the ground and spread along it. They were seldom more than two stories high and usually one. They discharged children quickly into the open and were thus both more pleasant and safer as they reduced the threat of fire or of accidents on stairs. They sought natural light and orientation, ventilation from the prevailing breezes, courted flexibility, removed the barriers between outside and indoors, tore down the earlier sense of confinement and restraint which had been the hallmark of the old school buildings. Campus-type plans were almost inevitable, there was gaiety and color. So it came to pass that the finest living and aesthetic experience in the life of many American children came to them in their schools. It was not hard to see that American taste might be much altered after they had grown up. There were those like Dorothy Thompson who remembered with pleasure the rigors of confinement of their school days, who deprecated the lack of educational discipline in the new school world and who, associating the two, concluded with the *non sequitur* that the buildings were to blame, while also inappropriately extravagant. But most Americans had more sense.

Thus the dreary stacked-up school of the '20s and '30s gave way to the finger-plans of the '30s and '40s. Individual classrooms sprang from the spine of a central corridor, while landscaped courts and gardens separated the individual units. Such plans were revealed by schools like Franklin and Kump's Acalanes Union High School at Lafayette, California, of 1940-1941. Here the dispersed plan with an outlying gymnasium and cafeteria made handsome yet functional use of a large rural site. Maynard Lyndon's Elementary School at Vista, California, combined the finger-plan with clerestory lighting and well-made covered walkways scaled to the dimensions of a child. Ernest Kump's High School at San José of 1952 had a denser finger-plan but its concrete framed buildings had a crisp Miesian appearance that created a mature environment suitable for additional use as a community center.

As the applications of the theories matured, the schools became steadily more attractive. In the early '50s John Lyon Reid in California, one of the very best of the school designers, provided the Garfield Elementary School at Carmichael, California, where classrooms were arranged about grass and paved courts, and where covered walkways, low eaves, color, and small detail gave a strong sense of shelter. Donald Barthelme's elementary school at West Columbia, Texas, built in 1952, provided a tall block at the center contained a theater, library, arts studio, washrooms and clinic; two-storied wings east and west of the central block contained classrooms opening to an interior court. The structural details of the girders and bar joists in the steel frame were exposed for their decorative value, while colored panels enlivened the top-lighted classrooms.

In 1955 Reid invented a loft-plan high school with fluctuating room sizes to encompass the flexibility demanded by shifting departmental boundaries and the changing community of San Mateo, California. About 1953, the cluster plan became popular. In this there were separate pavilions of one to eight rooms, without corridors, with students separated into "age neighborhoods"

and a chance to isolate disparate activities. Perhaps the most publicized of these was Perkins and Will's Heathcote School at Scarsdale, New York, 1952, which had a core surrounded by little
schoolhouses containing hexagonal classrooms with natural light
on all four sides. An auditorium for a theater-in-the-round, a
cheerful library and a central hall for each group of four classrooms completed this attractive school which also demonstrated
that school problems, managed with more ease in the favorable
climate of California and the Southwest, could also be solved
under the more stringent conditions of the East. In 1959 the long
·and effective pioneering work of William Caudill in the Southwest, made up of excellent propaganda pieces and fine and always
progressive buildings, was capped by his school at San Angelo,
Texas. Throughout the country choice modern schools could now
be seen and there seemed little doubt that America led the world
in this kind of architecture.

22

UNHAPPILY, the quality of primary and secondary school buildings was seldom matched by the buildings for American higher
education. If some school boards were forward-looking, most university trustees kept their eyes on the rear-view mirror. Before the
war there were few advanced college buildings to match M.I.T.'s
Swimming Pool by Anderson and Beckwith (1938) or the University of California's Stern Hall which William Wurster designed for Harvey Wiley Corbett, who had the commission. The
Museum of Modern Art and *Architectural Forum* sponsored modern design for college campuses as an aftermath to the ill-fated
competition of 1938 for a new art center at Wheaton College, but
little came of it. Although the Saarinens won a second prize in
the competition for Goucher College in 1938, the award went to
a firm of modified traditionalists whose campus site plan gave
birth to a set of homely buildings. Colleges and universities generally remained impervious to modern architecture until after the
war and resistant after that, often belying by the new buildings
they acquired the principles of what they were teaching in their
own architectural schools. After 1957 the wave of acceptance

could be seen to be sweeping over all but the most adamant. A modern building on an ancient campus was no longer noteworthy and the *Architectural Record* could devote a whole issue to successful contemporary college and university designs. But this came to pass only a long time after modernism was firmly in the saddle elsewhere.

Trustees at universities and colleges who were becoming bold with respect to their corporate architecture or even their personal houses remained naïvely traditional when they were acting as custodians of education. For a time they were supported in this by their own architectural schools. There men like Everett Meeks, Leopold Arnaud, William Emerson and Paul Cret, at Yale, Columbia, M.I.T. and Pennsylvania, all traditionalists, wielded strong influence through the '30s and '40s. To be sure, leading young American moderns often emerged from these conservative schools. But, characteristically, their contact with modern design had come through magazines and visiting lecturers or travel. As faculties were renovated, some schools offered strong support for modern design. When William Wurster became dean at M.I.T. in 1944 he found already installed a force for modernism centering around Professors Lawrence Anderson, John Lyon Reid, and Herbert Beckwith, products of the older ways but navigators of their own revolution, and this encouraged M.I.T.'s continued experimentation with contemporary design which had begun with the Swimming Pool of 1938 and now was continued with additional works by Anderson and Beckwith and others by Aalto, Saarinen, Rapson, Koch, DeMars, Stubbins, Bunshaft and Pei with only occasional backsliding into more conventional hands. A few other architectural faculties assumed some leadership in addition to the obvious excitement at Harvard and IIT. Yale, North Carolina, Minnesota and Oklahoma were examples, but they were not followed by Cornell, Columbia, Princeton or California very soon.

Meanwhile, even where the faculties had at least some interest in contemporary principles it was rare that presidents and trustees did. At Wheaton College in 1946 a new president, disliking modern architecture, appointed a traditional firm despite strong protest from members of the faculty, notably the head of the art

department who resigned. Thus execution of the building along
the lines of the modern entry by Richard M. Bennett and Caleb
Hornbostel which had won the competition of 1938 was first
postponed and then abandoned. It was even rumored that its
public success had led to the downfall of the president who sponsored it. This was unhappily a typical story. Princeton rested cozy
in its Gothic. The relatively modern Firestone Library was encased in a pseudo-Gothic stone cloak. Even as late as 1960 the
distinguished Italian modern architect Enrico Peressutti, after
years of patience, resigned publicly from the architectural faculty
as a reproach to the archaic architectural policy of Princeton's
trustees. President Goheen took this into thoughtful consideration but for a while at least the freeze continued. But there was a
thaw almost everywhere else.

Even before the war a few colleges had tentatively opened their
gates to the new design. They were likely however to be experimental places such as Black Mountain College. Here the students
and faculty collaborated to erect a new building designed by A.
Lawrence Kocher, who was professor of architecture there. About
1938 Florida Southern College at Lakeland offered Wright his
first opportunity to work for an institution of higher learning
when it commissioned him to plan eighteen units for its West
Campus, of which ten were built. It was his largest commission
since the Imperial Hotel in Tokyo but was not, unfortunately,
one of his most successful. A handful of other newly founded colleges toyed with modernism. But in many cases inadequate
finances, ill-defined curricula, internecine disputes thwarted the
efforts at obtaining fine new campuses.

Meanwhile the famous old institutions clung to the old terrain.
In 1934 John Russell Pope designed Calhoun College at Yale, the
seventh residential unit on that campus. Intended for about two
hundred undergraduates, the college centered on quadrangles and
the buildings formed walls to baffle the street noise from the interior rooms. The college construction was a modern steel frame.
This was covered with random ashlar in full Tudor Gothic detailing. The planning had come from English precedent. Its virtues
were attested by centuries of use, at least in England and at least
in earlier centuries. It occurred to no one to introduce a new way

of life by a new architecture; perhaps the question did not even arise whether Yale undergraduates were any longer living the life of medieval Oxonians or had any intention even of trying to live such a life; if it did the faculty and trustees answered the question with a resounding "Yes" or thought that the manifest masquerade in architecture did not matter for a university which obviously did not encourage masquerade in the more serious matter of scholarship.

Other universities did not fare much better, perhaps worse, when they timidly attempted a modern appearance produced by men who had no real affection for modern aesthetic or any respects for and belief in the convictions it asserted. In fact these pseudo-modern buildings may have helped to ruin fine campuses of another day. You could see them at Kresge Hall at Harvard, at the Woodrow Wilson School at Princeton, at Buckland Hall at Mount Holyoke College and many other places where the results would have been better had there been no attempt at modernism at all.

Aalto's Baker House dormitory at M.I.T. of 1948, whose serpentine plan offered views of the Charles River, dramatized some of the difficulties in producing modern architecture in an environment that was only partly friendly. The difficulties did not arise from the trustees or the senior administration but rather from the general building climate in Boston which required the Finn to be associated with a local firm whose affection for his skills was at best tepid. Aalto started with the premise that every room should have sun in the morning or the afternoon, that every room should have a view of the river. M.I.T. stipulated against multiple entries. The number of rooms required combined with the small size of the lot dictated that the rooms must look up and down the river and not straight across. The choice was then between a regimented set of chevroned pavilions set diagonally to the street which might have been most functional and the freer serpentine form which had always been part of Aalto's palette. He elected the latter. Rooms were thereby less standardized, many had to be pie-shaped, some were less convenient and certainly less conventional than they would have been on an orthodox plan. But the built-in furniture and the far greater interest of the building outweighed the inconveniences. Any reasonable person had finally to admit that the combination of reason and intuitive caprice had produced something fine. Student affection for the building, despite its defects, supported the view. By 1960, acclaimed from Zurich to Tokyo as one of Aalto's greatest buildings, Baker House remains a landmark in American university architecture.

An influential version of college architecture appeared on Chicago's South Side when Mies van der Rohe was appointed to develop the campus of IIT. He began there with the Metals and Minerals Building of 1943, and on this campus worked out his style. The whole was a formal group of precisely designed research buildings, classrooms, chapel, boiler plant and dormitories. Steel frames, buff-colored filler bricks between the columns and beams, defined the prisms. The result was a somewhat cold but precision-calibrated campus homogeneous, meticulously detailed. As time went on Mies steadily refined the details. No doubt he failed, as we have suggested, with the chapel which seems almost an afterthought. As of 1960 the handsomest of the buildings was Crown Hall built for the Department of Architecture. It was here that Mies was able to follow his own theories most closely, to accept the fewest limitations by permanent partitions or other encroachments on free and flexible space. His attitude, formalism, necessarily involved a lessened attention, some thought an irresponsibility, toward utility, especially as regards privacy, noise, storage, control of light, and circulation. It remained to be seen whether the Miesian flexibility would work out well for a library and administration building. Those who admired purity of design excused the faults; those who disliked the forms were able to recount only the troubles. But Illinois Tech offered a first-class foretaste of things to come for town and gown. The main lines were soon recapitulated by Saarinen at Drake, and by Skidmore, Owings and Merrill at Smith College, at M.I.T., at Grinnell and at the Air Force Academy in Colorado Springs, and by many others in less excellent demonstrations. These later buildings were often more colorful, better planted, even more agreeable, but the principle of their designs was set forth unequivocally and first by

Mies. Thus IIT attained almost overnight an internationally famous campus.

Such ultra-modern university buildings were naturally viewed with mixed emotions. It took considerable courage for old institutions to break with tradition for any building that had to be financed by alumni subscriptions. Led by President James B. Conant, Provost Paul Buck and Dean Erwin Griswold, Harvard, for example, erected modern dormitories for law and other graduate students in 1950. The site plan by The Architects Collaborative was masterful; eight buildings were arranged to form three well-shaped quadrangles with good planting, interesting vistas and changes of level, all reminiscent in modern terms of the scale and surprise of the old Harvard Yard and suggested by it. The dormitories had concrete frames enclosed with buff-colored brick and artificial limestone trim. The Commons was a separate building with lounges on the first floor and a large, subdivided dining room opening off the cafeteria in the second story. There and in the lounges of one dormitory, modern artists, Miró, Arp, Kepes, Albers, and Bayer made murals while Lippold provided sculpture for the focal point in the sunken quadrangle in front of the curved wall of the Commons. The best features of the Graduate Center were unsurpassed even by the buildings in the Yard. The scale of buildings and spaces was fine, the color of brick brought the Harvard campus to excellent conclusion at the north, the site plan was excellent. But even the admirers of those matters could not approve all the details. Cramped and squeezed quarters were not adequate for students, no provisions had been made for book storage; corridor lights bothered students trying to sleep; and economical cinder-block partitions combined with paired top-hinged windows to conduct noise from one part of the building to the next. Students accustomed to living in dormitories like Harvard's houses complained about the poor performance of the bedrooms and lounges, and ultimately in 1956 when the University tried to raise money for a new house, an official pamphlet admitted the functional shortcomings of the Graduate Center.

It was a disappointment to the friends of modern architecture; so much had been accomplished there, but those who were predisposed to dislike the design never forgave lapses in performance which they took for granted in conventional work. Hence they were heartened to see a resurgence of pastiche Georgian at Radcliffe and the Harvard Business School, where misscaled buildings, bad site planning, and even plywood pilasters (which would soon raise maintenance problems) were readily overlooked, as sentimental eyes melted at the sight of red brick, white trim and multi-paned windows.

Contrasted to these the Graduate Center was fresh and alive, strong in its convictions, able to rest its case on having provided the strongest community among modern buildings yet achieved. Until Wurster completed his picturesque retreat, the Center for Advanced Study in the Behavioral Sciences at Palo Alto, there was no better example of modern collegiate design than the Graduate Center, which was courageously pioneered under the administration of a college president who rose above his own predilections in the arts and set an example that other presidents of many kinds of institutions might profitably follow.

Thereafter the college and university afforded more frequent bright spots. Brandeis, a new institution, sought to house itself in an almost completely new and modern campus. Settling on only a fair campus plan, it acquired a collection of fair to undistinguished buildings, though the three chapels for separate faiths, designed by Abramovitz in 1955, made a noble effort to cover and express the needs of diverse rituals; and the latest buildings by TAC and Stubbins were beginning to tie things together. Oberlin acquired a new auditorium as early as 1943, also designed by Harrison and Abramovitz, but its funnel-shaped walls lacked the scale that should have subordinated this "Moby Dick," as the students called it, to the old green. By 1959 this college was commissioning other buildings by Yamasaki and Bunshaft. In 1951 Marcel Breuer completed his Cooperative Dormitory at Vassar College. In 1954 Saarinen produced the distinguished and much discussed auditorium and chapel at M.I.T., a move in the direction of circular freedom. At Detroit, Minoru Yamasaki produced a new site plan for Wayne State University, and his jewel-like McGregor Memorial of 1958 provided a monumental yet personal glass-roofed central court, a highly sculptured building set above a Japanese-like garden with pools. Attempting to avoid the rigor of a single idiom, such as had dominated IIT, Yamasaki retained control over the site plan but embarked on a stated policy of encouraging the administration to invite other architects to design some of the individual pieces, though he soon diminished his own McGregor Memorial by his adjacent School for Education which recalled the Ca d'Oro in Venice in everything except its appropriateness and its excellence.

Other efforts to free the forms were made by Paul Rudolph at Wellesley College and Eero. Saarinen at Yale University. Rudolph, associated with Anderson and Beckwith, produced the Jewett Art Center at Wellesley in 1957. Here he had to deal with a dominant existing Gothic architecture. He carried the bay-and-gable theme of a neighboring Gothic quadrangle into a programmatic building housing galleries, an auditorium, work spaces and offices and achieved a bold yet sympathetic transition of appearances though at some cost to the lighting of the gallery. Saarinen's Ingalls Ice Rink at Yale, in 1958, was not dominated by the old campus. Here he provided one of the most spectacular forms of present time, a great parabolic central rib swelling like the inverted keel of a Viking ship, supporting a roof which fell away from it in a modified catenary. There was no doubt about the elegance of the space once the occupant was in his seat at a hockey game or on his runners on the ice, but entrances, washrooms, and the appearance from the back were perhaps a little casual. There were in this building moments of drama and moments of failure and the ultimate judgment would have to be postponed. What it did say resoundingly was that when universities did succumb, they succumbed wholeheartedly. Nowhere in the whole range of modern American architectural experiment were so many fantastic buildings now to be found as on the campuses of the land. In a few years more Yale would have controversial and mutually inconsistent new buildings by Saarinen, Bunshaft and Rudolph. Harvard would have comparable adventures with Yamasaki, Sert, Caudill and Le Corbusier. Few pockets of resistance remained, even at Old Nassau. Exciting

chaos had taken the place of revivalism, while the desired symbolism was that of seeming up-to-date. The campus had become a
microcosm of the city with a vengeance.

Still, up to 1960, the steel-framed cage dominated the college
field. This was most dramatically exposed in Netsch's complete
campus for the United States Air Force Academy at Colorado
Springs. Here whole hills were bulldozed down and new mesas
graded up to provide the platforms against which the Miesian
idiom, now at massive scale, could be displayed against the backdrop of even more massive mountains. Here the architects had to
yield convictions obtained in other systems of education. That
group marching must influence the design might perhaps be
taken for granted by anyone who had visited Gothic West Point
or Beaux-Arts Annapolis. But that all the cadets must eat in a
common mess hall and at one time to achieve "togetherness," instead of aiming for it as they would in the intimate commons of
the halls of ivy, was a new idea. From it came one of the most
interesting buildings, perhaps the only one that was very differentiated, save the chapel which began to rise in 1960. The dining
hall was one great free space, enclosed by glass, covered by a massive and projecting roof and referred to by English critics as possibly the Parthenon of a new Acropolis. In any event the Air Force
Academy uttered a stentorian shout to the effect that modern
design had won the battle of the campuses as it had earlier won
the battle of the residence, of the factory, of the office building,
of the church, of the school.

23

THE federal government proved a harder nut than the universities.
The competition for the Federal Reserve Board Building at
Washington in 1935 was closed to any except conservative firms.
The prize-winners, Cret, Pope and Rogers, were all classically disposed. In 1937 Pope's proposal for the Jefferson Memorial raised
a stormy discussion. Critics balked at the proposed destruction
of cherry trees, at the secrecy surrounding the selection of the
architect. They might have balked at more important things.
Pope's Roman rotunda, absurd as it was, was defended by Harvey

ORLANDO R. CABANBAN

Chicago, Illinois, University of Illinois, Chicago Circle Campus,
Phase I, 1964-1966, Skidmore, Owings and Merrill, archs.

Collegeville, Minnesota, St. John's Abbey Church, 1953-1961,
Marcel Breuer, arch., Hamilton-Smith, associate

SHIN KOYAMA

Washington, D.C., Arena Stage Theater, 1961,
Harry Weese and Associates, archs.

Minneapolis, Minnesota, Tyrone Guthrie Theater, 1961-1963,
Ralph Rapson, arch.

New York, Philharmonic Hall at Lincoln Center, 1958-1962,
Harrison and Abramovitz, archs.
© 1962, Lincoln Center for the Performing Arts

Chantilly, Virginia, Dulles International Air Terminal, 1960-1963,
Eero Saarinen and Associates, archs.

New Haven, Connecticut, Yale University, Stiles and Morse
Colleges, 1960-1962, Eero Saarinen and Associates, archs.

Houston, Texas,
Texas Instruments Company,
Semi-Conductor Building, 1959,
O'Neil Ford Associates
and Richard S. Colley,
associated arch.

Cambridge, Massachusetts, Harvard University, Francis Greenwood Peabody Terrace, 1964-1965, Sert, Jackson and Gourley, archs.

Philadelphia, Pennsylvania, Society Hill, 1963, I. M. Pei and Associates, archs.

Philadelphia, Pennsylvania, University of Pennsylvania,
Richards Medical and Biological Laboratory Building, 1961-1965.
Louis I. Kahn, arch.

New Haven, Connecticut, Yale University, Art and Architecture
Building, 1962, Paul Rudolph, arch.

Lincoln, Nebraska, University of Nebraska, Sheldon Art Gallery, 1963,
Philip Johnson, arch.

Andover, Massachusetts, Phillips Andover Academy,
Thomas M. Evans Science Building, 1963,
The Architects Collaborative, Inc., archs.

Corbett and by McKim, Mead and White. Senator William Borah and Frank Lloyd Wright spoke against the whole idea of spending three million dollars on a monument but Wright's reasons were aesthetic and Borah's economic. Wright called it "an arrogant insult" to the memory of Jefferson — which was probably true, though Jefferson might have liked it. It memorialized his lesser side. Educators protested against it, led by Columbia's faculty of architecture including Hudnut, Bauer and Mumford. It was a waste of breath. The rotunda went through and no doubt pleased the taste of those legislators who ever looked at it. As we have already pointed out, the winning modern design for the Smithsonian was laid on the shelf until nineteen years later it could be replaced by a dull compromise.

Once in a while a modern post office or fire station could be found in some small community such as Orchard Heights, Washington. Yeon's Tourist Center at Portland, Oregon, of 1949 was a sophisticated sign for the city. Brazos County Courthouse in Texas was built by Caudill in 1958 as an excellent adaptation of school-campus planning to a county political complex. But all this was spotty and things certainly moved faster at the local than at the federal level.

Cret's Federal Reserve Bank of 1937 still seemed progressive to most official Washingtonians who admired the Supreme Court and the National Archives Buildings. It might have been hoped that a new National Gallery would lead the way; but Pope's confection of 1939-1941 was an outdated extravaganza of multiple-returned cornices, pilasters and entablatures intended to provide genteel backgrounds for fine Italian primitives but not really well suited for the exhibition of any art, architecture or sculpture, ancient or modern. Building for the Army and Navy were bombastic assertions of crude forms: the Pentagon in Washington had an efficient plan, less bewildering than it was sometimes accused of being, easy for a familiar to use and much less complicated than any comparable arrangement of the integrated housing of so many offices might have been; but it lacked all other distinction. The earlier War Department Building, later to serve the State Department, verged on the German neo-classic so much beloved by Adolf Hitler.

P

European urban and national governments especially in Scandinavia had long supported excellent modern design; Communist Russia, Nazi Germany, Fascist Italy and Democratic America remained the most ardent supporters of classicism. The American symbol of government threatened to house the United Nations in a sterile and monumental package. In 1946, when the United Nations was expected to rise upon a site at Flushing Meadows Park, architects in New York made a design in which a dome for the General Assembly was raised on a slab platform, and it was fronted by a long mall of courts approached between a row of pylons. The pompous quality in the scheme prompted the *Architectural Forum*'s editors to emerge from an anonymous objectivity; the pylons standing knee-deep in a moat-like reflecting pool seemed "to introduce the *memento mori* note," and the hollow, formal group was "a guileless admiration for pageantry." A reasonably clear form did not emerge until the Rockefellers had given land for the UN, and an international commission of architects had been set up, chaired by Wallace Harrison. Le Corbusier almost certainly provided the main elements of the ultimate design but in the end he, and his friends, asserted that he had been deprived of influence and his design emasculated beyond recognition by Harrison. Certainly it did not have the powerful connotations of buildings the Swiss had done alone. But the combination of forms was unique; and in the end it became an emblem for the United Nations that no one ever mistook.

Solely American governmental work continued to limp at home, but farther away from the cynosure of Senatorial eyes it might be bolder. By a fortunate chance, in 1954, and responding to much persuasion, the Foreign Buildings Operations of the Department of State wisely appointed the architects Shepley, Walker and Belluschi to give advice about government buildings abroad, where America's classical embassies had often denoted imperialism, perhaps more than conservatism. The advisers encouraged the State Department to appoint outstanding modern architects, sometimes on the basis of competitions, as in the case of the London Chancellery, 1956, but more successfully without competitions, and the architects were encouraged to seek regional expressions appropriate to the countries in which the new embassies, chancelleries, consulates, information centers and staff quarters would be built. In a marked turn from the few examples of International Style architecture Harrison and Abramovitz had pioneered at Havana and Rio de Janeiro, and Rapson and Vandermeulen had built at Neuilly, Stockholm and Copenhagen, the designs for new buildings tended to develop modern interpretations of regional motifs. Financed by foreign debts from Lend Lease, sales of surplus property, and Marshall Plan funds, the buildings broadcast the work of Ketchum, Gina and Sharp (Morocco), Kump (Korea), Raymond and Rado (Indonesia), Warnecke (Thailand), Neutra and Robert Alexander (Pakistan), Yamasaki (Kobe), Saarinen (England and Norway), Rudolph (Amman, Jordan) and Harry Weese (Ghana). Of all these designs, the leaders were Edward Stone's Embassy for New Delhi, Warnecke's for Bangkok, Sert's for Baghdad and Gropius's for Athens. These were unities, attentive to scale and local forms though none had the boldness of Le Corbusier's Chandigarh. They should have encouraged better work for governmental architecture at home even though they did not escape criticism from modernists who found them too "pretty."

Indeed, none of these buildings transcended criticism. Rapson's were thought to be too indifferent to the mores of Stockholm. Saarinen's London building was badly castigated for its vulgar use of metal and its bombastic eagle. Of Breuer's new one for The Hague, J. J. Vriend wrote in *Bouw*: "We see here a once truly functional architect losing himself in modern '*l'art pour art*' in a fashionable dressing up of essentially elementary space and form."

All this criticism was no doubt justified. It was an expression of the concern that was mounting as to the trend of American contemporary work in 1960. But to those who brought a less apprehensive eye the whole foreign program could look only admirable in the light of what might so easily have been a proliferation of Williamsburg all around the world.

Thus it seemed that real strides were being taken and this was endorsed by Hugh Stubbins's dramatic Conference Hall for the Berlin Exposition of 1955 and Stone's American pavilion at Brussels of 1958. But it was easy to underestimate the strength of tradition, particularly in this field. Perhaps Henry Hope Reed, Jr., was not very important as he preached a return to classic forms, displaying drawings by his New York associate John Barrington Bayley to convince New York that it would be improved by tall classic and baroque skyscrapers topped by statues of Minerva. But behind these patent absurdities there were other and quieter people who shared Bayley's hope that the classical architectural idioms might find an appropriate use in the twentieth century city. Even more felt that what might do for commerce was not worthy of the dignity of the government.

Some of these broke their silence at the first sight of the designs for the chapel for the Air Force Academy, prepared by Walter Netsch in the Chicago office of Skidmore, Owings and Merrill. Now the halls of Congress resounded to the complaints of Representative Fogarty and others; and of their special witness, Frank Lloyd Wright, who denounced the advisory commission of Saarinen, Belluschi and Becket as a team of a small boy, a schoolteacher and a man who had done a great deal of harm to American architecture. Congressman Hardy of Virginia thought the Academy looked like a cigarette factory. Senator Flanders was not alone in calling the chapel sacrilegious. President Eisenhower, whose sophistication and taste in architecture were not great, is said to have "flushed with anger" when he learned that the proposed design of the chapel was seriously advanced. In spite of this, the chapel was built to remain a source for critical dispute on different grounds, from those of pure aesthetics to the absurd conclusion of Allan Temko that a library and not a chapel should have offered the main symbol for a modern Air Force Major-General.

In 1957 the Eighty-fifth Congress, under the stimulus of men like Representative Frank Thompson of New Jersey, entertained proposals for creating some form of legislation fostering the arts. Representative Thompson cannot be held responsible for the tenor of the discussions that followed. On September 8, 1957, the *New York Times* printed a rendering of "A National Theater Project for Washington, D. C.," a fully Roman building, much like the Supreme Court, only more massive and gross, the proposal of Eggers and Higgins, stalwart and thriving survivors of the

Beaux-Arts days. Government buildings still required appropri-
ations and members of Congress still liked to make speeches ex-
hibiting the poverty of their aesthetic judgments. Most of these
indicated ominously enough the village mind that still prevailed
in the Capitol, but it was not different at the other end of the
Avenue, as President Eisenhower showed in 1960 when he proposed to Congress a project for a $24,000,000 monument, the
Freedom Shrine, to be built on federal park land overlooking the
Potomac River, adjoining Arlington National Cemetery. Designed by Eric Gugler, the colossal structure was an innocuous
fascist version of classic tombs and temples, intended to enclose a
pompous court, approximately 327 feet long and 24 feet wide,
shielded by walls 68 feet high decorated with historic reliefs and
inscriptions carved by Paul Manship. The building might in the
end not be approved. But the contrast between the public going-
over imposed on the Air Force Academy chapel and the under-
the-rug treatment of this proposal was glaring.

The *New York Times* permitted Ada Louise Huxtable to criticize the project and the procedure for obtaining it. But even with
public criticism there was no assurance that the arts could survive
federal patronage. This was discouraging to sincere men who entered the competition for a memorial to F.D.R., announced in
May, 1960; even if the excellent jury should award a modern design the prize, a Commission, a Congress, a President might still
impose a third-rate village taste, accepting only watered-down tradition as has always been the tendency where art lies under the
domination of conservative but uninformed laymen. There was
more hope in President Kennedy and his appointment of Karel
Yasko as architecture adviser; and in the winning design for the
Boston City Hall.

24

MEANWHILE the face of the American city seemed likely to be
determined more by the appearance of its housing than by the
elegance or the mediocrity of its new monuments which were
drowned in the flood of residential building. This was particularly
evident on the urban peripheries where monuments were scarce

but the expanding population pressed everywhere as the urban core degenerated and failed to offer the income needed for metropolitan services. The overlapping of independent municipal units no longer dealt effectively with sprawling metropolitan regions, particularly where the suburbs straddled state lines or clung like leeches to the dying city. All these problems could be seen clearly in the physical form of urban environment. No architect could escape them, but many tried to forget.

The short supply of housing in the postwar period brought a boom in large urban housing projects. There had been some good precedents for apartment towers like George Fred Pelham's Castle Village, Manhattan, of 1939, which developed a superb site north of 181st Street on Riverside Drive with five cross-shaped towers twelve stories tall. Much improvement might have been made upon its judicious planting and the plastic grouping of the towers. But, more typically, developers like the Metropolitan Life Insurance Company built gargantuan projects with colossal buildings that overcrowded the land. Peter Cooper Village contained a whole city of people without adequate areas for shopping, schools, playgrounds and entertainment. Stuyvesant Town became the classic pedagogical warning of what not to do. Built in 1947 on seventy-five acres of land between 14th and 20th Streets on the East River, it was a housing colossus of eighteen blocks with 8759 apartments that were intended for 24,000 persons. The buildings were towers raised upon a cross-plan; their staggered alignment on the site was so dull and mechanical that the three-acre park and ten small playgrounds did little to alleviate it. The city had given a twenty-five-year partial tax exemption to the insurance company to help finance the project; still, it contained no schools, forced the high density of 390 persons per acre, and did not include a shopping or cultural center.

But it was not impossible to treat such projects considerately. William Ballard showed this in the community center, auditorium, shop and nursery schools at the Queensbridge Houses, New York, where the residential buildings were sited so as to provide central parks and play areas. The James Weldon Johnson Houses in New York presented fifteen-story apartment buildings, severely simple in their lines, serving to accent vistas, define open areas and parks, and to supply a neutral background for sensitive planting. Smaller buildings were even more successful. The Fort Dupont housing at Washington was an excellent community with its variety, its domestic scale and its communal parks. Two-story row housing was handled well at Arthur Brown's Holly Courts at San Francisco in which low, cubic buildings with sensitive fenestration were set on terraces so that changes in level separated playgrounds and planting areas and sunlit courts were attractive and homelike. Some of the projects were further enriched as by the sculpture in the Jane Addams Housing Project in Chicago (John A. Holabird, Chief Architect), which brought life and scale to the buildings.

About 1950 considerable interest was awakened in the field of elegant high-cost apartments. Two of the more interesting buildings in that field were done in Cambridge, Massachusetts, and Chicago. The Cambridge building was the apartment house at 100 Memorial Drive, designed by Robert Kennedy, Carl Koch, Vernon DeMars, Ralph Rapson and William Brown of the M.I.T. faculty. Sited so that its entrance and bedrooms stood on a relatively traffic-free and quiet street, the building was an eleven-story slab with two wings projected southward to form a large open court on the side that overlooked the Charles River and the skyline of Boston. Apartments were entered from a corridor on every third floor from which vestibules and private stairs led to upper or lower apartments. The skip-floor elevator system reduced corridor space, provided cross-ventilation to apartments and enabled them to have large living rooms with glass walls and large balconies overlooking the court and the river. The traffic and living pattern was faithfully displayed in the exterior form, whose strip windows indicated the corridors. Strongly varied colors adorned the balcony ends. Some criticized the building for being a jumble of many different forms, telling enough, but cluttered and awkward. But the "clutter" was orderly; it was enhanced rather than disturbed by the individual idiosyncrasies of apartment dwellers whose varied interior decorations, Christmas trees, lighting, and personal vagaries regarding curtains and blinds strengthened the design, rather than producing the customary disruption. Such an approach permitted charming over-all effects without regimenting the tenant. It was one of the few modern buildings with gaiety, to be compared with Hans Scharoun's joyful Romeo and Julia apartments in Stuttgart.

The opposite approach was attempted by Mies van der Rohe at 860 Lake Shore Drive, Chicago, of 1951. There, two tall glass prisms, abstract enough to look like drawings, announced a radical departure from functional expression. To keep the glass façades uniform in color, reflection, and pattern, all apartments were equipped with gray curtains. Tenants were permitted to install their own curtains behind those. At most, their effect upon the buildings' appearance was to create varied Mondriaanesque patterns within the grid of windows as the gray curtains were drawn or opened. Thus the variety of apartment interiors was denied expression on the exterior. A further turn away from functionalism appeared in the sheathing. Both buildings were steel frames embedded in concrete, but the concrete was not expressed on the exterior. Steel I-beams painted black were applied to the façades to serve as window mullions and to provide vertical accents. These two towers were the closest approximation America had yet made to Le Corbusier's city schemes of the '20s. They formed an impressive group on the shore of Lake Michigan, prophesying a formalism which became increasingly dominant after 1952. The open spaces beneath them gave free views to the lake; the high style of the fenestration pattern made them supreme examples of Miesian doctrine. The tenants suffered some discomforts not to be met in more traditional quarters and felt some exultations that were simply not possible in the older buildings. If you prized average convenience more than exultation perhaps you moved out. But few of the critics of the apartments were themselves tenants and whether for snobbish or other reasons there was always a waiting list even for the new units that were not completed.

Mies seemed about to achieve a comparable success in Lafayette Park, Detroit, with a combination of row houses and a high apartment slab. But following the death of its promoter and his long-time supporter Herbert S. Greenwald in 1959, this seemed less likely. For architecture requires talented clients as well as talented architects.

Whether cities could be talented clients for their own redevelopment was about to be tested in San Francisco in 1960. If ever the test might be made on favorable terms it was in that Parnassian city.

Directed by Justin Herman and the San Francisco Redevelopment Authority, the Golden Gateway Project drew nine competing proposals from syndicates of developers and architects, who submitted plans for turning twenty of an eventual forty acres of the city's blighted produce district into a park with 2200 apartment units, parking garages, landscaped malls, and an office or apartment tower. Exceptionally fine schemes were the hierarchically scaled winning submission by the team of Wurster, Bernardi and Emmons and DeMars and Reay (with Perini-San Francisco Associates) and the monumental project proposing three curved twenty-two-story apartment slabs, the work of Skidmore, Owings and Merrill (Golden Gateway Center Corporation); one exceptionally refreshing series of terraced apartments was submitted by Jan Lubicz-Nycz, a Polish designer (collaborating with John Collier, Philip Langley, Sidney Leiken Enterprises and Theodore G. Meyer and Sons). The competition established an important principle: that intense and prolonged public scrutiny should be given the plans, which were well published in advance of the judgment. The intention was to enlist public enthusiasm for an imaginative proposal that would go beyond financial returns to investors. In striking contrast was the contemporaneous near-secrecy that surrounded plans for the Prudential Center at Boston or the later competition for the Boston City Hall. The San Francisco precedent was not only more democratic but better for it put some trust in the people.

Between the Lafayette Park·demonstration of Miesian order and the "human" romance of the San Francisco proposals of Wurster, Warnecke or Becket there was a considerable gap of theory. But each showed, if in a polar way, that architects were able to come to grips with the problem of middle-sized housing groups just as they could and had come to grips with the problem of grouping a few large buildings as in Rockefeller Center. The question remained whether they knew how to deal with the problem when it was presented at still larger scale.

P*

25

WHATEVER else they might fail to do, local and national governments were interested in providing still larger channels for the flow of automobiles. As an effort to solve the traffic problems within cities, decayed areas were redeveloped as freeways beginning with the urban expressway that opened in St. Louis in 1936. Interurban and interstate transportation improved with the building of great turnpikes like the Pennsylvania which opened in 1940. Many graceful bridges appeared as the suspension spans became longer. Daring engineering produced new vehicular tunnels without always providing easy egress at bridge or tunnel head.

More hope for the future of the airport as a gateway to the city began to appear about 1954 when dramatic shells leaped across spaces with some of the enthusiasm an air traveler might expect. The earliest to be admired was Hellmuth, Yamasaki and Leinweber's terminal at St. Louis where three pairs of intersecting concrete barrel vaults of 120-foot spans sprang from small point supports. The new Idlewild Airport proposed in December 1957 to erect even more dramatic terminals for United Airlines by Skidmore, Owings and Merrill, for American Airlines by Kahn and Jacobs, for Pan-American Airlines by Tippetts, and for Trans-World Airlines for which Saarinen proposed a thin shell, almost birdlike in its wingspread. But on the scale of Idlewild there was doubt whether the experience could ever be that of a gateway but only that of arriving at a sort of elegant way station, to be hoisted by bus to mid-Manhattan as soon as possible. It was not yet clear in 1960 whether airports would in the end, and quite consistently, develop a fine architecture. The Dulles National Airport at Washington, one of the most brilliant works of our day, was about to prove that in great hands they could. But even if they should, they would be peripheral to the central city or independent of it. Meanwhile the central city was being eaten alive by the ubiquitous and proliferating automobile.

26

INDEED, no other instrument so affected the American landscape. It spawned highway architecture from Maine to California and all the architecture was alike and most of it bad. Highway strips soon became the scene of the worst imaginable visual abuse. Roads once attractive and safe became hazards under the acts of *laissez-faire* development. New highways built by local, state and federal money were quickly exploited as sites for diners, stores, factories, nurseries, hardware shops, car washers, gas stations, garages, doughnut stands, for hubcap salesmen. National concerns worked with mediocre iconographic emblems such as Howard-Johnson's standard orange-tiled roofs which joined the clashing signs and colors that vied to catch the motorist's eye. The sincere efforts of national gasoline companies to provide respectable, clean stations, designed by Teague, Loewy or Bel Geddes, did not often survive the housekeeping of the proprietors or the sales efforts of the local offices who flooded the buildings with flapping pennants, gas-war signs, tire bargains, and gadget-filled windows that weakened the architectural lines and efficiency of the plans. Car-hop restaurants, flourishing in Los Angeles before the war, adopted futuristic and exhibitionistic roofs to attract the hot-rod crowd that flashed its headlights for service and ate in cars from trays brought by girls in cowboy boots or on roller skates. Roadside diners and drive-ins, begun in the early '20s, appeared as architectural problems at schools in 1934, and even the Beaux-Arts Institute of Design assigned the problem of a refreshment stand for a highway in 1939. Motels sprouted rapidly. Originally called roadside cabins, auto camps or auto courts, they made their initial architectural appearance in the *Architectural Record* of 1933, and 30,000 were estimated to be in the United States in 1952. They steadily grew in size, comfort and cost and by 1957 some had pushed the intown hotels in most matters of convenience and comfort at tariffs, which were also nearing those of downtown, while also beginning to acquire the inconvenience as well. Indeed, the motels themselves began to appear on downtown sites and perhaps the hotel of the future might be a new type, developed by a merger of the advantages of a Ritz-Carlton and a Holiday Inn, now that the travails of the city were reducing the value of downtown land so that it was economical to run a motor park on it and thus a downtown builder might begin after a century to think again in horizontal rather than vertical terms.

Trailer occupancy flourished as migratory farm workers followed harvests, industrial workers moved among defense projects, and drifters followed the sun southward to Florida and California as whole trailer towns developed to reveal a low standard of American living. In 1934 the first drive-in theater was built at Camden, New Jersey, in accordance with a design patented by R. M. Hollingshead, Jr. They became increasingly frequent appendages to the highway as young people acquired cars in which they lived most of the day and, until television became general, married couples found that they could have entertainment without leaving their children at home with a baby sitter. Very little of this highway architecture was as beautiful as Raphael Soriano's attractive Garden Center for the Hallawell Seed Company on Sloat Boulevard in San Francisco of 1942. Few states attempted to control it, and even Connecticut's magnificent Merritt Parkway, with clean, official service stations, attractive landscaping and borders zoned against the commercial development, did not encourage neighboring states like Massachusetts to develop similar parkways, until toll turnpikes were created to take the drive from Boston to New York to Chicago with never a grade crossing, a stop light or even a toll-house from entrance to final exit. Occasionally a pretzel or giant cloverleaf on the ramped approaches to Triborough Bridge afforded almost futurist vistas that were powerful sculptures, and nowhere were these more brilliant than in automobile cities like Detroit or Los Angeles. Indeed, the freeways of the latter may have become its noblest architecture, until they, too, choked with cars. But freeways without interesting nuclei to stop at would hardly be enough.

The planned shopping center was therefore potentially a most important development in highway architecture. Initial ideas for such centers began with studies like one of neighborhood shopping facilities that Clarence Stein and Catherine Bauer published in the *Architectural Record* of 1934. One of the earliest building-type studies of the shopping center appeared in the *Architectural Record* of 1940. Its examples emphasized the mall-type plan in which buildings were arranged around the sides of an open court. This plan appeared in the Shopper's World at Framingham, Massachusetts, designed by Ketchum, Gina and Sharp, who specialized in this sort of complex. An attractive variation upon the mall-type was that in the shopping center for Linda Vista, California, of 1944. Neatly tailored store fronts with discreet signs surrounded a central landscaped area in which one side was enclosed by an arc of shops. The small space devoted to recreational use within that arc became an increasingly larger element in later centers, signalized by Victor Gruen's article in *Progressive Architecture* of 1952 in which he wrote that the ideal shopping center would also be a cultural center containing an auditorium, governmental offices, lecture halls, exhibition rooms, reading rooms, theaters, restaurants and lounges. Even without all these some of the new shopping centers had distinctly cultural implications. Perhaps the most famous was Gruen's Northland Shopping Center at Detroit of 1952, a commercial center for pedestrians. Its plan contained a series of connected open courts, walks and small stores that were clustered around Hudson's large department store. Its 165 acres housed eighty-one stores with a total rentable area of more than a million square feet. Sixty-eight acres were reserved for auto-parking areas, strategically located to reduce the walk from car door to store door. Generous colonnades, fourteen feet wide, connected the malls and courts. These had sculpture by many artists, fountains and planting of rhododendron, azaleas, flowering cherries and magnolias laid out by landscape architect Edward Eichstedt. Despite the indifferent quality of its art, it was such a magnet that many Detroiters had the habit of visiting it, even on Sunday when only the restaurants were open. (They might have gone but did not go to the Civic Center instead.) It was possible that they might offer clues for a new and good urbanism. But they were slow in coming and the usual shopping center had none of this scale, none of this taste, none of this pleasure, offering another somber example of the termite that the real estate developer had become. And none of them approached the amenity of the garden of the Palais Royal.

Fine shopping centers, extended in purpose and sophistication, might indeed become the patterns for new central cities but before that could happen some other problems needed to be solved. Few of these were architectural. It was becoming banal to say that cities were dead. Yet it seemed to be true, if urbanity were to be the measure of the city. Measured on other terms the city was very much alive even if it were changing drastically. The amorphous structure and unprecedented size of the new metropolitan areas, increasing as populations were drawn to the cities and as the urban birth rate mounted, accentuated problems of cost, management and democratic government; they suggested the creation of political super-authorities such as those organized for the ports in New York and New Jersey or for the power of the Tennessee Valley; but they did not answer how these new and larger authorities would be understood or supported by a people which had been apathetic about smaller, more intimate and more comprehensible units. Technological change had removed the necessity for some of the things that had determined the earlier city: poor communications, conditions of defense, strategic or economic location, diversity of occupational opportunity, the necessity that populations be concentrated in centers of mass production and mass distribution. But not all kinds of production or distribution could get along without such concentrations, unless television, for example, were to be a satisfactory substitute for all other aspects of the visual arts and hi-fi to replace live music.

So, as some of the earlier forces for urban living were weakened they opened opportunity for those who had, perforce, dwelt in cities, but had never cared for urbane living, to leave the city and thus free the urban scene for those who really admired it, for those who craved what it had to offer. What it had to offer, if it could be realized, was that the metropolis was uniquely fitted to facilitate the free interchange of ideas among people of diverse temperaments, vocations and habits. The communication might be in matters of sports, of food, of the arts as well as in matters of the intellect. Those who sought no such interchanges were better off on the periphery with their small plots of anemic grass and their thin patches of personal sky; those who craved the urbanity might look forward to a time when it too could be combined with a way of life that permitted quiet conversation, sauntering, the song of birds even in the heart of the metropolis. Thus many urban projects, notably those for convention centers, arts centers, entertainment centers, and office groups, proposed after mid-century, were intended to capitalize on this need for civilized communication without the intervening censorship of uncivilized radio and television monitors. It was what lay at the bottom of Victor Gruen's proposal for the center of Fort Worth which would have kept private transportation out of the hub altogether and put the public transportation below the surface, thus restoring the land to people. All this would have been admirable and attainable had enough people wanted it enough, just as in Boston the Public Garden and the Boston Common stood as a daily challenge to the lethargy of the citizens and the selfishness of the abutters. But no such plan could be complete unless enough people wanted it enough. It had also to presuppose that many of those who craved the urbane life, would come back to live in the city, that they need be of a number of different income levels and not just all rich or all poor. The formula for such a combination of living had not been well developed in America, as it had for example in such a subcenter as Vållingby at the end of the Stockholm subway.

Furthermore while the truck and automobile weakened the tie of the manufacturing plant to the urban area and its tracks and waterfronts, and industrial plants began to cluster on the peripheries in belts of almost autonomous factories, the high cost of transporting retail goods over long distances coincided with the growth of the large peripheral populations and large local markets capable of supplying at least most of the needs of the peripheral men. Thus national companies were encouraged to establish satellite plants close to the large cities, particularly on circumferential highways which all too often had originally been planned for recreation but over which adequate controls had not been placed. Thus while manufacturing generally tended to quit the center of cities, businesses that offered services had either to be nucleated so as to serve a substantial number of automobile-borne customers or remain in the central city itself. The only services that could be different in the central city were those which met the extraordinary need. It no longer required an urban center to support a complete Rexall store; but it might be different for some specialized commodities.

What this meant in logical terms was beginning to become clear as 1960 approached. Logically it suggested that the peripheral family, all of whose aspirations were met by the mass supermarket, the mass drive-in movie, the mass television set, need never incur any of the "disadvantages" of the city but instead could live out its conforming yet peripheral life sleeping in a peripheral suburb, working in a peripheral factory, shopping in a peripheral market and never penetrating to the center at all. Indeed this was becoming the lot of many suburbanites and, so far as it was the lot they wished and enjoyed, it seemed absurd for sociologists and social philosophers to go on viewing suburbia with alarm. Suburbs did indeed offer political problems and economic problems and even problems of the national tone if, as some thought, a nation mostly of conformists was inevitably a weak nation. But had not all nations been made up mostly of conformists and was this on the whole a bad thing?

The problem was actually a different one, the problem of Gresham's Law. Perhaps the massive conformity of the periphery would make it impossible to have vital diversity at the center. For the individuals with individuality the center might be a mecca if it could ever arise. But as it was, the central city was not rising in this form. Instead it was becoming a place for a few very rich people who sent their children out of town to grow up, and a great many very poor who were far from urbane and would escape to the periphery as soon as their personal economics permitted. If they could be poured out of the central city and the non-suburbanites who lived in the suburbs be brought back to town there might yet be an elegant and urbane civilization in some American cities which would lift the level of the whole civilization. But it was much easier to speculate about it and to write about it and even to draw about it than it was to make serious and effective efforts to bring it about. Whether Lincoln Center was or was not to be a fine achievement for the performing arts of New York City when it was ready in the '60s might not matter much if the problems of uptown Manhattan were not solved. Nor would a high office building on top of Grand Central Terminal automatically lure more commuters back to the waning commuter services.

Major civic surgery was needed, surgery and grafting; fantastic cooperation between financial powers; brilliant new political machinery and courageous and foresighted politicians; in the end it surely meant abandonment of much private interest in favor of a greater and communal urban interest.

But any such major efforts could hardly be made until there was more agreement as to what was wanted. If it was true that architects could no longer think of cities as collections of independently designed buildings with spaces between them but had also to inject the dimension of time and the dimension of the motor car, it was also true that no one knew what to do about the automobile which Americans loved so much. And it was not only Americans who were seduced. The automobile was as disruptive to Rome and to Tokyo as it was to New York. No one really liked what was happening; but no one really wanted to give up anything either. Reyner Banham of the *Architectural Review* probably summarized the general attitude when he said in 1960: "Yet most citizens — including those called upon to plan — are determined to have the best of both worlds. They expect to be able to drive straight down an Autoroute de l'Ouest, straight through the Arc de Triomphe, and into a Champs Elysées that still has the urbanity of a sequence from *Gigi*." He might have added, "and then stop there for a personal errand."

Such a possibility was remote and it was not even a possibility save through some drastic action such as making the automobile a public utility or excluding it from large areas of human life. Yet any drastic action required either dictatorial powers or democratic unselfishness at a pitch the democracy had never displayed save in moments of obvious local catastrophe or national crisis. The catastrophe of the automobile was just enough short of disaster so that it did not insist upon unselfishness. In such circumstances one could have only a limited enthusiasm for a single brilliant achievement in architecture. The gnawing question remained whether the Americans were prepared to abandon private interest in favor of a greater communal urban interest. It did not seem likely.

This was the more frightening for the growth of the problem had been so fast as to outrun even the doomsayers. Time had seemed to be available until the recovery of 1935 and perhaps even until the population explosion that followed World War II.

Having sprawled into the country with their quaint Colonials and Garrisons and later with their ranch houses, the population now drained the metropolis for services, and congested the transportation lines leading into shopping districts and business centers. The site planning of office buildings gained increasing importance as the density of tall structures diminished the well-lighted open spaces on city streets. Unfortunately building codes were not amended to prescribe limited land coverage as well as limited height and setback. Rockefeller Center remained the single example of excellent site planning. Even that was marred after 1935 when additional buildings like Number 11, Time and Life and International crowded the area to the west of the main plaza, ignoring the site-planning lessons of the original group. Major skyscrapers like Chicago's Field Building of 1935 and Boston's John Hancock preserved no unbuilt land. Many businessmen still doubted the advertising advantages to be gained by having people swarm around the symbol of a national concern. This may have been some of the justification for Lever House, which rose from only a fraction of its land squarely in the middle of opulent and costly mid-Manhattan.

This site plan and others like the plazas of the Alcoa Building were pale reflections of the proposals Le Corbusier and city planners had advocated for many years. No city in America passed legislation or established the agencies that would have guided the future growth of industries, commerce and residences along lines that the elder Saarinen or Le Corbusier had proposed during the '20s. Even in the hardest hour of the climb back from the depression, urban and federal governments failed to grasp the opportunity for planned decentralization and urban renewal. The city planning proposals of men like Hilberseimer and Stein were consistently ignored in Washington. There were exemplary instances of partial metropolitan planning such as Robert Moses's Port Authority and recreational program at New York, and even some outstanding instances of interstate action in the preservation of areas like Bear Mountain Park and the Palisades, offset by Moses's ruthless projection of more and more highways and more and more bridges, disdainful of much else. The appalling fact was that so little interest seemed to be aroused in the possibilities of reform. A brilliant exhibit in Philadelphia in 1947, designed by Oscar Stonorov and Edmund Bacon, was one of the few attempts at alerting citizens, and its educational power was attested when Penn Center and other projects gave Philadelphia a new face in 1955-1957.

27

IF one wanted to gain some idea about what the city might become, he might go to Penn Center, begun in 1955, to Denver's Mile High Center (1955), or to Pittsburgh's Golden Triangle Gateway Center (begun in 1953). There he would find much to like in the reservation of space for pedestrians, in clean buildings, but he would still be disheartened by the failure of modern architects to build harmoniously with each other, to create fine spaces, to use sculpture and painting effectively, to gain a scale that was personal and to control large areas of the metropolis, or to lure people to their new plazas as they came naturally to those of Venice, Paris or Göteborg. For visions of what might have been, he would turn to unexecuted projects: Wright's baroque cylinder for the Golden Triangle, his Ninth Symphony, which remains only a great drawing on sheets of rice paper, or Boston's Back Bay Center as proposed by Belluschi, Gropius and a group of Boston architects. For each of these a banal design was substituted, often because it seemed more "practical," more functional; and even the fine designs seemed to disclaim the fountain and the trees.

But if the architect of the '50s had learned anything about art, it was surely to take a maturer view of functionalism. The best designers now recognized what had been formerly neglected in doctrinaire modernism, that an essential function of architecture is to be a work of art. Hence the purely programmatic expression of a building's function no longer dominated the artist. Beginning about 1948, architects and critics began to search for a new artistic and monumental expression. In that year London's *Architectural Review* predicted that the future of modern architecture would be a broadening of functionalism to include a building's emotional functions; Hitchcock spoke of our needs for durability, solidity, dignity, testimonials, fundamental emotional impact; and Giedion wanted a monumental architecture "representing . . . social, ceremonial and community life . . . more than a functional fulfillment . . . the expression of . . . aspirations for joy, for luxury and for excitement." In 1951 Mumford decried the mechanical solution and "self-imposed poverty" and applauded subjective impressions and expressions, even the willful, the capricious and those deficient in common sense. Rudolph, Yamasaki and other architects joined the critics, and their point of view was best summarized in Matthew Nowicki's dictum, "Form follows form," in which he meant to suggest that functions arise because of form if the form is expressive and commanding.

Such ideas led designers toward two contrasting viewpoints: the first was the single-form, single-space composition achieved through the use of monumental thin shells and curved geometry, as in Nowicki's Stock Pavilion at Raleigh, Saarinen's Auditorium at M.I.T. and Hockey Rink at Yale, or Yamasaki's Airport at St. Louis. The space might be rectilinear and universal, as in Mies's Crown Hall at IIT, and sometimes it might be associated with separate service cores as in Louis Kahn's Art Gallery at Yale. The opposite approach was to try to unify a composition by using overall patterns such as decorative screens, either to envelop a classically composed building as a single unit with well-defined base, terminations and cornice, as in Stone's embassy at New Delhi, or to provide a mantle across the face of a building whose interior was subdivided programmatically, as in Rudolph's Art Gallery at Wellesley. Each of these promised a future for art in modern architecture so that Yamasaki, for example, created the McGregor Memorial Building at Wayne State University employing features of the single-form building, the decorative sculptural roof and column, and the screen. "If we stop at function," he had said in 1955, "and function only, we have not even commenced with architecture." And some of those who saw his buildings were convinced that a full art had now blossomed; nor were they surprised that this modernist should have sat before so venerable a building as the Taj Mahal, drinking in its proportions, its symphony of consonances, its development of beautiful detail amidst perfect concept and proclaimed, "I believe it is without peer . . . pure joy to behold."

Outside such classicizing tendencies stood an opposing point of view, held by architects who were less concerned with the serene monument or climax of a composition than with creating vigorous background architecture, but free of the Miesian idiom. Again, much of the lead was European, and not only from Le Corbusier's Ronchamp and La Tourette, but from buildings that seemed urgent, even violent, like those of Vittoriano Vigano in Italy, André Wogensky in France, and Alison and Peter Smithson in England, who wanted to make strong structures legible, expose rough concrete, and gain abruptly ruptured silhouettes by faceting their buildings into coarse blocks that were randomly projected, recessed, raised and lowered.

In his less classic moments, Paul Rudolph seemed to be well on the way toward such syncopated rhythms, hurtling horizontals and rocketing verticals, as his gallery at Wellesley and high school at Sarasota, Florida, suggested. They were an architecture intended to stand with the classic, unified building, indeed to be its foil; any campus or city needed both. Thus Louis Kahn drew international attention for his work in Philadelphia. After a long and quiet and studious career in which he had been much appreciated by a few architects and critics for his adventurous theory of served and servant spaces and his insistence upon accommodating mechanical equipment usefully and handsomely, Louis Kahn capped his work at Philadelphia's CIO Medical Center, Trenton's Jewish Community Center, and Yale's Art Gallery, with a great lunge toward boldness, the Richards Medical Research Building at the University of Pennsylvania, completed in 1960. Its clusters of jagged towers were built in brick and treated as salient masses, over-sized and stark, brazenly offering unflinching contrasts to the irregular voids exposed by Vierendeel trusses. It was the one architectural experience on a campus where the bland monument or the banal historicism had stifled space. It was more the pity that as time went on the researchers it housed found it harder to forgive the difficulties it raised for them simply because of the nice things it did for the street. It seemed that we were reverting to a new kind of façadism and that research was still looking for its honest bricklayer.

There remained a second and more difficult bridge. Every previous important architecture had used sculpture and painting profusely — and integrally. Modern architects had not tried very often and had almost never really succeeded to do more than add casual if charming punctuation marks. Gropius had not really achieved what he dreamed in the Harvard Graduate Center; nor had Breuer come out much better in his more elaborate experiment for the new Unesco Building in Paris. Noguchi's stones for Bunshaft's Connecticut General seemed almost an irrelevancy; Lippold's wires in the Inland Steel lobby were inadequate in a lobby that was itself inadequate; the fountains of Seagram's were trivial. Indeed some architects, like Mies van der Rohe, formally thought the attempt to use artists was undesirable. Work like Rudolph's denied the other arts. Some few like Le Corbusier were sculptor, painter and architect rolled into one, and all too many architects who were not such complete artists tried to be. But it was clear for all the effort that the other arts were not playing the role they had in Athens, Byzantium, India, Cambodia, Rome, Burgundy, the Île de France, Tuscany or Guatemala. Was it the fault of a time which was too much concerned with words to care for visual messages? Was it the fault of artists who had so divorced themselves from life that they had nothing to say to the public? Was it the fault of the architects who had become so arrogant that they could ignore art? Or was it all unimportant anyway since whatever history might say about other times it had nothing whatsoever to say about ours? You could hear many different answers. What was clear was that the merger did not exist, although there were hints of success in the collaboration between Arp, Léger and Villanueva at the University of Caracas in Venezuela.

28

So the period 1933 to 1960 saw America develop a modern architecture by assimilating still another immigrant art form and gradually modifying it to its characteristic institutions and thereby
making it as American as any architecture was likely ever to be.
The art was not so pure as when it had arrived; it was nothing like
what Wright would have had it; it had not learned enough from
Le Corbusier or even from Aalto; but it was assuredly an art of
and for the times. It could be designed and built with some conviction, perhaps best when it was in a state of hectic uncertainty
and change — for that, too, was the spirit of the times. Though
the areas of agreement among the most talented architects
seemed to be growing smaller, it was true that many individually
exciting and even beautiful buildings were being made for an age
which had lost its critical anchors. But these fine buildings accounted for a minuscule fraction of everything that was being
built. A great many of the others caused American as well as foreign observers to think that the American landscape was getting
worse, not better. The highwayscape was wretched, the urban
approaches were worse, the cityscape deteriorating. Few Americans should have taken offense at the long photographic essay
which appeared in 1952 in London's *Architectural Review* showing "the mess that is man-made America" or been consoled that
an equally damning essay with fewer good contemporary alleviations could have been photographed in England.

The tragedy lay in the fact that things could have been so
much better. The architects and planners awaited a franchise, one
that would come not only from local and national governments
but from bankers and school treasurers and university trustees,
most of all from subdivision speculators and the merchants of the
highway strips. We had too long postponed a mature answer to
the question of how to control our visual environment. We had
too long cowered at the suggestion that beauty was an expensive
frill, and repose or silence a threat to a way of life built on the
consumption of gasoline.

But there was one encouraging thing in the scene of 1960 that had not been visible fifty years before. This was that Americans could now see superior examples of what good building could be and in any part of the land. There was enough brilliant architecture and it was widely enough distributed so that Americans could easily learn what they would be able to do if they ever got around to wanting to do it.

They could see this, at least, in individual buildings and in small collections of buildings. They might not be so readily able to see it if they could peer into the minds of architects. For there uncertainties were prominent; modern architecture had triumphed but what, now, was modern architecture? Was it being atomized along with the rest of society? Must architects follow the lonesome path of the painters? In the end would each talented man go his solitary way to the confusion of cities and societies and ultimately of himself? Could architecture continue to get along without other artists? But these were almost the trivial questions. There were others that cut deeper.

How could an architect now be educated so that, retaining his aesthetic intuitions unblunted, he would know enough to plan wisely or to coordinate those who, as specialists, must advise him? Could he really trust his personal intuition in matters of complex social behavior? If not, could he ever learn to be a good enough economist, sociologist, psychologist, engineer, political scientist, even demagogue — and remain an artist at all? If not, could he as artist survive, much less remain as the coordinator of building? Was he, was any team, capable really of dealing with urban enterprises of the size they now seemed to demand without losing all contact with human reality? The good architects knew they were not ready in 1960; the question they had to ask was whether they could ever be ready or must lose the game to the package builder who was even less ready but was more prepared to sell his gilt as gold.

Mountaineers know the annoying moment when, after hours of toil on an unknown terrain, they triumphantly reach the top — of the false summit. This was the predicament of the architects of 1960, all over the world. The problem was evident in Italy and Scandinavia and England and Japan — and it would have been evident in the USSR too had there been any architecture there.

The men who stood on the false summit seemed to have won an architectural victory. Far below lay the crevasses they had crossed. But the true summit seemed perhaps farther away than the false summit had thirty years ago. Could they whip their energies again, or find new resources and new and younger talents for the next assault? Even when they reached the goal would it yet be the true summit? These would be interesting things for someone to report in 2007, when the American Institute of Architects would meet for its 150th celebration. If meanwhile the architects had not learned how to manage enormous affairs, if the public had not come to want a great architecture, there might be little to celebrate. One might call, then, for a return to Shirley Center. But Shirley Center would not be there.

Epilogue

On the big scale of history it is evident that great styles in art, especially architecture, have taken a long time to develop and this suggests the question whether we should expect too much from an America that has only a three-hundred-year history. Many things have accelerated now and the new ways may develop and die more rapidly, even too rapidly. But up to now the periods of gestation, fruition and decay have run into centuries. The Greek temple was on the way to development at least as early as 700 B.C., had its finest hour at around 400, and though it has never died away altogether ceased to be a vital form by the first or second century of the Christian era. It was an architecture of a millennium.

Early basilicas that paved the way for the Romanesque and thus the Gothic had taken a recognizable form by the reign of Constantine. They were well developed by the eleventh century; they reached their peak in the Gothic of the Île de France in the thirteenth century; like the Parthenon, they never died away but they stopped being a living force towards the end of the fifteenth century. Thus their span was also a millennium. The buildings that are genuinely Renaissance began with the fifteenth century and they have been moribund perhaps since the eighteenth, and surely after the Crystal Palace of 1851. This leaves us four or five hundred years for the Renaissance-baroque-Georgian stream. The Roman architectural reign was about as long.

One cannot extrapolate with confidence to guess how long it will take to evolve an architecture of the industrial revolution. It did not begin to be suggested until well after the industrial changes were under way. When did the modern movement begin? Was it as early as the first uses of iron by Frenchmen in the Galerie d'Orléans and similar structures, near the beginning of the nineteenth century? With the Crystal Palace of 1851? With the reconstruction of Chicago after the Great Fire of 1871? With the first writings and speculations of Le Corbusier, Mies van der Rohe or Gropius? In any event, a new attitude toward building has been held for not much over a century at most; and it has been widely acceptable, even inevitable, only since the Second World War. It is not yet ubiquitous; there are those who yearn for the fancied elegance of yesterday. All the battles are not won, any more than they were when Chartres was completed. But it is also clear that the significant battles have been won and that rear-guard actions will not matter in the end.

This does not mean at all that the new architecture is perfected, that it has been distilled into its classic forms. We cannot really say that we are in the center of the history of the new great style, much less that we are seeing it at its apogee. What is certain is that we are watching the development of the first potentially great architectural period in which America has had a chance to participate in a major way.

Great building periods have always focused on the creation of one or two, and usually not more than two, important building types on which the people were prepared to lavish all their greatest architectural skills. This attention was possible because the belief was there. These were not the conditions in nineteenth-century America. The society was not wealthy enough, though it was becoming so. It was not powerful in the world sense, though it was getting ready to reach such power. It had no very clear purposes, it was vigorously discussing everything. It was not prone to waste money on the arts, it did not have a single dominating admiration for which it wanted to build the best buildings that could be built. It may not even have cared to build any "best" building. The evolution of its architecture had come at second hand and colonially at that. If the conditions of Chartres and the Parthenon were essential conditions for a great architecture, nineteenth-century America could not be expected to produce one. It would be hard even in the mid-twentieth.

The greatest architectures have arisen in support of religion. It is possible that this is not essential but that the important thing is that there should be a strong common belief, religious or not. But the great models of history suggest that the greatest artistry has come in times with unifying concepts, even *a* unifying concept, about which most people, *including the artists*, agreed. This proposes questions for Americans. When were Americans near to such unity? Were they ever near to it? Are they nearer or farther now? Is it true, as Mencken insisted in a dark period of America, that artists are always in rebellion against their time? Or is this a late and unhappy state of the Western world, not experienced before Galileo, Machiavelli, Montaigne and Luther, ominously growing through the nineteenth century and into the twentieth? Is a former American unity proclaimed by the New England village green or the manor on the James? Was the confused, even bad American architecture of the nineteenth and early twentieth centuries simply a reflection of the turmoil of a people who had lost the values of a unitary, agrarian, Protestant society and were trying to come to terms with a pluralistic, technological-urban, heterogeneous, Catholic or rabbinical one? If there was a schism, was it the artists or was it the people who were the wiser?

Had any building types emerged that seemed so desirable to Americans that they would lavish upon them kindred sacrifices of extra money, extra labor, extra love, such as we think were brought to the Acropolis or to Mont St. Michel? If there were no such dominant types, was the pluralistic society nonetheless reaching towards an agreement on some common values to be expressed by many architects, ordinary and extraordinary, to be accepted, even admired, by many people, not only by a few self-indoctrinating critics and connoisseurs, to be offered and accepted as a record not only of what the times *might* have .been like in twentieth-century America but also of what the times *were* like?

These were the continuing problems. If the American work was not often good work, it may be explained quite as much by the uncertain dialogue that was going on in America as by any lack of talent in the unfortunates who, in a given moment, were trying to make architecture. If the newer work has promise, its promise is partly related to the fact that Americans in general may be almost ready to decide what is worth while, admit the decision, and then lavish effort on it. Our study has been, then, less one of great achievements than one of great debates.

As soon as the serenity of tidewater colonialism was disturbed by the thrust across the Alleghenies, the American architect's life began to be complicated by the perplexing questions that rose from these debates.

How was he to work with an enormous and varied terrain, and its multifarious materials and climate? Should he try to preserve the innate regional qualities or should he deliberately negate them? Should he seek personal uniqueness or a classic result which might be called a "carbon copy"? Should he let his work be controlled by nature, or should he as a "pilgrim of power" seek to control nature? What would his genesis be; how much should he let others affect him; how much should he accept from other countries, how much attempt to stand as an American? How could he manage to produce first-class architecture in a nation of the middle class? What would happen to his profession as bigness was laid upon it? What limitations would be put upon his work by the "rural" or "village" mind?

How much should he subscribe to the Emersonian dream of unique America? In the great debates, where was he to take his stand? Would he be for tradition or innovation, for the frontier or the cultivated area, for preservation or demolition, for evolutionary or revolutionary change, for classicism or originality, for big cities or for villages? Should he believe in and try to serve an egalitarian or an aristocratic taste? How much should he be willing to satisfy the docility of his society, how much should he affront it? Was any other building worth more of his love than a church, and if so what should it be, and why? What position would he take between the hand and the machine? How much should he condone frugality? Should he suppress or reveal any ecstasy he felt in this work? What was to be his stance with sculptors and painters? Should he woo them or repel them? Control them or be guided by them? Use them as collaborators or as tools? Or should he reject them altogether on the ground that architecture was now its own sculpture and painting, the architect a better sculptor than the sculptor, a better painter than the painter, an artist complete and self-sufficient?

These were the questions he had to meet and to answer. Sometimes he answered them one way, sometimes another. But all the time it was quite a slalom course to run. Not very many American architects got to the bottom with all the flags still flying.

Acknowledgments

First of all, we are indebted to The American Institute of Architects. In June 1955 a committee on the Centennial observance was planning the celebration which was to take place on May 12-17, 1957. Dean Burchard was approached by a subcommittee appointed to deal with the problem of a history for the Centennial observance and he agreed to develop such a book, subject to two important reservations: first, that it would be quite impossible to do a respectable job in the time before the Centennial date, and secondly that he wished Professor Bush-Brown as co-author. Both of these were agreed to and the A.I.A. then made a grant in support of research leading up to the book, in return for which they took title to the manuscript.

During all the intervening years we have been much indebted to the friendly and patient understanding and help of some members of the A.I.A. Notably, these were William Wilson Wurster and the two other members of his subcommittee on the book, Frederick T. Hannaford and David T. Witmer; Alexander S. Cochran, chairman of the parallel committee on the Centennial Exhibition; Alexander C. Robinson, III, chairman of the parent committee on the Centennial observance. In the Octagon itself we owe special thanks to Philip Will, Jr., President of the A.I.A.; to J. Roy Carroll, Jr., Secretary; to Edmund R. Purves, Executive Director; to Arthur B. Holmes, Director of Convention Activities; to Joseph Watterson, Editor of the A.I.A. Journal; and to Henry H. Saylor, beloved Editor Emeritus of the Journal.

Next we are indebted to a group of influential advisers. As soon as the work was undertaken we wrote to some thirty friends and colleagues who have in their own work dealt with the whole of our subject or a significant part of it or with relevant historical materials in other fields. It speaks well for the camaraderie of the academic community that more than half of them provided suggestions of real importance and we have pleasure in listing them here and thanking them for their early aid: James S. Ackerman, the late Catherine Bauer (Wurster), John M. Blum, Julian P. Boyd, J. Bronowski, Carvel Collins, John P. Coolidge, Thomas H. Creighton, Donald D. Egbert, Naum Gabo, Sigfried Giedion, Frederick Gutheim, Oscar Handlin, Douglas Haskell, Henry-Russell Hitchcock, Richard Hofstadter, Stephen W. Jacobs, Howard Mumford Jones, Robert W. Kennedy, Elting E. Morison, Stephen C. Pepper, J. M. Richards, David Riesman, the late John Knox Shear, the late E. Baldwin Smith, James Johnson Sweeney. They are obviously not responsible for any interpretation we have made of their suggestions.

Next, we are indebted to a large number of architects scattered throughout the country. In the early stages of the study Dean Burchard traveled for months visiting architectural monuments in all parts of the United States to supplement the knowledge he already had. This involved looking at a great many buildings that would generally be called obscure. To do this he solicited the aid of individual architects in many communities. Almost every one of these people devoted a good deal of time to preparing for the visit in such a way that the work could be done efficiently, and usually acted as guides and advisers as well. This was an indispensable part of the preparation which in the end meant that the authors had seen the buildings of every state in the union, and we wish to thank here the extensive list of architects and a few others who assisted us in this endeavor: Ray Alderson, San Diego; Robert E. Alexander, Los Angeles; Harris Armstrong, St. Louis; Silvio L. Barovetto, Sacramento; Rex L. Becker, St. Louis; Robert L. Bliss, Minneapolis; J. Palmer Boggs, Norman; Ernest O. Brostrom, Kansas City, Missouri; John Albury Bryan, St. Louis; Harold E. Burket, Ventura; G. M. Cameron, Stockton; Georgius Cannon, Salt Lake City; Norman Chrisman, Jr., Lexington; Grady Clay, Louisville; Colonel Harry F. Cunningham, Lincoln; George R. Eckel, St. Joseph; William H. Hartmann, Chicago; Roger Hayward, Pasadena; Maurice Hefley, Oklahoma City; Earl T. Heitschmidt, Los Angeles; George F. Hellmuth, St. Louis; Frank J. Hoffman, Racine; Edward D. James, Indianapolis; Perry B. Johanson, Seattle; Roy W. Jones, Minneapolis; Edgar Kaufmann, Jr., Pittsburgh; W. J. Keenan, Columbia, South Carolina; Frank Latenser, Omaha; Samuel E. Lunden, Los Angeles; Edwin

H. Lundie, St. Paul; W. G. Lyles, Columbia, South Carolina; Harlan E. McClure, Clemson; Fred T. Meyer, Sainte Genevieve; R. G. Miller, Oklahoma City; Joseph D. Murphy, St. Louis; Walter A. Netsch, Jr., Chicago; Gyo Obata, St. Louis; Louise M. Pedersen, Tacoma; W. F. Petty, Columbia, South Carolina; Buford L. Pickens, St. Louis; Charles S. Pope, San Francisco; W. H. Porter, La Jolla; Lutah M. Riggs, Santa Barbara; Marion D. Ross, Eugene; Paul Rossiter, Dubuque; W. F. Ruck, Los Angeles; Eero Saarinen, Detroit; Robert W. Schmertz, Pittsburgh; Albert Simons, Charleston, South Carolina; Seven Skaar, Nevada City, California; Whitney R. Smith, Pasadena; Clifford C. Sommer, Owatonna; Philip Souers, Eugene; Henry P. Staats, Charleston, South Carolina; Glenn Stanton, Portland, Oregon; Donald J. Stewart, Portland, Oregon; Charles R. Strong, Cincinnati; John Sullivan, Jr., Dayton; Paul Thiry, Seattle; Charles Truax, Dayton; Robert J. Upshur, Columbia, South Carolina; Walter K. Vivrett, Minneapolis; Grant W. Voorhees, Des Moines; James E. Webb, Oklahoma City; Harry Weese, Chicago; Harry C. Weller, Pullman, Washington; Ronald Whiteley, Manhattan, Kansas; Wayne R. Williams, Pasadena; Henry Withey, Sherman Oaks; Muriel H. Wright, Oklahoma City; William Wilson Wurster, Berkeley; Minoru Yamasaki, Detroit.

Every book of this sort requires extensive library reference and every scholar knows the debt he owes to librarians in time of need. This book is no exception. We cannot list all the librarians who helped us but we had an unusual amount of help from Irma Y. Johnson, Reference Librarian, Massachusetts Institute of Technology; H. Katherine McNamara, Librarian, Graduate School of Design, Harvard University; and Caroline Shillaber, Librarian, Rotch Library, Massachusetts Institute of Technology.

We are grateful to Emily Morison Beck and Peter H. Davison of the Atlantic Monthly Press for steady and imaginative reading and editing of the manuscript. John Rackliffe did wonderful service with his sympathetic and helpful editing of copy.

On the home front, the late Margaret C. Hopkins did an enormous amount of work at all stages, including a great deal of redaction, and saved us from many errors.

Index

Chandigarh, Punjab (Le Corbusier), 326, 362, 421
CHANDLER, Joseph, 45
Chandler Farms, Arizona (De Mars), 328
Chanin Building, New York (Sloan), 283
Channel Heights Housing, San Pedro (Neutra), 335
Chapel, Princeton University (Cram), 313
Chapel, USMA, West Point (Cram), 176
Charles River Basin, Boston, 108
Chartres Cathedral, 278, 355, 448
CHASE, Frank D., 274
Château, Blois (François I), 111
"Château au Mer," Newport (Hunt), 116
Chatelet, Paris, 122
Chatham Village, Pittsburgh (Stein), 298
CHÉDANNE, Paul, 205
Cheney Building, Hartford (Richardson), 135
CHERMAYEFF, Serge, 373
CHERSANAZ, Luciano, 389
Chicago, University of (Cobb), 224, 226
Chicago Theater, 256
Chicago Tribune Building (Hood), 277, 279, 280, 281, 282, 284, 290
Chinese Pagoda, Kew (Chambers), 43
Christ Church, Cambridge (P. Harrison), 20
Christ Lutheran Church, Minneapolis (Saarinen), 360, 407
Christian Science Church, Berkeley (Maybeck), 177, 223
Christian Science Church, 96th St., New York, 219
Chrysler Building, New York (Van Alen), 283, 318
Church, Bryn Athyn, Swedenborgian (Cram), 221
Church, Cedar Rapids (Sullivan), 223
Church of the Advent, Boston (Sturgis), 122

Church of Christ, Lancaster (Bulfinch), 39
CIAM, 271, 357, 358, 371, 372, 373, 374
CIAMPI, Mario, 406
CIBA plant (Rudolph), 397
CIO Medical Center, Philadelphia (L. Kahn), 439
City Hall, Albany (Richardson), 132
City Hall, Boston, Competition, 423, 427
City Hall, Los Angeles (Parkinson), 284
City Hall, San Francisco (Bakewell), 213
City National Bank, Mason City (Wright), 223
Civic Center, Chicago, 213
Civic Center, Cleveland, 212, 213, 297
Civic Center, Denver (Robinson), 297
Civic Center, Manila, 213
Civic Center, Philadelphia, 297
Civic Center, San Francisco, 213, 297
Claremont College, Music Auditorium (W. T. Johnson), 388
Clare Street Station, Baltimore, 37
Clark House, Aptos (Wurster), 394
Clark Mansion, New York (Chedanne), 205
CLÉRISSEAU, C. L., 45
Cleveland, Henry, 49
Cleveland Tower, Princeton University, 227
Cloisters, Ephrata, 14
Coal Exchange, London (Bunning), 31, 61, 199
COBB, Henry Ives, 192, 207, 226
Cole, Thomas, 29, 55, 125
Colonnade Buildings, New York (Underhill), 34
Colorado, University of (Klauder), 315
Columbia, California, 73
Columbia University Campus (McKim), 225, 226
Commodore Hotel, New York (Warren), 288